The World in the Head

The World in the Head

Robert Cummins

OXFORD
UNIVERSITY PRESS

OXFORD
UNIVERSITY PRESS

Great Clarendon Street,
Oxford OX2 6DP

Oxford University Press is a department of the University of Oxford.
It furthers the University's objective of excellence in research, scholarship,
and education by publishing worldwide in

Oxford New York

Auckland Cape Town Dar es Salaam Hong Kong Karachi
Kuala Lumpur Madrid Melbourne Mexico City Nairobi
New Delhi Shanghai Taipei Toronto

With offices in

Argentina Austria Brazil Chile Czech Republic France Greece
Guatemala Hungary Italy Japan Poland Portugal Singapore
South Korea Switzerland Thailand Turkey Ukraine Vietnam

Oxford is a registered trade mark of Oxford University Press
in the UK and in certain other countries

Published in the United States
by Oxford University Press Inc., New York

British Library Cataloguing in Publication Data

Data available

Library of Congress Cataloging in Publication Data

Library of Congress Control Number: 2009938566

Typeset by SPI Publisher Services, Pondicherry, India
Printed in Great Britain
on acid-free paper by the
MPG Books Group, Bodmin and King's Lynn

ISBN 978–0–19–954803–3 (Hbk.)

1 3 5 7 9 10 8 6 4 2

Preface

This is primarily collection of papers on mental representation. There are four exceptions. 'What is it Like to Be a Computer?' is a paper about consciousness, written in the mid-1970s for a convocation at my alma mater, Carleton College, but never published. Beside the fact that I kind of like it, it is included to explain why, as a philosopher of mind interested in mental representation, I have never written about consciousness. The answer, in a brief phrase, is that I think that consciousness, or at least what David Chalmers has called the 'hard problem,' isn't ready for prime time (Chalmers 1995). The other three—'"How does it Work?" vs. "What are the Laws?": Two Conceptions of Psychological Explanation,' 'Cognitive Evolutionary Psychology without Representational Nativism,' and 'Biological Preparedness and Evolutionary Explanation'—are obviously about psychological explanation. They are there because a guiding principle of my work on representation has been that a philosophical account of representation should, first and last, account for its explanatory role in the sciences of the mind. As I argue in 'Methodological Reflections on Belief,' it should *not* be about the semantics of propositional attitude sentences or its implications. 'Connectionism and the Rationale Constraint on Psychological Explanation' is apparently about psychological explanation, but it is motivated by the idea that connectionist representation does not sort well with propositional attitude psychology.

Philosophers of mind come in many flavors, but a useful broad sort when thinking about the philosophy of mental representation is the distinction between philosophers of science, whose science was one of the mind sciences, and philosophers of language, whose interest in the verbs of propositional attitude led to an interest in the contents of beliefs. This latter route to the 'theory of content' can seem natural enough. We have beliefs, and their semantic contents are propositions, and so one naturally comes to wonder how a belief, considered as a psychological state rooted in the brain, could come to have one proposition rather than another as its content, and to wonder what is for a belief to *have* a content at all. This can even look like philosophy of science if you think that scientific psychology does or should be propositional attitude psychology. This whole issue is discussed in 'Meaning and Content in Cognitive Science.'

Most of the papers in this collection, however, do not assume that the propositional attitudes will have a central role in a mature science of the mind. They focus, therefore, on non-propositional representations and their role in our understanding of cognitive success and failure. The result is an attempt to replace the true–false dichotomy appropriate to propositional representations with a graded notion of accuracy along an number of simultaneous, and perhaps competing, dimensions, and to explore the virtues of a distinction between accuracy and effectiveness. The thought is that accuracy is expensive and accurate representation is often intractable, while less accurate representation is often cheap and easy to manage, hence more effective.

Underlying this approach is a healthy respect for the fact that our representational resources and their deployments are the result of a complex interaction between evolution, development, and learning. Learning, I am beginning to suspect, is not fundamentally distinct from development, even when development is conceived strictly as physiological growth. To learn anything, synapses have to be altered. To alter a synapse, something has to grow. Proteins have to be synthesized. Protein synthesis is orchestrated by the genes, and especially by their expression. Because gene expression is always responsive to the local environment, so is growth. The DNA in your stomach is the same as the DNA in your mouth, yet you do not grow teeth in your stomach, unless something goes seriously wrong. Because the brain has, via the senses, a broadband connection with the whole body and beyond, growth in the brain can be, and generally is, responsive to distal events and conditions. When distal influences loom large, and especially when their effects on changes in the brain can be modeled as inference, we have a paradigm case of learning. But the underlying mechanisms for replacing kidney cells are basically the same as those for growing binocular columns or a capacity to speak a language or to do algebra.

If anything like this is even close to right, the role of the propositional attitudes and their semantically tracked interactions is going to be limited at best, and often deeply misleading. I am not an eliminativist (see Ch. 11, 'Meaning and Content in Cognitive Science'), but it is becoming increasingly clear that Paul Churchland was right to warn us against propositional attitudes (Churchland 1981). As I argue in Chapter 5 ('Methodological Reflections on Belief'), we should beware of reading the structure of cognition off the structure of a propositionally based epistemology, and the structure of mental representation off the logical form of belief sentences.

If you like the propositional attitudes, you will like the Language of Thought as a theory of mental representation. The propositional attitudes have propositions as contents, and sentences are just the thing for representing propositions. If, like me, you are suspicious of the propositional attitudes and the language of thought, then you are likely to be attracted to the idea that mental representations are more like maps than like sentences, and are built up from indicators—detector signals—in a way quite distinct from semantic composition. This is the theme of Chapter 7 ('Representation and Indication').

The papers in this volume are not ordered by date of publication, but by topic and, where possible, by an attempt to put papers that presuppose x after papers that explain x.

References

Chalmers, David, 'Facing up to the Problem of Consciousness', *Journal of Consciousness Studies,* 2/3 (1995), 200–19.

Churchland, Paul, 'Eliminative Materialism and the Propositional Attitudes,' *Journal of Philosophy,* 78 (1981), 67–90.

Acknowledgments

These papers span decades; I cannot possibly acknowledge all the colleagues, students, and referees who have contributed ideas and criticisms. A few specific acknowledgments are in order, however. First and foremost, I want to thank Denise Dellarosa Cummins. Without her role as a collaborator, and constant source of a truly amazing river of information about the mind and how it works in humans and other species, this body of work would not have been possible. In particular, her ideas about the role of natural selection, and its interaction with development and learning, completely changed the way I frame the problems of mental representation and psychological explanation. She showed me that biology generally, not just neuroscience, matters to the mind. Thanks also to Ty Fägan who helped prepare the manuscript, found figures, and did the index.

I wish also to thank the Philosophy Department at the University of California at Davis who allowed me to count the weekly meetings of my research group against my teaching commitments. The participants in that group show up as co-authors on a number of papers in this volume.

The work leading to 'Unexploited Content,' 'Representation and Indication,' and 'Truth and Meaning,' was supported in part by NSF grant 0137255. The work leading to 'Atomistic Learning in Non-Modular Systems' was supported in part by NSF grant 9976739. The work leading to ' "How does it work?" vs. "What are the laws?" Two conceptions of psychological explanation' was supported in part by NSF grants 9896194 and 999976739.

Sources of the papers in this volume are acknowledged at the beginning of each paper.

Contents

1

What is it Like to be a Computer?

1.1. The question

Well, not just any old computer; one that is programmed just right. *Could* a computer be programmed so that it was like something to *be* it? And how could we possibly know? And even if we knew it *was* like something, how could we know *what* it was like?

The 'what is it like to be an x?' formulation is due to Thomas Nagel (1974). It is wonderful, but it is cumbersome. So I'll abbreviate: I'll say of something that it has the Nagel property if it is like something to be that thing. Or I'll simply say it is conscious, though this is really not equivalent at all.

Computationalism—the doctrine Haugeland (1986, 1981) has elegantly expressed as the doctrine that the mind is an automatic formal system—entails that the answer to the first question be yes. Of course, one can imagine a kind of philosophically de-sexed computationalism that says something much weaker, viz., that to be a cognitive system is to be an automatic formal system. Thus conceived, computationalism is just a theory of cognition. A mind, complete with *consciousness* and *a subjective point of view*—the Nagel property, in short—may after all be more than a mere thinker, more than a mere cognitive engine. Descartes held that the essence of mind is thought, Locke that it is the capacity for thought. But it never occurred to these thinkers that thought without consciousness—thought without the Nagel property—might be a serious possibility. But it might be a serious possibility, for all of that. And if it is, then computationalism might be the correct theory of it. The existence of such a thing—cognition without consciousness—would be terrifically important, and it would be terrifically important that it could be captured computationally. From the point of view of cognitive science, this would vindicate computationalism. A sober, scientific computationalism will surely avoid the Nagel property if it possibly can.

But maybe a science of cognition can't avoid consciousness. And anyway, *philosophers*, for the most part—those who aren't (like me) just philosophers of cognitive science—will want to ask the questions I began with anyway. Could something be conscious (have the Nagel property) in virtue of exercising its computational capacities?

1.2. Methodology

How could we hope to find answers to these questions? Even if we build terrifically impressive programs, so impressive that the computers that execute them (probably special purpose jobs that have the program hard-wired) are indistinguishable from normal adult humans on a battery of cognitive and other psychological tests, won't we be left wondering if it is all mere *imitation*? Won't we still be left wondering it if really is like something to be that computer, and, if so, *what* it's like?

Well, probably not, really. The temptation to *intentionalize* the things we interact with is overwhelming. Most of us, at times, treat our cars, our appliances, and even really inanimate objects like show shovels, as persons. We blame them, for example. And once you *intentionalize* something, you just naturally start to think of it as *like us*—at least a little—and hence as conscious, as something with the Nagel property. But, for philosophy, if not for common (and sensible) life, this is a kind of intellectual weakness. Even if we found the temptation irresistible to think of the computer as, in the relevant respect, one of us, we'd want to ask the question anyway, to force the issue into the open.

So, yes, we *would* be left wondering if it was all mere imitation. How could the underlying doubts be resolved?

If there is a received answer to this question, it goes like this. Maybe *we* will turn out to be automatic formal systems. When we read this result in *The Science News*, we will, each one of us, know what it is like to be an automatic formal system: we will each be in a position to think, *it's like being me!*

But I don't think this line of thought really cuts any ice, because I'm pretty sure the scientists are going to have to beg the very question at issue—or find a substantive answer to it—in order to be in a position to announce the result in question. For how will they know it is specifically the *computational* capacities of the brain that are responsible for the Nagel property? The obvious methodology is the method of differences: build something whose only significant similarity to the human brain is computational architecture and see if *it* has the Nagel property. But *that* methodology is no help unless we can dismiss the possibility of *mere imitation*. And, on the face of it, it seems impossible to be certain *from the outside* whether some behaving system has the Nagel property or not.

1.3. The issue is empirical

I think the received answer just rehearsed (if that's what it is) has its heart in the right place in insisting that the issue is not one to be settled by a priori speculation. To show that the issue is, at bottom, an empirical issue, one that could be settled by experiment, I want to borrow a famous thought experiment from Dennett's 'Where Am I?' (Dennett 1978). My version will be slightly different, but only in such inessential details that make its application to the present issue obvious.

1.4. A Dennettesque thought experiment

A bit of personal history will help here. Some time ago, I was craft-wrecked on an alien planet. Fortunately, the natives proved friendly and, despite rather large biological differences, I learned to communicate and become a useful member of their society. One day, however, a friend confided to me that there was a faction who suspected me of being a mere robot. I was insulted, but not daunted, for my craft's computer had survived, and it contained a copy of HUMIND, a computer program that had passed every psychological imitation test devised on Earth. I presented it to the doubters and told them: 'This embodies the ultimate theory of the mental capacities of me and my kind.' They studied and mastered the HUMIND, which they found impressive. 'But,' they said, 'how is one to know whether being something satisfying this theory—running HUMIND—is like being one of us, or even like anything at all? As your immortal Locke pointed out, one cannot tell simply by understanding a complete chemical description of pineapple whether tasting something satisfying the description is like tasting pineapple. You shouldn't expect us to be able to tell, merely by *understanding* an objective scientific theory of your psychology, whether being you is like being one of us, or like anything at all. A scientific theory can never give that kind of knowledge, but it's just that kind of knowledge we're after when we wonder if you're a mere robot!'

The aliens were right, of course. In the matter of the pineapples, I reflected, we can find or construct something satisfying the suspect description and *try it*. If it tastes like pineapple, we have reason to accept the hypothesis that something tastes like pineapple because it has the chemical description in question. Or at least that satisfying the description is sufficient. But it seemed to me that nothing analogous would work in the psychological case: the aliens couldn't try satisfying my psychology to see how it is to be me.

For a while, I despaired. Sometime later, however, one of my new friends consoled me. 'You shouldn't feel bad,' she said. 'These doubters are hypocrites. No one let on, but HUMIND is recognizable as an implementation of best theory our scientists have been able to devise for *us*. So, you see, they really have no more business doubting your consciousness than each other's.'

Well, this not only cheered me up, it gave me an idea. Recalling my Dennett, I suggested that the 'brain' of an alien volunteer be removed, kept alive in a life support system, and linked with her perceptual and motor systems via radio. Meanwhile, HUMIND would be run on an advanced special purpose alien computer, and its data bases stuffed, stacked, and tuned until the result simulated perfectly and in real time the I/O of the volunteer's brain, running 'in sync.' with it. The set up is shown in Figure 1.1.

One of the doubters volunteered. The operation was a success, and, after several months of fiddling, we managed to get the brain and the computer synchronized. 'Now,' I said to the volunteer, 'you may wonder if the computer process is mere simulation, or synthetic mentality—a synthetic you, in fact. It passes all the objective tests, to be sure, but: what's it like to *be* something running HUMIND, and thus satisfying a computational theory?' Curious? Well, before you are five switches. Four are fakes, but one breaks the radio link between your brain and your body that allows your brain to control your body, and substitutes a link that allows the computer to control you body. The links from your body back to you brain and to the computer are not affected. The switches all automatically reset in five minutes, so there's no serious danger. Your body amputation was far more serious. I wonder if you can tell which is the real switch?'

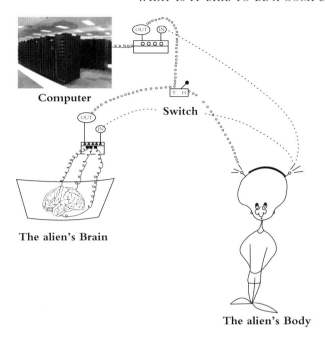

Computer

Switch

The alien's Brain

The alien's Body

Figure 1.1 Signals from the alien's body go to both brain and computer. Signals from the computer and brain reach the alien's body depending on the setting of the switch

In the event, the alien couldn't tell the dummy from the real thing. At first, she suspected that they were all fakes, but after exposing the circuitry, she was forced to concede that instantiating the theory—running HUMIND, in fact—is a sufficient condition for alien consciousness as she knew it, for the only relevant fact about the computer was that it instantiated the computational theory that I and the alien scientists claim specifies the computational powers in virtue of which we all are what we are— conscious persons with a subjective inner life.

A few months into the trial, she came up with an objection. 'Suppose,' she said, 'that the seat of my consciousness remains in my brain. When control of my body is switched to the computer, everything seems normal *to me*, because, as the human philosopher Leibniz pointed out, as long as a perfect parallelism is maintained between the control signals from my brain, and those from my body, it will *seem to me* that I am in control. I intend to raise my arm, and my arm goes up. I think scary thoughts, and my pulse rate goes up. It would. The synchronization guarantees it.'

I started to say something, but she held up her hand. 'I thought this could be resolved by spoiling the synchronization between my brain and the computer. If consciousness does reside only in my brain, then it will be obvious to me that I have lost control when the computer is controlling my body. To *you,* of course, there will seem to be two persons sharing my body in turns, but *to me,* the issue will be resolved.'

'Not really,' I replied. 'Think: If we disrupt the synchronization while the computer is in control, and there is a seat of consciousness in the computer, then it will seem to you, and to us, that nothing has happened. If the disruption occurs when the brain is in control, then, again, it will seem to you, and to us, that nothing has happened.'

'I see that,' she replied, 'but if my consciousness resides in my brain, then it will seem to me that I have lost control of my body when control is switched to the computer. But it will seem to me that I have regained control, not lost it, when control is switched to the brain.'

'Well, yes,' I said. 'But if there is a seat of consciousness in the computer, then it will seem to *that* person—the one whose seat of consciousness is in the computer—that she is not controlling her body when the brain is in control.'

This conversation continued for some time, without significant progress. A week later, however, she returned again.

'This could be settled,' she said, 'by destroying my brain, or simply by drugging it into unconsciousness while the computer is under control. If I cannot tell that this has happened—if my stream of consciousness remains unbroken—then my objection is refuted. Under this condition, I will have the same reasons I have now, and have always had, to think I have survived *any* event in my life.'

So, with her permission, we put her brain under with drugs while the computer was under control. She says she noticed no difference. She—or it—*would* say that, of course. When the brain is under control these days, she doesn't remember the chess match we played while her brain was under. So, when her brain is under control, she says she lost consciousness when her brain was under. When the computer is under control, she insists that she noticed no difference when the brain was put under, and, therefore, that she, or rather her seat of consciousness—*her* seat of consciousness—resides in the computer now. She acknowledges that a personal fission has taken place, and that another person supervenes, in part, on the processes going on in '*that brain.*'

I am pretty sure someone—one of those persons who started out as my volunteer—knows from first person experience that the right computation suffices for consciousness. It follows from this that the right computation *does* suffice for consciousness. And it also follows that the issue is an empirical one, one that can be settled by observation, even though getting in a position to make the relevant observation is a bit, well, *odd*.

1.5. Remarks about the experiment

Notice, by the way, that the experiment could have failed. I'm not sure how to describe a failure from either a first or third person point of view except that, unlike the success we achieved, failure wouldn't be just like flipping a dummy switch. Lacking a positive description of failure, I won't presume to say how a failure ought to be interpreted. But, my 'success' does resolve, for me, the question of whether computationalism is true of false, because, to repeat, I am quite certain that my former chess partner knows, from first person experience, that computationalism is true.

Contemporary anti-materialist writers are correct in supposing that there's a kind of knowledge or understanding of thought that might not be provided by an intellectual grasp of a computational (or any other) *theory* of thought, but this does not establish that materialist theories of mind must 'leave something out.' Perhaps, through weakness of imagination or technology, we cannot know, for any arbitrary psychological theory, what it would be like to satisfy it. But, as my recent experience demonstrates, it is possible to discover that satisfying some particular theory is like being one of us, and that is surely enough to show that whether the theory 'leaves out' something essential to possession of the Nagel property is an empirical question at bottom. Intellectual grasp of the theory may not tell us whether it is like anything to satisfy the theory, but there are other ways to tell. In principle, we could 'try it on.'

1.6. Knowing it's true isn't understanding it

Having said all this, I must admit that there might be something 'left out' by the sort of theory lately experienced by the alien volunteer. We could, I think, be in the position of knowing beyond serious doubt that our consciousness results from our programming, yet have no understanding of how this could be. We would, of course, know what sort of phenomenon it is, viz., that it is the sort of thing that supervenes on having been programmed in a certain way. In that sense, the ontological issue would have been settled empirically. But we might still be quite in the dark as to *how* consciousness does or could supervene on that or *any other* physically specified design. We might have no idea, in fact, what sort of intellectual tool it would take to understand this fact. We might not know whether we should be doing phenomenology, neuroscience, AI, or what.

An analogy will help us focus on the possibility I have in mind. A seventeenth-century physicist might well have wondered why pounding a nail makes it hot. (Galileo did.) She would realize that the kinetic energy of the hammer must be transformed into heat in the nail, and even have the case subsumed under an excellent quantitative causal law. But as to *how* the hammer's kinetic energy is transformed into heat, she is in the dark, and consequently unable to explain why her excellent equation is satisfied. What she needs, of course, is our deep analysis of temperature as molecular motion. Without it, she knows *that* pounding induces a rise in temperature. She can predict it with great quantitative accuracy. But she can't understand it—she can't explain how *pounding* could change *temperature*. This, I suppose, is just where we all stand today with respect to the basic laws of quantum electrodynamics. Perhaps we will never understand this. But, then, that is how things must have seemed to our seventeenth-century physicist.

In just the same way, we might know *that* computation underlies consciousness but be in the dark as to *how* consciousness could supervene on mere symbol manipulation. Like Leibniz (*Monadology*, §17), we might wander through the computational mill and never encounter the Nagel property. The existence of this possibility has an interesting implication: *No conclusion about the ontology of consciousness can follow from premises concerning what it would take to understand it*. In particular, from the fact, if it is one, that a

computational theory of thought wouldn't make us understand consciousness or subjectiveness—at least not in the sense in which we understand why
pounding a nail makes it hot but don't understand why the laws of quantum
electrodynamics hold—nothing follows about what these things *are*.

1.7. Conclusion

To sum up: a priori arguments against the possibility of a computational
synthesis of something with the Nagel property are pervasive—even believers
are not untouched. More subtle thinkers than we are have been tempted to
conclude something about the ontological nature of consciousness from the
supposed impotence of certain explanatory strategies to make us understand
how being a machine could be like being one of us. But these aprioristic
tendencies need to be resisted. Reflection in the form of the thought
experiment lately described reveals that the issue is empirical at bottom.
Non-empirical arguments against the possibility of a computational (or
connectionist, or whatever) synthesis of consciousness are ultimately self-
defeating. Lacking an empirically tested theory of thought, our only intellectual line on the concept is ostensive, and that line is too weak to support
non-empirical argumentation. By the same token, current announcements
of successful synthesis of thought are equally unfounded, depending—as
they must at this stage—on some rather arbitrary a priori theory of thought
rather than on an empirically tested theory of the ostensively identified
phenomena.

If this is on the right track, then to argue back and forth at this stage about
whether it can be like anything to be a computer is premature: we know
what we are talking about, but we are only just beginning to know how to
talk about it. Two hundred years ago, John Locke lamented that he could
identify the real essence of gold ostensively—it's whatever accounts for the
causal powers of the stuff the last guinea coined was made of—but he
couldn't *conceptualize* it except in very vague and abstract terms as some
sort of micro-structure (*Essay Concerning Human Understanding*, 3. 6. 19).
Cognitive science is just about where physical chemistry was in Locke's day:
we know what phenomena we're after, and we have several nifty ideas
about the sort of theory that will do the job. And we're making progress on
some special and rather artificial cases. To argue now about whether

consciousness (or thought, or intentionality) *could* be computational is rather like arguing in Locke's day about whether the properties of gold *could* depend on its micro-structure. It's worth remembering that many argued confidently at the time—on a priori grounds—that they could not.

References

Cummins, R., *The Nature of Psychological Explanation* (Cambridge, Mass.: MIT Press/Bradford Books, 1983).

Dennett, D., *Brainstorms* (Cambridge, Mass.: MIT Press/Bradford Books, 1978).

Fodor, Jerry, *RePresentations* (Cambridge, Mass.: MIT Press/Bradford Books, 1981).

—— *The Modularity of Mind* (Cambridge, Mass.: MIT Press/Bradford Books, 1983).

Haugeland, J. (ed.), *Mind Design* (Cambridge, Mass.: MIT Press/Bradford Books, 1981).

—— *Artificial Intelligence: The Very Idea* (Cambridge, Mass.: MIT Press/Bradford Books, 1985).

Hofstadter, D., and Dennett, D. (eds.), *The Mind's I: Fantasies and Reflections on Self and Soul* (New York: Basic Books, 1981).

Nagel, T., 'What is it Like to Be a Bat?', *Philosophical Review*, 83 (1974), 435–50.

Pylyshyn, Z., *Computation and Cognition* (Cambridge, Mass.: MIT Press/Bradford Books, 1984).

2

The LOT of the Causal Theory of Mental Content

The thesis of this chapter is that the *causal theory of mental content* (hereafter CT) is incompatible with an elementary fact of perceptual psychology, namely, that the detection of distal properties generally requires the mediation of a 'theory.' I'll call this fact the *nontransducibility of distal properties* (hereafter NTDP). The argument proceeds in two stages. The burden of stage one is that, taken together, CT and the *language of thought hypothesis* (hereafter LOT) are incompatible with NTDP. The burden of stage two is that acceptance of CT requires acceptance of LOT as well. It follows that CT is incompatible with NTDP. I organize things in this way in part because it makes the argument easier to understand, and in part because the stage two thesis—that CT entails LOT—has some independent interest and is therefore worth separating from the rest of the argument.

2.1. Stage one: the conjunction of CT and LOT is incompatible with the nontransducibility of distal properties

Let us begin by clarifying some terms. By LOT, I mean the hypothesis that the human scheme of mental representation satisfies the following conditions:

(1) It has a finite number of semantically primitive expressions individuated syntactically.
(2) Every expression is a concatenation of the primitives.

Originally published in *Journal of Philosophy*, 94 (1997), 535–42. This paper appears with the kind permission of the *Journal of Philosophy*.

(3) The content of any complex expression is a function of the contents of the primitives and the syntax of the whole expression.

The *locus classicus* of this thesis is Jerry Fodor's *The Language of Thought*.[1] I shall also use 'LOT' to refer to the language of thought itself rather than the hypothesis. The context will resolve any ambiguity this might otherwise introduce.

By CT, I mean the doctrine that the contents of the semantic primitives in the human scheme of mental representation are determined by their role in detection. The basic idea is just that the content of a primitive r in a system $\sum$ is the property P if there is the right kind of causal connection between instantiations of P and tokenings of r by $\sum$'s detectors. Causal theories come in a variety of flavors.[2] I am simply going to assume familiarity with these theories in what follows.[3] The only feature of the theory that will play a role in the discussion that follows is the following uncontroversial feature: assuming LOT, CT requires that every property represented by a primitive in LOT be detectable.

Now for NTDP. Distal properties generally cannot be directly transduced.[4] Instead, the detection of distal properties must be mediated by what we might as well call a theory about that property.[5] To detect cats (an instantiation of catness) requires a theory that says, in effect, what sorts of proximal stimuli are reliable indicators of catness. To detect cats visually, you have to know how cats look. The same goes for colors, shapes, and sizes: for these to be reliably detected visually under changes in perspective,

---

[1] Fodor (1975).

[2] See Stampe (1977); Dretske (1981); Millikan (1984); Papineau (1987); Fodor (1990a). Some readers might wonder at the inclusion of adaptationist theories like those of Papineau and Millikan as flavors of CT. These theories differ from other causal theories only in using adaptational role to select those causal connections that are content-fixing.

[3] A review can be found in Cummins (1989).

[4] 'Transduced' in the sense of Pylyshyn (1984), ch. 6. The central idea is that transduction is a cognitively primitive operation that maps physical events at the sensory surface onto computational events 'upstream.' It is controversial whether there *are* any transducers in this sense in human functional architecture. It is not controversial that transducers thus conceived are not responsible for distal property detection. This 'engineering' conception of transduction is to be distinguished from that found in the mathematical theory of computation where a transducer is just any finite automaton.

[5] It is controversial in psychology just what the form and exact content the mediating theory might turn out to have. It might turn out to be a point in weight space—e.g. Churchland (1989), chs. 9–11. According to LOT, if it is learned, it will be a set of sentences in LOT. If it is innate, it might, in some sense, be implicit in the architecture. For a review of some ways such information might be implicit, see Cummins (1986: 116–26), Ch. 6, this volume.

lighting, and distance requires knowledge of such facts as that retinal image size varies as the inverse square of the distance to the object.

Much of the knowledge[6] that mediates the detection of distal properties must be acquired: we are, perhaps, born with a tacit knowledge of Emmert's Law, but we are not born knowing how cats look, or with the ability to distinguish edges from shadows. We must, then, learn the theory that mediates cat recognition. Learning the theory will require formulating and confirming hypotheses such as these:

(A) Cats have whiskers.
(B) Cats have four legs.
(C) Cats have fur.

According to LOT, these hypotheses are represented as sentences in LOT. As such, they require for their formulation, a symbol for cats, that is, a |cat|.[7] But, according to CT, you cannot have a |cat| until you have the ability to detect cats. According to psychology, you cannot have the ability to detect cats until you have a theory of cats. According to LOT, you cannot have a theory of cats until you have |cat|s. So, you cannot make the conjunction of LOT and CT compatible with psychology.

Objections and replies

Objection one   That is all right for |cat|s, but what about |square|s? What reason is there to believe that we have to learn a theory of squares to recognize them?

Reply one   Suppose the objection is right about squares and circles and some other stuff. What are you going to do about cats? Your only option is to suppose that |cat| is not a primitive symbol in LOT. But if it is not a primitive symbol in LOT, then it must be a complex symbol in LOT, that is, a Tarskian combination of other symbols in LOT. This implies that |cat| can be defined in LOT in terms of symbols for properties whose detection

---

[6] I use 'knowledge' here as it is used in cognitive psychology, which does not require that what is known be true or justified. Knowledge in this sense is information that is treated as if it were reliable by the system that uses it. This is what allows us to say that the visual system must know such things as that retinal image size varies as the inverse square of the distance to the object even though, in the ordinary sense of 'know', this was not widely known in Europe until the 17th cent.

[7] A |cat| is a mental representation whose content is the property of being a cat.

does not require a learned theory. Good luck: this kind of reductionism has a dismal history; if you want to revive it, you are on your own.

Reply two   The only argument on offer for the idea that you *do not* have to learn a theory of squares to recognize squares is that you *could not* learn it. Indeed, Fodor argues quite correctly in *The Language of Thought* that you could not learn to recognize any property represented by a primitive of LOT, the argument being, in effect, just the one given above. But this cuts as heavily against LOT as it does against the idea that squares can be detected without the aid of acquired information.

Objection two   The thing is done by degrees. You start out with some relation between distal stimuli and *R*. Since you don't yet know much about cats, *R* cannot mean catness. It means, as it might be, *p*catness ('*p*' for proximal). Since your theories have to use the symbols you have got, you have hypotheses like these: *p*cats have whiskers;[8] *p*cats have four legs; *p*cats have fur. As the theory gets elaborated, eventually, we are able to recognize cats reliably.

Reply one   Why should the theory become elaborated? There is not, after all, an error signal that says, in effect, that the theory is not right yet. By hypothesis, the theory is, at any stage you like, as right as it could possibly be for *p*catness. This is because CT implies that you cannot have |*p*cat|s in the theory unless you have a good enough theory of *p*cats to underwrite the connection between *p*cats and some symbol in LOT. To elaborate the theory in the right direction, you have to know that the theory isn't yet a good enough theory of catness, and that, it would seem, requires having |cat|s in your repertoire, applying them to various things—for example, *p*cats—and finding out that they are not cats.

It is easy to get confused about this, because one imagines someone who has not yet learned to recognize cats reliably looking at a cat and having the same percept as you and I would have. As George Berkeley would have said, he hath his eyes and the use of them as well as you and I; and surely that percept is a percept of a cat.

---

[8]   There is, of course, a corresponding problem for whisker detection and consequently for |whisker|s. So, perhaps, (1) should read, '*p*cats have *p*whiskers.' We then work on |whisker| and |cat| simultaneously.

Quite right. But (*a*) it is not a |cat| since, as Berkeley also pointed out, it represents some particular cat of definite color, shape, and so on, whereas a |cat| represents any cat whatever; and (*b*) the structural similarities between the percept and the cat that make it so tempting (rightly, I would argue) to suppose it represents the cat before you are completely irrelevant to its representation content according to CT. What matters, according to CT, are the causal relations between the representation and the property of being a cat; the intrinsic structural features of the representation are irrelevant. NTDP says nothing in your head has a chance of standing in the requisite causal relation to the property of being a cat unless you have a theory of cats. Lacking such a theory, nothing in your head can represent that property, perceptually or any other way.

Objection two reformulated   What you do is try to acquire a theory that will underwrite a mental representation that translates the public language word for cats. While learning about cats, you are also learning about 'cat.' You say 'cat' whenever your detectors generate the symbol R. You keep refining the theory that mediates your detection system's tokening of R until you are saying 'cat' in the presence of the distal stimuli that prompt 'cat' in your language community.

Reply one   This objection falsely implies that only humans (and other language users, if any) can mentally represent the property of being a cat. Cats recognize conspecifics, and hence, according to all but the most hopelessly chauvinistic version of LOT, cats represent catness.[9] Moreover, nonverbal children can recognize cats, as discrimination experiments show. Furthermore, you can recognize things for which your language has no word. The objection under consideration will require that all of these be things for which you have a completely adequate paraphrase. This is surely an empirical question. Moreover, it is the sort of empirical question that a theory of content should leave open. Whatever the arguments are for LOT and CT, they should not settle issues like this.

---

[9] Maybe cats could get by with a |same species/variety as me|. Maybe. But (1) there is evidence that |me|s might be problematic for cats; and (2) in the context of the larger argument, acquiring a theory that will underwrite a |same species/variety as me| is going to be just as problematic as acquiring a theory that will underwrite |cat|s.

Reply two   The objection currently on the table implies that the acquisitions of 'cat' and |cat| are coeval. But it is a hypothesis dear to the hearts of LOTers that the acquisition of 'cat' is a matter of figuring out which mental representation best translates 'cat.' According to this view, learning the meaning of 'cat' is a matter of confirming the hypothesis that 'cat' means |cat| (that is, confirming '|"cat" means cat|'), and this is evidently ruled out by the scenario under consideration. Since I am not fond of the translation theory of language acquisition myself, I regard this as merely a polemical point, and I include it here only to sow the seeds of doubt in the opposition.

2.2. Stage two: CT entails LOT

CT entails that mental representation is arbitrary in the following sense: any primitive representation could mean anything. You get this feature in CT for the following reason: if you can build a *P*-detector at all, you can arrange for it to output any symbol you like when it detects *P*.[10] So far as CT is concerned, then, any primitive symbol could mean any detectable property.

CT also entails that there are finitely many semantically primitive representations in the scheme of mental representation. To see this, begin with the observation that CT requires a detector for each primitive representation. Detectors do not have to be componential or functional units. All that is required is that, for each primitive representation, there is a mechanism/ process that detects its target property. Since a finite system cannot incorporate infinitely many such mechanisms/processes, the question reduces to this: can one process/mechanism detect infinitely many target properties?

It might seem so. Consider a planar array of photo-sensors. If we assume that a square pattern, regardless of location, size, or orientation on the array, is a representation of squareness, and make a comparable assumption about every shape, then this system will (depending on density, and discounting 'viewing angles' other than those normal to the array) detect and represent infinitely many shapes. But notice that CT could not possibly underwrite

---

[10]   It is tempting to suppose that the state of the detector when it detects *P* is the symbol in question, but this cannot be right, for then every time the system tokens that symbol, it will think it has detected *P*, and that will rule out thoughts like this: 'Well, it is not a cat, but if it were, it would pounce on that mouse.'

such a representational scheme. For what we have done here is assume that any square pattern represents squareness regardless of its regular causes. To see this, notice that a particular pattern will only be caused by some squares, namely, those with the right location, orientation, and size–distance combination relative to the array. The causal theory will say that the pattern represents only those squares, not squareness. To fix this problem, we shall have to map each square pattern onto some single arbitrary symbol. To do that, we shall have to introduce an algorithm that abstracts from size, orientation, and location on the array. It will have to look for a closed pattern with four straight sides. To distinguish square patterns from trapezoids and parallelograms, it will have to test for right-angled corners; to weed out rectangles, it will have to test for side equality. It will, in short, have to know about squares. Ditto for any other shape that is represented by a primitive in the system. Since there is only a finite amount of memory available, this knowledge will have to be finite. So, the system can only map a finite number of shapes onto primitive representations.

It is clear that this argument generalizes. NTDP requires, in effect, a theory of P for the detection of P, and CT requires the detection of P as a precondition of the primitive representation of P. In a finite system, there is only so much room for theory, so it follows that there can, at any given time, be only a finite number of primitives in play. CT allows for a scheme in which the set of primitives is unbounded in the sense that, given enough memory, another can always be added.[11] But it does not allow for a scheme in which the number of primitives is infinite.

This may seem a pretty trivial result, but other stories about content do not have this consequence. As the shape example shows, if a representation represents everything structurally isomorphic to it,[12] then it is possible to have a scheme with as many primitive shape representations as there are shapes (or something isomorphic to them) for the representations themselves to have. Finite precision will make it impossible for any actual system to exploit all that primitive representational power, but the scheme has it for all that.

Thus, CT implies that the scheme of mental representation has a finite number of arbitrary primitives. Moreover, since the scheme of mental

[11] Even this may be allowing too much, since, as every PC owner knows, the architecture typically limits how much memory you can add.
[12] See Cummins (1996a).

representation needs to be productive, it follows that there must be a way of combining the semantically arbitrary primitives into complex representations such that the meaning of the complex is a function of the meaning of the constituents and their mode of combination. A scheme of finitely many semantically arbitrary primitives that allows for an unbounded set of semantically distinct complex representations whose contents are determined by their constituents and mode of combination is LOT as near as makes no difference.[13] So CT entails LOT.[14]

2.3. Conclusion

I have argued that, taken together, CT and LOT are incompatible with the nontransducibility of distal properties; and I have argued that CT entails LOT. It follows that CT is incompatible with the nontransducibility of distal properties. Since distal properties are not transducible, it follows that CT is false. Since the argument uses only a generic form of CT, it follows that CT is false in all its forms.

The conclusion can be generalized a bit. Nothing in the argument given here depends on the content-fixing relation being causal; any covariationist semantics will face exactly the same problem, since (1) NTDP says that the only way to get reliable covariation between a mental state and a distal property is to have a theory of that property, and (2) covariational accounts make representation arbitrary in the sense required by the argument of stage two.

In *Representations, Targets, and Attitudes*,[15] I argue that CT is a restricted form of functional-role semantics. CT is what you get when you restrict the functional roles that determine content to the roles a representation plays in detection. The question therefore naturally arises as to whether functional-role

---

[13] There is nothing in CT to guarantee that the combinatorics have to be Tarskian, but, then, neither must advocates of LOT insist on Tarskian combinatorics. It is just that Tarskian combinatorics are the only ones currently available for combining arbitrary symbols productively. LOT is Tarskian by default, not by inner necessity.

[14] Strictly speaking, what I have argued is that CT plus finite detection resources plus productivity entails LOT. The finiteness of detection resources is, I suppose, an empirical premise, but it is uncontroversial. Productivity is an empirical premise as well, but it is a pretty secure premise, and it is a premise that both CTers and LOTers typically accept.

[15] Cummins (1996a).

semantics generally is incompatible with NTDP. I do not know the answer to that question. What is clear, however, is that nothing like the argument just rehearsed will work against functional-role semantics generally, since that argument turns essentially on facts about the detection of distal properties, and detection has no privileged role to play in functional-role theories of mental content.

References

Churchland, P. M., *A Neurocomputational Perspective* (Cambridge, Mass.: MIT Press, 1989).

Cummins, R., 'Inexplicit Information', in M. Brand and R. M. Harnish (eds.), *The Representation of Knowledge and Belief* (Tucson, Ariz.: University of Arizona Press, 1986).

—— *Meaning and Mental Representation* (Cambridge, Mass.: MIT Press, 1989).

—— *Representations, Targets, and Attitudes* (Cambridge, Mass.: MIT Press, 1996a).

Dretske, F., *Knowledge and the Flow of Information* (Cambridge, Mass.: MIT Press, 1981).

Fodor, J., *The Language of Thought* (New York: Thomas Y. Crowell, 1975).

—— *A Theory of Content and Other Essays* (Cambridge, Mass.: MIT Press, 1990a).

Millikan, R., *Language, Thought, and Other Biological Categories* (Cambridge, Mass.: MIT Press/Bradford Books, 1984).

Papineau, D., *Reality and Representation* (Oxford: Basil Blackwell, 1987).

Pylyshyn, Z., *Computation and Cognition* (Cambridge, Mass.: MIT Press/Bradford Books, 1984).

Stampe, D., 'Towards a Causal Theory of Linguistic Representation', in P. A. French, T. E. Uehling, and H. K. Wettstein (eds.), *Midwest Studies in Philosophy*, ii. *Studies in the Philosophy of Language* (Minneapolis: University of Minnesota Press, 1977), 42–63.

3

Systematicity

Jerry Fodor and various colleagues[1] have argued that the human scheme of mental representation exhibits a certain sort of constituent structure—a *classical* structure—on the grounds that the systematicity of thought and language, alleged to be evident and pervasive, is best explained on the hypothesis that mental representation is classical. It turns out to be more difficult than one would expect to specify either what it is for thought to be systematic or for a representational scheme to be 'classical' in the required sense. The definitions in the literature are quite hopeless, and when the deficiencies are corrected, the thesis that thought is systematic is seen to be problematic at best, and the argument from the systematicity of thought to the alleged classicalness of representation collapses. The systematicity of language, on the other hand, is relatively unproblematic, but it turns out that sensitivity to the systematicity of language can be explained without appeal to classical representation. Moreover, there are other systematicities—for example, in vision—that must receive some explanation or other. If the argument from linguistic systematicity to classical representation is accepted, then we should also accept an exactly parallel argument from visual systematicity to nonclassical representation. The argument from human sensitivity to systematicity to classical representation is therefore self-defeating if it is meant to establish that *the* scheme of mental representation in humans is classical.

Originally published in *Journal of Philosophy*, 93 (1996), 591–614. This paper appears with the kind permission of the *Journal of Philosophy*.

[1] Fodor and Pylyshyn (1988); Fodor and McLaughlin (1990c); Fodor and Lepore (1992).

3.1. Classical representation

Let us begin with the idea of a classical representational scheme. Here is the preferred definition: a representational scheme is *classical* in the intended sense if tokening a complex representation requires tokening its constituents.[2] On the obvious reading, this is surely a tautology, since what makes a representation complex is just that it has constituents. A representation that does not have constituents will not count as complex. We can rescue this notion from triviality only by supposing that a token of a complex representation can 'have' a constituent that is not tokened. Tim van Gelder[3] suggests that we might broaden the notion of compositionality so that x might count as a constituent of y even if tokening y does not require tokening x, provided that you can reliably get from x to y and back again. He calls this *functional compositionality*. But this appears to leave the notion of complexity in some obscurity. As P. Smolensky, G. LeGendre, and Y. Miyata[4] show, we can represent arbitrarily complex structures as vectors of activations, but the complexity of the resulting vectors does not correspond to the complexity of the structure represented. Indeed, all the vectors in such a scheme are of equal complexity (since they are of the same dimension). The only sense in which one representation in this scheme is more complex than another is that some decode into more complex structures than others. This relativizes the complexity of a representation to a decoding. Since there may be more than one decoding possible, and these need not be semantically equivalent, it also makes complexity an implicitly semantic notion, rather than a purely formal notion. If we reject the dubious notion of functional compositionality, the criterion of classicalness proposed by Fodor and Brian McLaughlin will make every scheme classical. Evidently, we need a different approach.

Another way of getting at the idea of classical representation is that a scheme is classical if representing a complex content requires a correspondingly complex representation, with each constituent of the representation corresponding to each constituent of the content represented. This is certainly operative in the discussion of systematicity in Fodor and

---

[2] Fodor and Pylyshyn (1988); Fodor and McLaughlin (1990c).   [3] van Gelder (1990).
[4] Smolensky *et al.* (1992).

Pylyshyn's[5] classic discussion, for example. Following C. Swoyer,[6] I shall call representational schemes that satisfy this condition *structural schemes*. Fodor and Pylyshyn's discussion of systematicity suggests that classical representation is structural representation. But the idea that classical representation is structural representation faces two serious difficulties. First, this formulation requires that propositions be complex—complex, moreover, in just the way that the representations are complex. And, second, it precludes abbreviation ($r = df\ p\ \&\ q$), which is surely not intended. The first consequence—that propositions themselves have a constituent structure that mirrors the constituent structure of some favored representational

---

[5] Fodor and Pylyshyn suggest that a connectionist might get simplification by having a node representing $p\ \&\ q$ activate nodes representing p and representing q. (See Figure 3.1.)

p & q

p   q

Figure 3.1 Fodor and Pylyshyn's suggestion for a network that does conjunction simplification

Since each node has (let us suppose) no semantically relevant internal complexity, it follows that the representation of $p\ \&\ q$ is no more complex than the representation of p, and certainly does not contain a representation of p as a constituent. The question arises, however, as to why the whole three-node net does not count as a classical representation of $p\ \&\ q$. (Notice that it misses the point of this proposal to argue that we could cut the connections, or change the weights, allowing activation of the top node, hence tokening $p\ \&\ q$, without tokening either p or q.)

The obvious response to this sort of proposal is to argue that it is unfair to build, as it were, the entailments into the representation. This response is unavailable, however, to anyone who, like Fodor himself, is an advocate of functional-role semantics for the logical connectives. To say that logical connectives are identified by their functional role is just to say that logical form is determined by what inferences get made. Functional-role semantics says that what makes something a conjunction is precisely connections to other formulas. So what makes it appropriate to label the top node '$p\ \&\ q$' is just that it is connected in the proper way to nodes labeled 'p' and 'q' (among other things). This is not quite the same as saying that the whole net is the representation of $p\ \&\ q$, but it is as close as makes no difference. If you accept functional-role semantics, then nothing that does not work pretty much the way the net does will count as a representation of $p\ \&\ q$, and that is as close as makes no difference to saying that the whole net is a classical representation of $p\ \&\ q$ by the criterion offered in Fodor and Pylyshyn and in Fodor and McLaughlin: whenever you token a representation of $p\ \&\ q$, you are bound to token one of p, since, if you do not, you do not have the causal relations in place that make something a conjunction in the first place. Since Fodor himself accepts functional-role semantics as an account of the content of the logical connectives, it is hard to see how he could object to this construal. Those who think the meanings of logical connectives are fixed functionally are therefore committed to accepting van Gelder's idea that functional compositionality is as good as the 'real thing.' I would prefer to take this as a reductio against a functional-role approach to the connectives.

[6] Swoyer (1991).

scheme—is controversial, and I propose to set it aside for the moment. But the second consequence defeats the proposal outright. In the sort of scheme Fodor and others have in mind, differences in complexity need not correlate with differences in content. We want to be able to hold with Fodor that 'Jocasta is eligible' and 'Œdipus' mother is eligible' have the same content in spite of having different constituents. It will not do, then, to suppose that a representation is classical just in case representations of complex contents require correspondingly complex representations.[7]

What Fodor has in mind, of course, is a language, a language with the sort of syntax and semantics that admits of a Tarskian truth theory. So, perhaps with some de jure but no *de facto* loss of generality, I shall call a scheme *classical* if (1) it has a finite number of semantically primitive expressions individuated syntactically; (2) every expression is a concatenation of the primitives; and (3) the content of any complex expression is a function of the contents of the primitives and the syntax of the whole expression.

3.2. Systematicity in thought

Recent discussion in the literature has centered around language processing.[8] A system is said to exhibit systematicity if, whenever it can process a sentence *s*, it can process systematic variants of *s*, where systematic variation is understood in terms of permuting constituents or (more strongly) substituting constituents of the same grammatical category. Systematicity in this sense has been amply demonstrated in connectionist systems that do not use classical representational schemes.[9] Niklasson and van Gelder are surely right to claim that the issue is now the difficult empirical one of determining (i) what systematicity humans actually exhibit in their language processing; and (ii) what sort of architecture best models it.

I shall return shortly to systematicity in language. First, however, I want to consider the alleged systematicity of thought. The usual formulation (for example, Fodor and Pylyshyn's) goes like this:

---

[7] See Fodor (1990*a*: ch. 6). Notice that, for a language of thought theorist, chunking is abbreviation. Since chunking is essential to every orthodox computational architecture that has any pretensions to psychological relevance, abbreviation is an ineliminable feature of 'classical' schemes.

[8] Hadley (1994); Niklasson and van Gelder (1994).

[9] See Smolensky *et al.* (1992); Niklasson and van Gelder (1994).

> (To) Anyone who can think a thought of the form *Rab* can think a thought of the form *Rba*.

This is hopeless as it stands because it presupposes that thoughts have forms corresponding to the forms of classical representations, and this is precisely the point at issue.[10] To be non-question-begging, we need a formulation like this:

> (T1) Anyone who can think a thought with a content of the form *Rab* can think a thought with a content of the form *Rba*.

This evidently faces a difficulty encountered above and set aside, namely, that contents may not have the relevant forms or any form at all. We can sidestep the issue by reformulating the condition:

> (T2) Anyone who can think a thought with the content c can think a thought with the content c^*, where c^* is any systematic variant of c.

Intuitively, the idea is that c^* is a systematic variant of c if c^* is a content you can express by permuting the constituents of your expression of c.[11] This allows (on the face of it, anyway) for the possibility that contents themselves are unstructured or not structured in a way that happens to mirror the structure of your representations. For example, it permits, but does not require, that anyone who can think the set of possible worlds picked out by 'John loves Mary' can also think the set of possible worlds picked out by 'Mary loves John.'

This approach evidently relativizes the systematicity of thought to the choice of some representational scheme that allows for the permuting of constituents. That consequence is disturbing. The systematicity of thought ought to depend only on the structure of the mind, not on the structure of the representational scheme we, as theorists, choose to use in representing the contents of thoughts. We could defend a particular choice of scheme, of course, if we knew it reflected the structure of the propositions thought, but

---

[10] Of course, sometimes one thinks thoughts in one's natural language. In this case, one could argue that thoughts are represented in a classical scheme since they are represented in, say, English, which is classical. In this case, the systematicity of thought simply reduces to the systematicity of language, which I shall take up below.

[11] Depending on how you do your grammar, allowable grammatical permutations may not yield an expression with a content. 'The hill went up Jack' is, perhaps, an allowable permutation of 'Jack went up the hill,' but may not express any proposition at all.

the motivation for (T2) is precisely to avoid having to make any such dubious commitment.[12] Still, I think it is pretty clear that (T2) is what underlies intuitions about the systematicity of thought, such as they are, for those intuitions clearly depend on one's natural language. The intuitions in question are claims like the following:

(1) Anyone who can think that *John loves Mary* can think that Mary loves John.

The systematicity of thought that this is supposed to illustrate is clearly derived from the systematicity of the language—in this case, from the fact that 'John loves Mary' is a permutation of 'Mary loves John.' The intuitive force of (1) would obviously disappear or change if we could substitute either unstructured or differently structured classical representations for the propositions, or if we could substitute nonclassical representations for the propositions. Consider:

(2) Anyone who can think *Mary's favorite proposition* can think that Mary loves John.

On the obvious assumption, the italicized phrase in (2) refers to the same proposition as the italicized phrase in (1). But (2) elicits no systematicity intuitions precisely because the italicized phrase in (2) is not a permutation of 'Mary loves John.'

One might object at this point that (2) does not tell us what Mary's favorite proposition is, and hence that we are in no position to determine whether her favorite proposition is a systematic variant of the proposition that Mary loves John. This is fair enough, perhaps, but it underlines the fact that identifying the propositions in question requires the mediation of an appropriate representation. It is the structure of the mediating representation which determines whether or not we see systematicity in the thoughts. (2) seems like cheating because it does not give us canonical representations

---

[12] One might think that propositions have classical forms on the grounds that they are expressible by classical representations. This appears to be Fodor's line in *A Theory of Content*. But one might equally think that propositions have pictorial forms on the grounds that they are expressible by pictorial representations. (The proposition represented by a picture is the set of possible worlds it accurately depicts. For example, the picture on your driver's license picks out the set of possible worlds in which someone looks like you do in that picture.) Moreover, it is a notable feature of classical schemes that representations of radically different forms can express the same proposition. Indeed, since logical equivalence is not decidable, it is not even decidable in a classical scheme whether two forms express the same proposition.

of the propositions in question. But that is just my point: (1) gets all of its appeal from the fact that it incorporates linguistic expressions for the propositions that are interderivable by permutation. You get the same dialectic if you put in Gödel numbers or activation vectors: once you lose the relevant constituent structure in the expression of the propositions, you lose the intuition for systematicity. The apparent obviousness of the systematicity of thought looks to be an illusion created by reading the structure of contents off the structure of their representations.

A comparable point can be made by noticing that thought may appear systematic relative to one scheme but not systematic relative to another. Consider:

> (3) Anyone who can think that a face is smiling can think that a face is frowning.

This looks pretty implausible. But imagine a palette scheme for constructing cartoon faces (Figure 3.2).

Under the influence of this scheme, (4) looks pretty plausible:

> (4) Anyone who can imagine a smiling face can imagine a frowning face.

Absent some representation-independent access to the structure of propositions, which propositions seem to be systematic variants of each other will depend on one's preferred scheme for representing propositions. If you linguistically represent the contents to be thought, then you will want

Figure 3.2 Two cartoon faces that are systemic varients involving non-semantic constituents

mental representation to be linguistic, since then the systematicities in thought that are visible from your perspective will be exactly the ones your mental scheme can explain. You can make things look hard for (some) connectionists by (*a*) covertly relativizing systematicity to a natural language; and (*b*) reminding them that they favor a nonclassical scheme of mental representation. If you can get them to accept this 'challenge,' they will then labor away trying to show that a user of a nonclassical scheme might still exhibit the systematicities visible from a classical perspective. Getting connectionists to accept this challenge is nice work if you can get it, and apparently you can. There may still be job openings in this area if you want employment in the confidence business.

The preceding argument depends on the claim that something like (T2) is the only way to get at the systematicity of thought. Actually, there is another way. One supposes that thoughts are relations to mental representations. According to the standard story, believing that *p* is harboring a representation that *p* in the belief box; desiring that *p* is harboring a representation that *p* in the desire box; and so on. Thoughts then inherit the forms of their associated representations, and the systematicity of thought is just a reflection of the systematicity of the scheme of mental representation. If you think that mental representation is classical, then you are entitled to:

> Anyone who can think a thought of the form *Rab* can think a thought of the form *Rba*.

But equally, if you think mental representations are activation vectors, then you are entitled to:

> Anyone who can think a thought of the form $<\ldots a \ldots b \ldots>$ can think a thought of the form $<\ldots b \ldots a \ldots>$.

The whole point of the appeal to systematicity was to argue from systematicity to a conclusion about the form of mental representation. Everyone gets a free explanation of whatever systematicities are exhibited by the scheme of mental representation they hypothesize. You only get independent leverage on what sort of scheme the mind uses if you have a trick for independently identifying systematicities in thought, that is, a trick that does not depend on any assumptions about the scheme of representation the mind uses.

3.3. Sentence processing

What the systematicity argument requires is a domain D of things such that
(*a*) some members of D are systematic variants of others; and (*b*) it is an
empirical fact that anyone who can represent a member of D can represent
its systematic variants. The problem we are having is that we have no non-
question-begging way of saying which propositions are related by systematic
variation. This suggests that the problem is with propositions, not with systematicity. Surely, there are other domains that loom large in human cognition
and whose members exhibit systematic relations. This is one reason why the
debate has tended to focus on the issue of language processing. Sentences are
systematically related in various ways, so it might seem that the issue could be
joined meaningfully in that venue, where the claim at stake is this:

> (L) Anyone who can understand a sentence of the form F can under-
> stand a sentence of the form F^* (where F and F^* are systematic
> variants).[13]

No one, of course, is in a position to say definitively what sort of
representational scheme might be required for understanding sentences.
But we are in a position to ask whether various sentence processing tasks
that are plausibly supposed to be necessary conditions of systematic understanding are possible for systems employing nonclassical representational
schemes. So we can wonder about (L1), for example:

> (L1) Anyone who can parse a sentence of the form F can parse a
> sentence of the form F^*.

As noted above, it is now pretty clear that (L1) holds of systems that do not
employ a classical representational scheme, or any scheme that structurally
represents sentences or their grammatical forms.

It is interesting to reflect on what makes this possible. The answer, in a
word, is complete *encoding*. By an encoding of a domain D (which might
itself be a representational scheme), I mean a recursive mapping of the
members of D onto the representations in a scheme S whose members do
not preserve the internal complexity (if any) of the members of D. Gödel
numbering of sentences is an encoding in this sense, since it does not

---

[13] See Niklasson and van Gelder (1994) for various levels of systematic variation that might be plugged
in here to give claims of different strength.

preserve constituent structure, while Morse code is not an encoding since it is simply an alternative alphabet, preserving the same letters in the same order, which is sufficient to preserve the syntactic structure of a (written) sentence. An encoding is *complete* if it provides a representation of every member of the target domain.

Unlike an encoding, a *structural representation* (SR) is an isomorph of the thing it represents, so a scheme of structural representations does preserve the structure of the items in the represented domain. The issue between connectionists and classicists concerning the explanation of (L1) is whether structural representation is required—that is, whether the representations of F and F^* required by the parser must themselves be systematic variants—or whether an encoding of the target sentences is sufficient. Classical representation gets into the debate only because it happens that classical schemes can (but need not) provide structural representations of sentences.[14] It has seemed to classicists that structural representation of sentences is required to account for (L) and its corollaries (for example, (L1)).

The work of Smolensky *et al.* (1992) demonstrates that a complete encoding is sufficient, for they prove an equivalence between a parser written in TPPL, a LISP-like language that uses classical representations, and a network using fully distributed representations. The network devised by Niklasson and van Gelder (1994) appears to demonstrate the same point. Structural representation of sentences is not required for parsing tasks, and since the only reason for preferring classical schemes in this case is that they can provide structural representations of sentences, the argument to classical representation from language processing appears to collapse.

3.4. Systematicity

Friends of the systematicity argument need not throw in the towel just yet, however. They can legitimately complain (though they have not) that (L)

---

[14] Recall that a classical scheme can represent sentences without structurally representing them. There is abbreviation (s = 'John loves Mary') and there is logical equivalence ('John loves Mary' equivalent to 'the sentence s such that s = 'John loves Mary' or '$1 + 1 = 2$'). It is also important to keep in mind that it might be possible structurally to represent sentences without classically representing them. If so, then an argument from sensitivity to sentence structure to structural representation of sentences is not yet an argument for classical representation.

and (L1) are incautiously formulated. The explananda in this debate have the form:

(S) Anyone who can represent c can represent c^*.

where c and c^* are systematic variants in some domain D.[15] The problem is that (S) will be satisfied by any system employing a representational scheme that is complete for D. Being able to represent systematic variants is a trivial consequence of being able to represent everything. So, for example, if you can represent every sentence of L, it will follow that if you can represent $s \in L$ you can represent its systematic variants. This is evidently not what is wanted for the systematicity argument, since the whole idea is that a system handles systematic variants in some way that is special. What is needed is the idea that, in a system sensitive to a systematicity in D, generating a representation of c^* from c is easy or principled in a way that moving from one representation to another generally is not. This is what makes structural representation a natural candidate for explaining sensitivity to systematicity: to get from a representation of c to a representation of c^*, all you have to do is to permute constituents of the representation of c; you do not have to start from scratch.[16]

A system is sensitive to a systematicity in D, then, if there is something about its processing of representations of systematic variants in D that is special. There must be, in short, some effect E that a system exhibits when it processes representations of systematic variants and does not exhibit otherwise. A system might, for example, get from a representation of c to a representation of c^* faster than to a representation of d. Or perhaps the time required to move from a representation of c to a representation of c^* is constant or independent of the complexity of c^*. Moving between representations of systematic variants might be less error prone or prone to some characteristic sort of error. All of these would count as exhibiting sensitivity to systematicity in D, and they are the sorts of effects one would expect if the system employs a structural representation, since permuting elements of c should be simpler than constructing a new representation.

---

[15]   (L1) does not actually have this form, but it entails something of the right sort, since it says, in effect, that anyone who can represent a parse of F can represent a parse of F^*, and these will be systematic variants of each other on the assumption that F and F^* are systematic variants.

[16]   I am reading 'permute' liberally here to include turning over the 'smile' in a cartoon face, as well as, say, exchanging it with an eye to give a surprised person winking.

With this rudimentary understanding of systematicity, we can see that the success of connectionist parsers does not really settle the question. On the other hand, to my knowledge, no definite question has been posed. That is, no one has specified a systematicity effect human parsers exhibit that does not simply reduce to the ability to parse any grammatical sentence that does not overload short term memory. Perhaps there are such effects—they may even be well-known—but they have not made their way into the systematicity debate as yet.

The relation between systematicity and classical representation is only a bone of contention between classicists and connectionists because connectionists (some of them) believe in nonclassical representation. The deeper issue is whether any nonclassical system—any system using nonclassical representation—can achieve sensitivity to systematicity. As we have just seen, we have a substantive systematicity effect if a system exhibits some characteristic effect when moving from a representation of c to a representation of c^*, a systematic variant of c. Within a broadly computationalist framework, there are two ways in which effects can arise: (I) they are computed; (II) they are incidental, that is, side-effects. An effect is computed just in case exhibiting the effect is a matter of computing the characteristic argument-to-value pairs; it is incidental just in case exhibiting it is, as it were, a by-product of computation: not a matter of which values are computed from which arguments, but a matter of some effect of doing the computation, such as how long it takes, how much the system heats up, or how much sugar is metabolized. An example will make the distinction clear and, at the same time, introduce a methodological problem that arises in drawing it.

Consider two multipliers, M1 and M2. M1 uses the standard partial products algorithm we all learned in school. M2 uses successive addition. Both systems exhibit the *multiplication effect*: given two numerals, they return a numeral representing the product of the numbers represented by the inputs. M2 exhibits the *linearity effect*: computation is, roughly, a linear function of the size of the multiplier. It takes twice as long to compute $24 \times N$ as it does to compute $12 \times N$. M1 does not exhibit the linearity effect. Its complexity profile is, roughly, a step function of the number of digits in the multiplier. The linearity effect is incidental; the multiplication effect is computed.

Of course, the linearity effect might be computed. We could design a system M3 that not only computes products, but computes reaction times as well, timing its outputs to mimic a successive addition machine. M3 might be quite difficult to distinguish from M1 on behavioral grounds. It need not be impossible. The timing function might be disabled somehow without disabling the multiplier. More subtly, computation of the relevant output times might itself be nonlinear, in which case M3 will not be able to fool us on very large inputs (assuming it can process them at all). Or it might be that the linearity effect in M3 is cognitively penetrable.[17]

This last possibility is important, because it reminds us that incidental effects, being architecture dependent, cannot be cognitively penetrated. Since a difference in representational scheme is precisely a difference in architecture in the relevant sense, it follows that two systems using different representational schemes cannot exhibit all the same incidental effects. It follows further that classical systems and distributed connectionist systems cannot exhibit all the same incidental effects. It seems clear that proponents of the systematicity argument are thinking that systematicity effects are incidental.[18] They are thinking, recall, that you can easily get from a representation of the sentence 'John loves Mary' to a representation of the sentence 'Mary loves John' because (I) you represent these structurally—classical

---

[17] Pylyshyn (1984).

[18] Suppose the effects in question are computed by a system that uses a scheme of structural representation. Then they can be computed by a system that uses an encoding scheme. Let D be some domain exhibiting systematicity, and let f be a computational procedure that manipulates structural representations of members of D in such a way as to exhibit sensitivity to the relevant systematicity. Now let e be an encoding of the structural representations manipulated by f, and define f^* as follows: $f^*(x) = e(f(e^{-1}(x)))$. The function f^* is evidently computable, since f, e, and e's inverse are computable. Any relation f imposes on the things its structural representations represent will be imposed on those things by f^* as well. If you have a classical explanation of computed systematicity effects, you can have a nonclassical explanation, too. I have heard the following objection: 'If the only way to compute f^* is to decode into structural representations, then you do need structural representations to do the job.' But there is no reason to assume that the only way to compute f^* involves computing e. Indeed, there are bound to be other ways of doing the job. Without loss of generality, we can suppose e to be a numerical encoding. Since f^* is a recursive function that takes numerical arguments and values, it follows that it can be defined in terms of the standard arithmetical functions plus minimalization and composition. There is therefore an arithmetical algorithm Af^* for computing f^* which traffics only in numerals, never having anything to do with their decodings. We can think of Af^* as manipulating numerical encodings of D directly, since an encoding of a scheme of structural representations of D is easily exchanged for an encoding of the relevant structures of D themselves. Let h be a function taking elements d of D onto their structural representations. Then h^* encodes D directly, where $h^*(d) = e(h(d))$. Evidently, $f^*(h^*(d)) = h^*(d')$ if and only if $f(h(d)) = f(h(d'))$. So we can think of Af^* as operating on a direct encoding of D.

Connectionists, of course, must do more than merely provide an encoding of a classical grammar if they are to explain (LI). They must provide an encoding into activation vectors, and they must demonstrate that a network can compute the appropriate star function. (This is exactly the approach of Smolensky et al. 1992.) These are, of course, nontrivial tasks. But the possibility of Af^* is enough to demonstrate that structural representation of a systematic domain is not required to explain sensitivity to that systematicity.

schemes providing structural representations of sentences—and (II) given a structural representation of one sentence you can get a structural representation of the other simply by permuting constituents, a much simpler operation, one might suppose, than constructing a new representation, as a system that encodes sentences must do. Indeed, a system that encodes sentences will have to compute the relevant effect. As we will see shortly, this may make an encoding explanation of the effect ad hoc in a certain sense, but it need not invalidate it. When it comes to systematicity, some encoding explanations are inevitable, as I will argue in the next section.

3.5. Nonlinguistic systematicity

If we focus exclusively on systematicities in language, classical representation occupies a kind of favored position, because it affords structural representations of sentences. Structural representation is not the only way to go, as we have just seen, but it is a natural way to go. If you want to explain sensitivity to structure in D, it is natural to hypothesize a representational scheme whose members preserve (that is, actually have) the relevant structure.

Sensitivity to nonlinguistic systematicities appears to abound in human psychology, however. Consider, for example, the perception of objects in space: anyone who can see (imagine) a scene involving objects o_1 and o_2 can see (imagine) a scene in which their locations are switched:

> (SP) Anyone who can see (imagine) a scene involving objects o_1 and o_2 can see (imagine) a scene in which their locations are switched.

Again, any system employing a complete scheme will satisfy (SP), but it is surely the case that spatial representation underlies a number of substantive systematicities as well. One might well take the extensive literature on imagery to provide examples. Indeed, the imagery literature appears to put the shoe on the other foot, the friends of imagery arguing that imagery effects are best explained as incidental effects of employing a structural representation of space, while opponents argue that they are computed by a system employing an encoding in a classical scheme.

Once we see that there is sensitivity to systematicity in nonlinguistic domains, an argument parallel to that given for the classical representation of language would be available for the nonclassical representation of these other domains. The perception of objects in space appears to be a case in point. A map in three dimensions that has object representations as constituents would provide a structural representation of the domain, and hence allow for a 'simple' explanation of the systematicity effects suggested by (SP). A classical scheme of representation will have its work cut out for it, however, since three-dimensional scenes are not isomorphic to Tarskian structures, that is, to the kind of structure a representation must have to be subject to Tarskian combinatorics—the kind of structure we are calling classical. No scheme can structurally represent both sentence structure and spatial structure, since these are not isomorphic to each other. Friends of the Fodorian argument that moves from sensitivity to linguistic systematicity to classical representation ought to be friendly to an analogous argument that moves from sensitivity to spatial systematicity to nonclassical representation, for the Fodorian argument is really just an argument from sensitivity to systematicity in *D* to structural representation of *D*. If you like this kind of argument, you had better be prepared for as many schemes of mental representation as there are structurally distinct domains with systematicities to which we are sensitive. People can transpose music and color schemes as well as spatial scenes and sentences. One flavor of representation will not fit all.

Of course, there is no exclusive choice that has to be made here. Maybe there are three schemes of structural representation (sight-touch, smell-taste, hearing) and a lot of encoding to boot. Maybe there are two structural schemes, or twenty-five. My point here is just that you cannot regard the need to explain a substantive version of (L) as decisive for classical representation unless you also regard the need to explain a substantive version of (SP) as decisive for nonclassical representation. Seeing that much is enough to show you that you cannot get from human sensitivity to systematicity to the conclusion that human mental representation is exclusively classical.

3.6. An argument for structural representation

There is another Fodorian argument that goes like this.

> You can get sensitivity to systematicities in a domain without structurally representing its members. But an explanation in terms of structural representation is better, other things equal, because

postulating structural representations constrains which systematicities you are going to get, namely, the ones mirrored in your representational scheme. Roughly speaking, given structural representations, you are going to get sensitivity to the mirrored systematicities whether you like it or not. The encoding hypothesis, on the other hand, leaves it open which systematicities you are going to get. With encoding, it all depends on the processing: you program in just the systematicities you want and leave the others out. So the encoding approach is ad hoc, while the structural representation approach is principled.[19]

This argument was intended to favor classical schemes over (distributed) connectionist schemes. But, given the fact that we have nonisomorphic domains to deal with, not all systematicity can be explained by appeal to the structural properties of any single scheme. If you favor an explanation of sensitivity to systematicity in terms of structural representation, then you are going to have to postulate at least one nonclassical scheme. If you want to stick with a classical scheme, then some systematicity effects will have to be explained via a nonstructural encoding of the domain. As an argument for classical representation and only classical representation, therefore, the proposed tactic is doomed by the fact that we are sensitive to quite distinct systematicities. Still, it is worth investigating the idea that explanations of sensitivity to systematicity are ad hoc unless they appeal to structural representation. There are two reasons why we need to get straight about this. First, there is the fact that connectionist explanations of sensitivity to systematicities in language do not appeal to structural representations of language. And, second, there is the diversity of systematicities to which we are sensitive: if we do not postulate a different representational scheme for each case, then some systematicity is going to need an encoding explanation, and those are going to be ad hoc by the standard currently on the table.

In what sense, then, are encoding explanations supposed to be ad hoc? To get at what is behind this idea, we need to return to the fact that structural representation schemes are themselves systematic. It is a defining characteristic of structural representation that systematicity in the represented domain is mirrored by a corresponding systematicity in the representational scheme.

---

[19] This is a generalized version of an argument found in Fodor and McLaughlin, systematically translated into my terminology, of course.

Whenever two elements of the domain are systematic variants of one another, their representations are systematic variants of one another as well. It follows from this that whenever the scheme can represent c, it can represent its systematic variants, and this seems to be just what is wanted for explaining systematicity effects.

As we have seen, however, the point is not just that whenever you have a representation of c you are guaranteed to have a representation of its systematic variants, for any complete scheme of representation can make this claim.[20] The point is rather that generating a representation of c^* from a representation of c is easy and principled in a scheme of structural representation but not in an encoding scheme. The idea is that you can state a formal rule that captures the systematic variation, and that rule can, as it were, be made a principle of cognition. For example, you can easily imagine a scene with the positions of two objects swapped because it is a simple matter to generate the required representation: you just swap the object representations in the scene representation. You cannot do this in an encoding scheme, because encodings are arbitrary: there is no formal relation an encoding of c bears to an encoding of c^* iff c and c^* are systematic variants.

> *Objection*: there is the following relation. If c and c^* are systematic variants, then the system using the encoding scheme will simply compute the relevant effects rather than have them as incidental behavior. Assuming, for example, that the encoding is numerical, there will be some arithmetical relation A that holds of r and r^* just in case these are encodings of systematic variants. A system that can compute A can exhibit the relevant effects. Any systematicity effects exhibited by a system using structural representations can be mimicked by a system using a nonstructural encoding.

The objection is overstated, since not all incidental effects can be mimicked by a system that must compute them. But the objection misses the point of the argument in any case. The relation A is not determined by the

---

[20] There might be some worry about how the scheme is known to be complete. In a scheme of structural representation, we are guaranteed representations of all the relevant variants. What is the corresponding guarantee in an encoding scheme? Well, think of Gödel numbers: you have a representation for every sentence, so you have a representation for every systematic variant of s for variable s. This example shows that there are ways of guaranteeing the completeness of an encoding scheme.

representations, but must be programmed independently in your computational model. Since you can program in whatever A you want, the resulting explanation is ad hoc. The only constraint on which A you program in is data coverage.

Of course, the permutation rules that drive the explanation of sensitivity to systematicity in a system using structural representation have to be programmed in as well; they do not come for free. But the theorist is constrained by the form of the representations: you can only write permutation rules when there are permutable constituents. Models using encoding schemes have no way of enforcing a comparably principled constraint. To get a feel for this, consider a vector encoding. Vectors can, or course, be systematic variants of each other, but since we are assuming an encoding scheme, we are assuming that systematic variation in a vector does not mirror systematic variation in what it represents.[21] But vectors do stand in spatial relations to one another, and this might make it possible to state rules of the form: given a representation of c, construct a representation of a systematic variant by performing spatial transformation T. It is easy to see, however, that this sort of rule is not comparable to the permutation rules available to users of structural representations. Suppose we have: given a scene containing o_1 and o_2, generate a representation of the same scene with o_1 and o_2 swapped by performing transformation T. But now suppose we want a representation in which o_2 and o_3 are swapped. We need a new and independent transformation. Because representation of the objects is not separable from the representation of the scene, we cannot state the rule in terms of the objects whose representations are to be swapped.[22]

Being principled is a virtue in explanation. But the virtue is purely methodological. Principled explanations are easier to test, but they are no more likely to be true. If there are independent reasons for preferring a

---

[21] The use of vector encoding in connectionist systems is therefore different than the use of vector representation in mechanics, in which systematic variation in direction and magnitude does mirror systematic variation in the quantity represented. Vector schemes are structural schemes in mechanics, whereas they are typically encoding schemes in connectionist systems.

[22] Permutation rules can be defeated by context sensitivity. Constituents of cartoon faces are thoroughly context sensitive, since whether something counts as a nose, an eye, or a mouth depends solely on its relative position in the whole face. If I try to swap the mouth and the left eye, I get a winking face with a tongue sticking out, not a face with a mouth where the eye should be. (See Figure 3.3.) If I make the features sufficiently realistic, however, the effect of context vanishes and the swap works. This, presumably, is because a 'sufficiently realistic' feature is just a feature with enough internal complexity to constitute a complete picture in itself.

 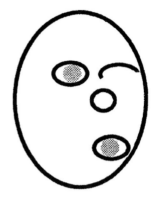

Figure 3.3 The two cartoon faces are systematic varients, but the constituents do not retain their representational significance when swapped

connectionist architecture (as there clearly are), then the methodological weakness of the ensuing explanations of our sensitivity to systematicity in language must simply be swallowed. If you are convinced that the mind is a network, you should not be dismayed by the fact that your explanation of our sensitivity to linguistic systematicity is not as easily tested as the other guy's. To repeat, there is no relation between being easily tested and being true. And anyway: no single representational scheme can structurally represent every domain exhibiting systematicities to which we are sensitive. If the other guys have not got a different scheme for each case, then some of their explanations are going to be exactly as ad hoc as yours.

3.7. Productivity

It is generally supposed that structural representation buys you a lot if the systematicity in the target domain is unbounded. Finite systematicity can be handled by a look-up table, and encodings are as good as structural representations in a look-up table. Structural representation begins to pay off as the amount of targeted systematicity grows large, because structural representation allows you to represent variations in a structure by corresponding variations in the elements of its representation. Permuting a small number of elements in the representation yields great representational power at low cost. Given enough time or memory, you get unbounded expressive power with finite means.

Reflecting on this familiar fact, it might seem that encoding strategies are bound to run into trouble in dealing with unbounded capacities to mirror systematicities. For the point about nonstructural representation is that you cannot rely on intrinsic properties of a representation r to construct a representation r^* that represents something systematically related to the thing represented by r. So you cannot get sensitivity to systematicity via a rule that applies to an unbounded set of representations in virtue of their shared form. Because nonstructural representations are arbitrary, it is tempting to conclude that getting r to generate r^* whenever the content of it is systematically related to the content or r^* is going to require something like a look-up table, and hence be essentially bounded.[23] If each element of D is represented by an arbitrary number, how in the world could you effect, with finite means, an unbounded set of pairings among those numbers that mirrors the unbounded systematicities in D?

We have already seen the answer to this question: at least sometimes, you can compute the effect directly. There is a more interesting answer, however, that is relevant to the dispute between connectionists and their detractors. Connectionists, of course, represent with vectors, and vectors stand in spatial relations to one another. Hence, if c and c^* are systematically related, the possibility arises that vector representations of c and c^* might stand in a characteristic spatial relation. For some arbitrary c in D, then, it might be possible to find a systematic variant of c by effecting a characteristic spatial transformation on its representation. In this way, the structure of the vector space itself can be used to mirror the desired systematic relations, even though the systematically related items have no structural representations in the system.

No actual physical computing system can compute an unbounded function, of course. When we say that our adding machines compute addition, we must be understood to mean that they would compute addition given freedom from resource constraints and from physical wear and tear. The point is that the algorithm is perfectly general; the boundedness of performance arises solely from resource constraints and physical disintegration. Talk

---

[23] Notice that the problem is not the lack of unbounded representational power. Suitable encodings do provide unbounded expressive power with finite means. The example of Gödel numbering shows this nicely: you get a unique decimal numeral for each sentence, and you get it with finite means. The game is still permuting elements, of course, but without any correspondence between those permutations and corresponding permutations in the target domain. The trouble with encoding is not that you run out of representations. The trouble, such as it is, is that it is structurally arbitrary.

of unbounded computational capacity (or productivity, as it is sometimes called) thus makes sense only when it makes sense to distinguish algorithm from resources. G. Schwarz[24] has recently argued, however, that this distinction is not available to connectionists. The argument is simple. Imagine a connectionist device Σ that computes some finite restriction of an infinite function f. To add memory to Σ, you have to add either nodes or precision to already existing nodes. In either case, you must reconfigure the weights to keep performance consistent with f. But changing the weights amounts to building a new device; for it is only the weight matrix that distinguishes Σ from the infinite class of nets having the same number of nodes and the same activation functions. Think, for example, of training a net to compute a certain function. After training, it computes f; before training, it does not. But the only thing that has happened is that the weights have changed. But if we can change an adding machine into a multiplier by changing weights, then weight change is surely change of algorithm. The evident underlying principle is: different function computed implies different algorithm executed.

Tempting as this argument is, I think it has to be rejected. The flaw is in thinking of the function computed as a function from input to output—addends to sum, factors to product—as we typically do when thinking about calculators,[25] rather than as a function from input and initial state to output and final state as we must when we are thinking about cognitive systems. Consider any AI system. The input-to-output relation it exhibits is a function of its stored knowledge. Change what the system knows and the same input will yield a different output. An airline reservation system cannot price a plan involving a flight it does not know about. But fortunately, given the fact that flights are added and deleted every day, you do not have to reprogram the system every time a new flight becomes available or an old one is dropped. More seriously, you cannot think of learning algorithms as pairing inputs and outputs, for the whole point of a learning algorithm is to replace ineffective input–output pairings by better ones. Leaning algorithms, by definition, remain constant over changes in input-to-output relations.

---

[24] Schwarz (1992).
[25] We can get away with this because the internal state is generally the same. Forbid use of the clear button, however, and the illusion quickly vanishes.

There is nothing wrong with the principle that a different function computed implies a different algorithm executed. The problem is in thinking of the function computed by a connectionist system as a function from inputs to outputs rather than as a function from an activation vector and point in weight space to another activation vector–weight space pair. We should think of a point in weight space as a point in stored knowledge space. From this point of view, we do not build a new network when we change weights any more than we build a new rule-based system when we change its stored knowledge.

The productivity issue, as we have seen, turns on whether it makes sense to idealize away from memory constraints, and, for connectionism, this depends on how connectionist networks are individuated. Schwarz is quite right in supposing that if we make identity of computational route from input to output a necessary condition of system identity, then we cannot coherently idealize away from memory constraints in connectionist systems. But the argument proves too much, for if we make identity of computational route from input to output a necessary condition of system identity, we cannot coherently describe learning in either classical or connectionist systems, nor, more generally, can we coherently describe any system whose behavior depends on stored information.

3.8. Inferential coherence

Fodor and Pylyshyn illustrate what they take to be the advantage of the classical view with examples of inference.

Because classical mental *representations* have combinatorial structure, it is possible for classical mental operations to apply to them by reference to their form. The result is that a paradigmatic classical mental process operates upon any mental representation that satisfies a given structural description, and transforms it into a mental representation that satisfies another structural description.[26] (So, for example, in a model of inference one might recognize an operation that applies to any representation of the form P & Q and transforms it into a representation of the form P.) Notice that

[26] Their statement here is a bit sloppy. Vector transformations apply to vectors in virtue of their (spatial) form as well. The point is rather that when you have a correspondence between form and meaning, as you do in any scheme of structural representation, similar formal transformations produce similar semantic transformations. This, as emphasized above, is what structural representation buys you.

since formal properties can be defined at a variety of levels of abstraction, such an operation can apply equally to representations that differ widely in their structural complexity. The operation that applies to representations of the form $P \& Q$ to produce P is satisfied by, for example, an expression like '(A∨B∨C) & (D∨E∨F)', from which it derives the expression '(A∨B∨C)'.   (1998: 13)

We can reconstruct such truth preserving inferences as *if Rover bites then something bites* on the assumption that (a) the sentence 'Rover bites' is of the syntactic type Fa, (b) the sentence 'something bites' is of the syntactic type. x(Fx), and (c) every formula of the first type entails a corresponding formula of the second type...

(1988: 29)

You can see this as a point about systematicity if you take the domain in question to be propositions (and maybe properties or propositional functions), together with their semantic relations. The claim is then that classical representation provides a structural representation of that domain, and thereby facilitates an explanation of our sensitivity to the systematicity it exhibits. The underlying idea is just that logical notation provides a structural representation of interpropositional entailment relations, and hence looks to be a good theory of representation on which to ground a story about human inference.

Two troubles loom. First, there is an undefended assumption here that standard logical notation does, in fact, provide a structural representation of propositions and other inferentially related contents. This assumption is bound to remain undefended pending an independent account of the structure of propositions and other inferentially related contents. You cannot take the soundness and completeness of standard logic as an argument that it provides a structural representation of the domain, since encodings of the standard notations will do as well. Since you do not need a scheme isomorphic to standard logical notation to capture all and only the valid inferences—you can do it with Venn Diagrams, for example[27]—there can be no argument from standard logic and our sensitivity to inferential relations to classical representation.

The second trouble looming is that there is ample empirical evidence that our sensitivity to the inferential relations captured by standard logic is extremely limited.[28] Humans are a good deal better at modus ponens than

[27] Shin (1994).
[28] See e.g. Braine (1978); Braine *et al.* (1984); Evans (1989); Braine and O'Brien (1991); Johnson-Laird and Byrne (1992); Rips (1994, 1990); D. Cummins (1995); Cummins *et al.* (1995).

they are with modus tollens, a fact that classical schemes will have to explain in some relatively ad hoc way.[29] For similar reasons, it is an embarrassment to classical schemes that structure-sensitive processing, unless constrained in some way, will treat '$(A \lor B \lor C)$ & $(D \lor E \lor F)$' in the same way it treats '$(P$ & $Q)$.' I am not sure about this particular example, but no one who is up on the human reasoning literature could think that humans are very good at detecting sameness of logical form.[30] Classical schemes based on standard logical notation appear to predict far more sensitivity to entailment relations than humans actually exhibit. Nonclassical schemes might do much better in this regard for all anyone knows at this time. The unwanted predictions generated by classical schemes have to be blocked in some relatively ad hoc way, a fact that appears to level the playing field on which classicists and their opponents have to play.[31]

3.9. Conclusion

So-called classical representational schemes get into the debate about systematicity only because they provide structural representations of linguistic expressions. Moving away from an exclusive focus on language (sometimes misleadingly disguised as a focus on thought) allows us to see that the real issue has to do with whether sensitivity to systematicity is better explained by appeal to structural representation than by appeal to encoding schemes.

While the alleged systematicity of thought is problematic because there is no uncontroversial way of specifying the structure of propositions, there are many domains that do exhibit systematicities to which we are sensitive. Since not all of these are isomorphic to each other, it follows that either some sensitivity to systematicity cannot be explained by appeal to structural representation, or we must postulate a separate scheme of structural representation for every distinct

---

[29] See e.g. Rips (1994).

[30] If there is a classical language of thought, then it might be that unconscious automatic processing is supremely sensitive to identities of logical form. But this is beside the present point, which has to do with whether humans are observed to be sensitive to systematicities in some independently identified domain.

[31] Here is an example of how to block a prediction of too much sensitivity: the effect disappears when the representations get complex, because you run out of short-term memory. This would be perfectly legitimate if logical breakdowns occurred when classical representation requires more than seven chunks. Unfortunately, things break down much earlier. No one thinks the problem with modus tollens is a resource problem.

systematicity to which we are sensitive. It is certainly possible to account for sensitivity to systematicities by appeal to nonstructural encodings of the domain. Although the resulting models will be methodologically ad hoc in a certain sense, they are no less likely to be true for all that.

References

Braine, M. D. S., 'On the Relation between the Natural Logic of Reasoning and Standard Logic', *Psychological Review*, 85 (1978), 1–21.

—— O'Brien, D. P., 'A Theory of If: A Lexical Entry, Reasoning Program, and Pragmatic Principles', *Psychological Review*, 98 (1991), 182–203.

—— Reiser, B. J., and Rumain, B., 'Some Empirical Justification for a Theory of Natural Propositional Logic', in G. H. Bower (ed.), *The Psychology of Learning and Motivation*, xviii (New York: Academic Press, 1984).

Cummins, D. D., 'Naive Theories and Causal Deduction', *Memory and Cognition*, 23 (1995), 646–58.

—— Lubart, T., Alsknis, O., and Rist, R., 'Conditional Reasoning and Causation', *Memory and Cognition*, 19 (1991), 274–82.

Evans, J. St. B. T., *Bias in Human Reasoning* (Hillsdale, NJ: Lawrence Erlbaum, 1989).

Fodor, J., *A Theory of Content and Other Essays* (Cambridge, Mass.: MIT Press, 1990).

—— Lepore, E., *Holism: A Shopper's Guide* (Oxford and Cambridge, Mass.: Basil Blackwell, 1992).

—— McLaughlin, B., 'Connectionism and the Problem of Systematicity: Why Smolensky's Solution Does Not Work', *Cognition*, 35 (1990c), 183–204.

—— Pylyshyn, Z., 'Connectionism and Cognitive Architecture: A Critical Analysis', *Cognition*, 28 (1988), 3–71.

Hadley, R., 'Systematicity in Connectionist Language Learning', *Mind and Language*, 9 (1994), 247–72.

Johnson-Laird, P. N., and Byrne, R. M. J., *Deduction* (Hillsdale, NJ: Erlbaum, 1992).

Niklasson, L., and Van Gelder, T., 'On Being Systematically Connectionist', *Mind and Language*, 9 (1994), 288–302.

Pylyshyn, Z., *Computation and Cognition* (Cambridge, Mass.: MIT Press, 1984).

Rips, L. J., 'Reasoning', *Annual Review of Psychology*, 41 (1990), 321–53.

—— *The Psychology of Proof* (Cambridge, Mass.: MIT Press/Bradford Books, 1994).

Schwarz, G., 'Connectionism, Processing, Memory', *Connection Science*, 1 (1992), 207–26.

Shin, S.-J., *The Logical Status of Diagrams* (Cambridge: Cambridge University Press, 1994).

Smolensky, P., LeGendre, G., and Miyata, Y., 'Principles for an Integrated Connectionist/Symbolic Theory of Higher Cognition', Tech. Report 92-08 (Institute of Cognitive Science, University of Colorado, 1992).

Swoyer, C., 'Structural Representation and Surrogative Reasoning', *Synthese*, 87 (1991), 449–508.

Van Gelder, T., 'Compositionality: A Connectionist Variation on a Classical Theme', *Cognitive Science*, 14 (1990), 355–84.

4

Systematicity and the Cognition of Structured Domains

ROBERT CUMMINS, JIM BLACKMON,
DAVID BYRD, PIERRE POIRIER,
MARTIN ROTH, AND GEORG SCHWARZ

The current debate over systematicity concerns the formal conditions a scheme of mental representation must satisfy in order to explain the systematicity of thought.[1] The systematicity of thought is assumed to be a pervasive property of minds, and can be characterized (roughly) as follows: anyone who can think T can think systematic variants of T, where the systematic variants of T are found by permuting T's constituents. So, for example, it is an alleged fact that anyone who can think the thought *that John loves Mary* can think the thought *that Mary loves John*, where the latter thought is a systematic variant of the former.

4.1. Background

The systematicity of thought itself, of course, cannot be directly observed. But it is easy to see why it is widely assumed. Anyone who can *understand* a

Originally published in *Journal of Philosophy*, 98 (2001), 167–85. This paper appears with the kind permission of the *Journal of Philosophy*.

[1] The debate was instigated by Fodor and Pylyshyn (1998). In the present article, we mainly focus on that paper and on Fodor and McLaughlin (1990c) and Smolensky *et al.* (1992). See n. 2 for other papers detailing Fodor's position and n. 6 for papers detailing Smolensky's. Other important participants in the debate were: Chater and Oaksford (1990); van Gelder (1990); Butler (1991, 1995); Horgan and Tienson (1992); Chalmers (1993); Hadley (1994a, 1994b, 1997a); Matthews (1994, 1997); Niklasson and van Gelder (1994); Cummins (1996b); Aizawa (1997); Hadley and Hayward (1997b).

sentence *S* can understand its systematic variants. Since understanding *S* requires having the thought it expresses, anyone who can think the thought expressed by a sentence *S* can have the thought expressed by the systematic variants of *S*. The systematicity of all thought expressible in language seems to follow: If you can understand 'John loves Mary,' you must be capable of the thought *that John loves Mary*. Since anyone who can understand 'John loves Mary' can understand 'Mary loves John,' it follows that anyone who can have the thought *that John loves Mary* can have the thought *that Mary loves John*.

To derive the thought one must have to understand the systematic variants of 'John loves Mary,' permute the words in 'John loves Mary' (while maintaining grammaticality), and preface the result with 'that.' This leads to what we might call the *orthodox position*, which Jerry A. Fodor, Zenon W. Pylyshyn, and Brian P. McLaughlin[2] defend concerning the explanation of systematicity, namely that it is best understood as involving two parts:

(1) *The representational theory of thought*: having the thought that *p* is having a *p*-expressing mental representation in a certain cognitive role.

For example, having a belief *that p* amounts to having a mental representation *that p* in the belief box.[3]

(2) Mental representation is 'classical': mental representation has a language-like combinatorial syntax and associated semantics.[4]

Putting these two parts together, we get that anyone who can think *that John loves Mary* can think *that Mary loves John*, since (i) thinking 'Mary loves John' involves tokening a representation of the proposition *that Mary loves John*; and (ii) that representation has constituents corresponding to Mary, John, and the relation of loving, which can simply be permuted to yield a representation, and hence a thought, corresponding to the proposition *that John loves Mary*. FPM thus conclude that the human system of mental representation must be 'classical,' that is, a language-like scheme having the

---

[2] FPM's position is fully laid out in the following articles: Fodor and Pylyshyn (1988); Fodor and McLaughlin (1990c); McLaughlin (1993a, 1993b); Fodor (1997). Hereafter, 'FPM' is used in the text to refer to the authors' position, result, and the like; otherwise, their full names are used.

[3] This assumption of the Representational Theory of Thought is controversial. One might think that a person can have the thought *that p* without having the representation *that p*. See Cummins (1996a).

[4] We call these schemes 'classical' in what follows (one could also call them 'Tarskian'). See Tarski (1936, 1944).

familiar kind of combinatorial syntax and associated semantics first introduced by Alfred Tarski.[5]

An unfortunate consequence of the way FPM have characterized the systematicity of thought is that any theory that accounts for understanding every sentence will account for systematicity trivially: if one can understand every sentence, one can understand every systematic variant of any given sentence. If the domain of sentences to be understood is finite, nonclassical schemes could be complete in the relevant sense, and hence account for systematicity. For instance, a look-up table that uses arbitrary names to represent each sentence of the domain would account for it.

A natural reply to this point would be to claim that only representational schemes employing something like classical combinatorics could be complete for an unbounded domain like the domain of thought-expressing sentences in a natural language. But Paul Smolensky, Géraldine LeGendre, and Yoshiro Miyata[6] have proven that for every classical parser—that is, a parser defined over classical representations—there exists a tensor-product network that is weakly (input–output) equivalent to the classical parser but does not employ classical representations.[7] Thus, it appears that the classical explanation and the tensor-product explanation explain the systematicity of thought equally well.

There are two *philosophical* responses to the SLM result that we want to surface briefly and put aside. The first, due to Georg Schwarz,[8] is that

---

[5]   Tarski (1936).

[6]   SLM's position is fully laid out in the following articles: Smolensky (1987, 1990, 1991, 1995); Smolensky *et al.* (1992). Hereafter, 'SLM' is used in the text to refer to the authors' position, result, and the like; otherwise, their full names are used.

[7]   Tensor-product encoding is a general-purpose technique for binding fillers to roles (object to properties/relations). An activation vector representing the binding of a filler f to a role R is obtained by taking the tensor product of the vectors representing R and f. The resulting vector can then be added to (superimposed on) others representing bindings of fillers to roles, yielding a single vector that represents the binding of many fillers to many roles. SLM use this technique to construct recursive representations of binary trees. Matrices effecting the vector operation for constructing a tree from its left child p and right child q (or for decomposing it) are then defined, making possible direct implementation in one layer of connection weights.

This connectionist representation of trees enables massively parallel processing. Whereas in the traditional sequential implementation of LISP, symbol processing consists of a long sequence of car, cdr, and cons operations, here we can compose together the corresponding sequence of W_{car}, W_{cdr}, W_{cons}, W_{cons1} operations into a single matrix operation. Adding some minimal nonlinearity allows us to compose more complex operations incorporating the equivalent of conditional branching (Smolensky *et al.* 1992). The matrices can then be straightforwardly combined to yield a single layer of connection weights that implement parse-dependent predicates and functions.

[8]   Schwarz (1992).

networks like that designed by SLM do not really have an unbounded competence. The second, suggested by FPM and discussed briefly by Cummins,[9] is that, while both parsers[10] can account for the systematicity data, the SLM explanation is unprincipled because the tensor-product parser is handcrafted to achieve systematicity, whereas the classical parser is not. We discuss these briefly in turn.

4.1.1. Unbounded competences in connectionist networks

Georg Schwarz has argued that connectionist networks that are not simply implementations of classical architectures cannot have unbounded competences. According to Schwarz, we take an ordinary calculator to have an unbounded competence because it employs perfectly general numerical algorithms for addition, multiplication, subtraction, and division. Consequently, its competence is limited only by time and memory.[11] We can add more memory to the calculator, and let it run longer, without altering the algorithms it exploits. But, Schwarz argues, the same does not hold of a connectionist calculator, for the only way to add memory is to add more nodes, or to add precision to the nodes. Doing either of these will require retraining the network, however, which amounts to programming a new system that, in effect, executes a different algorithm. The fact that processing and memory are fully integrated in connectionist networks blocks the standard idealization away from memory limitations that licenses attribution of unbounded competences to classical systems whose controlling algorithms remain unchanged with the addition or subtraction of memory.

We believe this argument should be rejected for reasons given by Cummins.[12] The culprit is the assumption that the function computed is a function from input to output rather than a function from input and initial state to output and final state. The input-to-output relation exhibited by a classical parser, for example, is a function of its stored knowledge. Change what the system knows and the same input will yield a different output.

---

[9] Cummins (1996b).

[10] Smolensky, Legendre, and Miyata do not in fact construct a parser. What they do is show how to construct networks effecting parse-dependent functions and predicates (e.g. active–passive) that correspond precisely to arbitrarily complex parse-dependent LISP functions/predicates. In the context of the current discussion, this amounts to showing that classical representation is not required for systematic and productive capacities defined over the constituent structure of a sentence.

[11] It is also limited, ultimately, by wear and tear, but this raises no special problem for connectionists.

[12] Cummins (1996b), Ch. 3, this volume.

Therefore, the input–output relation is seldom a function. This is particularly obvious when we consider learning algorithms. These cannot be conceived as functions pairing inputs and outputs, for the whole point of a learning algorithm is to replace ineffective input–output pairings with better ones. By definition, learning algorithms remain constant over changes in input-to-output relations.

We accept the principle that a different function computed implies a different algorithm executed. But the function computed by a connectionist system must be conceived as a function from an activation vector and point in weight space to another activation vector–weight space pair. From this point of view, we do not build a new network when we change weights any more than we build a new rule-based system when we change its stored knowledge.

4.1.2. *Connectionist data coverage is 'unprincipled'*

The idea here is that classical representational schemes *predict* systematicity, whereas connectionist schemes at best *accommodate* it.

To get a concrete sense of this objection, suppose a classical system generates a phrase marker for 'John loves Mary.' Since 'Mary loves John' has precisely the same phrase marker, except that 'John' and 'Mary' have exchanged positions, the system is bound to be able to parse 'Mary loves John' if it can parse 'John loves Mary': the grammatical structure is the same, and so are the lexical resources (Figure 4.1).

By contrast, so the argument goes, a connectionist network could be trained to parse 'John loves Mary' but not 'Mary loves John.'

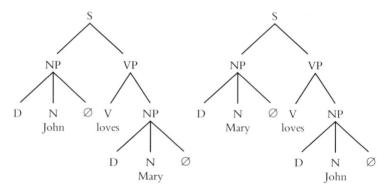

Figure 4.1 Parse trees for 'John loves Mary' and 'Mary loves John'

An obvious reply is that while a classical system might be programmed to exhibit the very same incapacity, the resulting system would be obviously ad hoc. The incapacity does not appear ad hoc in the connectionist framework, however, since the representations of the sentences do not themselves have constituents corresponding to the relevant lexical items. It might seem, therefore, that there is no reason why the network would have to process the two representations in a similar way. They are simply different activation vectors, and hence there will be no special problem with a training set that simply declares the second parse unacceptable. Bias against a systematic variant of an acceptable sentence will present no learning problem different in principle from bias against any other unacceptable sentence—for example, 'Loves Mary John.' A classical system, however, will give both parses if it gives either, unless some special rule is added to the grammar to block one or the other. There will be no rule or process in the deviant connectionist system that is special to this case. The same setting of weights that deals with every other sentence, whether acceptable or unacceptable, will deal with the deviation. There will, in short, be no principled distinction between the way it rejects 'Mary loves John' and the way it blocks 'Loves John Mary.'

Here is a different but related way to see the alleged problem. Imagine a classical system that can parse 'John loves Mary' but cannot parse 'John despises Mary' because 'despises' is not in its lexicon. It seems intuitively plausible to suppose that a simple learning algorithm will add 'despises' to the lexicon, and that this will suffice to yield the new parse. The SLM result shows that, for each of these classical systems, there is a weakly equivalent connectionist system. It is silent, however, about the relation between these two connectionist systems. In particular, it is silent about whether the one that handles 'despises' is in any sense a natural extension of the one that does not. For all the SLM result shows, the post-learning correlate would have to be built from scratch rather than on the basis of the pre-learning correlate. By itself, the theorem proved in SLM does not show that the networks corresponding to the pre- and post-learning stages lie on any common connectionist learning trajectory. It shows only that *any* set of parses that can be captured by a classical system can be captured by a connectionist network. This at least suggests that the connectionist network does not parse the systematic variants of S *because they are systematic variants of an acceptable sentence*, but rather that it parses them simply because they are among the sentences in the target set defined by the classical system to be emulated. We have, in short, no reason to think that all the systematic variants of S are parsed in the same way. Rather, the prediction that the network will parse a systematic variant of S is derived simply from the facts (i) that the systematic variants of S are acceptable if S is; and (ii) that the network parses all the acceptable sentences.[13]

We shall come back in a later section to the merits (and demerits) of the objection that connectionist data coverage is unprincipled. But notice that, at this point, the debate has shifted from empirical considerations of what best covers the data to philosophical considerations of what constitutes a principled explanation. We propose, therefore, to reformulate the issue in the hope of finding a way of retaining its essentially empirical cast.

4.2. The issue reformulated

The fact that a system cognizes a domain will manifest itself in a variety of psychological effects. By an *effect*, we mean a nomic regularity in behavior (what Ruth Garrett Millikan[14] calls a law *in situ*, that is, a law that holds of a system in virtue of the special structure and organization of that system). For instance, the fact that humans cognize the color domain is manifested by the fact that humans make such and such discriminations (and fail to make others), by the fact that they will eat some foods and not others, and so on.

We take it as uncontroversial that some domains are cognized via a grasp of their underlying structure. For example, we can recognize the melody of 'Mary had a Little Lamb' whether it is played by an orchestra or on a kazoo, regardless of what key it is played in, and, within limits, regardless of tempo. Sensitivity to melody across differences in timbre, tempo, and key suggests that we process melody by processing information about the structure and

---

[13] This problem is an instance of a more general problem we address elsewhere and will be pursued in further publications. See Poirier *et al.* (1999); also McCloskey and Cohen (1989). Connectionist systems using distributed representation cannot learn atomically, that is, they cannot add single representations, such as the predicate 'despise,' to their belief box or knowledge base without having to relearn everything they previously learned. Surely, this is not the way we acquire new representations in many domains (but, for a possible solution, see McClelland *et al.* (1995).

[14] Millikan (1984).

arrangement of notes in a composition. Word problem-solving in algebra is another case where grasping the underlying structure of a domain is required for cognizing the domain. Students are better able to solve word problems involving distances, rates, and times when they see the problems as having the same structure as problems with which they are already familiar. For example, students who can solve problems involving wind speeds but have difficulty solving problems involving current speeds are able to perform well on the latter when it is pointed out that current is analogous to wind.[15] Only when students recognize an underlying structure with which they are familiar do they seem able to give the correct answer (this suggests that sensitivity to structure is learned in some cases, or at least affected by prior knowledge). We also take it to be uncontroversial that some domains are cognized without grasping any significant underlying structure: knowing the capitals of twenty US states is no help in divining the capital of an unstudied state. Our ability to learn the state capitals does not depend on being sensitive to underlying structural features of states and their capitals. With respect to the previous distinction, we call an effect a *systematicity effect* if it is a psychological effect that implies sensitivity to the structure of the domain cognized.[16]

Is it possible to draw any conclusions about the form of mental representation from the presence of systematicity effects? We think it is. Recall that our main methodological objective here is to keep the issue at an empirical level in the hope that it can be solved there. Our first conclusion proceeds from the observation that not all systematicity effects are created equal: some may be computed by the system, and some may be incidental effects of whatever algorithm is being computed. We call the first type of systematicity effect *primary* and the second *incidental*, and in the next section

---

[15] D. D. Cummins (1992).

[16] These examples are meant to represent the extreme cases. There are likely to be cognitive tasks that require grasping varying degrees of structure depending on the domain, so the distinction between structured and unstructured is not all or nothing. Also, some cognitive tasks will be hybrid cases, where some aspects require grasping structural information while others do not. Cognizing language appears to be an example, since mastery of the primitive lexicon is surely more like learning the state capitals than like mastering the syntax. One must also be careful not to confuse structure in the domain with structure in the way a problem or question is posed. When a teacher requires that I learn the capital of California, the structure of my answer is determined in part by the structure of the question itself. Similarly, one can imagine a state-capital learning device that represents states as one place predicates such that only one capital could be matched with any state. In this case the structure of the answer is partly determined by the way states are represented in the system.

we address the distinction and what it tells us about mental representation.[17] Our second conclusion rests on a finer analysis of the SLM tensor-product representations. Unlike classical representations that preserve information about the structure of represented elements by actually sharing that structure, tensor-product representations do not share structure with what they represent yet still manage to preserve structural information and make it available to processors. This allows a possible solution to a problem raised by Cummins[18] against classical representations—namely, that they cannot possibly share structure with every domain in which we find systematicity effects—but the price for that solution may be one FPM are not ready to pay. We address this issue in section 4.4.

4.3. Primary vs. incidental systematicity effects

The distinction between primary and incidental effects captures the important fact that a system's behavior results not only from the function it computes, but from a variety of other factors as well. Compare a system that multiplies by partial products with a system that computes products through successive addition. What the two systems have in common is the *multiplication effect*, that is, the fact that they both produce the same products from the same arguments. They differ, however, in how long it takes them to compute the value for a given argument. In the case of the successive adder, the response time is roughly proportional to the size of the multiplier: computing ten times some number will take approximately twice as long as computing five times that number. The other system, in contrast, does not display such a linearity effect. Its response time is, roughly, a step function of the number of digits in the multiplier, indicating how many partial products need to be added in the end.

The two systems have the same primary systematicity effects, since every argument pair leads to the same value in both systems: they are both multipliers. But their incidental systematicity effects are different. For instance, the partial products multiplier will take approximately the same amount of time to multiply N by 10 as it will to multiply N by 99, whereas the successive

---

[17] The distinction between primary and incidental systematicity effects is introduced in Cummins (1996b) and also discussed in Cummins (2000a).

[18] Cummins (1996b), Ch. 3, this volume.

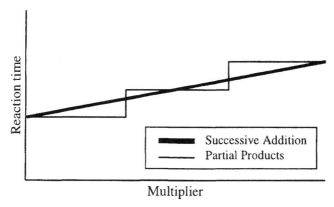

Figure 4.2 Products are computed (primary). Reaction time is incidental

addition multiplier will take roughly 10 times longer to multiply N by 99 as it will to multiply N by 10. In general, two systems that compute the same function using different algorithms will display different incidental effects, although they will be weakly equivalent in Pylyshyn's sense.[19]

One important source of incidental effects thus lies in the algorithm producing the primary effects. But systems that implement the *same* algorithm may exhibit different incidental effects. If the underlying hardware is sufficiently different, they may operate at greatly different speeds, as is familiar to anyone who has run the same program on an Intel 486 running at 50 MHz and on a Pentium III running at 750 MHz. A significant difference in response time between two systems, in other words, does not entail that they implement different algorithms; it may be a direct result of a difference at the implementation level. Hence, two systems that have identical primary effects may exhibit different incidental effects either because they compute different algorithms or because the identical algorithms they compute are implemented in different hardware.

Incidental effects are not restricted to the complexity profiles of the algorithm or the constraints imposed by the implementing matter on the execution of the algorithm. Continuous operation will heat up the calculator, an incidental effect that is normally irrelevant to the system's performance. Nonetheless, when things get too hot, the system will start malfunctioning and ultimately break down. As a consequence, two systems that differ in performance do not necessarily compute different functions; one of the systems may simply have been subject to extraneous factors, such as overheating, fatigue, or attention deficit disorder. By the same token, the general physical makeup of a system also determines the extent to which environmental conditions will have an impact on the system's ability to operate. The occurrence of a strong magnetic field, for example, will interfere with the operation of an electronic calculator but not with that of an abacus. In the case of single-purpose machines, this last kind of incidental effect is primarily relevant for explaining why a system fails to display its primary effects on certain occasions. But in the case of more complex systems, such effects have proven useful as an explanatory tool as well. Consider the fact that cognitive processing in the human brain is generally correlated with increased metabolic activity, a fact that has proved critical for the use of imaging technology (for example, PET, fMRI) that studies which cortical areas are involved in the processing of these tasks. Yet metabolic activity as such is not specific to the neural implementation of whatever computations are performed.

It is evident that the effects of implementation details and environment complicate inferences from sameness of incidental effects to sameness of underlying functional architecture. In what follows, however, we shall make use only of the inference from differences in incidental effects to differences in functional architecture in cases in which implementational and environmental influences are not at issue.

Now, SLM have proven that a connectionist tensor-product parser and the classical parser can exhibit the same primary effects (they are weakly equivalent, like our two multiplication algorithms). Any parse a classical parser computes can be computed by a corresponding connectionist parser. If systematicity effects are primary effects, then SLM have demonstrated, mathematically, that systematicity effects in language parsing can be accounted for without any appeal to classical representations. Hence, if the systematicity effects at issue are primary effects, then nothing can be concluded concerning whether the mental representations involved are classical or connectionist in form. As we saw, the consequence of that empirical deadlock has been to turn away from empirical considerations to philosophical issues concerning what constitutes a principled explanation. The SLM tensor-product parser employs a different algorithm than the classical parser, however, and thus the two systems are bound to exhibit different incidental effects. If the systematicity effects observed are incidental, then, barring cosmic coincidence, at most one of the two parsers can account for them. In particular, the classical explanation can gain leverage over the SLM explanation if the form in which information is represented is important to explaining the effect. An incidental effect of using classical representations in language processing might, for instance, involve priming. Since the lexical items and sentential structure of a recently processed sentence S may be easily accessible (they may still be in short-term memory, for instance), the recent processing of S may allow the system to process systematic variants of S faster than it would process sentences that are not systematic variants of S. An incidental effect of using connectionist representations is the flat temporal profile of parsing with a tensor-product parser. Since the latter will process all sentences, no matter how complex, in one step, it will process all of them in exactly the same amount of time. Should the empirical evidence show that subjects exhibit the kind of priming effect described above or a temporal profile different from the one we would expect from the use of a tensor-product parser, then, weak equivalence notwithstanding, FPM have a good argument in favor of their claim that classical representations better explain the systematicity of thought. Of course, should the evidence show that the incidental effects are those one would expect from an SLM-type parser, then it would seem that classical representations are not the source of the systematicity of thought.

FPM and their supporters cite no evidence of incidental systematicity effects, nor do their opponents. It seems likely that there are relevant effects reported in the literature on language processing, but they have not, to our knowledge, been brought to bear on this issue.[20] It should be emphasized, however, that systematicity effects of the sort FPM had in mind are clearly not incidental but primary:[21] they do not argue from evidence that processing 'Mary loves John' makes it easier to process 'John loves Mary' to the conclusion that mental representation is classical. They simply argue from

---

[20] We are in the process of searching the literature for such evidence. Meanwhile, the fact that the SLM parser accomplishes all parses in a single step, regardless of the complexity of the sentence parsed, is surely suggestive.

[21] This is put misleadingly in Cummins (1996b: 603), Ch. 3, this volume. The point is that proponents of the systematicity argument are thinking of systematicity effects as primary when they should be thinking of them as incidental.

the availability of a given thought (sentence understood) to the possibility of its systematic variants.

4.4. Representational pluralism and structural encodings

The inference from systematicity effects in language to classical representations involves three steps:

(1) The observation of systematicity effects in language.
(2) An inference from the presence of these effects to the conclusion that mental representations must preserve and carry information about the structure of the domain.
(3) An inference from that conclusion to the further conclusion that the information about structure must be carried by classical representations.

Most will readily agree that systematicity effects in language can be observed. We noted in the previous section that care should be taken to distinguish primary from incidental systematicity effects in language since only the latter will allow conclusions to be drawn about the nature of representations. Step (2) is also uncontroversial. In unbounded domains (see above), how else can these effects be produced? It is step (3) of the inference, from the preservation of structural information to the necessary presence of classical representations, that we wish to address here.

Sensitivity to the structure of a domain is best explained by a scheme of mental representation that carries information about the structure of that domain. One such scheme involves structural representations of the domain in question. A representation R is a *structural representation* of its target just in case R and its target share structure. Scale models, photographs, and maps are typical examples of structural representations. As Cummins[22] points out, it is natural to explain the systematicity effects we find in language, vision, and audition by positing structural representations of each of the respective domains. The obvious virtue of structural representation is that structural transformations and permutations of the representations yield representations

---

[22] Cummins (1996b), Ch. 3, this volume.

of the systematic variants of the corresponding targets in the cognized domain. For every operation defined over elements in a domain there can be a corresponding operation defined over elements in the representational scheme. Thus, the representation of an item in the domain can be used to construct a representation of its systematic variants. The sensitivity to structure that is required to cognize certain domains is accomplished by actually having the structure of the domain in the representations. We are now in a position to appreciate that the FPM classical representations are a case of a scheme of structural representation for the linguistic domain. The idea is that, in order to be sensitive to the combinatorial syntax and associated semantics of a language, there must be a system of internal representations that has the same (or corresponding) syntactic and semantic features.

This way of explaining systematicity effects, however, limits classical schemes to the explanation of systematicity effects exhibited by the cognition of language-like domains, since these are the only domains that classical schemes can structurally represent. This leaves the systematicity effects we find in other differently structured domains to be explained by appeal to non-classical schemes. Since we apparently grasp the underlying structure of domains structurally distinct from language, we would require structurally distinct representational schemes to cope with each of them in the same way that classical schemes are supposed to facilitate coping with language. Apparently, structural representation comes at the price of (perhaps massive) representational pluralism.

The problem of representational pluralism was first noticed by Cummins (1996). Roughly, representational pluralism is the idea that for every differently structured domain for which we show a systematicity effect, we employ a scheme of mental representation that shares structure with that domain. Thus, if we exhibit systematicity effects in cognizing three differently structured domains, we employ at least three differently structured schemes of mental representation. FPM can make a plausible argument from systematicity effects in language processing to the conclusion that some mental representation is classical. There are other systematicity effects, however, such as those found in vision and audition, that cannot be accounted for by structural representations if all mental representation is classical, since the structures of the domains in language, audition, and vision are different. Since the inference from systematicity effects in domains other than language to nonclassical, structural representations is on par with the inference from systematicity effects in language to classical representations, the systematicities in vision and audition are good evidence for some non-classical, structural representations. Thus, if the FPM inference is sound, it constitutes a good argument for representational pluralism. The only way FPM can retain the idea that mental representation is monistic is by allowing that some systematicity effects can be adequately explained without recourse to a corresponding scheme of structural representations. Some systematicity will have to be explained by appeal to mere *encodings*. An encoding of a domain D is a mapping of the members of D onto the representations in a scheme R whose members do not share the structure of their images in D. Classical representations structurally represent linguistic structure, but they only encode the structure of music. By allowing some encoding, however, friends of FPM would forfeit the objection that connectionist data coverage is unprincipled, since encoding, on their view, forces us to be unprincipled somewhere. So it seems that either the objection must go, or FPM are forced to accept representational pluralism.

The SLM parser shows, however, that representational monism is compatible with an adequate account of primary systematicity effects. To see this clearly, we need a taxonomy of representational schemes that (i) makes evident what property holds of structural representations in virtue of which they account for primary systematicity effects; and (ii) identifies an alternative sort of scheme that can be seen to have this critical property.

Our taxonomy relies on two distinctions. The first distinction has to do with whether a representational scheme represents its domain by making available representations that share structure with the items of the domain represented. Shared structure involves two things. First, the representations have constituents that represent the constituents of the domain. Second, these representational constituents are structurally related in a way that represents the ways in which the constituents of the content are structurally related. We call any scheme in which representations represent items in its target domain in virtue of sharing structure with the things they represent a *structural representational scheme* for that domain. We call schemes that represent a domain, but not in virtue of shared structure, an *encoding* of the domain. So the first distinction separates entities that represent in virtue of shared structure, that is, structural representations, from those that represent by some other means, that is, encodings.

The second distinction we need requires the notion of a *recovery function*. A recovery function is a function from a representational scheme to a domain. Intuitively, these functions allow one to recover contents from representational schemes. Recovery functions are not necessarily employed by cognitive systems; they may remain purely theoretical constructs with which we may interpret representational schemes. We distinguish between recovery functions that are *systematic* and those that are not. A recovery function is systematic if there is a general/productive algorithm for mapping the scheme to its contents. In such a case, the function does not need to be defined by a list of pairs each containing an element of the scheme and a content. If the recovery function is systematic, then the representational scheme is structural. If the recovery function is not systematic, then the representational scheme is pure or arbitrary.

This taxonomy allows us to distinguish three categories of representational entities: structural representations, structural encodings, and pure encodings. Schemes that belong to either of the first two categories are such that the information about the structure of the domain is systematically recoverable. This is relevant because, if structure can be recovered systematically from a scheme, the scheme has preserved information about the structure of the domain. The possibility of systematic recovery implies the preservation of structure.

One obvious way of preserving structure is for the representational scheme simply to share the structure of the domain. This is what structural representations do. But this is not the only way. Structural encodings preserve structure without sharing it. Gödel numbering and tensor-product schemes are both examples of structural encodings. In the Gödel scheme for encoding sentences, words are assigned natural numbers while their positions in the sentence are assigned prime numbers in ascending order. A number m in position n yields the number n^m. We can say that n^m stands for

Table 4.1 Representation and Encoding

	Systematic Recovery Function	No Systematic Recovery Function
Do not share structure	Structural Encodings	Pure Encodings
Share structure	Structural Representations	

the word numbered m standing in the place numbered n. This number is uniquely factorable into n, m times. The Gödel string of a sentence is determined by multiplying all these uniquely factorable numbers together. This yields a number, expressed by a Gödel string, which is uniquely factorable into a list of numbers. An example of a Gödel string is '1,093,500' which factors into $2^2 \times 3^7 \times 5^3$ which breaks down further into a list of 2s, 3s, and 5s. The values of these numbers have been assigned to places, and the number of occurrences of any number has been assigned to words. We may suppose the string encodes the sentence 'Mary loves John' where 'Mary,' 'loves,' and 'John' are assigned the numbers 2, 7, and 3, respectively. The Gödel string itself does not share structure with its content; however, this structure is systematically recoverable and thus the representation has preserved information about the structure of the sentence. The SLM tensor-product representations have the same property. The tensor-product activation patterns themselves do not share structure with their contents, but the existence of recoverability functions for such schemes entails that such schemes preserve structure.

Structural encodings permit recovery but do not share structure with their domains. Pure encodings do not permit systematic recovery and so do not preserve structure. If, for example, we were to take the names of the state capitals as encodings of the names of the states, we would be employing a pure encoding scheme, for there is no systematic way by which the names of the states could be recovered from the names of the capitals.[23] In this case, a look-up table is required, and no information about structure is preserved.

Structural encodings, as opposed to pure encodings, are adequate to account for primary systematicity effects because, under such schemes, information about structure is preserved and that is all that is required. This is, in fact, the property of structural encodings and structural representations in virtue of which it is possible to construct architectures using either one that exhibit systematicity effects. To take our previous example, any system capable of processing 1,093,500 (the Gödel string for 'Mary loves John') is also capable of processing 437,400 (the Gödel string for 'John loves Mary'). The parallel with the previous symmetric phrase markers is perfect.

---

[23] Another way to see the same point: given a new capital name, there is no way to infer what state name it corresponds to.

The SLM tensor-product scheme is a structural encoding, not a pure encoding as FPM seem to assume, and this is how SLM are able to prove their otherwise puzzling result. It is only when cognitive systems employ such structure-preserving schemes that they can be causally sensitive to the structure of the domain cognized and thus exhibit systematicity effects. Systems employing pure encodings cannot exhibit such effects because there is no common form or structure to which the system could be causally sensitive.

Once we see that structural encoding is adequate to account for systematicity effects—at least the primary ones—we are free to cleave to representational monism. Since a tensor-product scheme like that employed by SLM need not share structure with the domains it represents in order to account for primary systematicity effects, such a scheme could, in principle, account for primary systematicity effects in a variety of structurally distinct domains. The same point can be made about classical representation: since it can be used to structurally encode domains such as music that are structurally unlike language, a classical scheme could account for primary systematicity effects in nonlinguistic domains. Since classical and nonclassical structural encodings are evidently on equal footing in this respect, we conclude again that there is no sound argument from primary systematicity effects to classical representation. There is, of course, a sound argument from systematicity effects against pure encoding, but that should come as no surprise. What is important to systematicity is preserving information about the relevant structure of the target domain. It does not much matter how that information is encoded, provided an architecture exists that is capable of exploiting the information in that encoding. SLM demonstrate that connectionist networks can exploit such information as encoded in tensor-product activation vector schemes.

The staunch defender of classical representations may object at this point that there still is a methodological virtue in accepting classical representations-plus-pluralism over encodings-plus-monism, because it is the lawfulness of systematicity that needs to be explained and encodings just do not account for it. But it is not clear that they do not. We agree that, with pure encodings, there could be minds that encode 'Mary loves John' without encoding 'John loves Mary,' since the ability to encode the former does not imply the ability to encode the latter. With structural encodings such as the tensor-product scheme employed by SLM, however, matters are different.

Since the encodings are generated recursively from the filler and role vectors, the ability to encode 'Mary loves John' does imply the ability to encode 'John loves Mary,' since the two encodings employ the same filler and role vectors. The only difference between them is how the vectors get multiplied and added to create the respective tensor-product encodings of the two sentences.[24]

References

Aizawa, K., 'Explaining Systematicity', *Mind and Language*, 12 (1997), 115–36.

Butler, K., 'Towards a Connectionist Cognitive Architecture', *Mind and Language*, 6 (1991), 252–72.

—— 'Compositionality in Cognitive Models: The Real Issue', *Philosophical Studies*, 78 (1995), 153–62.

Chalmers, D. J., 'Connectionism and Compositionality: Why Fodor and Pylyshyn were Wrong', *Philosophical Psychology*, 6 (1993), 305–19.

Chater, N., and Oaksford, M., 'Autonomy, Implementation and Cognitive Architecture: A Reply to Fodor and Pylyshyn', *Cognition*, 34 (1990), 93–107.

Cummins, D. D., 'The Role of Analogical Reasoning in the Induction of Problem Categories', *Journal of Experimental Psychology: Learning, Memory, and Cognition*, 5 (1992), 1103–24.

Cummins, R., *Representations, Targets, and Attitudes* (Cambridge, Mass.: MIT Press, 1996*a*).

—— 'Systematicity', *Journal of Philosophy*, 93 (1996*b*), 591–614.

—— ' "How does it Work?" versus "What are the Laws?": Two Conceptions of Psychological Explanation', in F. C. Keil and R. A. Wilson (eds.), *Explanation and Cognition* (Cambridge, Mass.: MIT Press, 2000*a*), 117–44.

Fodor, J., 'Connectionism and the Problem of Systematicity (Continued): Why Smolensky's Solution Still Doesn't Work', *Cognition*, 62 (1997), 109–19.

—— McLaughlin, B., 'Connectionism and the Problem of Systematicity: Why Smolensky's Solution Doesn't Work', *Cognition*, 35 (1990*c*), 183–205.

Fodor, J. and Pylyshyn, Z., 'Connectionism and Cognitive Architecture', *Cognition*, 28 (1988), 3–71.

[24] Versions of this article were presented before the Society for Philosophy and Psychology (June 1999), CogSci99 (July 1999), the APA (April 2000), and at various universities. We thank audiences and commentators for their helpful remarks. Research was funded by NSF Grant # 9976739.

Hadley, R., 'Systematicity in Connectionist Language Learning', *Mind and Language*, 9 (1994*a*), 247–72.

—— 'Systematicity Revisited', *Mind and Language*, 9 (1994*b*), 431–44.

—— 'Cognition, Systematicity, and Nomic Necessity', *Mind and Language*, 12 (1997*a*), 137–53.

—— Hayward, M. B., 'Strong Semantic Systematicity from Hebbian Connectionist Learning', *Minds and Machines*, 7 (1997*b*), 1–55.

Horgan, T., and Tienson, J., 'Structured Representations in Connectionist Systems?', in S. Davis (ed.), *Connectionism: Theory and Practice* (New York: Oxford University Press, 1992), 195–228.

Matthews, R. J., 'Three-Concept Monte: Explanation, Implementation, and Systematicity', *Synthese*, 101 (1994), 347–63.

—— 'Can Connectionists Explain Systematicity?', *Mind and Language*, 12 (1997), 154–77.

McClelland, J. L., McNaughton, B. L., and O'Reilly, R. C., 'Why There Are Complementary Learning Systems in the Hippocampus and the Neocortex: Insights from the Success and Failures of Connectionist Models of Learning and Memory', *Psychological Review*, 102 (1995), 419–57.

McCloskey, M., and Cohen, N. J., 'Catastrophic Interference in Connectionist Networks: The Sequential Learning Problem', *The Psychology of Learning and Motivation*, 24 (1989), 109–65.

McLaughlin, B. P., 'Systematicity, Conceptual Truth, and Evolution', in C. Hookway and D. Peterson (eds.), *Philosophy and Cognitive Science* (Cambridge: Cambridge University Press, 1993*a*).

—— 'The Connectionism/Classicism Battle to Win Souls', *Philosophical Studies*, 71 (1993*b*), 163–90.

Millikan, R., *Language, Thought, and Other Biological Categories* (Cambridge, Mass.: MIT Press/Bradford Books, 1984).

Niklasson, L. F., and van Gelder, T., 'On Being Systematically Connectionist', *Mind and Language*, 9 (1994), 288–302.

Poirier, P., Cummins, R., Blackmon, J., Byrd, D., Roth, M., and Schwarz, G., 'The Epistemology of Non-Symbolic Cognition: Atomistic Learning and Forgetting', *Technical Report Phil99-3* (University of California at Davis, 1999).

Pylyshyn, Z., *Computation and Cognition* (Cambridge, Mass.: MIT Press/Bradford Books, 1984).

Schwarz, G., 'Connectionism, Processing, Memory', *Connection Science*, 1 (1992), 207–26.

Smolensky, P., 'The Constituent Structure of Connectionist Mental States', *Southern Journal of Philosophy Supplement*, 26 (1987), 137–60.

Smolensky, P., 'Tensor Product Variable Binding and the Representation of Symbolic Structures in Connectionist Systems', *Artificial Intelligence*, 46 (1990), 159–216.

—— 'Connectionism, Constituency and the Language of Thought', in B. Loewer and G. Rey (eds.), *Meaning in Mind: Fodor and his Critics* (Oxford: Blackwell, 1991).

—— 'Constituent Structure and Explanation in an Integrated Connectionist/ Symbolic Cognitive Architecture', in C. Macdonald (ed.), *Connectionism: Debates on Psychological Explanation* (Oxford: Blackwell, 1995).

—— LeGendre, G., and Miyata Y., 'Principles for an Integrated Connectionist/ Symbolic Theory of Higher Cognition', *Technical Report 92-08* (Institute of Cognitive Science, University of Colorado, 1992).

Tarski, A. (1936), 'The Concept of Truth in Formalized Languages', in J. H. Woodger (ed.), *Logic, Semantics, Metamathematics* (Oxford: Oxford University Press, 1956).

—— (1944), 'The Semantic Conception of Truth', in H. Feigl and W. Sellars (eds.), *Readings in Philosophical Analysis* (New York: Appleton, 1949).

Van Gelder, T., 'Compositionality: A Connectionist Variation on a Classical Theme', *Cognitive Science*, 14 (1990), 355–84.

5

Methodological Reflections on Belief

5.1. Intentional realism

Let's suppose there really are such things as propositional attitudes. And let's understand this claim as Putnam (1975) would have us understand claims about natural kinds so that it could turn out that most of what we believe about the propositional attitudes might be mistaken in one way or another. Or, if that is going too far, let's at least understand the claim in such a way that any particular thing we believe about the attitudes might turn out to be false. This, it seems to me, is the way we have to understand the claim that there are such things as propositional attitudes if we are to take the claim to be an empirical one on all fours with such claims as that there are elephants, genes, or crystals. Otherwise, we can legislate against surprising empirical discoveries about the attitudes by claiming that the discoverers have merely changed the subject. 'Computationalists can't be talking about belief,' we might say, 'because beliefs are individuated, at least in part, by social factors, and computational states are not. At best, they are talking about 'shmaliefs', not beliefs.'

The trouble with this sort of move is that the philosopher who makes it runs the risk that he or she is talking about nothing at all. If philosophers insist, for example, that beliefs are socially individuated, while good empirical theory insists that computational states are what there are, then it is open to the computationalist to say that the empirical evidence suggests that there are no beliefs as the philosopher chooses to define them.[1] Scientists who have

Originally published in R. Brogdan (ed.), *Mind and Common Sense* (Cambridge University Press, 1991), 53–70. This paper appears with kind permission of Cambridge University Press.

[1] The situation is comparable to Dretske's (1981) insistence that mental states get their representational content during a learning period when they are perfect indicators of the properties they are said to represent. The theory runs the risk that no mental states have representational content as defined, or

no stomach for a fight over words will either cease talking to philosophers, or they will simply invent a new word. The philosophers will quite rightly be perceived as having won a petty squabble over semantic territory at the price of cutting themselves off from serious empirical research.

5.2. Methodology: intentional realism and the philosophy of science

Lots of philosophers, I suspect, resist realism about the attitudes—in practice, if not explicitly—because it threatens to lead to unemployment. How, after all, can a philosopher who toes the realist line hope to discover anything about the propositional attitudes? Doesn't being a realist about the propositional attitudes amount to conceding them to the scientists?

The same thing might be said about space and time. If we are realists about these matters, shouldn't philosophers concede that the natures of space, time, and space–time are empirical matters and stop poaching on the physicist's preserves? Yes, of course. But accepting that answer hasn't put philosophers out of the space and time business. Rather, it has led philosophers to treat the issues as issues in the philosophy of physics. Instead of asking what the nature of space and time are—a question philosophical methodology cannot properly address—the philosopher of physics asks, for example, how space must be conceived if some well-articulated physical theory or theoretical framework is to deliver the explanatory goods it advertises. How must we conceive of space if general relativity is to be true and explanatory? Should we be substantivalists? Is space a thing? Or is it a property of things? This kind of inquiry is especially pressing when the target is an explanatory primitive of the theory or theories that harbor it. Hence, a good deal of the philosophy of science is concerned with explicating the 'foundations' of this or that theory or framework or research paradigm.

All this applies straightforwardly to the philosophy of psychology. Philosophers may, without concern for a misfit between their methodology and

---

anyway no content worth bothering about, since it might turn out that no mental state is ever a perfect indicator of distal states of affairs.

their conclusions, identify some theory (or theoretical framework or research paradigm) that invokes propositional attitudes and then ask how we should understand them if the invoking theory is to be true and explanatory. Thus, if our target is computationalist theories, and we determine that computational states are not individuated by social factors, then we may conclude that beliefs, at least as invoked by computationalists, had better be asocial too. We can then go on to attempt to construct an appropriate asocial conception of belief.[2]

5.3. Methodology and belief attribution

What I've been describing is not what philosophers have been doing. What they have been doing instead is trying to turn semantics into psychology. Here is a familiar example.[3]

5.3.1. Burge: belief and linguistic affiliation

'Brisket' applies to cuts of breast meat generally. Tyler, however, believes that it applies only to breast of beef. Tyler[*] is just like Tyler except that he lives in a language community in which 'brisket' applies only to breast of beef. Tyler and Tyler[*], we may suppose, are molecule-for-molecule identical, for, though their language communities differ slightly, Tyler has, in point of fact, never encountered the sort of situation that could distinguish him from Tyler[*], for example, reading a dictionary entry for 'brisket.'

---

[2] In a similar vein, we might ask what belief must be if folk psychology is to be true and explanatory. To this I have no objection, but two comments are in order. First, to explicate the concepts of folk psychology one must begin by determining what folk psychology is. In practice, this is usually a matter of gesturing apologetically to some simple examples of alleged folk psychological explanation, examples that are generally conceded to be seriously flawed in some way. The assumption seems to be that we just know what folk psychology is. Psychologists who want to know what folk physics is (e.g. what people would say about the trajectories of falling objects) do some controlled experiments to find out. Philosophers who make claims about folk psychology don't feel the need. Perhaps they are right: perhaps folk psychology is rather more explicit in daily practice than folk physics. But I don't think this is what's really going on. Philosophers don't need to know what folk psychology is because they never appeal to it. It never matters to the philosophical arguments what the principles actually are—only that there are some. This is suspicious in itself: how can you know what the explanatory role of belief is in folk psychology if you don't know or care what folk psychology is? Second, it is worth knowing what belief must be if folk psychology is to turn out true and explanatory only if there is some reason to think folk psychology might turn out to be true and explanatory. It is amazing how certain philosophers are that folk psychology is true and explanatory given their avowed ignorance of its alleged principles.

[3] The following example is taken from Burge (1979).

In spite of their mereological identity, however, it seems we are prepared to attribute beliefs about brisket to Tyler but not to Tyler*. For when Tyler* says, for example, 'Brisket is better than tenderloin,' he is making a statement that has a different truth condition than the statement Tyler makes with the same words. Tyler's statement is about breast of beast; Tyler*, using the same words, makes a statement about breast of beef. But it seems obvious that what goes for the statements must go for the beliefs they express: the belief Tyler expresses when he says, 'Brisket is better than tenderloin,' is about breast of beast; the one Tyler* expresses is about breast of beef. It is concluded from all this that beliefs are not entirely 'in the head.' They are not, in fact, psychological states as psychologists normally conceive them, since they are individuated in part by such extrapsychological factors as the rules of one's language,[4] even in cases in which the relevant facts about the language have had no causal impact whatever on the believer.

How exactly is this sort of thought experiment supposed to lead to conclusions about the nature of belief? Can this sort of 'intuition pump' (Dennett 1980) really show that beliefs are not psychological states,[5] that psychologists are mistaken to try to use 'believes' to characterize mental processes in a way that abstracts away from such things as the subject's linguistic affiliation?

I'm going to need a name for the methodology implicit in this sort of thought experiment. I'll call it the CRHS methodology for *c*onsidered *r*esponse to a *h*ypothetical *s*ituation. It is difficult to see how CRHS can deliver the goods about belief. What we've got to go on is just whether we would say that Tyler but not Tyler* has beliefs about brisket. But how could this tell us anything about their beliefs? Isn't this like inferring that objects dropped from an airplane have a straight-line trajectory (relative to the earth) because that's the trajectory people tend to attribute in such cases?[6] Or isn't it like inferring that the rate of free-fall is a function of weight from

---

[4] A psychologist will treat the rules of the language as a psychological factor only to the extent that they are represented in the speaker (or implicit in the speaker's functional architecture somehow).

[5] Burge, of course, would not accept my description of these factors as 'extrapsychological,' nor would he condone my speaking of beliefs widely individuated as 'not psychological states.' I hope it is clear that, in the present context, this is merely a matter of terminology. I don't think I've begged any substantive questions. In the context of a particular explanatory framework, we can get around this terminological issue by saying that if beliefs are individuated in part by linguistic affiliation, then they are not computational states, or neurophysiological states, or whatever the framework in question holds to be the relevant way to specify the 'substrata' of mentality.

[6] See e.g. McCloskey (1983); Kaiser *et al.* (1986).

the fact that people's attributions of rate are sensitive to the supposed weight of the falling object? Why assume that people are any better authorities about belief than about the trajectories or rate of free-fall of falling objects? Perhaps people can, within limits, tell you what they believe with fair reliability. But even if people were incorrigible about what beliefs they had, it wouldn't follow that they had any special knowledge about the nature of belief.

How could it even seem that investigating the conditions of belief attribution could yield conclusions about belief? The answer seems simple enough: if we know, for example, that

(A) Tyler and Tyler* are psychologically equivalent,

and that

(B) Tyler and Tyler* have different beliefs,

then it follows that,

(C) individuation of belief is a function of extrapsychological factors.[7]

The trouble, of course, is B: what entitles us to the claim that Tyler and Tyler* have different beliefs? CRHS serves up B for us: reflecting on the story, we attribute different beliefs to Tyler and Tyler*. But why should we take our belief attributions seriously in a tough case like this, uninformed, as they are, by good empirical theory?

There are two reasons for caution. To see what they are, we need to look more closely at the underlying situation. Here's the plot outline:

(i) It is stipulated that Tyler and Tyler* are psychologically equivalent.
(ii) We are moved, on reflection, to attribute different beliefs to Tyler and Tyler*.
(iii) It follows that our belief attributions are sensitive to extrapsychological factors—linguistic affiliation in this case.
(iv) We conclude that the truth conditions of belief attributions contain extrapsychological factors, and hence that beliefs are individuated (in part) by extrapsychological factors.

---

[7] Again, I don't mean to beg any questions by the use of 'psychological' here. For a computationalist, the issue could be put this way: If we know that (A) Tyler and Tyler* are computationally equivalent, and that (B) Tyler and Tyler* have different beliefs, then it follows that (C) individuation of belief is a function of extrapsychological factors.

But (iv) doesn't follow from (iii). Extrapsychological considerations may be legitimate *evidence* for belief attributions, yet not be implicated in their truth conditions.[8] In this case, we are moved by the fact that what Tyler states when he says, 'Brisket is better than tenderloin,' is different than what Tyler* states in uttering the same words in the same circumstances. People generally believe what they sincerely state to be the case. What people sincerely state therefore provides a good bet concerning what they believe. But what someone states in uttering a sentence is a function of the meanings of the words in the sentence, and that in turn is a function of the language they are speaking. So here we have an uncontroversial case of an extrapsychological factor—word meaning in the language—counting as legitimate evidence for a belief attribution.

But it is only evidence. From the fact that attributions of belief are properly sensitive to extrapsychological factors, it doesn't follow that extrapsychological factors figure in the truth conditions of belief attributions. All we are entitled to conclude is that extrapsychological factors figure legitimately as evidence for belief attributions. In the particular case under discussion, it is easy to see why we shouldn't move to a conclusion about truth conditions. Why, after all, should we assume that Tyler means exactly what his words are conventionally suited to express?[9] Why, that is, should we assume that what Tyler says is an exact reflection of what he believes? Tyler *thinks* his words express what he believes, but, of course, he is wrong about this, for it is part of the story that he doesn't know what 'brisket' means in the language he is speaking. Corrected about this matter, it seems likely that Tyler would change his story: 'Oh, I see. Well, then, it's breast of beef I like, not brisket! I really haven't given any thought to what you call brisket. Quite a mixed bag, after all.' Or he might simply pull a Humpty-Dumpty: 'That's not what *I* mean by "brisket." What I mean is breast of beef.'

---

[8] If you thought the CRHS methodology could lead to conclusions about the evidence conditions for belief attribution, and you assimilate truth conditions to evidence conditions, then you would have a route to conclusions about belief. This route, however, is bound to be unattractive to those who have learned Quine's lesson: if anything can be evidence for anything else (via intervening theory), then reflection on what might justify a belief attribution is not likely to tell you much about the truth conditions for belief attribution.

[9] If there is such a thing: actually, it is just *stipulated* that Tyler's words mean that breast of beast is better than tenderloin.

The point of the foregoing is not so much to argue that Tyler and Tyler* don't have different beliefs, but rather to emphasize that we cannot move from premises about our considered belief attributions to conclusions about the truth conditions of belief attributions. There is, of course, a kind of consistency argument available: *if* you agree that Tyler and Tyler* have different beliefs, then you must agree that beliefs are individuated by extrapsychological factors. But this won't carry much weight with thoughtful realists, for they will be rightly suspicious of their 'intuitions' in cases like this. They will remember that plausible belief attributions may yet be false. They will remember that even justified belief attributions may yet be false.

More radically, they will remember what intelligent, well-informed people who happen to be innocent of mechanics say about things dropped from airplanes. People generally attribute incorrect trajectories to hypothetical objects dropped from hypothetical airplanes. They do this, presumably, because they have false beliefs about the trajectories of objects dropped from airplanes. Subjects with a knowledge of elementary physics don't make this sort of mistake. Similarly, people with false beliefs about belief can be expected to make mistaken attributions of belief in real and hypothetical situations. 'Perhaps,' the realist will think, 'it is best to let well-motivated empirical theory inform our attributions of belief as it ought to inform our attributions of trajectories.' Well-motivated empirical theory, of course, is just what CRHS cannot provide. If belief is to be a serious explanatory construct, then we had better put the *serious* explanations in the driver's seat and let our intuitions go along for the ride. If we are wrong about belief, we will make mistaken attributions. In the end, the only way to know about belief is to study belief. Studying belief attributions will, at best, tell you only what people believe about belief.[10]

It might seem that the problem with the Burgean argument is not with the methodology—not with CRHS—but with the mistaken assumption that sincerity is enough to guarantee a match between what someone states and the underlying belief. But this *is* a problem with the methodology: our considered responses to hypothetical situations will depend on what we consider. It turns out that we should have considered the fact that sincerity isn't enough to match what is stated to what is believed. What else should

---

[10] 'At best' means empirically, under controlled conditions. CRHS is bound to yield biased conclusions, for your *considered* responses will depend on what you consider, including your philosophical theories.

we consider? This is just the sort of question that science is supposed to answer better than common sense.

The Burgean argument is instructive in part because we can *see* that we have been misled. Lacking a good empirical theory of belief, we normally have no really satisfactory way of knowing whether CRHS is yielding questionable attributions. But in this case, we are told that Tyler doesn't know what 'brisket' means in his language. Since we know that what one states is a function of the meanings of the words one uses, we can be pretty sure that Tyler doesn't succeed in stating what he intends to state, so we can be pretty sure that what he does succeed in stating isn't likely to be a perfect reflection of what he believes. Having come this far, it is tempting to say that, *on further reflection*, we can see that what Tyler believes is not that brisket is better than tenderloin, but that breast of beef is better than tenderloin. There's no harm in yielding to this temptation, provided that we don't suppose that *further reflection* has got round the need for empirical theory after all. CRHS isn't going to tell us how to individuate belief, unless the *further reflection* in question is adequately informed reflection. Only a good empirical theory of belief could seriously justify confidence that our reflections are adequately informed.

5.3.2. Putnam: belief and environmental affiliation

It is tempting, as I've just pointed out, to suppose that the difficulty we've uncovered is special to the sort of argument given by Tyler Burge for the relevance of linguistic affiliation to belief. The Burgean argument simply assumes that what is stated is what is believed:

(B-1) If S sincerely states that p, then S believes that p.

But (B-1) is false. In the case lately imagined, is seems plausible to suppose that what Tyler states (viz., that breast of beast is better than tenderloin) is not what he intends to state (viz., that breast of beef is better than tenderloin). What he actually states is, of course, a function of the meanings of his words. But he is, by hypothesis, mistaken about the meaning of 'brisket' in his language. Hence he chooses the wrong words to express what he intends to state. The difficulty, one might suppose, is not with the methodology; the problem was just that it was an inadequately informed application of the methodology. Even if we accept the view that adequately informed reflection is reflection informed by good empirical theory, perhaps there is enough good empirical theory in hand to allow CRHS to yield the targeted result, namely *true* attributions of distinct beliefs to psychologically equivalent subjects. Consider Putnam's Twin Earth case (Putnam 1975). Twin Earth is an exact duplicate of earth except that where we have H_2O they have *XYZ*. When Hilary says, 'Water is better than Pepsi,' he makes a statement about H_2O. When Twhilary (Twin-Hilary) says, 'Water is better than Pepsi,' he makes a statement about *XYZ*. Once again, it is concluded that Hilary and Twhilary express different beliefs. But since, by hypothesis, the twins are molecule-for-molecule duplicates, it follows that beliefs are individuated by extrapsychological factors.

In this case, it seems we cannot object that one of the characters in the story fails to state what he intends to state on the grounds that one of them is mistaken about the meanings of the words he uses. It seems that neither character is mistaken about the meaning of 'water' in the language he uses. Both speak sincerely. It seems to follow that what each states is what each intends to state. Since what one sincerely intends to state is what one believes, both state what they believe. Since the statements are different, so are the beliefs. QED.

Should we concede that the CRHS *can* deliver the conclusion that beliefs are individuated by extrapsychological factors? How is this possible? Haven't we just reinstated armchair science? A realist about belief will surely want to give this argument very close scrutiny.

The argument makes use of a crucial assumption:

(P-1)   What the twins state is what they intend to state sincerely.

(P-1) is bolstered (though of course not entailed) by (P-2):

(P-2)   Neither twin is mistaken about the meaning of 'water.'

(P-2) looks harmless enough. In the Burge case, it is an explicit assumption that Tyler is mistaken about the meaning of 'brisket', but there is no comparable assumption operative in the Twin Earth case. Still, (P-2) is not as harmless as it appears.

Let's begin with the fact that the twins are, in a certain sense, ignorant of the reference of their words: Twhilary doesn't know that the referent of 'water' in Twinglish is *XYZ*. How, one might wonder, can Twhilary sincerely intend to state something about *XYZ* given that he doesn't know that what he calls water is *XYZ*? Aren't we simply assuming about intention what we are trying to prove about belief?

It seems that (P-2) is wrong if it is understood to imply that the twins are fully informed about the reference of 'water' in their respective languages: while it is surely uncontroversial that, *in some sense*, Twhilary knows what 'water' refers to in Twinglish, it doesn't follow that he is fully informed about the nature of the stuff he refers to with his uses of 'water.' There is, therefore, a certain sense in which he doesn't know what he is talking about, viz., he doesn't know what proposition he is expressing when he says, 'Water is better than Pepsi.' It would seem to follow that he cannot sincerely intend to express that proposition in uttering those words. Hence, (P-1) cannot be invoked to yield a conclusion about what he believes. Once again, it appears that the argument depends on a dubious psychological assumption linking what one believes to the reference of what one says. Here's how the trick is done:

> (1) The meanings of one's words are determined by extrapsychological factors,

hence,

> (2) the truth conditions of one's statements are determined by extrapsychological factors.

But,

> (3) one's sincere statements express what one believes,

hence,

> (4) the truth conditions of one's sincere statements are the same as the truth conditions of one's beliefs.

I have no quarrel with (1) and (2), but (3) is false, as we've seen, and so is (4). Something close to (3) is plausible, namely,

> (3′) one believes what one intends to state sincerely.

But (3′) merely shifts the burden from belief to intention. It may be true that the truth conditions of what one intends to state sincerely are the same as the truth conditions of what one believes. But this won't help you get a conclusion about the truth conditions of beliefs from premises about the truth conditions of statements, unless you already have a link between the truth conditions of intentions and the truth conditions of statements. Shifting the focus to intention is no help because there is no more reason to say that Twhilary intends to state that *XYZ* is wet than to say that he believes that *XYZ* is wet. On the contrary, the shift to intention makes the trick a little easier to spot.

That's not the end of the matter, of course. The Twin Earth case is different from Burgean cases in that we are still left wondering what Twhilary *does* believe, whereas we are pretty sure we know what Tyler believes. We will have to come back to this.

5.4. Semantics and psychology

5.4.1. *The psychological reality of semantic values*

There is, of course, an intellectual tradition according to which you *can* discover the truth conditions for belief attributions without knowing anything about belief. Formal semantics in the Tarskian tradition espoused by Davidson (1967) is supposed to yield truth conditions for whatever it is that is truth-valuable in natural languages. But this kind of traffic in truth conditions isn't supposed to be the sort of thing that could supply fuel for the antiindividualist fire. For *that* you need to be able to discover such things as that the truth-value of a belief attribution can depend on an extrapsychological factor. If Tarskian semantics is serving up conclusions like that, then it is certainly doing more than telling us about the language, and is therefore overstepping the boundaries set by its original charter. No one in that tradition thought of semantics as the sort of thing that could overlap the psychology of belief.

Yet this crossing of boundaries—doing philosophy of mind, and even psychology, by doing philosophy of language—has become a small industry. What gives the trespassers such confidence?

I think a lot of the trespassing (or what I'm contentiously calling trespassing) began with the hypothesis that semantic values are psychologically real.

> (Psychological reality of semantic values—PRSV): to understand (or know the meaning of) an expression requires knowing its semantic value.

Examples of PRSV are (*a*) the claim that to understand a statement requires knowing its truth condition; (*b*) the claim that to understand a proper name requires knowing its sense; (*c*) the claim that to understand a proper name requires knowing its reference; (*d*) the claim that to understand a general term requires knowing what property it expresses; (e) the claim that to understand a statement requires knowing what proposition it expresses. Two clarifying remarks are essential.

First, *understanding* is to be construed psychologically in the PRSV: for example, (b) is to be construed as the idea that one must represent the sense of a name, and represent it as the sense of that name, in order to be a party to successful communicative episodes that employ that name. A corollary of PRSV is the assumption that learning a language involves learning the semantic values of its expressions.[11]

Second, *semantic values* are, in the first instance, to be understood in the model theoretic sort of way that is central to the Tarskian tradition: they are whatever one needs to assign to things in order to capture systematically the entailment relations that hold among things that are truth-valuable. The paradigm case is the assignment of satisfaction conditions to the primitive terms of a first-order language in such a way as not only to enable a truth definition, but to account for the entailment relations among statements. It is the fact that semantics aims for, and is constrained by, a proprietary goal independent of psychology that gives PRSV its bite: PRSV is the hypothesis that the stuff that tracks entailments is an essential part of the stuff a system needs to know in order to use and understand a language. This is how PRSV links semantics with psychology: since the stuff that tracks entailments is the stuff that (in part) drives use and understanding, when we do the semantics we have done a good deal of the psychology as well.

Meaning and semantic values   I suspect that some have been seduced into accepting PRSV by the following line of thought: to understand an expression is just to know what it means. But to know what an expression means is to know its meaning (that is, to know its semantic value).

I suppose there is an innocent sense in which people who know English know the meaning of 'elevator' and 'rescue'. Perhaps they can even tell you what these words mean. I've asked a few people about 'elevator' just now. The best answer I got was this: 'An elevator is like a closet. You go in, press one of several buttons with numbers on them, and the thing travels up a

---

[11] Since you can't learn an infinite list, the corollary amounts to the claim that learnable languages must be *finite-based*: there must be a finite number of primitive terms, and a finite number of rules, such that learning the semantic value of each of the primitives, and learning the rules, allows one to generate the semantic value of any expression of the language. (See Davidson 1965.)

vertical shaft in the building, stopping at the floor corresponding to the number on the button you pushed. Faster and easier than stairs.' This person certainly knows what 'elevator' means. But does this person know the semantic value of 'elevator'? Does she know which whatnot 'elevator' must be associated with in order to track the entailments of expressions in which 'elevator' occurs as a constituent? Maybe. But the fact that she knows, in this ordinary way, what 'elevator' means does not, on the face of it anyway, show that she does (or must) know, even tacitly, what semanticists want to know about 'elevator'.

Maybe the *psychology* works like this: when you encounter an 'elevator' you generate a pointer to a frame that allows you to access, more or less reliably, everything you know about elevators. On this rather plausible view, your ability to use and understand 'elevator's is closely related to your ability to use and understand elevators: it rests on what you know about elevators. You have the concept of an elevator, on this view, when you have a frame whose semantic value is (let's say) the property of being an elevator but whose psychological content is just whatever you know about elevators.[12] The crucial point is that there is a strong distinction between the psychological content of a concept and its semantic content. The psychological content is the *knowledge[13] in (or accessible via) the relevant data structure; the semantic content (what I've been calling the semantic value) is the sort of thing that enters into truth conditions. I'll call this view of concepts the encyclopedia view of concepts to emphasize the idea that the psychological content of a concept is like an encyclopedia entry rather than a dictionary entry (that is, an entry that specifies a meaning).

I think there is a good deal of empirical evidence for the encyclopedia theory of concepts. However that may be, the point I want to make is that it is incompatible with PRSV. Since the encyclopedia theory of concepts is plainly an empirical theory, so is PRSV. It doesn't follow, of course, that philosophers are not allowed to assume PRSV, but it does mean that they

---

[12] Or perhaps, whatever knowledge or misinformation in fact drives your use and understanding of 'elevators' and elevators. If it is mostly or all misinformation, perhaps we say you don't have the concept of an elevator. Or perhaps we say that everything you believe about elevators is wrong. In that case, we credit you with a frame whose semantic value is appropriate to 'elevator.' A consequence will be that whether you have the concept of an elevator will not depend on the psychological content of the frame in question at all (or only minimally—perhaps it must be the frame accessed in response to encounters with 'elevators' if not to elevators).

[13] By *knowledge I mean something that functions like knowledge, but needn't be true or justified or conscious.

are required to acknowledge the empirical loan they are taking out when they do assume it. No argument that assumes PRSV, for example, can be used to criticize the encyclopedia theory of concepts.

Belief and the PRSV   Even if we know something about the semantic values of such things as beliefs or mental representations, nothing will follow about the psychological content of those representations or states unless we assume something like PRSV. If you have the semantics straight, you will be able to track the semantic relations among mental states. But it doesn't follow that you will be able to track their psychological relations. We should therefore be cautious of moves from premises about the truth conditions of belief attributions to substantive conclusions about belief. If the PRSV isn't true, then semantic values (for instance, truth conditions) aren't in the head. The semanticist will be able, in one sense, to draw conclusions about mental states (viz., conclusions about their semantic values). But nothing will follow about the psychological contents of those states. Hence, even if, contrary to fact, philosophy were in a position to establish that Tyler and Tyler* have beliefs with different semantic contents, it wouldn't follow that they have beliefs with different psychological contents. Hence it wouldn't follow that they have, in any sense of interest to psychology, different beliefs. Empirical science must be left free to individuate its states in whatever way conduces to good theory. Philosophers can insist that states individuated by psychological content rather than semantic content are not beliefs, but this won't be worth taking seriously unless and until they catch psychologists using what they call beliefs in a way that assumes that they are semantically individuated.[14]

5.4.2. *The old and the new semantics*

I have already emphasized that if philosophers are to be able to move from semantical theses to psychological theses, there has to be a sense in which semantics is independent from psychology. That is, it had better be the case that semantics has its own proprietary goals and constraints. Only thus will it be possible to establish some semantical thesis *and then* expose its

---

[14] This is harder than it sounds. Psychologists *seem* to acquiesce in the semantic individuation of beliefs, but they don't mean by *semantics* what philosophers (and some linguists) mean by *semantics*. When psychologists talk about semantics, they typically have in mind *how something is understood, what it means to the subject*; they don't have model-theoretic considerations in mind at all.

implications for psychology. Semantics, I have supposed, is the theory of entailment. Semantic values are whatever one needs to assign to statements (or whatever is truth-valuable) to systematically track entailment relations.[15] So the idea behind what I have contentiously called philosophical trespassing on psychological turf can be put this way:

> (Easement): get the semantics of belief attribution right (that is, find out what it takes to track their entailments) and this will put constraints on belief and, hence, on psychology.

From this perspective, it is possible to see how the Twin Earth argument depends on a rather recent conception of semantics. Twenty years ago, it would have been natural to respond to the argument along the following lines.

The old semantics   If the point is to track entailments, then the semanticist should not think of the reference of 'water' in English as H_2O, since 'This is water' doesn't entail, 'This is made up of hydrogen and oxygen.' Semantics, like any other science, must choose its theoretical specifications carefully. In this case, specifying the reference of 'water' as H_2O is the wrong choice for semantics, though it is the right choice for chemistry. Of course, 'water' does refer to H_2O (in English), but that is the wrong way to specify its reference if you are interested in tracking entailments, though it is the right way if you are interested in tracking chemical interactions. Thus, although Hilary and Twhilary are referring to different things when they use the word 'water,' this is not a difference that semantics will notice. And what goes for reference goes for truth conditions: good semantic theory will not use the term 'H_2O' in specifying the truth conditions for statements containing 'water.' From the fact, then, that two beliefs or statements are about different things, it doesn't follow that good semantics will distinguish them. One shouldn't assume that a proper scientific specification of what a belief or statement is about is a proper semantic specification. Semantics, in short, is an autonomous discipline.

The new semantics   Nowadays, most of us would object to the claim that Hilary's statement that water is better than Pepsi doesn't entail that H_2O is

---

[15] Perhaps there is a better way to characterize the proprietary goal of semantics, though I rather doubt it. What matters here, in any case, is just that semantics *has* a proprietary goal that is independent of psychology.

better than Pepsi. Of course, you cannot *formally derive* 'H$_2$O is better than Pepsi' from 'Water is better than Pepsi' without adding something like 'Water is H$_2$O,' but entailment is supposed to be a semantic notion, not a formal one. What we need to know, then, is whether 'H$_2$O is better than Pepsi' is true in every possible world in which 'Water is better than Pepsi' is true. Now, if 'Water is H$_2$O' is true in every possible world if it is true at all, as Kripke and Putnam have made plausible, then the entailment is unproblematic.

Here, of course, the sentences in quotation marks are assumed to be bits of English. If they are assumed to be bits of Twinglish, we get quite different results. In Twinglish, 'Water is *XYZ*' expresses something true in every possible world, so in Twinglish, 'Water is better than Pepsi' entails '*XYZ* is better than Pepsi.'

I have a lot of sympathy with this line of thought. But notice that if we understand entailment in this way, semantics is no longer an *autonomous* discipline: our knowledge of what entails what must wait on such things as chemistry. Since we have enough chemistry in hand to know that water is H$_2$O, we know that beliefs about water are beliefs about H$_2$O. Twhilary certainly has no beliefs about H$_2$O, so his beliefs will be semantically distinct from Hilary's—Twhilary believes that *XYZ* is better than Pepsi—even though he is Hilary's computational (or neurophysiological) twin. From this perspective, the PRSV seems preposterous. People don't need to know the chemistry of water to use and understand 'water.'[16] And yet I think there are many who accept some form of the PRSV, at least tacitly, while embracing the new semantics. The problem is that we have updated our conception of semantics without noticing that it requires us to abandon PRSV, a view that made sense only against the background of a conception of semantics as an autonomous discipline. If you accept the conception of semantics that underlies the Twin Earth argument, you must abandon the PRSV. Hence Putnam's claim that meanings (semantic values, not psychological contents) aren't in the head.

The individuation of belief   If we accept the new semantics and reject the PRSV, what motivation could we have to *individuate* beliefs semantically? If we are realists about belief, we will want to individuate beliefs in whatever

---

[16]   This is Fodor's point (in Fodor 1980).

way conduces best to good psychological theory. Adherents of the new semantics should scoff at the idea that indexing beliefs to propositions will track their psychological relations. They will scoff precisely because it is so obvious that tracking entailments requires factors irrelevant to psychology. 'Intentional realism' is therefore a potentially misleading name for contemporary realism about belief, for it suggests that we should take seriously the idea that psychology should individuate beliefs semantically. Of course, 'intentional individuation' doesn't *have* to mean semantic individuation, but it is an easy enough identification to make 'intentional realism' a dangerous name for realism about belief. For the doctrine we are now considering is the doctrine that propositional attitudes should not be individuated in psychology by propositions. From the fact that p and q are distinct propositions, we cannot conclude that the belief that p is distinct from the belief that q.[17]

How should we individuate concepts (psychologically construed) and beliefs? You shouldn't ask me: I'm a philosopher. You wouldn't ask a philosopher what water is. Don't ask a philosopher what belief is either.

5.5. Folk psychology

This chapter has been mainly a complaint against armchair psychology disguised as the philosophy of mind or as the philosophy of language. The recent interest in so-called folk psychology is, I think, largely due to the fact that it provides philosophers an excuse to do psychology without having to bother about sound empirical method. If by 'folk psychology' you mean the psychology of the folk—a theory on all fours with folk physics (and as likely to be true)—then I have no objection to *studying* it—that is, investigating it in the way psychologists study folk physics: empirically. There can be no serious talk of vindicating the psychology of the folk until we have some empirically justified account of what it *is*.

But, of course, this is not what philosophers typically mean by folk psychology. What they mean is some sort of psychological theory—the details are left unspecified because they are irrelevant—that makes central

---

[17] Everyone has known for a long time that it doesn't work the other way: from the fact that p and q are the same proposition, it doesn't follow that the belief that p is the same as the belief that q.

explanatory appeals to belief and desire. Folk psychology in this sense will be 'vindicated' if it turns out that empirical psychology has some serious use for belief and desire. Now this *looks* to be a question for empirical psychology itself, or for the philosopher of science who asks whether any serious extant empirical theory in psychology makes use of something close to belief and desire—GOALS and KNOWLEDGE, say. And that is exactly the sort of question it is.

Yet that is not how philosophers have been treating the question, for what philosophers have been doing is (i) conceptual analyses of belief; and (ii) the semantics of belief attribution. But it is hard to see how (i) and (ii) could bear on psychology at all. For, first, there is no evident reason why a serious empirical psychologist should care what the ordinary concept of belief is any more than a serious physicist should care what the ordinary concept of force is.[18] And, second, the good semanticist will want to describe the way scientists use their concepts, not dictate to science how a certain concept must be used. If Putnam is right in his claim that the reference of 'water' waits on chemistry, then the reference of 'belief' must wait on psychology. But it isn't just reference that waits on science. Physicists created a sense for 'force'; they didn't just discover the reference of an ordinary concept or term. We can expect psychologists to do the same. When philosophers appreciate this point, they will be forced concede that the semantics of ordinary belief attribution has essentially no relevance to psychology at all.

Still, philosophers will want to know what is involved in semantically characterizing mental states. This is fine, provided it isn't construed as a question about the 'ordinary concept of belief' or the semantics of belief attribution, but as a question in the philosophy of science analogous to this: what is involved in the noncontinuous and nondeterministic characterization of the states of subatomic particles? And philosophers will want to know whether belief-desire explanations can be turned into good science. This question, I say, is analogous to another: can alchemy be turned into good science? Chemists solved that question; let the psychologists solve the other one.

---

[18] A serious psychologist might, of course, be interested in how people conceive of belief. But (i) no serious psychologist would employ the method of reflective equilibrium in such an investigation (I hope); and (ii) no one in their right mind would suppose that the way to construct an important explanatory concept in science is to discover what the 'ordinary concept' is.

References

Burge, T., 'Individualism and the Mental', in P. A. French, T. E. Euhling, and H. K. Wettstein (eds.), *Studies in the Philosophy of Mind: Midwest Studies in Philosophy,* 10 (Minneapolis: University of Minnesota Press, 1979).

Davidson, D., 'Theories of Meaning and Learnable Languages', in Y. Bar-Hillel (ed.), *Proceedings of the 1964 International Congress for Logic, Methodology, and Philosophy of Science* (Amsterdam: North Holland, 1965).

—— 'Truth and Meaning', *Synthese*, 17 (1967), 304–23.

Dennett, D., 'Comment on Searle, "Minds, Brains and Programs" ', *Behavioral and Brain Sciences*, 3 (1980), 417–24.

Dretske, F., *Knowledge and the Flow of Information* (Cambridge, Mass.: MIT Press/ Bradford Books, 1981).

Fodor, J., 'Methodological Solipsism Considered as a Research Strategy in Cognitive Science', *Behavioral and Brain Sciences*, 3 (1980), 63–109.

Kaiser, M. K., Jonides, J., and Alexander, J.,'Intuitive Reasoning about Abstract and Familiar Physics Problems', *Memory and Cognition*, 14 (1986), 308–12.

McCloskey, M., 'Intuitive Physics', *Scientific American*, 24 (1983), 122–30.

Putnam, H., 'The Meaning of "Meaning" ', in H. Putnam, *Mind, Language and Reality: Philosophical Papers,* ii (Cambridge: Cambridge University Press, 1975), 215–71.

6

Inexplicit Information

6.1. Introduction

In a recent conversation with the designer of a chess playing program, I heard the following criticism of a rival program: 'It thinks it should get its queen out early.' This ascribes a propositional attitude to the program in a very useful and predictive way, for as the designer went on to say, one can usually count on chasing that queen around the board. But for all the many levels of explicit representation to be found in that program, nowhere is anything roughly synonymous with 'I should get my queen out early' explicitly tokened. The level of analysis to which the designer's remark belongs describes features of the program that are, in an entirely innocent way, emergent properties of the computational processes that have 'engineering reality.'   (Daniel Dennett)

Before discussing the issue raised by this passage, we need to do a little house-cleaning. We are not interested, or shouldn't be, in what representations exist in (are tokened in) the program. Our interest is rather in what representations exist in the system as the result of executing the program, that is, with representations constructed by the system or that exist in one of its data bases at run time. Thus, although the program Dennett is discussing might contain nothing explicitly about queen deployment, the system might well construct such a representation at run time. For example, the system—call it CHESS—might begin by executing a rule that says, in effect,

(1) Whenever circumstance C obtains, construct the goal DEPLOY THE CURRENTLY HIGHEST RATED PIECE.

Given the way CHESS typically opens, C regularly obtains early in the game, when the Queen is the highest rated piece. Hence, it typically

Originally published in M. Brand and R. M. Hamish (eds.), *The Representation of Knowledge and Belief* (University of Arizona Press, 1986), 116–26. This paper appears with kind permission of the University of Arizona Press.

happens early in the game that the system constructs the goal DEPLOY THE QUEEN.

It is all too easy to write programs that do unintended things like this, so it is all too likely that the case Dennett is actually discussing is like this. But if it is, it is boring. To keep things interesting, I will assume that the system never constructs or uses a representation having the content DEPLOY THE QUEEN. Surely that is the case Dennett intended.

Given that the system never constructs the goal to deploy the queen, what are we to make of the characterization 'It thinks it should get its queen out early'? What kind of characterization is that? Dennett's point might be simply that the device behaves *as if* it were executing a program with the explicit goal of early queen deployment. A more interesting interpretation, however, is that information to the effect that the queen should be deployed early is in the system in some sense relevant to the explanation of its performance, but is not explicitly represented. It is this interpretation I want to pursue, so I'll assume it's what Dennett meant.[1]

What's interesting about this interpretation, of course, is that it assumes the propriety of a kind of intentional characterization—a characterization in terms of propositional content—in the absence of any token in the system having the content in question. I agree with Dennett that it is common and useful to intentionally characterize a system even though the system nowhere explicitly represents the propositional content figuring in the characterization. I have doubts, however, about Dennett's 'intentional systems theory' that would have us indulge in such characterization without worrying about *how* the intentional characterizations in question relate to characterizations based on explicit representation. How does 'The queen should be deployed early' relate to what is explicitly represented by the system? What determines the content of an intentional characterization at this level of analysis?

In what follows, I will try to distinguish and clarify various distinct types of what I will call *inexplicit information*, that is, information that exists in a system without benefit of any symbolic structure having the content in question. 'Untokened' might be a better term than 'inexplicit' for what I have in mind, but it just doesn't sound right. I also have qualms about 'information.' As Dretske (1981) uses the term, a system cannot have the

---

[1] Perhaps Dennett doesn't distinguish these two interpretations, being an instrumentalist about goals. But he should, as the sequel will show, I think.

information that p unless p is the case. I see much merit in this usage, but in the present case it won't do. As I use the term below, information may be false information.

6.2. Types of inexplicit information

6.2.1. Control-implicit information

There are many cases in which the natural thing to say is that some piece of information is implicit in the 'logic' or 'structure' of the flow of control. Imagine a circuit fault diagnosis system so organized that it checks capacitors, if any, only after verifying the power supply, and suppose that it is now executing an instruction like this:

(2) CHECK THE CAPACITORS.

Given the way the program is structured, the system now has the information that the power supply is OK. It has this information because it cannot execute instruction (2) unless it has verified the power supply. There may be no explicit representation of this fact anywhere in memory—no token having the content, 'The power supply is OK'—but the fact that control has passed to rule (2) means that the system is in a state that, as Dretske would say, carries the information that the power supply is OK. Programmers, of course, constantly rely on this sort of fact. The system doesn't need to explicitly represent the power supply as being OK because this fact is implicit in the current state of control. This type of implicit information is ubiquitous in almost every computer program.

It isn't difficult to imagine how early queen deployment could be at least partly control implicit in CHESS. The easiest way to see this is to consider how one might exploit control structure to prevent early deployment of the queen. To imagine a trivial illustration—this would be a very bad way to build a chess system—suppose use of the pieces is considered in order, lowest rated pieces being considered first. Only if no acceptable move is found involving a lower rated piece does the system consider moving a higher rated piece. In this way, it might seem, we will avoid queen deployment except when it's really needed. But now suppose that the move evaluation routine was designed with the middle and end game primarily in mind, parts of the game where one might want to rate 'aggressiveness' fairly heavily.

As a consequence, very few moves in the early part of the game score high, since it is more difficult to make aggressive moves early on. A side effect will be that control will be passed to consideration of queen moves in circumstances that we assumed would occur only in the middle game but which in fact regularly occur earlier. Passing control to a consideration of queen moves amounts to assuming that other moves are insufficiently aggressive, and this assumption will be made much too early in the game.

This sort of possibility comes close to fitting Dennett's original description. Although, in the case imagined, we don't have 'Deploy the queen early,' we do have the system deciding that only a queen move will do, and doing this early in the game, and doing it without explicitly representing anything like early queen deployment as a goal.

6.2.2. Domain-implicit information

With a few degenerate exceptions, the information we think of a system as having is always to some extent lodged in the environment. Suppose I write a program, execution of which will get you from your house to mine. Now, in some sense, the program represents me as living in a certain place, perhaps correctly, perhaps not. Where does it say I live? Well, nothing like the proposition

(3) Cummins lives at location L

need be explicitly represented; the program may *fix* the location in question in that execution of it will get you to my house from yours. But nowhere need there be anything remotely like (3), either in the program itself or constructed at run time.

It is easy to get confused about this and suppose that the location in question must be *inferable* somehow from the location of your house, together with information given in the program. But this is seriously mistaken. I could give you a perfectly precise program for getting to my house from yours, and another for getting from your house to Paul's, and you could not, without executing them, determine so much as whether Paul and I live in the same place. I could do this by, for example, relying exclusively on LEFT, RIGHT, counting intersections, and counting houses. In such a case, the location of my house just isn't going to be a consequence, in any sense, of premises supplied explicitly. The only way you could use the program to figure out where my house is would be to execute it, either in real space or using a sufficiently detailed map. The information in question is as much in the map or geography as it is in the program; the program is completely domain dependent for its success. Nevertheless, given the terrain, the program does carry the information that my house is at a certain place: if you follow it and wind up at the bus depot, you have every right to complain that I gave you the wrong information.

The phenomenon Dennett describes could be like this. Imagine a set of tactics designed to achieve early control of the center. Suppose they aren't very good; most good opponents can frustrate them, and really good opponents can exploit the situation to draw out the queen, queen deployment being, in the situation that develops, the only way CHESS can protect its knights. Here, the analogue of the geography is the opponent's play. It shifts from game to game, but given the way CHESS plays, good opponents are going to respond in similar ways. The resulting interactions typically result in CHESS deploying its queen early. The analogy becomes closer if we imagine that I used *parked cars* as landmarks in my directions. Given that you seldom leave for my house before seven and that most people are home from work by six-thirty and typically park in front of their houses, the result will be that you typically get to my house. But sometimes you will get to the bus depot, or the deli, or somewhere else.

If the phenomenon Dennett describes *is* like this, then it is misleadingly described. If early queen deployment is domain implicit in CHESS, then neither the programmer nor the device executing the program thinks in general, or momentarily, that the queen should be deployed early. Early queen deployment is rather an unintended, unexpected, and perhaps even unnoticed artifact of a variety of factors in the system that have nothing to do with the queen interacting with factors in the 'environment' that do. Intuitively, the goal is 'in the environment'—that is, in the opponent's play. Indeed, it's the opponent's goal! Nevertheless, the flaw—early queen deployment—is a flaw in the program; it's in the program in just the way that information about the location of my house is in the program consisting of 'Two lefts, a right, opposite the blue Chevy station wagon.'

6.2.3. *Rules, instructions, and procedural knowledge*

Once upon a time, there was something called the procedural–declarative controversy in Artificial Intelligence. This controversy had to do with whether it is better to represent knowledge as a procedure—that is, as a program applying it—or as a set of declarative propositions. What everyone decided was that it all depends on what's convenient for the programming purposes at hand. In short, the controversy died for want of an issue. In a well-known article ('Artificial Intelligence Meets Natural Stupidity'), Drew McDermott (1976) enjoined us never to talk about it again. Nevertheless, I intend to follow a long philosophical tradition of ignoring the injunctions of such courts and prod these dead issues a little bit anyway.

Let's begin with an example. Suppose we set out to build a system called FIXIT that diagnoses faults in appliances. Expert system programs—programs designed to duplicate the performance of an expert in some domain such as appliance failure diagnosis—are written as sets of *productions*. A production is a rule of the form IF C THEN A, where C is some condition and A is some action. Whenever something in working memory matches C, A is performed. In the simplest case, the rules are unordered; the flow of control is determined solely by which conditions happen to be matched, together with some simple conflict resolution routines that determine what happens when more than one condition is matched.

The rules of an expert system are supposed to formulate the knowledge of humans who are expert at the task the system is to perform. FIXIT, for example, would probably have a rule like this:

(R) IF APPLIANCE DOESN'T START THEN FIND OUT IF IT IS PLUGGED IN.[2]

Most of *us*, on the other hand, probably begin with the goal to start the appliance, together with a belief like this:

(B) If the appliance isn't plugged in, then it won't start.

If the appliance doesn't start, we use (B) and some inference procedures to construct a subgoal: find out if the appliance is plugged in. Experts, unlike the rest of us, seem to have 'proceduralized' this business: they just execute (R). The difference is that novices must remember that an appliance won't start if it is unplugged and then reason from this to the conclusion that the plug should be checked. Experts don't have to figure out what to do: they simply check the plug when the thing won't start.

---

[2] Something must be done, of course, to prevent the left-hand side of this rule matching forever. The completed rule might read: IF A DOESN'T START AND NOT (PLUG CHECKED) THEN CHECK PLUG AND WRITE (PLUG CHECKED).

There are two ways in which a system can 'have' a rule like (R): (R) might be a rule that is represented in the system's memory, or (R) might be an *instruction*, that is, a rule in the program that the system executes. These are quite different matters. Let's take them in order.[3]

First, then, suppose that FIXIT has rule (R) represented in memory. (R), then, is one of the rules it 'knows.' But having access to (R) is evidently quite a different matter from having access to (B). A system that has access to (R) knows what to do if the appliance won't start. A system with access to (B) must *infer* what to do and hence must have some capacity for means–ends analysis. This is why a system operating on the basis of (R) can be expected to make different sorts of errors than a system operating on the basis of (B), and why a system operating on the basis of (B) can be expected to be slower than one operating on the basis of (R). It is precisely because a system with access to (R) doesn't need to infer what to do that it is a mistake to suppose its access to (R) amounts to knowing the same thing it would know if it had access to (B) instead. A system with access to (R) knows what to do, and a system with access to (B) instead does not: it must figure out what to do.[4]

So much, then, for the case in which (R) is represented in memory—a genuine rule. What about the case in which (R) is a rule in the program that the system executes—that is, an instruction? Let's move back to the original example derived from Dennett. Suppose the *program* executed by the *device* CHESS contains the following rule:

IF IT IS EARLY IN THE GAME THEN DEPLOY THE QUEEN.

Does CHESS—the *device* executing the program—believe that it should deploy its queen early? The programmer certainly believed it. And CHESS will behave as if it believed it too: hence the characterization Dennett reports. But CHESS (as we are now imagining it) simply executes the rule without representing it at all, except in the degenerate sense in which

---

[3] The literature on expert systems treats this distinction with a benign neglect. It only matters if we want the system to be able to alter its own productions, in which case they must be rules, not instructions.

[4] The received view is that we have the *same knowledge* represented in each case, but represented in different forms—a declarative form and a procedural form—and this difference is held to account for the characteristic differences in performance. But is this right? Is the difference only a difference in how the same thing is represented? It seems clear the difference is a difference in *what is known* rather than simply a difference in how what is known is represented. To make the point once again: the system with (R) knows what to do, whereas the other must figure it out. It is an important Kantian insight that representing something in a different form always changes what is represented.

rubber bands represent the rule IF PULLED THEN STRETCH, and masses represent the rule COALESCE WITH OTHER MASSES. Like the rubber band, CHESS simply executes its rule, and executing that rule amounts to having a behavioral disposition to deploy the queen early.[5] By contrast, it *does* represent the state of the game—for example, the positions of the pieces and the fact that it is early in the game—and it does that by executing a set of instructions that say, in effect, REPRESENT THE CURRENT STATE OF THE GAME. Moreover, the system not only represents facts about the game, but its representations of these facts play something like the role that functionally distinguishes belief from other intentional states, viz., availability as premises in reasoning and susceptibility to evidential evaluation (if CHESS is a learner). But CHESS (as we are now imagining it) does not represent the rule requiring early queen deployment, nor is anything with a comparable content available for reasoning or epistemic assessment. Consequently, I think we should resist the claim that CHESS thinks or believes or knows that it should deploy the queen early. The rules CHESS executes—what I've been calling its instructions— are quite different and have a very different explanatory role from the rules CHESS knows.[6]

A frequent reply to this point is that our system has *procedural knowledge* to the effect that the queen should be deployed early in virtue of executing a program containing the rule. Ordinary usage condones this line to some extent by allowing us to describe the capacities of cognitive systems as knowing how to do something even though there is no explicit tokening of the rules executed. Notice, however, that we aren't allowed this license when speaking of noncognitive systems: rubber bands don't know how to stretch when pulled. I think talk of procedural knowledge has its place—it's the case we discussed a moment ago in which we have (R) explicitly tokened in memory—but a system's procedural knowledge is not knowledge of the rules it executes. The rules a system executes—the ones making up its program—are not available for reasoning or evidential assessment for the simple reason that they are not represented to the system at all.[7]

---

[5] We might mark the distinction by saying that instructions are 'embodied' in the device that executes them. Cf. the notion of E-representation in Cummins (1977, 1983).

[6] For more on the explanatory role of appeals to instructions executed see Cummins (1977, 1983).

[7] When inference-dependent propositions like (B) are replaced by rules like (R) *in memory*, we have a kind of proceduralization that does yield knowledge but not the *same* knowledge.

Of course, if CHESS is implemented on a general purpose computer, rather than hardwired, the program itself will also be represented 'in' the system: it may be on a disk, for example. But these are not representations to CHESS; they are representations to the system that implements CHESS, typically an interpreter and operating system. The interpreter 'reads' these rules, not CHESS. The program file is not a data base for CHESS; it is a data base for the interpreter. CHESS doesn't represent its program; it executes it, and this is made possible by the fact that a quite different system *does* represent CHESS's program. If we hardwire CHESS, the program is no longer represented at all; it is merely 'embodied.' There is all the difference in the world between writing a program that has *access* to a rule codified in one of its data structures and a program that *contains* that rule as an instruction.[8]

The presence of our rule in CHESS's program, therefore, indicates something about the programmer's knowledge but nothing one way or the other about CHESS's representational states. Contrast a case that *does* tell us something about CHESS's representational states:

IF OPPONENT HAS MOVED THEN UPDATE THE CURRENT POSITION.

When this instruction is executed, CHESS will create a representation of the current position and store it for future access.

Once we are clear about the distinction between representing a rule and executing it, we are forced to realize that production systems demonstrate that a system can have a cognitive skill or ability—for example, the ability to diagnose appliance failure or to play chess—without knowing the sorts of things appliance fixers or chess players typically know. When knowledge is 'proceduralized,' it ceases to be knowledge, if by 'proceduralization' we mean that the rules in question become instructions in the program the system executes. Nevertheless, and here is the main point at last, even though the system doesn't represent such rules, the fact that it executes them amounts to the presence in the system of some propositionally formulable information, information that is not explicitly represented but is inexplicit in the system in virtue of the physical structure upon which program execution supervenes.

---

[8] From an AI perspective, this is trivial, of course: simply putting a rule in memory is not going to get it executed; we must somehow pass control to it.

If we turn back to Dennett's parable now, we find something of a muddle. Evidently, the case in which we have a rule explicitly tokened in memory is not the one at issue. In the case lately imagined, however, although we do have an instruction *in the program*, nothing like DEPLOY THE QUEEN EARLY is tokened *by the system*. This is the case we are interested in, but here it seems plainly incorrect to say that the system thinks or believes that it should deploy the queen early, though this does apply to the programmer. Instead, the correct description seems to be that in the system there is a kind of inexplicit information, information lodged, as it were, in whatever physical facts underwrite the capacity to execute the program. Explanatory appeals to this sort of information evidently differ radically from explanatory appeals to the system's representations—for example, representations of current position. Moreover, it is plain that it is the appeal to rules *executed*—that is, to instructions—that is the basic explanatory appeal of cognitive science. It is only in virtue of the instructions a system executes that the knowledge it has can issue in behavior. Indeed, it is only because of the instructions executed that it has any representational states at all.

6.3. Conclusion

We have now seen several ways in which it makes a kind of sense to describe a chess system in terms of informational contents that are not explicitly represented. Moreover, each type of inexplicit representation appears to have a bona fide—indeed essential—explanatory role, and, though the details want spelling out, each seems to supervene in conceptually straightforward ways on ontologically kosher features of program-executing systems. In general, once we realize that a system can have all kinds of information that isn't in its memory, information that *it* does not represent at all, we see that intentional characterization—characterization in terms of informational content—is not all of a piece and that the different pieces have radically different explanatory roles. Explanation by appeal to any of the three kinds of inexplicit information I have been discussing is always explanation by appeal to rules executed and hence is quite different from explanation by appeal to knowledge structures. Everyone realizes that what you can do is a function of what information you have, but not everyone in cognitive science seems to realize the importance of information that is not explicitly represented or stored in memory.

I've been making much of the distinction between representing a rule and executing it. Executing a rule, I've been urging, isn't knowing or believing it. And conversely, there is ample evidence that knowing a rule isn't sufficient for being able to execute it. Explicit information—knowledge and belief properly so-called—is a matter of which representations are created or exist in the system at run time and of how these are used by the system. If a representation of the world exists in the system, is available as a premise in reasoning, and is subject to evidential assessment, we have at least the salient *necessary* conditions for intentional characterization as knowledge or belief. *Inexplicit* information, on the other hand, is a matter of which rules or instructions the system executes—a matter of its program—and the environment the system operates in. A system can have much information that is *not represented by the system at all* and that doesn't function anything like knowledge or belief, even tacit knowledge or belief. When we formulate the content of this information and attribute it to the system, we intentionally characterize that system, and rightly so, even though the propositional contents of our characterizations are not represented by the system we characterize. But we are not characterizing what it knows or believes.

Current cognitive science, with its emphasis—nay, fixation—on 'knowledge representation,' has neglected (officially, if not in practice) the ubiquitous and critical information that isn't represented[9] (not represented by the cognitive system anyway). It *is* represented by the programmer, of course, and one of the important insights of the cognitive science movement is that a program is a theory. When we write a program, we are theorizing about our human subjects, representing to each other the rules we suppose they execute. When we do this, what we are doing to a great extent is specifying the inexplicit information that drives human as well as computer cognitive processes. Everyone recognizes the importance of what is represented. I've been urging the importance of what isn't.

---

[9] 'Knowledge representation' seems a misnomer: what we are interested in is how a cognitive system represents (or should represent) the world, not how to represent knowledge. 'How does S represent the world?'='How is S's knowledge *encoded*?' Cognitive science might be interested in knowledge representation in the following sense: how should we, as theorists, represent in our theoretical notation the knowledge a cognitive system has of, say, chess. This is a legitimate issue but not the one generally meant by 'knowledge representation.'

References

Cummins, R., 'Programs in the Explanation of Behavior', *Philosophy of Science*, 44 (1977), 269–87.

—— *The Nature of Psychological Explanation*. (Cambridge, Mass.: MIT Press/ Bradford Books, 1983).

Dennett, D., *Brainstorms* (Cambridge, Mass.: MIT Press/Bradford Books, 1978).

Dretske, F., *Knowledge and the Flow of Information* (Cambridge, Mass.: MIT Press/ Bradford Books, 1981).

McDermott, D. (1976), 'Artificial Intelligence Meets Natural Stupidity', in J. HAUGELAND (ed.), *Mind Design* (Cambridge, Mass.: MIT Press/Bradford Books, 1981).

7

Representation and Indication

ROBERT CUMMINS AND PIERRE POIRIER

7.1. Two kinds of mental content

This chapter is about two kinds of mental content and how they are related. We are going to call them representation and indication. We will begin with a rough characterization of each. The differences, and why they matter, will, hopefully, become clearer as the chapter proceeds.

7.1.1. Representation

Some authors (e.g. Schiffer 1987) use 'mental representation' to mean any mental state or process that has a semantic content. On this usage, a belief that the Normans invaded England in 1066 counts as a mental representation, as does the desire to be rich. This is not how we use the term. As we use the term, a mental representation is an element in a scheme of semantically individuated types whose tokens are manipulated—structurally transformed—by (perhaps computational) mental processes. The scheme might be language-like, as the language of thought hypothesis asserts (Fodor 1975), or it might consist of (activation) vectors in a multidimensional vector space as connectionists suppose (e.g. Churchland 1995). Or it might be something quite different: a system of holograms or images, for example.

On one popular theory of the propositional attitudes, having the belief that the Normans invaded England in 1066 involves tokening a mental representation with the content that the Normans invaded England in 1066—writing in the Belief Box a representation that means that the

Originally published in Philip Staines and Peter Slezak (eds.), *Representation in Mind* (Elsevier, 2004), 21–40. This paper appears with kind permission of Elsevier.

Normans invaded England in 1066.[1] That theory takes the content of the belief to be the same as the content of the implicated representation, but distinguishes representations from attitudes, taking representations, as we do, to be expressions in a scheme of representational types. We think this theory of the attitudes is seriously flawed (see Cummins 1996a), but one thing it surely gets right is that representations should be distinguished from attitudes.[2]

7.1.2. Indication

It is useful to begin with some influential examples.

- *Thermostats*: the shape of the bimetallic element (or the length of a column of mercury) is said to indicate the ambient temperature.
- *Edge detectors*: cells in the primary visual cortex (V1) strongly respond to edges in the visual field, that is, linear boundaries between light and dark regions.[3]
- *Idiot lights*: most cars have indicator lights that come on when, for example, the fuel level is low, or the oil pressure is low, or the engine coolant is too hot.

'Indication' is just a semantic-sounding word for detection. We are going to need a way to mark the distinction between the mechanism that does the detection and the state or process that is the signal that the target has been detected. We will say that the cells studied by Hubel and Wiesel (1962) are indicators, and that the patterns of electrical spikes they emit when they fire are indicator signals. Rather less obviously, a mercury thermometer is an indicator, and the length of the mercury column is the indicator signal.

---

[1] This way of putting things—that believing that it will rain and desiring that it will rain differ only in that a mental representation meaning that it is raining is in the Belief Box in the first case and in the Desire Box in the second—is due to Schiffer (1987).

[2] Conceptual role theories of mental content have difficulty distinguishing mental representations from the attitudes because they take the mental content of x to be a function of x's epistemic liaisons. Propositional attitudes have epistemic liaisons, but representations, as we use the term, do not. See Cummins (1996a: ch. 3) for a detailed discussion of this point.

[3] The cells were discovered by David Hubel and Torsten Wiesel (1962). They describe the behaviors of these cells this way: 'The most effective stimulus configurations, dictated by the spatial arrangements of excitatory and inhibitory regions, were long narrow rectangles of light (slits), straight-line borders between areas of different brightness (edges), and dark rectangular bars against a light background.'

Similarly, the bimetallic element found in most thermostats is an indicator, and its shape is the signal.[4]

7.2. Indication and representation contrasted

It is commonplace to think of indication as a species of representation. Indeed, one very popular theory of representational content has it that, at bottom, representation just is, or is inherited from, indicator content.[5] We think there are some good reasons to keep the two distinct.

7.2.1. *Indication is transitive, representation is not*

If S3 indicates S2, and S2 indicates S1, then S3 indicates S1. Aim a photosensitive cell at the oil pressure indicator light in your car. Attach this to a relay that activates an audio device that plays a recording of the sentence, 'Your oil pressure is low.' If the light going on indicates low oil pressure, so does the recording. Indeed, there is already a chain of this sort connecting the pressure sensor and the light. Representation, on the other hand, is not transitive. A representation of the pixel structure of a digitized picture of my aunt Tilly is not a representation of my aunt Tilly's visual appearance, though, of course, it is possible to recover the later from the former. To anticipate some terminology we will use later, a representation of the pixel structure is an *encoding* of my aunt Tilly's visual appearance.[6]

7.2.2. *Indicator signals are arbitrary in a way that representations are not*

This actually follows from the transitivity of indication. Given transitivity, anything can be made to indicate anything else (if it can be detected at all),

---

[4] Thermostats using bimetallic strips are usually designed so that when the bimetallic changes shape 'enough,' it closes a circuit that turns on the furnace, or air conditioner, or whatever. The electrical pulse that closes the furnace relay is also an indicator signal, but it doesn't indicate the temperature, except relative to a fixed thermostat setting.

[5] The theory is generally credited to Dennis Stampe (1977). Its most prominent advocates are Dretske (1981, 1988) and Fodor (1987, 1990a).

[6] It is also what Haugeland would call a recording of the picture. See Haugeland (1991). If r represents a representation r′ of t, r need not be a representation of t even though, as was argued in Cummins (1996a), representation is grounded in isomorphism, which *is* transitive. This is because the structure that r shares with r′ need not, in general, be the same as the structure r′ shares with t, as the pixel example illustrates.

given enough ingenuity and resources. (This is what makes it tempting to think of words as indicators: they mean something, but they are arbitrary.) It follows from the arbitrariness of indicator signals that disciplined structural transformations of them are not going to systematically alter their meanings. Susceptibility to such transformations, however, is precisely how representations earn their keep. Consider, for example, a software package that takes a digitized image of a face as input and 'ages' it, that is, returns an image of that face as it is likely to look after some specified lapse of time. Nothing like this could possibly work on an input that was required only to indicate a certain face, because there is no correlation between the physical characteristics something must have to be a signal that indicates the appearance of my face at age 18 and the physical characteristics of my face at age 18. You could design a device that *seemed* to do this, of course. Given a name and a target age, it would retrieve from memory its most recent picture of the person named (if it has one), and age it by the number of years equal to the target date minus the date the picture was taken. But surely(?), respectable cognitive scientists would not be fooled by such a device. They will know that you need a representation, not just an indicator signal, to get the job done, and they will infer the internal representation.[7] Similarly, while it could conceivably be useful to detect the utterance of a particular sentence ('Look out!'), there is no possibility of using a mere indicator signal to effect an active-to-passive transformation. A representation of the sentence's phrase structure, on the other hand, actually has, by hypothesis, the relevant structure, and hence formal transformations—transformations that systematically alter structure— of a representation of that phrase structure can easily be constructed to give a representation of the structure of the corresponding passive.

It is, therefore, a consequence of the nature of indication that the structural properties of an indicator signal (if it has any) have no significance.[8] Indicators 'say' that their targets are there, but do not 'say' anything about what they are like. Representations, on the other hand, mirror the structure of their targets (when they are accurate), and thus their consumers can cognitively process the structure of the target by manipulating the

---

[7] Actually, a structural encoding (Cummins *et al.* 2001, Ch. 4, this volume) of the information a representation would carry would do the trick as well. This does not affect the present point, which is that indicator signals would *not* do the trick.

[8] The structural properties of an indicator signal might be used to type-identify it. More of this shortly.

structure of its representation. But representations, unlike indicator signals, are typically silent concerning whether their targets are 'present': they are not, except incidentally and coincidently, detector signals.

7.2.3. *Indicators are source-dependent in a way that representations are not*

The cells studied by Hubel and Wiesel all generate the same signal when they detect a target. You cannot tell, by looking at the signal itself (the spike train), what has been detected. You have to know which cells generated the signal. This follows from the arbitrariness of indicator signals, and is therefore a general feature of indication: the meaning is all in who shouts, not in what is shouted.[9]

In sum, then, indication is transitive, representation is not. It follows from the transitivity of indication that indicator signals are arbitrary and source-dependent in a way in which representations are not, and this disqualifies indicator signals as vehicles for structure-dependent cognitive processing. Representation is intransitive, non-arbitrary, and portable (not source-dependent), and therefore suitable for structural processing. Indicator signals 'say' their targets are present, but 'say' nothing about them; representations provide structural information about their targets, but do not indicate their presence. Indicator signals say, 'My target is here,' while representations say, 'My target, wherever it is, is structured like so.'

7.3. Portable indicators and the language of thought

In principle, indicator signals can be distinguished into types so as to reduce source dependency. Rather than label the low fuel and low oil pressure lights, one could make the lights different sizes or shapes or colors. This amounts to building an arbitrary source label into the form of the signal. The result is a portable signal. It is not obvious, however, what advantage there might be to such a system beyond the fact that you could tell in the dark whether it is oil pressure or fuel that is low. To appreciate the value of portability, we have to imagine a more complex system.

Consider, then, the system called LOCKE (see e.g. Cummins 1989: 37 ff.) (Figure 7.1).

---

[9] We do not mean to imply here that the shape of a spike train is never significant. The point is rather that two indicators can have the same spike train, yet indicate different things.

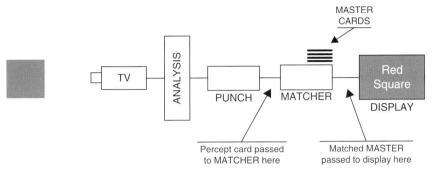

Figure 7.1 The LOCKE machine (from Cummins 1989)

A TV camera is attached to a card punch device. The pattern of holes punched in a 'percept' card depends on the structure of the optical stimulus. The matcher is equipped with a set of 'concept' cards. A match is achieved when every hole in a concept card matches a hole in a percept card (barring chads, of course). When a match is achieved, the word printed on the back of the concept card is displayed.

It would be no mean feat to build such a device. A frog detector, for example, would have to accommodate the fact that frogs come in various postures, colors, and sizes, against various backgrounds, with various neighbors, etc. Even color and shape detection will have to accommodate variations in distance, in lighting, and in angle of view. For LOCKE to work well, a huge variety of visual scenes whose only common feature is the presence of a frog or red or square will have to produce cards that have the same characteristic subpattern. The 'analysis' box thus amounts to a sophisticated vision system capable of detecting very 'high level' distal properties.

As this example illustrates, the physical characteristics of the signal—punch patterns—can be arbitrarily different from the physical characteristics of the detector itself, and from the physical characteristics of the target. Heat detectors do not have to get hot, nor must motion detectors move. Unlike the sorts of indicators studied by Hubel and Wiesel, however, LOCKE's indicator signals are type identified by their structural properties (their 'form'), and are therefore potentially source independent. This makes it possible to compare concept cards to each other to yield such judgments as that sisters are female, or even that frogs are green, even though none of the corresponding perceptual targets are in the offing. LOCKE, in short, has a crude language of thought, the primitive symbols of which are punch patterns—perhaps single holes—whose contents are fixed by their roles in detection. A punch pattern means *square*, wherever or whenever it is tokened, if it is the pattern LOCKE's detection system produces in response to squares.[10] One might then suppose that primitive patterns could be combined in ways that yield complex patterns whose meanings are functions of the meanings of their constituents and their mode of combination. The resulting complex representations will have the semantically primitive indicator signal patterns as constituents, but these will not, of course, function as indicator signals in this new role. Rather, they simply inherit their denotations from their other life as signals indicating the presence of the properties (or whatever) they are now taken to denote.

As things stand, LOCKE cannot represent bindings: it cannot represent the difference between a red square plus a blue triangle on the one hand, and a blue square plus a red triangle on the other. To overcome this limitation, and others like it—to exploit the possibilities of combinatorics—LOCKE will need some syncategorematic representational machinery. The forms that distinguish bindings and the like evidently cannot themselves have their meanings (semantic functions) fixed by their roles in indication. Rather, a complex representation will count as a conjunction or predication or whatever in virtue of how it is processed (Fodor 1987). The machinery of binding is just whatever form a representation has that causes it to be processed as a binding.

Portable indicator signals, then, provide one way of grounding the capacity to represent in the capacity to indicate (detect). The result is a Language of Thought (LOT) as it is defended by Fodor (1975). There is a characteristic approach to cognition entrained by LOT style representation. It is entrained by the fact that there are basically just three ways that arbitrary mental symbols of the Language of Thought variety can enter into cognitive explanations: as *triggers* for procedures, as *cues* for stored knowledge, and as *constituents* of complex representations. This simply follows from the fact that the structure of a LOT symbol serves only to type identify it. It carries no information about its target, not even the information that its target is present, since, freed from its source, it no longer functions as an indicator signal.

---

[10] Qualifications are required to turn this into an even mildly plausible definition of content. See Cummins (1989) for details.

Suppose you are to milk the cow. First you must find the cow. You wander around scanning until your visual system tokens a |cow|—an arbitrary mental symbol that refers to cows. But to visually recognize cows, you need to know how a cow looks. A |cow| contains no information about how cows look, and so it isn't what psychologists, at any rate, would call a visual concept. But knowledge of cows is what you need, for it is knowledge of cows, including tacit knowledge about the sort of retinal projections they tend to produce, that makes it possible for your visual system to token a |cow| when you see one. So the Mentalese |cow| does no work for the object recognition system, it just signals its output, functioning as an indicator signal.

Tokening a |cow|, we may suppose, *triggers* the next step in the plan. Needing to locate the udder, a mental word is totally useless unless it happens to function as a retrieval *cue* for some stored knowledge about cows. Faced with actually having to deal with a cow, the burden therefore shifts again from the symbol to your stored knowledge, because the symbol, being arbitrary, tells you nothing about cows. So it turns out that it isn't because you have a Mentalese term for cows that you find the cow and get the milking done, it is because you have some stored knowledge about cows—some in your visual analysis system, some higher up the cognitive ladder. Mentalese |cow|s could play a role in stored knowledge about cows only as constituents of complex representations—|cows have udders between their back legs|, for example—that are, on the Mentalese story, implicated in the possession of stored knowledge about cows.

LOT stories therefore lead inevitably to the idea that it is really stored knowledge, in the form of systems of LOT 'sentences,' that does the explanatory work. It is worth emphasizing that there is a big difference between appealing to the fact that one has a primitive mental symbol referring to cows, and appealing to the fact that one has a lot of knowledge about cows. LOT commits one to the view that representations of cows don't tell you anything about cows. On the contrary: having a mental symbol that refers to cows *presupposes* considerable knowledge about cows.

Perhaps it isn't so bad that LOT entails that the representations that are satisfied by cows have only an indirect role in the explanation of cow cognition, for there are always mental sentences to tell us about cows. But let's just be clear about what LOT is committed to here: the view we have arrived at is that cognition is essentially the application of a linguistically expressed theory. All the serious work gets done by sets of sentences that are internal tacit theories about whatever objects of cognition there happen to be. As far as cognizing cows goes, your |cow|s really don't matter; it is your tacit theory (or theories) of cows that does the work.

Enough has been said to suggest how the language of thought hypothesis provides for assembling representational structures from symbols whose semantic content is grounded in their functions as (portable) indicator signals. The strategy, however, has its limitations. Two are important for the present discussion. First, portable indicator signals that are assembled into complex representations, while a reality in digital computers, are surely not on the cards in the brain. As we have seen, complex LOT representations cannot have actual source-dependent indicator signals as constituents, for this would imply that every representation indicated the presence of the targets of each of its constituents. Such 'representations,' indeed, would not be representations at all, but simply bundles of simultaneous feature detections. The transition from indication to representation in LOT systems is mediated by source-independent signal types that, severed from their source, denote the properties whose presence they detect when functioning as indicator signals.[11] But such source-*independent* (portable) indicator signals are neurally implausible, to say the least. What formal characteristics could distinguish the signal types? There is no evidence to support the idea that a distinctive spike train produced by a neural indicator retains its semantic significance when produced elsewhere in the brain. It is more plausible to suppose that a distinctive pattern of activation in a pool of associated neurons might retain its significance if copied, or simply repeated, elsewhere. But there is no evidence whatever for the suggestion that such patterns are not only the distinctive outputs of detection circuits, but are also assembled into complex representations. The fear, voiced early and often by connectionist critics of LOT systems, that LOT systems have no plausible neural implementation, seems well-founded.

The second limitation of LOT systems has to do with their restricted representational power. Representations in the language of thought have whatever structure is implicated by their combinatorial syntax. In language

---

[11]   Or rather: they are, when things are working properly, processed as if they denoted the properties they detect when functioning accurately as indicator signals.

like schemes, the structure in question is logical form. While propositions arguably have structures isomorphic to logical forms, it is surely the case that many, perhaps most, representational targets of significance to cognitive systems have structures of entirely different sorts. Natural images of the sort studied by Olshausen and Field (1996), for example, certainly do not have logical forms, nor do problem spaces of the sort studied by planning theory in artificial intelligence (Newell and Simon 1972; see Cummins 1996a, for more on this theme). Representational systems whose non-syncategorematic elements get their meanings by inheriting denotations from their roles in indication are, inevitably, denotational schemes, schemes whose semantics is the familiar truth-conditional semantics. The only things such schemes can represent are propositions or complex propositional functions. Everything else is simply denoted. You can call denotation representation, provided you keep in mind the very real difference between something that merely labels its target, and something that actually provides information about it. Grounding representation in indication by promoting portable indicator signals into the semantic constituents of complex representations inevitably leads to a scheme that represents propositions and nothing else.

LOT schemes get around this limitation by encoding structure rather than representing it. To see the difference, compare LOT schemes for representing sentences in a natural or artificial language with Gödel numbering. A LOT scheme represents a target sentence S by tokening a sentence in the language of thought that has the same relevant structure—e.g. logical form—as S. In the Gödel numbering scheme, on the other hand, words are assigned natural numbers, and their positions in a sentence are encoded by prime numbers in ascending order. A word in position n assigned to m yields the number n^m. This number is uniquely factorable into n, m times. The Gödel number of a sentence is determined by multiplying all these uniquely factorable numbers together, yielding a uniquely factorable number from which the sentence can be recovered. For example, assume that 'John,' 'Mary,' and 'loves' are assigned 2, 3, and 4 respectively. Then 'John loves Mary' is encoded as $2^2 \bullet 4^3 \bullet 3^5 = 62208$. This number may be represented in any convenient number system. The result is a numeral that does not itself share structure with the sentence it encodes. Information about the constituent structure of the sentence is still there, though well disguised, and this is what makes it possible to devise arithmetical processes that manipulate the relevant structural information without actually recovering it and representing it explicitly. An active–passive transformation, for example, can be written simply as an arithmetic procedure.[12]

7.4. The assembly of complex visual representations

According to indicator-based theories of mental content generally, and to LOT theories in particular, mental representations either *are* indicator signals, or inherit their content from their roles, or the roles of their constituents, as indicator signals. We have seen however, that there are serious reasons for doubting that complex representations in the brain could be *semantically* composed of constituents whose meanings are inherited from their roles as indicator signals.

An entirely different relation between indication and representation emerges if we examine the way in which the sort of indicators discovered by Hubel and Wiesel are implicated in the assembly of visual images. One account of this is to be found in recent research by Field and Olshausen (Field 1987, 1994; Olshausen and Field 1996, 1997, 2000).

Natural images contain much statistical structure and many redundancies (Field 1987) and early visual processing functions to retain the information present in the visual signal while reducing the redundancies. In the 1950s, Stephen Kuffler (1952) discovered the center-surround structure of retinal ganglion cells' response and, forty years later, Joseph Atick (1992) showed that this arrangement serves to decorrelate these cells' responses. As Horace Barlow (1961) had suspected, sensory neurons are organized to maximize the statistical independence of their response. Bruno Olshausen and David Field recently showed that the same is true of neurons in the primary visual cortex. Hubel and Wiesel discovered that neurons in the primary visual cortex are sensitive to edges, hence their functional description as edge detectors, but could only guess at the functional relevance of this structure (Hubel 1988). According to Olshausen and Field, edge detection allows neurons in the primary visual cortex to respond to visual signals in a maximally independent fashion and thus produce sparsely coded representations of the visual field. To show this, they constructed an algorithm that could identify the minimal set of maximally *independent* basis functions capable of describing natural

---

[12] For an extended discussion of this theme, see Cummins *et al.* (2001), Ch. 4, this volume.

images (or small 12 × 12 pixel patches thereof) in a way that preserves all the information present in the visual signal. Because natural images tend to contain edges, and because there are reliable higher order correlations (three-point and higher) between pixels along an edge, it turns out that natural images can be fully described with minimal resources as composites of about a hundred such basis functions (see Figure 7.2).

Given the statistical structure of natural images in the environment, there had to be such a set of functions, but the important point is that these basis functions are similar to those Hubel and Wiesel found forty years earlier: spatially localized and oriented edges. Recently, O'Reilly and Munakata (2000) showed how to train a neural network using a form of Hebbian learning (conditional PCA) to produce a similar set of basis functions.

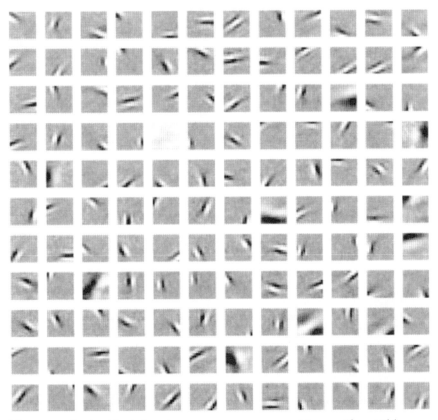

Figure 7.2 Optimal basis function set to represent natural images (from Olshausen and Field 2000)

To understand how visual representations are constructed out of these basis functions, consider a vector of V1 cortical cells[13] connected to the same retinal area via the same small subset of LGN cells.[14] Each cell has a receptive field similar to one in the minimal set of basis functions in Figure 7.2 above. Visual representations (of a small retinal area) can thus be thought of as a vector of cell activation, and an observed state of affairs (the inferred distal stimuli) as a linear function of a visual representation and some noise factor. A natural, but ultimately wrong, way to understand the construction of visual representations is as the activation of a subset of such basis functions *solely on the basis of the information each cell receives from the relevant retinal region.* In such a case, cells in the primary visual cortex would function as indicators of activity in the LGN and, ultimately, of properties in the visual field. Indeed, it would be easy to determine what state of affairs is currently observed if the basis functions were completely independent and the noise factor was known, but neither is the case. Because of this, many distinct visual representations (sets of basis vector functions) will account for the same observed state of affairs. Lewicki and Olshausen (1999) have shown, however, that it is possible to construct (infer) a unique visual representation given prior knowledge of the observed environment, that is, prior prob- abilities (the probability of observed states of affairs) and likelihood functions (the probability of visual representations given observed states of affairs). Instead of constructing a visual representation from a set of indicator signals, the visual system may infer the representation from indicator signals and relevant probabilistic knowledge of the visual environment.

Visual representations are thus constructed from retinal indicator signals, knowledge of the high-order correlational structure in the environment (coded in the LGN–V1 connections), and knowledge of relevant prior probabilities and likelihood functions. The picture that emerges here

---

[13] In reality, this vector is contained within a hypercolumn, which also contains a similar contralateral vector (for the other eye). All cells in a given hypercolumn respond to the same region of retinal space. Neighboring hypercolumns respond to neighboring regions of retinal space (Livingstone and Hubel 1988).

[14] The LGN (the lateral geniculate nucleus of the thalamus) is not a mere relay station en route to the cortex since it performs important computations of its own. But these will not matter here, as they are mostly concerned with the dynamic, as opposed to structural, aspects of vision and, owing to the massive backprojections from the cortex to LGN, with visual attention processes (it is estimated that there are ten times more backprojections from the cortex to the LGN as there are projections from the LGN to the cortex, Sherman and Koch 1986).

involves the construction of an image from a set of indicator signals that have the following characteristics:

- They are surprisingly few in number.
- They indicate multi-point correlations between adjacent pixels in the (whitened version of) the input.
- Their prowess as detectors of their proprietary targets is due, to a large extent, to recurrent circuitry that, in effect, computes a Bayesian function in which the prior probabilities are determined by the properties of neighboring areas of the developing image.
- Their representational content is semantically disjoint from that of the image they compose in the same way that pixel values themselves are semantically disjoint from the representational content of a computer graphic.

Like maps and scale models, image representations thus constructed have their meanings in virtue of their geometry rather than their origins. This is what gives them the source-independence characteristic of representations rather than indicator signals, and what allows for the possibility of disciplined structure sensitive transformations. Because such representations literally share structure with their targets, both static and dynamic structural properties of those targets can be mirrored by learning to transform the representations in ways that mirror the ways in which nature constrains the structure of, and structural changes in, the targets. Faces can be aged, objects can be rotated or 'zoomed,' projections into three dimensions can be computed. None of this is thinkable in a system in which visual representations are *semantically* composed from constituents whose contents are determined by their roles as indicator signals.

7.5. Representations and targets

We have been emphasizing the source independence that representations achieve in virtue of their distinctive internal structure which either mirrors or encodes the structure of what is represented, or encodes semantic combinatorics. To be useful, however, representations must typically retain a kind of source dependence. To understand this, we need to understand the relation between a representation and its target.

'x represents y' belongs to a group of relational semantic terms that are ambiguous. This can be seen by reflecting on a comment of Jerry Fodor's. 'Misrepresentation,' Fodor said, 'is when a representation is applied to something it doesn't apply to' (email exchange). It is obvious that 'applies to' has to be ambiguous if this remark is to make sense and be true, which it evidently does and is. Analogous observations apply to 'x refers to y,' 'x is true of y,' 'x means y,' and 'x represents y.' For example, you say, 'I used that map and found my way around the city with no problem.' 'Which city do you mean?' ('Which city are you referring to?') I ask. Here, I am asking for your *target*, the city against which that map's accuracy is to be measured. 'Here is the city map I was telling you about,' you say. 'Which city do you mean?' ('Which city are you referring to?') I ask. Here, I am asking for the *content*, that is, for the city the map actually represents—the city with which the map shares structure.

Though unmarked in ordinary vocabulary, the distinction between representational targets and contents is a commonplace. We are looking through my pictures of opera singers. You ask me what Anna Moffo looked like in her prime, and I hand you a picture, which happens to be a picture of Maria Callas. (It's hard to believe, but it is just a philosophy example.) We can distinguish here between the target of my representing—Anna Moffo, the singer the picture I handed you was supposed to represent on this occasion—and the content of the picture I produced—Maria Callas. The target of a representation on a particular occasion of its use is whatever it is supposed to represent on that occasion of use. The content of a representation is whatever it actually does represent.

So: a representation can be applied to something it doesn't apply to because there can be a mismatch between the content of a representation and its target on a particular occasion of its use, a mismatch between what it actually represents—its representational content—and what it is intended to represent on that occasion. Let's call something whose function is to represent some target or class of targets an *intender*. Intenders come in many forms. A clear example would be the process hypothesized by standard speech-recognition models whose function is representing the phrase structure of the current linguistic input. This process has a proprietary class of targets, viz., phrase structures of the current linguistic inputs. The accuracy of the representational performances of that process is to be judged by reference to the degree of match between the current target—the actual phrase structure of the current input—and the actual (as opposed to intended) content of the representation it produces on that occasion.

A representation's target, as opposed to its representational content, is source dependent. Processes downstream of the parser lately imagined—its clients—operate on the assumption that the representations it gets from that intender are representations of the phrase structure of the current linguistic input. To know that a token representation's target is the phrase structure of the current linguistic input amounts to knowing it was produced by an intender whose business it is to represent the phrase structure of the current linguistic input. If the representation were produced by a different intender, one whose business it is to represent move-trees in checkers, for example, it would need very different treatment (though it probably wouldn't get it in this case).

Exactly this sort of source dependency is exhibited by the visual representations built up in V1. Consumers of these representations other than mere enhancers need (typically) to operate on the assumption that they are processing representations of the current visual scene, and not, say, a remembered scene. This information is not encoded in the structure of the representation itself. To be available to a consumer that has more than one source, then, the information has to be carried by the fact that a particular intender produced the representation in question.

It is tempting to suppose that source information, hence target information, could be incorporated into the representation itself. To see the limitations of this idea, imagine labeling yearbook photographs with the names of the people represented. This gives us representations with contents of the form, 'Susan Smith looks like this <photo>.' There is nothing wrong with this scheme, provided consumers know that the targets of the complex representations—name plus picture—are true propositions about people's appearances.[15] But imagine someone using such a representation in a *reductio* argument. 'Suppose Maria Callas looked like this <photo>,' she starts out, exhibiting a photo of Anna Moffo. Her target is a false proposition about how Maria Callas looked. A consumer who does not realize this will get

---

[15] It actually isn't clear that the targets could be propositions, since the representations have pictures as constituents. See Cummins (1999), Ch. 10, this volume, for an argument against the view that pictures could have propositional contents. From the fact that pictures cannot have propositional contents, it doesn't *follow* that representations with pictures as constituents cannot have propositional contents. But it makes it seem problematic.

things seriously wrong. Labeling a photo just produces a new complex representation with a new content. Its target could be anything. Though most things, for example the number nine, will be non-starters as the target, it doesn't follow that they couldn't be the target. It is just unlikely that any intender would be that stupid. A representation cannot say what its own target is.[16]

Thus, representations have this in common with indicator signals: just as the information carried by an indicator signal depends on which indicator produces the signal, so the information carried by a token representation depends, in part, on the intender that produces it. Unlike indicator signals, however, representations carry lots of information about their targets beyond the fact that they are present. And this is precisely what makes them useful.[17]

7.6. Accuracy

There are two different ways in which indication can be accurate or inaccurate. Simple binary indicators of the 'idiot light' variety are either on or off, hence either right or wrong. An indicator signal in such a case cannot be more or less accurate. But the indicator that produces it may be said, somewhat misleadingly, to be more or less accurate as a function of its reliability.

Indicator signals often come in degrees, however. Thermometers can fail to be accurate because they have the amount of something as a target, and they can get the amounts wrong by a greater or lesser margin. The cells studied by Hubel and Wiesel present an interesting case of this kind. A cell firing at less than peak but more than is involved in normal background noise could be interpreted as indicating: (1) a probability that its target is present; or (2) how close the current stimulus is to the target. Both interpretations allow for individual signals having a degree of accuracy that is independent of the cell's reliability, since both involve indicating the amount of something (probability, nearness). On the other hand, it may

---

[16] This is why LOTers put LOT sentences into boxes like the Belief Box. An |I am rich| in the Belief Box is presumed to have a true proposition as target. Not so an |I am rich| in the Desire Box.

[17] There is much more to be said about intenders and target fixation. Some of this can be found in Cummins (1996a, 2000b).

be that less than peak firing is simply ignored, in which case the cells in question are, essentially, binary indicators.

Indicators say only whether (or how much of) their target is there; they say nothing about what their targets are like. Representations do carry information about what their targets are like, and this makes representational accuracy a far more complex affair than indicator accuracy.

Representational accuracy is a relation between representation and a target. Once we recognize that accuracy is a relation between a representation and its target on a particular occasion of its deployment, it becomes clear that representations are not accurate or inaccurate in their own right. What we are calling accuracy thus differs sharply from truth. A sentence may express a true proposition, yet be an inaccurate representation of its target. This is precisely the situation in *reductio* arguments, where the proposition targeted by the sentence expressing the supposition is (if the argument is successful) a false proposition. Similarly, if you are asked to specify some false proposition about the Eiffel Tower, your performance will be accurate only if you express a false proposition. In general, targets need not be actual states of affairs, objects, events, or whatever. The target a particular token representation is aimed at is fixed by the function of the intender that tokens that representation, together with the facts that happen to obtain at the time. Thus, an intender may have the function of representing the phrase structure of the current linguistic input, and that function, together with the actual (phrase) structure of the then current input will determine what the target of a particular token happens to be, and hence the standard against which the accuracy of the representation is to be measured.

Propositions are peculiar targets in that they cannot be represented with greater or less accuracy: they are either hit or missed. There is no such thing as varying degrees of accuracy when it comes to representing the proposition that the Eiffel Tower is in Paris. Someone might say it is in France, and claim that that is 'closer' than saying that it is in Europe or Australia. But this is evidently not a matter of getting closer to expressing the right proposition, but a matter of specifying a location that is closer to the correct one. Proposition expressing, at least as the going theory has things, is an all-or-nothing affair (Fodor and Lepore 1992). But most representation isn't like this. Pictures, maps, diagrams, graphs, scale models, and, of course, partitioned activations spaces, are more or less accurate representations of the targets they are applied to.

It follows from this observation that most representations cannot have propositional contents. It might seem that pictures could express propositions, because they could be said to hold in some possible worlds and not in others. It seems that one could take a video tape of a convenience store robbery, and alter it in various ways so that the variants held in possible worlds that were 'close' to the actual world, worlds in which everything went down just as it did in the actual world except that the perpetrator had a moustache, or the clock on the wall behind the clerk said ten-twenty-five instead of ten-twenty-two. Since a proposition can be conceived as a set of possible worlds (Stalnaker 1984), it might seem that a picture could be regarded as expressing the proposition that consists in the set of possible worlds it actually depicts accurately.

But no picture depicts with perfect accuracy. This is not just a consequence of rendering three dimensions in two. One might reasonably hold that the target of a photograph, for example, is not the three-dimensional spatial layout, but its two-dimensional projection at a certain plane. Even granting this, however, there is still the fact that getting the color right often requires inaccurate illumination and a sacrifice in resolution. Depth of field issues will inevitably render some things sharper than others. A video that gets the perpetrator's face in focus but blurs the clock on the wall behind him misrepresents the scene as having a blurry clock. We are not fooled, of course: we know clocks in convenience stores are not blurry. This makes it tempting to suppose that the photo doesn't really represent the clock as blurry. But it does: a photo of things we don't antecedently know about—one taken through a microscope, for example—can leave us wondering whether we have an accurate picture of a blurry object or a depth of field problem. Similarly, there are many compromises involved in shooting moving subjects with still shots, and even with movies or video. When we take all this into account, we no longer have a set of possible worlds corresponding to a given picture, but a smear of more or less similar worlds spreading out along various dimensions. Is the photo that nails the color of Aunt Tilly's hat while, inevitably, overestimating the intensity of illumination and blurring the features of the man running past her, more or less accurate than the one that allows us to identify the man but not the hat?[18]

---

[18] We could, perhaps, imagine a possible world whose natural laws dove-tailed with the constraints of a given representational scheme, so that, for example, things flattened into two dimensions when photographed, with objects originally at different distances losing various degrees of resolution themselves. These

Trade-offs of the sort illustrated by the depth of field problem in photographs are ubiquitous in non-symbolic representational schemes. Such schemes often represent many quantitatively variable properties simultaneously. Photos and models, for example, simultaneously represent color, relative distances, and sizes. It frequently happens that increasing accuracy in one dimension entails sacrificing accuracy in another. In human vision, sensitivity is in conflict with resolution and color accuracy because of the high density of the relatively insensitive cones at the fovea. (This is also why color blind individuals have better night vision.) Sentences (again, as construed by the tradition of truth-conditional semantics) can get around problems like this by abstracting away from some properties while focusing on others, and by abstracting away from troublesome differences in degree. 'Roma tomatoes are red when ripe,' is simply silent on size, shape, and variation in shade, intensity, and saturation. A photo or model cannot do this, nor can biological vision systems.

For those of us brought up to think of semantics in a linguistic setting, the striking thing about maps, diagrams, partitioned activations spaces, images, graphs, and other non-linguistic representations is that they are not true or false, and that their accuracy comes in degrees. A sentence either hits its propositional target or it fails. Nonpropositional representations require a graded notion of accuracy. Moreover, such representations are typically multidimensional. Images, for example, represent (relative) size, shape, color, and (relative) location simultaneously. The possibility thus arises that two image representations might be incomparable in overall accuracy, since one might do better on some dimensions—size and shape, say—while the other does better on others—color and location.[19] The fact that nonpropositional representations can simultaneously represent along many dimensions probably precludes any sort of 'all things considered' or 'overall' accuracy scores. The concepts of truth and falsehood, and the Tarskian combinatorial semantics we have come to associate with them, will be no help at all in understanding how these nonpropositional representations fit

would be radically counter-nomic worlds. The laws of our world, and every world satisfying anything like the same laws, preclude perfect accuracy for most representational schemes.

[19] It seems likely that high accuracy on one dimension will often have to be paid for in lower accuracy in others, given limited resources. The eye, for example, gains considerable resolution and color information via foveation, but loses light sensitivity in the process. A map that shows all the streets of London on one page will either be too big to use in the car or be viewable only with magnification.

or fail to fit their targets. Representational meaning for nonpropositional representations will have to be understood in different terms, as will their semantic structures. It is precisely this rich area of inquiry that is opened up when we distinguish representation from indication, and contemplate mechanisms other than those presupposed by the Language of Thought for assembling representations from indicator signals.

References

Atick, J., 'Could Information Theory Provide an Ecological Theory of Sensory Processes?', *Network*, 3 (1992), 213–51.

Barlow, H. B., 'Possible Principles Underlying the Transformation of Sensory Messages', in W. A. Rosenblith (ed.), *Sensory Communication* (Cambridge, Mass.: MIT Press, 1961), 217–34.

Churchland, P. M., *The Engine of Reason, the Seat of the Soul: A Philosophical Journey into the Brain* (Cambridge, Mass.: MIT Press, 1995).

Cummins, R., *Meaning and Mental Representation* (Cambridge, Mass.: MIT Press, 1989).

—— *Representations, Targets, and Attitudes* (Cambridge, Mass.: MIT Press, 1996a).

—— 'Truth and Meaning', in J. K. Campbell, M. O'Rourke, and D. Shier (eds.), *Meaning and Truth: Investigations in Philosophical Semantics* (New York: Seven Bridges Press, 1999).

—— 'Reply to Millikan', *Philosophy and Phenomenological Research*, 60 (2000b), 113–28.

—— Blackmon, J., Byrd, D., Poirier, P., Roth, M., and Schwarz, G., 'Systematicity and the Cognition of Structured Domains', *Journal of Philosophy*, 98 (2001), 1–19.

Dretske, F., *Knowledge and the Flow of Information* (Cambridge, Mass.: MIT Press/ Bradford Books, 1981).

—— *Explaining Behavior: Reasons in a World of Causes* (Cambridge, Mass.: MIT Press, 1988).

Field, D. J., 'Relations between the Statistics of Natural Images and the Response Properties of Cortical Cells', *Journal of the Optical Society of America A*, 4 (1987), 2379–94.

—— 'What is the Goal of Sensory Coding?', *Neural Computation*, 6 (1994), 559–601.

Fodor, J., *The Language of Thought* (New York: T. Y. Crowell, 1975).

—— *Psychosemantics* (Cambridge, Mass.: MIT Press, 1987).

—— *A Theory of Content and Other Essays* (Cambridge, Mass.: MIT Press, 1990a).

—— Lepore, E., *Holism: A Shopper's Guide* (Oxford: Blackwell, 1992).

Haugeland, J., 'Representational Genera', in W. Ramsey, S. Stich, and D. Rumelhart (eds.), *Philosophy and Connectionist Theory* (Hillsdale, NJ: Lawrence Erlbaum, 1991).

Hubel, D. H., *Eye, Brain, and Vision* (New York: Scientific American Library, 1988).

—— Wiesel, T. N., 'Receptive Fields, Binocular Interaction and Functional Architecture in the Cat's Visual Cortex', *Journal of Physiology*, 160 (1962), 106–54.

Kuffler, S., 'Neurons in the Retina: Organization, Inhibition and Excitatory Problems', *Cold Spring Harbor Symposia on Quantitative Biology*, 17 (1952), 281–92.

Lewicki, M. S., and Olshausen, B. A., 'A Probabilistic Framework for the Adaptation and Comparison of Images Codes', *Journal of the Optical Society of America A*, 16 (1999), 1587–601.

Livingstone, M., and Hubel, D., 'Segregation of Form, Color, Movement and Depth: Anatomy, Physiology, and Perception', *Science*, 240 (1988), 740–9.

Millikan, R., 'Representations, Targets, Attitudes', *Philosophy and Phenomenological Research*, 60 (2000), 103–11.

Newell, A., and Simon, H., *Human Problem Solving* (Englewood Cliffs, NJ: Prentice-Hall, 1972).

Olshausen, B. A., and Field, D. J., 'Emergence of Simple-Cell Receptive Field Properties by Learning a Sparse Code for Natural Images', *Nature*, 381 (1996), 607–9.

—— —— 'Sparse Coding with an Overcomplete Basis Set: A Strategy Employed by V1?', *Vision Research*, 37(1997), 3311–25.

—— —— 'Vision and the Coding of Natural Images', *American Scientist*, 88 (2000), 238–45.

O'Reilly, R. C., and Munakata, Y., *Computational Explorations in Cognitive Neuroscience* (Cambridge, Mass.: MIT Press, 2000).

Schiffer, S., *Remnants of Meaning* (Cambridge, Mass.: MIT Press, 1987).

Sherman, S. M., and Koch, C., 'The Control of Retino-Geniculate Transmission in the Mammalian Lateral Geniculate Nucleus', *Experimental Brain Research*, 63 (1986), 1–20.

Stalnaker, R., *Inquiry* (Cambridge, Mass.: MIT Press, 1984).

Stampe, D., 'Towards a Causal Theory of Linguistic Representation', in P. A. French, T. E. Uehling, and H. K. Wettstein (eds.), *Midwest Studies in Philosophy*, ii. *Studies in the Philosophy of Language* (Minneapolis: University of Minnesota Press, 1977), 42–63.

8

Representation and Unexploited Content

ROBERT CUMMINS, JIM BLACKMON, DAVID BYRD,
ALEXA LEE, AND MARTIN ROTH

8.1. Introduction

In this chapter, we introduce a novel difficulty for teleosemantics, namely,
its inability to account for what we call unexploited content—content a
representation *has*, but which the system that harbors it is currently unable
to exploit. In section 8.2, we give a characterization of teleosemantics. Since
our critique does not depend on any special details that distinguish the
variations in the literature, the characterization is broad, brief, and abstract.
In section 8.3, we explain what we mean by unexploited content, and argue
that any theory of content adequate to ground representationalist theories in
cognitive science must allow for it.[1] In section 8.4, we show that teleosemantic theories of the sort we identify in section 8.2 cannot accommodate
unexploited content, and are therefore unacceptable if intended as attempts

Originally published in Graham McDonald and David Papineau (eds.), *Teleosemantics* (Oxford
University Press, 2008), 195–207. This paper appears with the kind permission of Oxford University
Press.

[1] There are, of course, initiatives in cognitive science that are not representationalist—e.g. the dynamic
systems approach advocated by van Gelder and Port (1995) and others. If non-representationalist
approaches ultimately carry the day, then disputes about how mental representation should be understood
in cognitive theory will have been idle. For the most part, we simply assume in what follows that some
form of representationalism is correct. But, now and again, we phrase matters more methodologically, as
points about what representationalist explanations of cognition need to assume rather than as points about
what cognitive processes actually require.

to ground representationalist cognitive science. Finally, in section 8.5, we speculate that the existence and importance of unexploited content has likely been obscured by a failure to distinguish representation from indication, and by a tendency to think of representation as reference.

8.2. Teleosemantics

Teleological accounts of representational content identify the extension of a representation R with the class of things C such that, historically, it was applications of tokens of R to members of C that led to the selection and replication of the mechanisms that produced or consumed tokens of R. Accounts along these general lines are familiar from the writings of Millikan, Neander, Papineau, and others (Millikan 1984, 1986; Papineau 1984, 1987; Neander 1991; recent anthologies by Allen *et al.* 1998; Buller 1999; Ariew *et al.* 2002). For our purposes, the crucial point about all such theories is that a representation R can have the content C for a system only if it had, when selection took place, the ability to apply R to members of C. There cannot be selection for an ability that isn't there. The scenario underlying teleological accounts of content features a sub-population with a mechanism (what Cummins 1996*a* calls an intender) in the R-application business. It applies R to a variety of things, including, under certain circumstances, members of C. Those applications—the applications of R to members of C—prove adaptive enough to cause the mechanism in question to spread through the population over time.

It is no part of this story that the reliability of R applications (applications of R to Cs vs. non-Cs) or their accuracy (excellence of fit between a token of R and its target C) is ever very good, or improves over time. All that is required is that it is the applications of R to members of C that leads to the spread of the mechanism through the population. The trait—the characteristic pattern of R applications—may go to fixation even though R is applied somewhat inaccurately to members of C, and only under rather special or rare circumstances, and frequently applied to other things. We emphasize this to make it clear that the critique we elaborate in the next section does not depend on the reliability or accuracy of the selected representing or representation-consuming mechanisms. On the other hand, accurate enough applications of R to Cs cannot simply be random accidents: there must be a mechanism in the R-application business to select.

8.3. Unexploited content

By *unexploited content* we mean information or content carried by or present in a representation that its harboring system is, for one reason or another, unable to use or exploit. A common-sense example will help to introduce the basic idea. Imagine someone who learns to use road maps to find a route from point A to point B. A study of the map might lead to the following plan: make a left at the third intersection, then another left at the next cross street, followed by an immediate right. It never occurs to this person to use the map to extract distance information until, one day, someone suggests that the map shows a shorter route than the one generated. Prior to this insight, our imaginary subject uses the map in a way that would be insensitive to various geometrical distortions, such as shrinking the north–south axis relative to the east–west axis. If assignments of representational content are limited by the abilities its user actually has to exploit the map, we will have to say that there is no distance information there to be exploited until after the user has learned to exploit it. And this will evidently make it impossible to explain how the user could learn to effectively compare routes for length: you cannot learn to exploit content that isn't there. Indeed, it is evident that this story makes no sense at all unless we concede that relative distances are represented before the user learns to exploit that information. Even if the user never exploits relative-distance information, we are forced to allow that it is there to be exploited, since, under the right conditions, the user could have learned to use maps to compare distances. This would not be possible if the map did not represent relative distances.

How seriously should we take this sort of example? We think the lesson is far-reaching and fundamental. To begin with, the idea that a brain can learn to exploit previously unexploited structure in its representations is presupposed by all neural network models of learning. Such learning typically consists in adjusting synaptic weights so as to respond properly to input activation patterns. This whole process makes no sense unless it is assumed that input patterns represent proximal stimuli prior to learning, and that the

Figure 8.1 Depth from texture gradients

representational content of input patterns remains the same throughout learning. Prior to learning, the network cannot properly exploit input representations: that is precisely what the process of weight adjustment achieves over time.[2]

Having come this far, we can see that the problem of learning to exploit 'lower-level' ('upstream') representations must be ubiquitous in the brain, if we assume that the brain acquires new knowledge and abilities via synaptic weight adjustment. In perceptual learning, for example, proximal stimuli must be represented before the appropriate cortical structures learn or evolve to exploit those representations in target location and recognition.

As an example, consider the capacity to exploit texture gradients as visual depth cues. Representations in V1 contain texture gradients but the ability to exploit these as depth cues (as you do when you view Figure 8.1) develops later. Similarly, the ability to exploit retinal disparity in binocular vision as a depth cue develops along with the organization of binocular columns in the visual cortex. This process can be aborted by exotropy, but in such cases, binocular fusion without stereoscopic depth vision can still be achieved as the result of surgical correction and vision training, demonstrating that the retinal disparity information is still present in early visual representations, but unexploited for depth.

---

[2] We have heard it said that the network creates the content of its input patterns as learning progresses. But if we say this, we have no reason to say that early responses are errors. And if early responses are not errors, why change the weights in any particular direction? Indeed, why change them at all?

There is no need to multiply examples. Once our attention is drawn to the phenomenon, it is clear that there must be many features of representations, especially structural features, at nearly all levels of perceptual and cognitive processing, that require learning and/or development for proper exploitation.

8.4. Teleosemantics and unexploited content

Situating these facts in an evolutionary context immediately reveals a problem for teleosemantics. It is certainly possible, and probably common, that the abilities required to exploit various features of representations evolved well after those features appeared in the representations themselves. As just remarked, the ability to exploit texture gradients in early visual representation as depth cues might well have evolved well after well-defined gradients were available in those early representations. Now here is the point: the presence of texture gradients in early visual representations could not have been adaptive prior to the evolution of the processes that exploit them. Teleosemantics, however, implies that texture gradients did not represent depth until *after* it became adaptive for visual representations to include them. In general, content only becomes adaptive, hence a candidate for the kind of content-fixing selection contemplated in teleosemantics, when and if the ability to exploit it is acquired. Evidently, there can be no selection for an ability to exploit content that isn't there. The 'opportunity' to evolve the ability to exploit texture gradients in visual representations as depth cues simply cannot arise unless and until depth representing texture gradients become available to exploit.[3]

Reflection on this last point suggests that the same difficulty arises whether the ability to exploit some feature of a representation is learned or evolved. For concreteness, assume that the ability to exploit texture gradients as depth cues is learned. While the current state of neuroscience provides no definitive account of such learning, it is perfectly intelligible to suppose it involves the systematic adjustment of synaptic weights in some substructure of the visual cortex. Evidently, if the ability to *learn* to exploit

---

[3] The underlying general point here, that selection for a given capacity requires that the capacity already exist in some part of the population, is not new. See e.g. Macdonald (1989).

texture gradients itself evolved after texture gradients became available in early visual representations, we have a situation exactly like the one just rehearsed: teleosemantics assigns no content to unexploited features of representations, and this undermines the obvious explanation of how the ability to *learn* to exploit such features might later become adaptive.

To sum up: once our attention is directed to the phenomenon of unexploited content, it is natural to ask how the ability to exploit previously unexploited content might be acquired. Learning in the individual, and evolution in the species, are the obvious answers. Equally obvious, however, is that teleosemantics cannot allow for evolving the ability to exploit previously unexploited content: That requires content to pre-date selection, and teleosemantics requires selection to pre-date content.

8.5. Representation and indication

It seems likely that the very possibility of unexploited content has been overlooked in philosophical theories of content because of a failure to distinguish representation from indication. In this section, we digress a bit to explain how we understand this distinction, and conclude by suggesting how exclusive attention to indication tends to make the phenomenon of unexploited content difficult to discern.[4]

8.5.1. Terminology

Some authors (e.g. Schiffer 1987) use "mental representation" to mean any mental state or process that has a semantic content. On this usage, a belief that the Normans invaded England in 1066 counts as a mental representation, as does the desire to be rich. This is not how we use the term. As we use the term, a mental representation is an element in a scheme of semantically individuated types whose tokens are manipulated—structurally transformed—by (perhaps computational) mental processes. Such a scheme might be language-like, as the Language of Thought hypothesis asserts (Fodor 1975), or it might consist of (activation) vectors in a multidimensional vector space as connectionists suppose (e.g. Churchland 1995). Or it

---

[4] This section draws heavily from Cummins and Poirier (2004), Ch. 7, this volume.

might be something quite different: a system of holograms, or images, for example.[5] An indicator, on the other hand, simply produces structurally arbitrary outputs that signal the presence or magnitude of some property in its 'receptive field.'

8.5.2. Indication

We begin with some influential examples.

- Thermostats typically contain a bimetallic element whose shape indicates the ambient temperature.
- Edge detector cells were discovered by David Hubel and Torsten Wiesel (1962). They write: 'The most effective stimulus configurations, dictated by the spatial arrangements of excitatory and inhibitory regions, were long narrow rectangles of light (slits), straight-line borders between areas of different brightness (edges), and dark rectangular bars against a light background.'
- 'Idiot lights' in your car have come on when, for example, the fuel level is low, or the oil pressure is low, or the engine coolant is too hot.

"Indication" is just a semantic-sounding word for detection. Since we need a way to mark the distinction between the mechanism that does the detection, and the state or process that is the signal that the target has been detected, we will say that the cells studied by Hubel and Wiesel are indicators, and that the pattern of electrical spikes they emit when they fire are indicator signals. Similarly, the bimetallic element found in most thermostats is an indicator, and its shape is the signal.

8.5.3. Indication vs. representation

Indication is generally regarded as a species of representation. Indeed, causal and informational theories of representational content assert that representation is, or is inherited from, indicator content.[6] We think the two should be kept distinct.

---

[5] It is possible that the brain employs several such schemes. See Cummins (1996b) and Cummins et al. (2001), Ch. 4, this volume, for further discussion of this possibility.

[6] The theory is generally credited to Dennis Stampe (1977). Its most prominent advocates are Dretske (1981) and Fodor (1987).

Indication is transitive, representation is not   If S3 indicates S2, and S2 indicates S1, then S3 indicates S1. Imagine a photosensitive cell pointed at an 'idiot light' in your car, and attached to a relay activating an audio device that plays a recording: 'The oil pressure is low.' If the light indicates low oil pressure, so does the recording. Representation, on the other hand, is not transitive. A representation of the pixel structure of a digitized picture of the Statue of Liberty is not a representation of the statue's visual appearance, though the later may be recovered from the former.[7] To anticipate some terminology we will use later, a representation of the pixel structure is an *encoding* of the statue's visual appearance.[8]

Indicator signals are arbitrary; representations are not   This is implied by the transitivity of indication. Given transitivity, anything can be made to indicate anything else (if it can be detected at all), given enough ingenuity and resources. Because indicator signals are arbitrary, disciplined structural transformations of them cannot systematically alter their meanings. Such transformations, however, are precisely what make representations useful. Consider, for example, a software package that takes a digitized image of a face as input and 'ages' it, i.e. returns an image of that face as it is likely to look after some specified lapse of time. Nothing like this could possibly work on an input that was required only to indicate a certain face—a name, say—because there is no correlation between the physical characteristics something must have to be a signal that indicates the appearance of a face at age 18 and the physical characteristics of that face at age 18. It follows from the nature of indication that the structural properties of an indicator signal have no significance. Indicators 'say' that their targets are there, but do not 'say' anything about what they are like. Representations, on the other hand, mirror the structure of their targets (when they are accurate), and thus their consumers can cognitively process the structure of the target by

---

[7] Representation, on the view advocated by Cummins (1996a), is grounded in isomorphism. Since isomorphism is plainly transitive, it might seem that representation must be transitive too. In a sense, this is right: the things that stand in the isomorphism relation are structures—sets of 'objects' and relations on them. If S1 is isomorphic to S2, and S2 is isomorphic to S3, then S1 is isomorphic to S3. An actual physical representation, however, is not an abstract object; it *has* a structure—actually, several—but it isn't *itself* a structure. The connected graph structure of a paper road map is isomorphic to the street and intersection structure of a town, but not to the town's topology. The town's topology is isomorphic to the topology of a citrus grove. But no structure of the road map need be isomorphic to any structure of the grove.

[8] It is what Haugeland would call a recording of the picture. See Haugeland (1990).

manipulating the structure of its representation. But representations, unlike indicator signals, are typically silent concerning whether their targets are 'present': they are not, except incidentally and coincidentally, detector signals.

Indicators are source-dependent in a way that representations are not   The cells studied by Hubel and Wiesel all generate the same signal when they detect a target. You cannot tell, by looking at the signal itself (the spike train), what has been detected. You have to know which cells generated the signal. This follows from the arbitrariness of indicator signals, and is therefore a general feature of indication: the meaning is all in who shouts, not in what is shouted.[9]

In sum, then, indication is transitive, while representation is not. It follows from the transitivity of indication that indicator signals are arbitrary and source-dependent in a way in which representations are not, and this disqualifies indicator signals as vehicles for structure-dependent cognitive processing. Representation is intransitive, nonarbitrary, and portable (not source-dependent), and therefore suitable for structural processing. Indicator signals 'say' their targets are present, but 'say' nothing about them; representations provide structural information about their targets, but do not indicate their presence. Indicator signals say, 'My target is here', while representations say, 'My target, wherever it is, is structured like so.'

8.5.4. *Discussion*

If indication is your paradigm of mental content, as it is bound to be if you hold some form of causal theory, you are going to focus on what fixes the content of an indicator signal.[10] Whatever fixes the content of an indicator signal, it is *not* its structural properties. In this context, therefore, motivation is lacking for thinking about which aspects of a representation's structure can usefully be processed, and whether the ability to do that processing is learned or evolved or a combination of both. Maps rub your nose in the possibility of unexploited content; idiot lights do not.

---

[9] We do not mean to imply here that the shape of a spike train is never significant. The point is rather that two indicators can have the same spike train, yet indicate different things.

[10] See Cummins (1997), Ch. 2, this volume, for more on the marriage between causal theories, indication, and the Language of Thought.

There can, however, be unexploited indicator signals. Think of the color-coded idiot lights at intersections: you have to learn that red means stop, green means go. Before learning, this is also unexploited content (though not what we have been calling representational content), and, unsurprisingly, it makes trouble for teleosemantics. Teleosemantics implies that an indicator signal has no content until there has been selection for the indicator that generates it. But the ability to exploit, or to learn to exploit, an indicator signal can only evolve if the indicator is already there signaling its target.

Magnetosomes are magnetically polarized structures (typically ferrite surrounded by a membrane) in single-cell ocean-dwelling anaerobic bacteria. The orientation of these structures correlates with the direction of the earth's magnetic field. By following the magnetic orientation in a particular direction, organisms far from the equator can avoid aerobic water near the surface. For this to work, magnetosomes must be chained and attached at both ends of the cell to form a reasonably straight line in the direction of locomotion (see Figure 8.2). This is because the orientation of

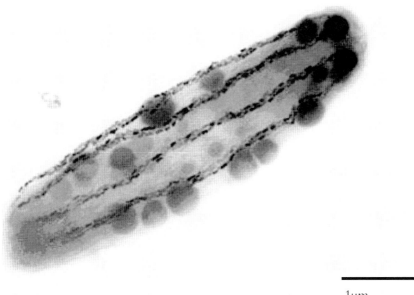

1μm

Figure 8.2 Magnetotactic bacterium from the Chiemsee, Bavaria, Germany (Bio-magnetism Group, University of Munich); dark blobs are sulfur granules

the organism is simply a consequence of the orientation of the chain of polarized molecules. The whole body of the bacterium is a floating compass needle. The organism swims, and will move in whatever direction it happens to point.

Chaining, of course, is simply a physical consequence of having a lot of little magnets suspended in proximity. They will stick together north to south. What is not so obvious is why the north pole of the string winds up attached at the 'front'—i.e. direction of locomotion—end of the organism. However this happens, it is certainly possible, indeed probable, that the attachment process evolved *after* magnetosomes themselves appeared within the cell body of anaerobic bacteria. Selectionist theories imply that magnetosome chains did not indicate the direction of anaerobic water until *after* it became adaptive to do so, i.e. only after the evolution of attachment. But surely it is in part because they *did* indicate the direction of anaerobic water that the attachment process was adaptive enough to be selected for.

8.6. Conclusion

A very natural response to the foregoing is to say that unexploited content isn't really *content*. After all, there is a lot of unexploited information in the *environment*, information that cognitive systems must acquire the abilities to exploit. We do not call *that* information *content*.

We are sympathetic with the comparison between learning or evolving an ability to exploit information in a representation or indicator signal and learning or evolving an ability to exploit information in the environment. We think these are, in fact, deeply similar. The importance of this similarity is obscured or lost in theories that essentially take representation to be *reference*. Theories of content that take representation to be reference perforce focus on devising the conditions that (allegedly) fix the references of semantically primitive terms, relying on the standard truth-conditional combinatorics to fix the references and truth conditions of complex expressions. Access to something that refers to horses—a primitive term in Mentalese however, tells you nothing about horses. Actual information about horses, therefore, is to be found only in the (or a) set of Mentalese sentences that contain a |horse| (a Mentalese term referring to horses) and appear in the Belief Box. The only sense in which such an account allows for unexploited content, therefore, is the sense in which a cognitive agent might not exploit all of its beliefs about horses on a particular occasion. While this is undoubtedly a case of unexploited information, it is not a case of the sort we have been discussing. Returning to our analogy, inability to extract relative-distance information from a road map is quite distinct from failing to read or utilize some of the sentences in a book. In the later case, the content of the unread sentences is unproblematically extractable from those sentences; they just are not noticed for one reason or another. The problem is not that one doesn't know how to read them. In the case of the map, a new skill is required to exploit the needed information. Unexploited information of the sort allowed for in Language of Thought (LOT) theories evidently poses no problem for teleosemantics comparable to the one we have been urging, since the mechanisms responsible for applying the primitive constituents and processing the relevant syntactical machinery may be selected for independently of their occurrence in any particular belief.

Cognitive systems need information. LOT accounts attempt to provide for this by giving indication a twofold role. First, indicator signals alert the organism to the instantiation of their target properties in their receptive fields.[11] Second, primitive terms of LOT inherit their references from the properties they are used to indicate in the context of detection. Cognition is understood as the application of theories expressed as organized sets of sentences in Mentalese, hence as a species of truth-conditional inference, implemented as computation over symbolic structures with Tarskian logical forms.

Perhaps something like this story makes sense for the 'higher' cognition of adult humans, especially if, like Plato, one is inclined to suppose that cognition is thinking and that thinking is essentially talking to oneself. But this picture is of little use for understanding phenomena like the capacity to exploit texture gradients in early visual representations as depth cues. When we turn to phenomena such as these, the truth-conditional semantics of propositional attitude contents is of dubious significance to cognitive science. Much more important, we believe, is the conception of representation and indication briefly introduced above. Representations, thus conceived, are of use to cognitive systems as an information source in addition to the

---

[11] See Cummins and Poirier (2004), Ch. 7, this volume, for a discussion of how indicators might become 'source-free' and function as terms.

environment (i) because they can be stored; and (ii) because they can be structurally transformed in ways that the environment typically cannot be. Sophisticated indicators are of use because they can signal the presence of environmental features—e.g. the presence of a predator or a mate—that are extremely abstract from the point of view of proximal stimulation. Representation and indication thus conceived are what make reference and the propositional attitudes possible. A theory that begins with the truth-conditional semantics of propositional attitude contents thus skips over most of the action and begins with a phenomenon that is just the sort of cognitive achievement that mainstream cognitive science seeks to explain in terms of representation.

We do not wish to quibble over whether the phenomenon we have called unexploited content is *really content*. We do contend, however, that what we are calling content *is* what ultimately does the work in representationalist cognitive science.[12] No doubt we need to mark the distinction between exploited and unexploited content. We think "exploited content" and "unexploited content" do the job nicely. Refusing to use the word "content" for as yet unexploited features of structured representations strongly suggests, wrongly, that those features are somehow different from those that are exploited. There is no intrinsic difference between texture gradients that are exploited and texture gradients that are not. To suppose otherwise would be like supposing that road maps cease to represent relative distances in the hands of those who cannot extract that information from them.[13]

In this chapter, we have urged what we think is a novel objection to teleosemantic theories, namely that they cannot accommodate unexploited content or information. Surely, a necessary condition for the plausibility of a theory of mental representation that hopes to ground representationalist

[12] An anonymous reviewer complained that we have not cited actual examples of cognitive scientists appealing to unexploited content. We are saying that they presuppose it whenever they assume that a representational capacity or ability is learned or evolved. Presumably, they were all learned or evolved.

[13] There is a temptation to think that an unexploited feature of a representation doesn't represent anything *to* (or *for*) the system that harbors it. This is surely right. But to assimilate representation to *representation to/for* will, like teleosemantics, make it impossible to understand how, for example, the ability to exploit texture gradients as depth cues could be learned or evolved. For more on the representation/representation- to distinction, see Cummins (1996*a*). Notice, by the way, that what is important about texture gradients is not just that they somehow covary with depth. It is their suitability for structural processing that makes them useful. When covariation is all that matters, an arbitrary indicator signal is all that is required.

cognitive science is that it accommodate unexploited content or information. For it *must* be possible for a system to be able to learn or evolve the capacity to exploit the information carried by a representation or indicator signal, and this implies that the information is there prior to acquisition of the capacity to exploit it.

References

Allen, C., Bekoff, M., and Lauder, G. (eds.), *Nature's Purposes* (Cambridge, Mass.: MIT Press, 1998).

Ariew, A., Cummins, R., and Perlman, M. (eds.), *Functions: New Essays in the Philosophy of Psychology and Biology* (Oxford: Oxford University Press, 2002).

Buller, D. (ed.), *Function, Selection, and Design* (New York: SUNY Press, 1999).

Churchland, P. M., *The Engine of Reason, the Seat of the Soul* (Cambridge, Mass.: MIT Press, 1995).

Cummins, R., *Representations, Targets, and Attitudes* (Cambridge, Mass.: MIT Press, 1996*a*).

—— 'Systematicity', *Journal of Philosophy*, 93 (1996*b*), 591–614.

—— 'The LOT of the Causal Theory of Reference', *Journal of Philosophy*, 94 (1997), 535–42.

—— Poirier, P., 'Representation and Indication', in H. Clapin, P. Staines, and P. Slezak (eds.), *Representation in Mind* (Oxford: Elsevier, 2004).

—— Blackmon, J., Byrd, D., Poirier, P., Roth, M., and Schwarz, G., 'Systematicity and the Cognition of Structured Domains', *Journal of Philosophy*, 98 (2001), 167–85.

Dretske, F., *Knowledge and the Flow of Information* (Cambridge, Mass.: MIT Press, 1981).

Fodor, J., *The Language of Thought* (New York: Thomas Y. Crowell, 1975).

—— *Psychosemantics: The Problem of Meaning in the Philosophy of Mind* (Cambridge, Mass.: MIT Press, 1987).

Haugeland, J., 'Representational Genera', in W. Ramsey, S. Stich, and D. Rumelhart (eds.), *Philosophy and Connectionist Theory* (Hillsdale, NJ: Lawrence Erlbaum, 1990).

Hubel, D., and Wiesel, T., 'Receptive Fields, Binocular Interaction and Functional Architecture in the Cat's Visual Cortex', *Journal of Physiology*, 160 (1962), 106–54.

Macdonald, G., 'Biology and Representation', *Mind and Language*, 4 (1989), 186–200.

Millikan, R., *Language, Thought, and Other Biological Categories* (Cambridge, Mass.: MIT Press, 1984).

—— 'Thoughts without Laws: Cognitive Science with Content', *Philosophical Review*, 95 (1986), 47–80.

Neander, K., 'The Teleological Notion of Function', *Australasian Journal of Philosophy*, 69 (1991), 454–68.

Papineau, D., 'Reality and Explanation', *Philosophy of Science*, 51 (1984), 550–72.

—— *Reality and Representation* (Oxford: Blackwell, 1987).

Schiffer, S., *Remnants of Meaning* (Cambridge, Mass.: MIT Press, 1987).

Stampe, D., 'Towards a Causal Theory of Linguistic Representation', in P. A. French, T. E. Uehling, and H. K. Wettstein (eds.), *Midwest Studies in Philosophy*, ii. *Studies in the Philosophy of Language* (Minneapolis: University of Minnesota Press, 1977), 42–63.

Van Gelder, T. J., and Port, R., 'It's about Time: An Overview of the Dynamical Approach to Cognition', in R. Port and T. van Gelder (eds.), *Mind as Motion: Explorations in the Dynamics of Cognition* (Cambridge, Mass.: MIT Press, 1995).

9

Haugeland on Representation and Intentionality

9.1. Targets and objects

Haugeland doesn't have what I would call a theory of mental representation. Indeed, it isn't clear that he believes there is such a thing. But he does have a theory of intentionality and a correlative theory of objectivity, and it is this material that I will be discussing in what follows.

It will facilitate the discussion that follows to have at hand some distinctions and accompanying terminology I introduced in *Representations, Targets, and Attitudes* (Cummins 1996a; *RTA* hereafter). Couching the discussion in these terms will, I hope, help to identify points of agreement and disagreement between Haugeland and myself. In *RTA*, I distinguished between the target a representation has on a given occasion of its application, and its (representational) content. *RTA* takes representation deployment to be the business of *intenders*: mechanisms whose business it is to represent some particular class of targets. Thus, on standard stories about speech perception, there is a mechanism (called a parser) whose business it is to represent the phrase structure of the linguistic input currently being processed. When this intender passes a representation *R* to the consumers of its products, those consumers will take *R* to be a representation of the phrase structure of the current input (because of where they got it).

There is no explicit vocabulary to mark the target—content distinction in ordinary language. Expressions like 'what I referred to,' 'what I meant,' and the like, are systematically ambiguous with respect to this distinction. Sometimes they mean targets, sometimes contents. Consider the following dialogue:

You: I used this map and got around the city with no problem.
Me: Which city do you mean? (or: Which city are you referring to?)

Here, I am asking for your target, the city against which the map's accuracy is to be measured. Now compare this exchange:

You: Here is the city-map I was telling you about.
Me: Which city do you mean? (or: Which city are you referring to?)

Here, I am asking for the content, that is, for the city the map actually represents.[1] The potential for ambiguity derives from the fact that there are two senses in which representations are semantically related to the world, the content sense and the target sense, but the distinction is not marked in ordinary vocabulary. The distinction is *there*, as the example just rehearsed makes clear, but it is marked only by different uses of the same expressions in ordinary language.

Representational error, then, is a mismatch between the representation produced and its target on the occasion in question. The obvious way to think of representational error, as Jerry Fodor once said to me in conversation, is this: error occurs when a representation is *applied to* something it is not *true of*, for example, when one applies a representation of a horse to a cow. The distinction in this formulation between what a representation is *applied to* and what it is *true of* is precisely the distinction between a representation's target and its content. The crucial point is that what determines what a representation is *true of* must be independent of what determines what it is *applied to*, otherwise error is problematic. It follows from this that a theory of representational content—a theory that says what it is for R to be *true of* T—is only part of the story about representation. We require, in addition, a theory of target fixation, a theory that says what it is for R to be *applied to* T. Since the target of tokening a representation is, as it were, the thing the representation is intended to represent, I shall say that representations *represent* their contents, but that a use of a representation *intends* its target. *Intentionality* is thus different from *semantic content*. The former is part of the theory of targets, while the latter is part of the theory of representational content. The *intentional content* of R is therefore not the actual content of R at all, but, rather, the *intended* content of some use of R.[2]

---

[1] The standard Twin-Earth cases simply trade on this ambiguity in semantic terms. See *RTA* 126 ff.

[2] 'Intend' is a technical term here. I do not, of course, suppose that cognitive systems generally intend their targets consciously, i.e. that whenever T is the target of a use of R in $\sum$, $\sum$ forms the intention to use R to represent T. But I do think the technical sense is a natural extension of this usual sense. In the case of conscious, deliberate use, intended content is quite literally the content one intends to represent.

I construe Haugeland's theory of intentionality and objectivity as a theory about targets. The theory has two internally related parts:

1. Intentionality: how are targets fixed—that is, what determines the target of a representation on a given occasion of its use?
2. Objectivity: what targets it is possible for a given system to have? (Because what will be an object—not a three-dimensional piece of furniture, but something that is objective, something that exists and has its properties for a given cognitive system—will depend on what targets it can have, not on what it can represent.)

By definition, a target of a representing is *normative* for the accuracy, on that occasion, of the representation deployed. If you have targets that you cannot represent accurately, you get what I called forced error in *RTA*. Accuracy and error come in degrees, of course. A certain amount of error is tolerable, sometimes even desirable, as when accuracy is traded for tractability or speed. Moreover, a given representation may be an accurate representation of one target and an inaccurate representation of another. Accuracy, then, is not intrinsic to a given representation. Indeed, representational types are not accurate or inaccurate. Only particular deployments of a representational type can be accurate or inaccurate, and the degree of accuracy is just the degree of match between the representation deployed and the target at which it is aimed.

To understand objectivity, then, we must understand how it is possible for a representing to be aimed at some particular target, and this is what makes intentionality and objectivity two sides of the same coin. To understand one is to understand the other.

Haugeland emphasizes that, in this inquiry, we must not take the objects for granted, and I agree. To see why, consider parsers once again. A parser is an intender whose function is to represent the phrase structure of the current linguistic input. Targets, then, are fixed by the representational function or functions of the intender mechanisms that produce or deploy them. So, when we ask what targets a system can have, we are asking what representational functions it can have.

Whatever your favorite account of functions, it is not going to be the function of any canid intender to represent chess positions. It follows that

As always, one may not succeed in doing what one intends, hence one may fail to represent what one intends to represent.

canids cannot have chess positions as representational targets, and hence that no chess position as such is normative for the accuracy of any canid representation deployment. In this sense, then, chess positions are not objects for canids. For exactly analogous reasons, it cannot be the function of any subcultural intender of which we have any experience to represent positrons. What representational functions something can have evidently depends in part on its conceptual sophistication and on its perceptual and inferential resources. This, then, is why the theory of intentionality cannot take the objects for granted. Nothing can be an object for me if I cannot have it as a target. I cannot have it as a target unless it can be the function of one of my intenders to represent it. But which intenders I can have depends, at least in part, on my sophistication and resources. How I am designed—my functional analysis—puts constraints on what can be an object for me.

Unlike representational content, function (and hence target fixation) is holistic in the sense that functions arise out of the organization of some containing system.[3] So, when Haugeland asks what perceptions are perceptions of, or what our thoughts are thoughts about, he is, I think, thinking of what I call target fixation. And he is right that target fixation is holistic. You cannot have chess positions as such as targets unless you have the sort of functional organization that supports an intender whose job is to represent chess positions. About intentionality and its relation to objectivity, then, we are in substantial agreement about the basics.

What about the details? Here, I am less confident. I propose to look at three different areas where I think that I must have misunderstood his position, or one of us must have misunderstood something about the phenomena themselves.

9.2. Seeing

I am pretty sure that Sheila, our canny Australian Shepherd cross, can see can openers and tennis balls. I am also pretty sure that it cannot be the

---

[3] Indeed, it is my view that holism in the theory of meaning is a response to the holism of target fixation. Since reference fixing, in *one* sense, is target fixing, and since Davidson (1967) turned the theory of meaning into the theory of reference, target fixation can look like the whole story about meaning. If you squint and don't move.

function of any canid intender to represent tennis balls or can openers. How is this dissonance to be harmonized?

It seems impossible to explain how Sheila could chase and catch a thrown tennis ball if she could not see it. But how can it make sense to say she sees it if it cannot be a target for her? Seeing is normative, an accomplishment. 'See,' as we used to say, is a success verb. If tennis balls cannot be targets for her, then they cannot be norms against which the accuracy of her perceptual representations is measured.

The overwhelmingly tempting move here is to say something like this: it certainly is the function of one of Sheila's intenders to represent the currently foveated thing, understood here as a coherent physical lump, and this thing could well be a tennis ball or a can opener. So, though she sees the tennis ball, she doesn't see it *as* a tennis ball. Realistically, she doesn't just see it as a coherent lump, either, since she can distinguish tennis balls from balls of other sorts of the same size and color, and will pick one out of a pile of assorted balls when asked to get the tennis ball. So she sees it as a ball (sphere?) of a distinct sort, pretty much as do young children who haven't a clue about tennis, but recognize the characteristic size, texture, and seam pattern of two interlocking bones wrapped around a sphere. In just this way, non-chess players can recognize standardized chess pieces. Because of this, terms like 'tennis ball' and 'chess piece' are ambiguous. There is a functional sense in which a salt shaker can be the white queen (or any other piece) in a chess game provided it is played (used) like one, and any ball of roughly the right size and elasticity can be a tennis ball in a game of tennis provided it is played (used) like one. But there is another sense in which these terms pick out objects with characteristic shapes and other intrinsic properties because these are the standard occupants of the functional roles in question. Sheila can see tennis balls in this latter sense, but not in the functional game-embedded sense.

The natural moral of this story seems to be that all seeing is seeing-as. Since seeing is an accomplishment, it must have an intentional object—a target— against which its accuracy is measured.[4] For a tennis ball, as such—that

---

[4] Representational accuracy should not be confused with perceptual or cognitive or behavioral success. Successful perception needn't be accurate perception. Indeed, to reiterate a point made earlier, accuracy can be expensive, hence undermine success. This means that no simple behavioral test is a test of representational accuracy. It also means that cognitive science has an extra degree of freedom to deploy in explaining successes and failures. In particular, it can distinguish between those failures that are due to the representations, and those that are due to an inability to exploit them. I will return to this point at length below.

is, taking the term functionally—to be a perceptual target, you have to be able to see it as a tennis ball. Hence, the only things against which the accuracy of your seeing can be measured are things that can be seen as something or other. Since all seeing is normative, if Sheila doesn't see the tennis ball as a tennis ball, she must see it as something else if she sees it at all. So all seeing is seeing-as. QED.

So what? It depends on what is built into seeing-as. Or better, it all depends on what it takes to have tennis balls and chess positions as targets. The capacity to see something as a tennis ball is just the capacity to have tennis balls as such as targets. So the question is what it takes to have an intender that has the function of representing tennis balls as such. Here, I think, Haugeland and I part company. I think his account over-intellectualizes target fixation and underestimates forced error. He writes: 'Surely no creature or system can see a given configuration as a knight fork without having some sense of what a knight fork is. To put in a familiar but perhaps misleading terminology, nothing can apply a concept unless it has that concept' (Haugeland 1996: 247). The respect in which Haugeland thinks this remark might be misleading is that it might suggest to some readers that seeing-as requires linguistic abilities. I am not even slightly tempted to think that having a concept—even a concept like the concept of a knight fork—requires having linguistic abilities, so I am not worried about being misled in this respect. My worry is, rather, the claim that having a knight fork as a perceptual target (or a target of thought, for that matter) requires having a concept of a knight fork, where this is meant to imply having at least a minimal knowledge, though perhaps not explicit knowledge, of chess in general and knight forks in particular.

To get a sense of why this worries me, consider a case of learning. What Haugeland's account rules out is a scenario like this: before learning, you have *T* as a target but do not know enough about it to successfully hit it. The errors you make, however, drive incremental improvements in aim, as back propagation does in connectionist learning. If this is possible, you must be able have targets you know next to nothing about. If the targets you could have were constrained by how much you knew about them, the size of the error would not decrease as you learned more. Indeed, your early shots would not be misses at all, since they wouldn't be aimed at the target you ultimately acquire.

Notice that I am not complaining about circularity here. It isn't that you need to know *about T* to have *T* as a target. I find this suspicious, all right, but I am sure some boot-strapping story, or co-constitution story, could leave me speechless, if not convinced. My complaint is rather that the account makes it impossible to articulate what it is that drives the learning process. NETtalk, for example, begins by knowing nothing about the phonetic values of letters in context (Sejnowski and Rosenberg 1987*a*, *b*). It learns the mapping by adjusting its weights as a function of the difference between its 'guesses' and the correct values. But this means that the correct values are targets right from the start, since it is the correct values against which the accuracy of the guesses is measured. Whether or not you think NETtalk is a good model of how letter-to-phoneme mappings are learned is not relevant here. If you think *any* perceptual or recognitional learning proceeds by adjusting one's knowledge to reduce the mismatch between one's targets and one's representational attempts, you have to have an account of target fixation that largely decouples it from what you know about the targets.[5]

9.3. Functions

How *can* systems have or acquire targets about which they know next to nothing? This is a question about representational functions, and hence depends to some extent on the theory of functions. I will discuss just two: Millikan's and my own.

On Millikan's (1984) account, an intender has the function of representing a T (for example, the phrase-structure of the current linguistic input) if it was selected for, historically, because, on various (perhaps rare) occasions, it did represent Ts accurately enough. How accurate is accurate enough? Enough to get selected. The point is that the intender got selected because, often enough (which might not be very often) it got however close it did

[5] A similar point can be made about representational contents. If you think, as all use theories (causal theories, conceptual role theories, selectionist/adaptationist theories) must, that there can be no more content in your representations than you can exploit, then you will be at a loss to even articulate the process whereby a perceptual system learns to exploit the information in its proximal representations to identify distal stimuli. Think now of the input end of NETtalk. Its input vectors carry information about the phonetic value of the targeted letter. Its job is to learn how to exploit this information. Since it cannot learn to exploit information that isn't there, it must be there prior to any ability to exploit it. Hence, input content must be independent of the system's sensitivity to it, contrary to all use theories of content. (See R. Cummins *et al.*, 2006, Ch. 8, this volume).

(which needn't have been very close) to an accurate representation of *T*s. *T*s are the targets, on this account, because it is *T*s as such, not something else, that are the standard you need to look at to see why the relevant intender was selected.

On this account it is plain that little if any knowledge of *T*s is required to have them as targets. What is required is just that *T*s were a good thing to get represented now and again, that the capacity to do that be heritable, and that competing lines didn't do it, or something even more important, better. Knight forks are bad candidates for canid targets because chess didn't figure in their evolutionary history, not because they don't have a clue about chess.

On my account of functions, an intender has the function of representing *T*s if its capacity to represent *T*s figures in a functional analysis of some capacity of a containing system. Consider, then, whatever complex capacity *C* of the whole organism made it more fit than the competition in the teleological scenario. The capacity to represent *T*s (to some degree of accuracy, with some reliability) figures in an analysis of *C*. And since Millikan's account didn't require knowledge of *T*s, neither does mine.

9.4. Commitment

Let's rehearse the plot. Haugeland and I agree that what targets a system can have—what it can intend—and, hence, what can be objects for it, depends, in part, and in a more or less holistic way, on the sophistication and resources of the system. So an account of intentionality and an account of objectivity are just two sides of the same coin. So far, we are both Kantians. In my view, however, Haugeland's account of intentionality over-intellectualizes intentionality by assuming that you cannot have targets you know next to nothing about, and underestimates the power of biological functions to make room for systematic error and therefore to ground targets and hence objectivity.

Given that Haugeland doesn't think biological function can ground targets, and hence objectivity, what does he think intentionality is grounded in? In a word, commitment; vigilant, resilient commitment. To see how this is supposed to work, we need to return to the chess example.

Nothing is a knight fork except in the context of a chess game. Nothing is a chess game unless the rules are in force. What enforces the rules? Nothing but a commitment on the part of the players not to tolerate deviations. You get a chess game, not when the rules are satisfied, but when the players take responsibility for their satisfaction.[6]

Thus, there are no knight forks unless there are players taking responsibility for the satisfaction of the rules and conditions constitutive of chess. When they do take such responsibility, and when the world cooperates well enough to make satisfaction possible—for example, by not having the pieces multiply and spread to adjoining squares—chess, and all that goes with it, is constituted. Haugeland thinks nothing less will do for objectivity generally, and consequently that mundane and scientific objects are on a par with chess positions when it comes to the grounds of objectivity. Hence genuine intentionality is possible only where there is not only the possibility, but the reality, of this sort of commitment. Since something comparable to human intelligence seems to be required for this sort of responsibility-taking—at least in many cases that we often think about—it seems to follow that animal and machine intentionality is ersatz.

Once ersatz intentionality is distinguished and characterized, however, it becomes apparent that there are candidates for it besides GOFAI robots. In particular, I want to suggest that (as far as we know) the intentionality of animals is entirely ersatz (except for purely tropistic creatures, whose intentionality is at best 'as-if'). That is, we can understand animals as having intentional states, but only relative to standards that *we* establish for them.   (Haugeland 1992: 303)[7]

---

[6] Compare this passage from Alston (1964: 41–2).

If we set out to analyze the concept of a serve in tennis, the problems we encounter will be very similar to those we have just discussed [in connection with the analysis of the illocutionary act of requesting someone to close the door]. To serve is not just to make certain physical movements, even given certain external circumstances. (I can be standing at the baseline of a tennis court, swinging a racket so that it makes contact with a ball in such a way as to propel it into the diagonally opposite forecourt, without it being the case that I am serving. I may just be practicing.) Nor are any specific effects required. A shot can have widely varying effects—it can inspire one's opponent with fear, despair, exultation, contempt, or boredom; these variations, however do not keep it from being true that one was serving in all these cases. Then what does change when, after a few practice shots, I call to my opponent, 'All right, this is it,' and then proceed to serve? The new element in the situation, I suggest, is my readiness to countenance certain sorts of complaints, for example, that I stepped on the baseline, hit the ball when my opponent was not ready, or was standing on the wrong side of the court. I take responsibility for the holding of certain conditions, for example, that neither foot touches the ground in front of the baseline before the racket touches the ball.

[7] I think Haugeland underestimates the capacities of social animals, especially those living in a dominance hierarchy, to take responsibility for the satisfaction of social norms. See D. D. Cummins (2000) and the papers referenced there.

It is tempting to agree with Haugeland that nothing less than this will do for the objectivity of knight forks. Knight forks, after all, are, well, pretty conventional objects. So it is not too surprising that they can exist only on the supposition that the conventions are somehow kept in force. And what could keep them in force other than the commitments of the players of the game? But surely you have to have illegal concentrations of transcendental philosophy in your veins to think nothing less will do for sticks and stones, conspecifics, smiles, and threats.

But this is unfair to Haugeland's position. Chess has to be playable, and this requires, to repeat, that the pieces do not multiply, that they do not move (in the chess sense) unless moved, etc., and these are not matters of convention. To give a very crude summary of a subtle and nuanced position, physics and chess differ in the extent to which the constitutive standards are matters of convention, but not at all in the grounds of *objectivity*, which have to do with a commitment to seeing that the standards are satisfied, not with their conventionality or lack of it.

And yet, surely this position vastly over-intellectualizes what it takes to have targets. And targets are all that objectivity requires, hence all that a theory of intentionality needs to accommodate. Targets are grounded in representational functions, and representational functions do not in general require either conceptual machinery or standard-grounding commitments. From this point of view, it seems it ought to be possible to see knight forks as such without having a clue about chess, and hence without being in a position to take responsibility for the satisfaction of its constitutive rules and conditions. It is tempting to give Haugeland knight forks, and hold out for stones, but I don't think this will do.

If target fixation is what I think it is, then, like Haugeland, I am committed to knight forks and stones being in the same boat. It is just that my boat is little more than a fleet of floating logs, while his is, well, the *Titanic*.

9.5. Functions Again

To make this contention stick, I need to show how an organism could have knight forks as targets on the cheap, as it were. To do that, I need to explain how it is possible for a relatively cheap intender to have as one of its functions the representation of knight forks. Haugeland points out that perceiving knight forks is a pretty abstract capacity.

These complementary considerations, that chess can be played in widely different media, and that widely different games can be played in the same media, together with the fact that knight forks can occur (and be perceived) in all the former but none of the latter, show that the ability to perceive knight forks presupposes some grasp or understanding of the game of chess—at least enough to tell when it's being played, regardless of medium.   (Haugeland 1996: 248)

What I find interesting about this passage, and the argumentation that turns on it, is the idea that what you do doesn't count as perceiving knight forks *unless you can do it all*, that is, recognize them in various media, and distinguish them from schnight forks (configurations that look like knight forks but are part of schness, not chess) in the usual media. But this conflates two very distinct issues:

1. How good is the system at recognizing knight forks?
2. Are knight forks among its targets, that is, are some of its representational efforts to be assessed for accuracy against knight forks?

I can, for example, be arbitrarily bad at recognizing colors (I am color blind), and yet have the color of the vegetable in my hand as a representational target. I won't hit it reliably, but it does not follow from this that it isn't my target. In order to understand error in learning, you don't want to think that your targets somehow depend on what you can hit.

Similarly, I can have the shape of the currently foveated thing as a target even though I always get it wrong to some degree (if, for example, I suffer from astigmatism). The mere fact that a dog or pigeon or novice human will be reliably fooled by schnight forks, and fail to see knight forks in esoteric media, is beside the point. You cannot, in general, argue that having T as a perceptual target is expensive because perception of Ts is expensive. Predator recognition systems tolerate a lot of false positives in the interest of speed. But when a prairie dog dives into its hole in response to a shadow made by a child's kite, this is a *false* positive, a mistaken predator identification, not an accurate shadow detection. This is not a point about the content of the animal's representations, which may not distinguish between shadows and predators, but a point about their targets. To understand what is going on, it is crucial to grasp that the targets are predators. Without this, you cannot even articulate the point about trading accuracy for speed.

9.6. Representation and intentionality

In general, you are going to vastly underestimate the representational (and other) functions a system can have if you do not maintain a principled distinction between representational accuracy on the one hand, and perceptual, cognitive, or behavioral success on the other. This distinction is precisely what grounds explanations in terms of trade-offs between accuracy on the one hand, and speed and tractability on the other. I think Haugeland misses this point when he writes:

> But there is another important distinction that biological norms do not enable. That is the distinction between functioning properly (under the proper conditions) as an information carrier and getting things right (objective correctness or truth), or, equivalently, between malfunctioning and getting things wrong (mistaking them). Since there is no *other* determinant or constraint on the information carried than whatever properly functioning carriers carry, when there is no malfunction, it's as 'right' as it can be. In other words, there can be no biological basis for understanding a system as functioning properly, but nevertheless misinforming—functionally right but factually wrong, so to speak.   (Haugeland 1998: 309–10)

Biological norms *do* enable this distinction, because it can be crucial to understanding the biological role of an intender to see that it is accuracy with respect to Ts that must be measured to judge its adaptiveness, even though it seldom or never gets Ts completely right.

If you miss this point, or just don't agree with it, then, like Haugeland, you will be forced to look elsewhere to find the resources to ground objectivity. You will be tempted to deal with my astigmatism and color blindness, either by claiming that I don't see colors or shapes (implausible), or by pointing out that I will take responsibility for corrections aimed at bringing my percepts (or, if that is not possible, my beliefs) into line with independently accessed color and shape information. Since prairie dogs don't take responsibility for their false predator recognitions, you will conclude that they don't see predators.

On the other hand, if you are on a budget and in the market for esoteric perceptual targets, here is how to get weak king-side defenses cheap. Imagine someone who is trying to learn to recognize them. They start with some crude criteria that don't work very well. Still, the function of those criteria is to enable recognition of a weak king-side defense. This is their function because the trajectory of the learning is tracked by the difference between the student's guesses and the actual weakness of the king-side defenses in the training set. The student needn't even be conscious of this. Indeed, it may well be that teachers who treat this as like a chicken-sexer case will have better success than their more cognitively explicit competitors.

Whether or not such learning could be successful, leading to reasonably reliable discrimination from foils in a variety of media is beside the point. What matters is that the relevant error is the gap between student guesses and weak king-side defenses. Nor need the students be committed to keeping the rules in force. For one thing, they may be spectators, not participants. More importantly, however, it isn't their commitments that count. They may be committed to anything you like, or nothing at all, provided only that it is differences between their guesses and the weakness of king-side defenses that must be compared to track the learning.[8]

If we are not careful, this talk of what *we* must do to track learning will make it look as if I have tried to pass off some ersatz intentionality for the real thing. Not so. It is the gap between weak king-side defenses and the student's guesses that drives the learning, whether or not anyone realizes this. It isn't that we make the learning intelligible by establishing this standard. It is rather that the learning becomes intelligible when we realize what the operative standard has been all along. The only reason to resist this point is the mistake about functions scouted above, the mistake rooted in the failure to distinguish representational accuracy from perceptual (cognitive, behavioral, reproductive) success.

Perhaps Haugeland thinks that *that* distinction, if viable at all, is a matter of *us* establishing standards for *them*, so that the functions in question are themselves ersatz functions. But I don't think it is. There is a subtle relationship between the accuracy of a representation and the success of its

---

[8] I don't mean to suggest that tracking learning trajectories is always the issue. I doubt that prairie dog predator recognition is learned at all. But thinking about learning highlights the difficulty because it is in the nature of the case that the target one is trying to learn to see (recognize, identify) is, in the early stages, beyond one's abilities. The novice learning about knight forks, and even some experts some of the time, will be stymied by non-standard media and fooled by schnight forks, as will a dog or a pigeon. All three may do quite well with the standard cases. And they may never get any better. The training may be discontinued, or the student inept. But the fact that acquiring the 'full ability' may be beyond certain non-human animals, and beyond certain humans, for that matter, is beside the point. Having a target doesn't require being able to hit it.

consumers. Once we see that accuracy can be sacrificed for speed or tractability in order to improve consumer performance, we will no longer be tempted to say, with Haugeland, that biological norms cannot enforce a distinction between success and accuracy.

9.7. Representational content

There is no free lunch, especially on a fleet of logs. The distinction I have been urging between representational accuracy and consumer success will collapse if you have a use theory of representational content. I said above that use theories of target fixation are not only acceptable, but inevitable. I also said that, to the extent that representational content is not distinguished from intentional content, use theories of representational content will seem inevitable. Use theories of representational content seem inevitable to almost everyone anyway. What could possibly endow a representation with a content that is completely independent of how that representation is used? And why should we care about such contents? These are large questions, and I will not address them here. But I do want to explain why use theories of representational content threaten to collapse the distinction between representational accuracy and consumer success. If I am right about this, then everyone who assumes a use theory of representational content should follow Haugeland in thinking that genuine intentional content is rare and expensive, rather than following me in thinking it is as common as dirt.

Use theories can be understood as applications of the following strategy:

1. Begin by noting that the content of R is whatever it is applied to in cases of correct application.
2. Provide a naturalistic—that is, non-question-begging—specification N of a class of applications that can be presumed to be accurate.
3. Identify the content of R with whatever it is applied to (its target) when N is satisfied.

The trick is in supplying the non-question-begging specification of a class of applications of R that can be presumed to be accurate. Use theories require that there be a sort of non-semantic natural kind of cases in which R is bound to be accurately applied to T. After the fact—with the definition in place—these will be cases in which application of R to T is accurate by definition.[9]

But: there *are* no non-question-begging conditions that guarantee accuracy. The best one can do is to require success or effectiveness. These are normative notions, but not semantic ones. So, for example, you get the suggestion that the content-fixing cases are those in which the producer of the representation and its consumers behave in the ways that account, historically, for their being selected (Millikan 1984). This fails because, to get selection, what you need is more effective representation than your competition, and this might require less accuracy, not more. Turning this point around, we can see that the account will work only if it is sometimes ok to collapse accuracy and effectiveness. So that is how use theories undermine the accuracy/effectiveness distinction.

Do all use theories do this? I think so, but I haven't the space to argue it here (see *RTA*). What about Haugeland's theory of representational content? Does it do this?

Haugeland doesn't explicitly endorse any theory of representational content. His concern is with intentionality and objectivity. He certainly seems to endorse holism about representational content, but this is difficult to pin down because the distinction I make between representational and intentional content is not in the forefront of his writing. Still, I will risk being irrelevant and ask whether holism about representational content is likely to grease (or clear) the path to Haugeland's position on intentionality.

Holism about representational content is essentially the idea that a representation gets its content from its role in a theory-like cognitive structure. It is, in short, conceptual role semantics, the idea that a representation's content is determined by the set of epistemic liaisons it enables.[10] The theory T in which a representation R figures determines what R will be applied to. False theories, of course, will not determine accurate applications of R. But we cannot, without circularity, require that R applies to—is true

---

[9] This is why all use theories give you some version of the analytic—synthetic distinction.

[10] The term 'epistemic liaisons' is Fodor's (1990*a*). It is important to realize that representations do not, by themselves, have epistemic liaisons. An attitude—an *application* of a representation in some particular cognitive role such as belief, desire, or intention—can be justified or rational in the light of others, but a representation cannot. So representations link to epistemic liaisons only via the attitudes they make possible. (See *RTA* 29 ff. for a full discussion.) I am going to slur over this in what follows because I can't see that it makes any difference.

of—those things a *true* host theory determines it will be applied to. So, what conditions *should* we place on T?

Notice that this is just the crux of every use theory, namely, specifying non-question-begging conditions under which content-fixing applications can be assumed accurate. What are the options here? If we say that every application licensed by the theory is content-fixing, we leave no room for error at all (Perlman 2000). Or rather, since the theory may license application of R to T yet be mismanaged or improperly deployed in some way, the only error allowed is whatever lives in the gap between well-managed and ill-managed theory.

But misrepresentation should not be confused with improper deployment on the part of the using system, nor bad luck in the results. These can diverge in virtue of the fundamental holism underlying what can count as a representation at all: the scheme must be such that, properly produced and used, its representations will, under normal conditions, guide the system successfully, on the whole. In case conditions are, in one way or another, not normal, however, then a representing system can misrepresent without in any way malfunctioning.

(Haugeland 1991: 173)

Well, what is proper deployment? Not deployment that licenses accurate applications, for this returns us in a circle again. It is rather something like this: all the inferences and calculations are done right. 'Done right' threatens circularity again. The only way out is to say something like this: *done right* means (*a*) done as they were designed to be done, which leads back to Millikan or Descartes's God; or (*b*) done *effectively*, that is, done in a way that leads to cognitive, behavioral, or reproductive success.

I think it is safe to conclude that there is no way to carry out step two of the use theory schema above without assimilating accuracy to effectiveness. I don't claim that Haugeland has done this; only that whatever pressures there are for use theories generally, and for holistic conceptual role theories in particular, are pressures to assimilate accuracy to effectiveness, hence to underestimate representational functions and overprice target fixation and intentional content. I don't think there is much pressure for holism about representational content once it is distinguished from intentional content. But there *are* pressures for use theories of content if you think that representations are structurally arbitrary in the way that words are, that is, that any structure of formatives could, in a suitable context, represent just about anything.[11] If representations are like words in this respect, what could fix their content other than use? My own view is that this is a good reason to reject the idea that representations are structurally arbitrary, but that is another story.

References

Alston, W., *Philosophy of Language* (Englewood Cliffs, NJ: Prentice Hall, 1964).

Cummins, D. D., 'How the Social Environment Shaped the Evolution of Mind', *Synthese,* 122 (2000), 3–28.

Cummins, R., *Representations, Targets, and Attitudes* (Cambridge, Mass.: MIT Press, 1996a).

—— 'Reply to Millikan', *Philosophy and Phenomenological Research*, 60 (2000b), 113–28.

—— Blackmon, J., Byrd, D., Lee, A., May, C., and Roth, M., 'Representation and Unexploited Content', in G. McDonald and D. Papineau (eds.), *Teleosemantics* (New York: Oxford University Press, 2006).

Davidson, D., 'Truth and Meaning', *Synthese*, 17 (1967), 304–23.

Fodor, J., *A Theory of Content and Other Essays* (Cambridge, Mass.: MIT Press, 1990a).

Haugeland, J., 'Representational Genera', in W. Ramsey, S. Stich, and D. Rumelhart (eds.), *Philosophy and Connectionist Theory* (Hillsdale, NJ: Lawrence Erlbaum, 1991).

—— 'Understanding Dennett and Searle', in A. Revonsuo and M. Kamppinen (eds.), *Consciousness in Philosophy and Cognitive Neuroscience* (Hillsdale, NJ: Lawrence Erlbaum, 1992).

—— 'Objective Perception', in K. Akins (ed.), *Perception: Vancouver Studies in Cognitive Science*, v (New York: Oxford University Press, 1996).

—— *Having Thought* (Cambridge, Mass.: Harvard University Press, 1998).

Millikan, R., *Language, Thought, and Other Biological Categories* (Cambridge, Mass.: MIT Press/Bradford Books, 1984).

Perlman, M., *Conceptual Flux: Mental Representation, Misrepresentation, and Concept Change* (New York: Springer, 2000).

Sejnowski, T., and Rosenberg, C., 'Parallel Networks that Learn to Pronounce English Text', *Complex Systems*, 1 (1987a), 145–68.

---

[11] There are some hints of this in Haugeland (1991). He clearly thinks that representational content is scheme-relative, and this suggests that a token with a given set of intrinsic structural properties could have arbitrarily different contents in different schemes.

10

Truth and Meaning

10.1. Introduction

Donald Davidson's 'Truth and Meaning,' revolutionized our conception of how truth and meaning are related (Davidson 1967). In that famous article, Davidson put forward the bold conjecture that meanings are satisfaction conditions, and that a Tarskian theory of truth for a language is a theory of meaning for that language. In 'Truth and Meaning,' Davidson proposed only that a Tarskian truth theory is a theory of meaning. But in 'Theories of Meaning and Learnable Languages,' he argued that the finite base of a Tarskian theory, together with the now familiar combinatorics, would explain how a language with unbounded expressive capacity could be learned with finite means (Davidson 1965). This certainly seems to imply that learning a language is, in part at least, learning a Tarskian truth theory for it, or, at least, learning what is specified by such a theory. Davidson was cagey about committing to the view that meanings actually *are* satisfaction conditions, but subsequent followers had no such scruples.

We can sum this up in a trio of claims:

(1) A theory of meaning for L is a truth-conditional semantics for L.
(2) To know the meaning of an expression in L is to know a satisfaction condition for that expression.
(3) Meanings are satisfaction conditions.

For the most part, it will not matter in what follows which of these claims is at stake. I will simply take the three to be different ways of formulating what I will call Davidson's Conjecture (or sometimes just The Conjecture).

Originally published in Joseph Keim-Campbell, Michael O'Rourke, and David Shier (eds.), *Meaning and Truth: Investigtions in Philosophical Semantics* (Seven Bridges Press, 2002), 175–97.

Davidson's Conjecture was a very bold conjecture. I think we are now in a position to see that it is probably false, but I do not expect many to agree with me about this. Since the publication of 'Truth and Meaning,' truth-conditional semantics has been pretty much all the semantics there is. In the current climate, therefore, it is something of a challenge to get philosophers of language to realize that The Conjecture is not obviously *true*. Generations of philosophers have been trained to regard The Conjecture as a truism. What else could semantics be? Surely, to understand an expression, one must know the conditions under which it is satisfied!

Prior to Davidson, semantics, at least in philosophy, was speech act theory: Austin, Grice, and their followers (Grice 1957; Austin 1962). That tradition either died, or was co-opted. Here is how the co-option went. The Gricean program, in the hands of Lewis (1969), Bennett (1973, 1976), Bach and Harnish (1979), Shiffer (1981, 1982), and their followers, reduces linguistic meaning to intentional psychology—i.e. to propositional attitudes. Fodor (1975), Schiffer (1981), and others then introduced what I call the representational theory of intentionality (RTI hereafter): the idea that an intentional attitude is a mental representation in a cognitive role—for example, a belief is realized as a sentence in Mentalese available as a premise in inference but not as a goal specification. So, meaning for public language reduces to the attitudes, and the attitudes reduce to cognitive psychology and a theory of mental representation. A theory of mental representation, in this tradition, is, in Fodor's words, supposed to tell us where truth conditions come from (Fodor 1987, 1990b). And that brings us back to Davidson's Conjecture. Meanings for Mentalese are to be given by a truth-conditional semantics, and the content of a propositional attitude is just the truth condition of its associated mental representation. Meanings for a natural language, then, are specified finally in terms of the truth conditions of the Mentalese constituents of the attitudes involved in linguistic communication.[1] Thus Gricean speech act theory ultimately rests on truth-conditional semantics. The substantive content of Speech Act Theory was relegated to 'pragmatics'—the business of distinguishing promises from threats, and specifying the contextual factors involved in determining truth conditions.

---

[1] There is a missing step here: Gricean stories provide only propositional contents, hence provide meanings for nothing smaller than a sentence. The Tarskian combinatorics, however, require satisfaction conditions for terms. See Cummins (1979) for a proposal about how to get the Tarskian combinatorics into a Gricean picture.

Of course, you do not need to be a Grician about meaning to get to this point. All you really need is the view that understanding[2] an expression *E* in a language *L* requires a mental state—either a representation or an intentional attitude—that has the same content as *E*. This reduces the theory of meaning and understanding the expressions of a language—the semantics anyway—to the theory of mental content. You then assume that a theory of mental content assigns truth/satisfaction conditions to mental states, either directly, or via the RTI. And that brings you back to Davidson's Conjecture.

So the philosophy of language turned into truth-conditional semantics, and the philosophy of mind labored to explain how mental representations could come to have the satisfaction conditions required. Thus it is that 'Truth and Meaning' set the agenda for the philosophy of language and the philosophy of mind, linking the two tightly together in the process.

The link is more important that it might first appear. Once you have a Davidsonian story about the semantics of natural language, it is nearly irresistible to conclude that intentional states or mental representations (or both) must have a truth-conditional semantics as well. How else could we hope to get a grip on how it is possible to mean and understand the expressions of a language? If the meanings of linguistic expressions are satisfaction conditions, and someone knows the meanings of those expressions, then surely they know satisfaction conditions for those expressions. The knowledge is tacit, of course, but can be tapped by suitable queries about what is 'intuitively' true under some specified set of hypothetical or actual circumstances. This is how we get the conclusion that mental representation must be 'classical' (Fodor and Pylyshyn 1988; Fodor and McLaughlin 1990*c*). It is worth setting this out explicitly.

- Davidson's Conjecture: the meaning of a linguistic expression is a satisfaction condition for it.

---

[2] I am going to use 'understanding' as short hand for 'meaning and understanding' or 'using and understanding.' The idea is to have a single word for whatever you need to be either party—speaker or hearer—in successful linguistic communication. Passive mastery and active mastery of language differ, with the former outrunning the latter, especially in young children, and this suggests that there is more to speaking the language than there is to understanding it. Still, you have to understand it to speak it, and it is at least plausible that whatever you have to add to understanding (passive mastery) to get active mastery, it isn't more *semantics*.

- To understand a linguistic expression that means M, you must be able to token a mental representation that means M. (For example, to have the thought that p you must be able to token a mental representation that means that p.)
- Hence, mental representations must have a truth-conditional semantics, i.e. they must be 'classical.'

This inference from The Conjecture to the nature of mental content carries a price.[3] To see what it is, we need to begin with a basic constraint on any theory of linguistic meaning.

> *Communicative Constraint*: the meaning of a natural language expression is whatever it is you have to know to understand that expression.

What I have just called the communicative constraint on linguistic meaning says, in effect, that linguistic meanings are whatever it is that have to be grasped or possessed for linguistic communication to be successful. Ultimately, a theory of meaning for natural language must dovetail with the psychology of linguistic communication.[4]

We can now see why the inference from Davidson's Conjecture to the nature of mental representation could be pricey. There are good reasons to think that the mental structures required for language understanding do not have a truth-conditional semantics. It is going to be the burden of this chapter to argue this point. If you accept the point, and you accept the Communicative Constraint on linguistic meaning, you will think that a theory of language understanding will make no use of truth-conditional semantics. It doesn't follow from this that natural languages don't *have* a truth-conditional semantics. But it does follow that there is no good reason to think that a truth-conditional semantics for natural language will have any place in a mature psycholinguistics.

So here is the bottom line: I think that Davidson's Conjecture is a mistake. I think that truth has little to do with meaning. Or rather, so that

---

[3] It ought to be darkly suspicious, too, since it is a license to do experimental cognitive psychology from the armchair. We begin by asking after the truth conditions of propositional attitude sentences, and wind up with conclusions about the structure and contents of psychological states. For more on this theme, see Cummins (1991a).

[4] This need not be the case for artificial languages, I suppose, since these need not be primarily in the communication business. They may be primarily in the business of expressing truths, and rely for whatever communicative efficacy they have on their connections with natural languages.

we won't simply slide into arguing over the word, I think that truth has little to do with speaking and understanding a language.

10.2. Communicative vs. referential meaning

Let's begin with some terminology. By the *communicative meaning* of a term in a language I mean whatever you have to have in your head to understand it.[5] By the *truth-conditional meaning* of a term in a language I mean its satisfaction condition, or its role in generating one in the pragmatic context of some particular production of it. We can now express the central question thus:

- Are communicative meanings truth–conditional meanings?

OK. So what do you have to have in your head to understand, say, 'elevator'? Well, you have to have a more or less adequate concept of an elevator. But this just names the problem. What do you have to have in your head to have a concept of elevators? I think it is pretty clear that what you need is some basic knowledge of elevators. If you ask someone what 'elevator' means, they will tell you what an elevator *is*. They might, if they are very forthcoming and articulate, say something like this:

> Imagine a little room like a closet that moves up and down in a vertical shaft in a building. You get in on one floor, and the thing moves up or down to other floors where you can get off. Faster and easier than stairs. I think it is done with pulleys. Modern ones are controlled with buttons inside, and you can summon it with a button by the door leading to it on any floor.

And they draw a diagram (see Figure 10.1).

This much, I think, would be plenty in ordinary life or a psychology experiment to demonstrate that the 'subject' has the (or a) concept of an elevator. And it would be enough precisely because it would demonstrate basic knowledge of elevators. So it seems clear that one can be said to have concepts in virtue of having a basic knowledge of their instances. If you

[5] For the picky: of course, you need to be awake, and to be smarter than a post. What we want is what you have to add to the mind to enable understanding of some particular expression not previously understood.

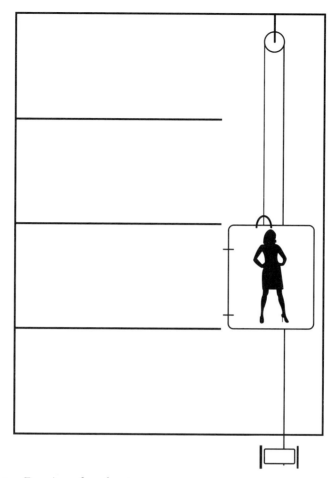

Figure 10.1 Drawing of an elevator

know what an elevator is, you have the concept of an elevator. Moreover, if you ask someone what 'elevator' means, the same answer will do the trick. If, in answer to the question, 'What does the word 'elevator' mean?' they demonstrate possession of a 'pretty good' concept of an elevator, then they know what 'elevator' means.

All of this knowledge one has that comes into play in connection with elevators is not just about elevators, of course. It is also about buildings and pulleys, for example. But the *topic* of the knowledge that one accesses when, as we say, one applies the concept of an elevator, is: *elevators*. Similarly, one can have an entire book about elevators. That book will also be about lots of other things, but the topic is elevators. I have no general analysis of what it is that determines the topic of a book or a body of knowledge. I don't think it is a very tight notion. Psychologically, the knowledge that gets accessed when a certain concept comes into play will vary from occasion to occasion and from person to person. My knowledge differs from yours, and my own is constantly changing. Moreover, which parts or aspects of my knowledge of a particular topic I happen to access on a given occasion will depend on the cues and on prior activation. But, given a reasonable amount of shared knowledge and stability over time, we can expect, in ordinary cases, a large overlap of core knowledge across persons and (reasonable) times.

On this view of things, the concept of a horse, and hence the communicative meaning of the word 'horse,' is not a mental representation the reference of which is horses or the property of being a horse. It is, rather, a body of knowledge loosely identified by its topic. Just as a book about horses has horses as its topic, but not its referent, so a concept of horses has horses or the property of being a horse as its topic rather than its referent. With some trepidation, I'm going to sum this up by saying that a concept (of horses, say) is a *theory* (of horses), the idea being that theories are organized bodies of knowledge that we identify in much the way we identify concepts—viz., by specifying a topic. One can have a theory of motion or a concept of motion; one can have a theory of pain or a concept of pain; one can have a theory of success or a concept of success. Theories, like concepts, are identified by their topics, not by their referents.[6] And they are, at least on the hoof, blessed with fuzzy boundaries that overlap other theories identified by other topics. Indeed, the identification of theories by topic, while useful, is a kind of heuristic in just the way I think the standard identification of concepts is a heuristic: it points you in the right direction if you want to look it up, but not much more.[7]

---

[6] I'm not sure what the referent of a theory would be. If you thought a theory was a set of sentences, which I do not, then, perhaps, the referent of a theory would be a proposition, viz., the proposition expressed by a conjunction of sentences used to express the theory.

[7] Psychologists, of course, have suggested a number of theories about the form our concepts take. (The classic review is Smith and Medin 1981. For a recent review of the literature, see Gelman 1996.) They all have in common, however, the idea that a concept of X is stored knowledge about X that mediates recognition of and reasoning about Xs. The dispute is over how that knowledge is stored and deployed, e.g. as a prototype or exemplar that is compared to instances in recognition and used to generate premises in inference, or as a frame, script, or semantic net. What you do *not* find in the psychological literature is the idea that concepts are terms in Mentalese that are satisfied by the instances of the concept in question. You do not find this because it wouldn't work, as we will see.

Concepts, conceived as (perhaps tacit) theories, are pretty clearly what you need to have in your head to understand terms such as 'elevator' and 'brown' and 'horse' and 'galloping'. They are also just what you need, along with the relevant sensory apparatus, to recognize elevators, horses, brown, and the gallop. And they are what you need to reason about such things. All of this is as it should be, since, when someone tells you not to ride the brown horse as he is likely to gallop, you don't want to avoid riding elevators. An immediate consequence of this view of concepts, and hence of communicative meanings, however, is the following:

> Concepts do not semantically combine in the way required by truth-conditional semantics.

The standard Tarskian combinatorics (Tarski 1956) suggests a mechanical process for combining a Mentalese term for being striped with a Mentalese term for being a fish, a process that yields a complex Mentalese term for being a striped fish. But no Tarskian process will semantically combine a theory of stripes with a theory of fish to yield a theory of striped fish. Even more obviously, the denial of a theory of fish is not a representation applying to all nonfish in the way that the denial of a Mentalese term for fish is (or would be if there were such a thing), precisely, a term applying to the nonfish. Tarskian combinatorics are hopeless in connection with the sorts of psychological structures concepts must be to do their jobs.

This is an instance of a widespread problem. The kinds of mental representations that are subject to Tarskian semantics are what Fodor and Pylyshyn (1988) call 'classical' representations: language-like concatenations of arbitrary primitive symbols whose syntactic rules of formation are directly exploitable by truth-conditional combinatorics. No one would dream of trying to exploit Tarskian truth-theory to cope with the semantic complexity and productivity of pictures, maps, graphs, or activation vectors. It only works for language-like schemes. Yet there is little reason to think that classical, language-like schemes have any real representational virtues. This is because there are basically just three ways that arbitrary mental symbols of the Language of Thought variety can enter into cognitive explanations: As *triggers* for procedures, as *cues* for stored knowledge, and as *constituents* of complex representations.

The point can be brought out by a simple example. You are asked to go milk the cow. You make a plan to carry out this request. Among your early subgoals is the subgoal to find the cow. You decide to look in the barn.

When you get to the barn, you walk around inside looking for the cow. You look in a stall, and token a |cow|—a mental symbol that refers to cows. But just how did this cow recognition work? To recognize cows, you need to know something about them. You need, at least, to know how they look. A mental symbol does not contain any information about how cows look, and so it is not what psychologists would call a concept. You need to deploy your knowledge of cows in order to recognize a cow. It is your knowledge of cows, including tacit knowledge about the sort of retinal projections they tend to produce, that makes it possible for you to token a |cow| when you encounter a cow. So the Mentalese |cow| did no work for the object recognition system, it just signaled its output.

But that is not all. Having tokened a |cow|, where do you stand in the great scheme of things? The |cow| tokening *triggers* the next step in the plan. Now that you have located the cow and are on the spot, you need to locate the udder. Here, something like a picture of a cow, an image, say, would be very helpful, whereas a mental word is totally useless unless it happens to function as a retrieval *cue* for some stored knowledge about cows. Faced with actually having to deal with a cow, the burden therefore shifts again from the symbol to your stored knowledge, because the symbol, being arbitrary, tells you nothing about cows. So it turns out that it is not because you have a Mentalese term for cows that you get the milking done, it is because you have a route—activated by a cue—to something else, some stored knowledge about cows. Mentalese |cow|s could play a role in stored knowledge about cows only as pointers to it, or as constituents of complex representations—|cows have udders between their back legs|, for example—that are, on the Mentalese story, implicated in the possession of stored knowledge about cows.

I do not think this should come as any real surprise to LOTers, for I think the view is widespread among them that it is really stored knowledge that does the explanatory work anyway. But it is worth emphasizing that there is a big difference between appealing to the fact that one has a primitive mental symbol referring to cows, and appealing to the fact that one has a lot of knowledge about cows. LOT commits one to the view that representations of cows don't tell you anything about cows.

Perhaps it is not so bad that LOT entails that the representations that are satisfied by cows have only an indirect role in the explanation of cow cognition, for there are always mental sentences to tell us about cows. But let us just be clear about what LOT is committed to here: the view we have arrived at is that cognition is essentially the application of a linguistically expressed theory. All the serious work gets done by sets of sentences that are internal tacit theories (ITTs) about whatever objects of cognition there happen to be. As far as cognizing cows goes, your |cow|s really don't matter; it is your ITT of cows that does the work.

But, of course, ITTs are not subject to Tarskian combinatorics. Indeed, it is pretty obvious that no psychological structure can play the roles characteristic of both a Tarskian term and concept. Concepts, for example, subserve object recognition. A concept of a fish (a FISH) is what enables one to recognize fish. To recognize fish, you need to know something about fish—you need a theory of fish, in short. Having a Mentalese term is of no use at all; you have to learn to token that term in response to fish, and that is just what knowing something about fish allows you to do, and what you cannot hope to do if you don't know anything about fish. Similarly, to understand the word 'fish,' you need to know something about fish. Having a mental term, by itself, would be no help at all, since having a mental term referring to something is not the same thing as knowing anything about it. You cannot understand 'fish' if you do not have a FISH, and your understanding of 'fish' is exactly as good as your FISH.

Mental terms in a language of thought, if there is such a thing, have satisfaction conditions: something counts as a |fish| just in case it is satisfied by fish. Consequently, mental terms in a LOT would be subject to semantic combination: you can combine a |striped| and a |fish| and get a |striped fish|. But having a |fish| at your disposal does not, by itself, endow you with any knowledge of fish, and hence does not enable you to recognize fish, or understand the word, or reason about fish. Expressions in a LOT might have the same truth-conditional meanings as the expressions of a natural language, but activating (tokening) a LOT expression that is truth-conditionally equivalent to an expression in a natural language could not possibly constitute *understanding* that natural language expression. To repeat, the story has to be that the Mentalese terms cue the corresponding theories.

10.3. Mental merging

I have been urging that communicative meanings are rather like theories. Since theories are not candidates for relevant sort of Tarskian combinatorics, it follows that a Tarskian truth theory cannot be a theory of communicative meaning. As I pointed out earlier, this does not refute Davidson's Conjecture, but it strips Davidson's Conjecture of most of its relevance to cognitive science. Even if a natural language could be fitted with a truth-conditional semantics, that would not help explain how it is learned or understood. Since natural language is a biological adaptation whose function is enabling communication—a fact philosophers of language sometimes forget and almost always neglect—the interest in such a semantics would be largely or completely orthogonal to the problem of understanding how we understand a language.

But if concepts do not have a Tarskian semantics, how do we combine our understanding of 'brown' and 'horse' to get an understanding of 'brown horse'? Theories do not simply merge, and the denial of a theory of horses is not a theory of nonhorses. Davidson's Conjecture, and its implications for language understanding, gave us a story to tell about how our understanding of complex expressions could be constructed from our understanding of their constituents. What shall we put in its place?

This problem would need facing even if you believed in a language of thought with a truth-conditional semantics. For suppose you have uttered, 'The man holding the brown shoe is my brother,' and my language understanding system has constructed a truth-condition for it. What it has, in effect, is a Mentalese translation of your sentence, containing Mentalese terms like |man|, |brown|, |shoe|, and |holding|. We can assume, for the sake of argument, that each of these activates the corresponding concepts, |man|s cuing MANs, |brown|s cuing BROWNs, and so on. But this is a far cry from having a conception of the state of affairs expressed by your sentence. How does one build up that conception from MANs, BROWNs, SHOEs, and so on, together with the truth-conditional combinatorics? Building a |brown shoe| form a |brown| and a |shoe| does not automatically give you a BROWN SHOE.

It is glaringly obvious, once the question is raised, that symbolically represented theories are not subject to Tarskian combinatorics. Truth-conditional combinatorics, therefore, allows you to explain how the truth-conditional meaning for a complex expression can be built up from the truth-conditional meanings of its components and its syntax, but it leaves untouched how the communicative meanings of complex expressions could be built up from the communicative meanings of their components. A truth condition for a complex expression provides no clue as to how one might build up the conception of the situation that expression so readily conveys to the mind of a mature speaker. We are thus led to ask whether there is some other way of representing the relevant knowledge—some nonlinguistic way of representing the knowledge involved in BROWNs and SHOEs, for example—which does allow the kind of relatively straightforward concept-merging that real-time language understanding so obviously requires.

In connectionist networks, long-term knowledge is stored in the connection weights. Whatever such a system knows about shoes and brown resides somehow in the pattern of connectivity and the associated weights.[8] It is, in the present state of play, a mystery how we should 'read' a pattern of connection weights. No one knows how to take a verbally expressed body of knowledge and express it as a pattern of connection weights. Indeed, if John Haugeland is right, and I think he is, this is impossible (Haugeland 1990). According to Haugeland, different genera of representational schemes allow for the expression of characteristically different contents. Pictures and sentences are intertranslatable only in the very roughest way. We should expect the same for sentences and patterns of connection weights. However, this message of incommensurability between verbal and connectionist representation is a *hopeful* message in the present context, because we know that the problem facing us has no ready solution—perhaps no solution at all—in its verbal form: logically combining verbally expressed theories, to repeat, has no hope of giving us what we want. This, perhaps, is enough to justify a bit of wild speculation in spite of our ignorance of the semantics of weight matrices.

Think, then, of a weight matrix as an encoding (doubtless idiosyncratic) of a kind of know-how. It might be knowledge of how to retrieve an item from memory given a cue of some sort. This is what we have in the famous Jets and Sharks network of McClelland and Rumelhart (1988). Or it might be knowledge of how to pronounce English text, as in Sejnowski and Rosenberg's NETtalk. Know-how, it seems, is naturally captured in a weight matrix. Can we think of concepts as know-how? Certainly. To

---

[8] Mathematically, we could reduce this to weights alone, dealing with connectivity by setting the weights between disconnected nodes to zero. But it is more intuitive to think in terms of what is connected to what, and how those connections are weighted. This allows us to think of a number of more or less independent nets that are only sparsely connected to each other.

possess the concept of a shoe is, to a first approximation, to know how to recognize one, to know how they are worn, and, if one is a linguistic creature, to know how to describe one. Knowing how to describe a shoe is, of course, know-how like any other. In particular, we should not assume that knowing how to describe a shoe requires a sort of 'declarative memory,' where this is conceived as a stored Mentalese description. The stored-description account has many failings, not the least of which is that we do not always describe the same thing in the same way. We get a more realistic account if we imagine a network that generates descriptions as outputs, with the description generated depending on the details of the input and the current state of activation—*set*, as it used to be called in psychology. In a similar vein, having a conception of the color brown is being able to recognize it, being able to give instances of brown things, being able to relate brown to other colors (e.g. darker than yellow and lighter than black), and so on.

Can we assemble the connectionist know-how that goes with SHOE and the connectionist know-how that goes with BROWN into the know-how that goes with BROWN SHOE? Notice that this is not a question in semantics at all, but a question about the mechanics of network building. We need a design that exploits the presence of a BROWN network and a SHOE network and generates, on the fly, and temporarily, a structure that exhibits the kind of know-how characteristic of BROWN SHOE possession.

It must be confessed that we are nowhere near to understanding how this might be done. But we do, I think, have a pretty good beginning on how the problem should be posed.

We start with a brief consideration of representation in connectionist networks, beginning with simple three-layer feed forward cases. Following Paul Churchland (1998), consider a network that learns to discriminate hillbilly families in terms of facial resemblance. Figure 10.2 depicts a simplified version of such a network, with the activation space at the hidden layer contracted to allow three-dimensional illustration.

The points in the space are what Churchland calls prototype points. They are centers of gravity around which cluster the points corresponding to related family members. They are a revealing way to represent the way that training the network partitions up the relevant activation space. The geometry thus revealed will be remarkably constant across different networks

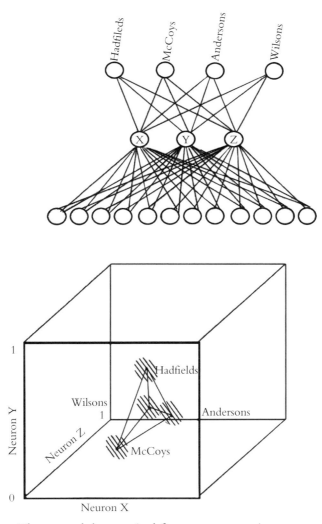

Figure 10.2 The network has acquired four prototype regions corresponding to facial family resemblance

trained to the same task, including ones with differing input codings and even ones with differently dimensioned hidden layers (Laasko and Cottrell 2000). We are thus led to the idea that there is an objective structure to the relevant face space, and that trained networks discover this and represent it via an isomorphic activation space. In such a space, it seems reasonable to think of the prototype points as something like individual concepts in a

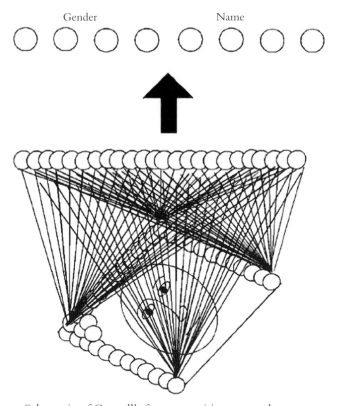

Figure 10.3 Schematic of Cottrell's face recognition network

conceptual space. This perspective becomes more compelling as the networks face more complex tasks. Cottrell's tiny face recognition network
(retina of 64 × 64 pixels; Figure 10.3) implicitly partitions its activation
space in such a way that female faces tend to be closer to each other than to
male faces and vice versa (Cottrell 1991).

Simple recurrent networks of the sort pictured in Figure 10.4 pose a
different case because they allow for dynamic representation. They are
probably best conceived in terms of paths in activation space rather than
points. This approach seems to work nicely for Elman's well-known grammar network, for example (Elman 1992).

Connectionist theory thus provides a compelling example of the kind of
representation by structural similarity that I recommended in *Representations,
Targets and Attitudes* (Cummins 1996a). It provides representations that
are structurally rich, representations that themselves guide cognition rather

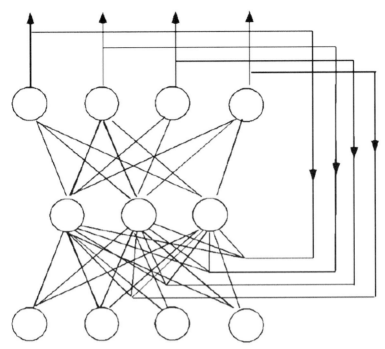

Figure 10.4 Simple recurrent network; projections from the output layer to the hidden layer give the network a kind of short-term memory of its immediate history

than function as mere indicators in detection. Unlike the representations posited by LOT theories, these representations are plausible candidates for concepts.

They are not, as yet however, plausible candidates for the sort of fleeting merges that seem to underlie language understanding. No cross-network associations between, for example, a color network and a shape network, will fill the bill here because, first, associations have to be learned, and, second, because they have to be unlearned to go away. A reference to yellow dogs early in your discourse makes it easier to understand talk of brown dogs later, not more difficult. There are powerful connectionist techniques for representing hierarchical bindings of the sort found in parse trees (Smolensky *et al.* 1992). It is tempting to suppose that vectors representing a parse could somehow be used to orchestrate the kind of conceptual liaisons we are after, but I think it is fair to say that no one currently knows how to do this.

10.4. The communicative function of language

A novel conception of the function of language emerges from the foregoing discussion. Davidson's Conjecture implies that language is a medium for the expression of propositions and their constituents. It serves its communicative function when the hearer figures out what proposition the speaker expressed (or perhaps which the proposition speaker intended to express). The approach I have been urging implies that language is primarily in the communication business, and only secondarily, if at all, in the expression business. Sentences, on this view, are like recipes for assembling chunks of know-how into a know-howish conception of the speaker's communicative intention, and of the situation as the speaker conceives it. Sentences, in effect, tell you how to cook up a thought, where the thoughts thus cooked up are as different from words as are the cakes and pies from the recipes that tell you how to cook *them* up.

Viewed this way, it is possible—indeed, likely—that language can be used to communicate things it cannot begin to express, something poets and good novelists have always known. You can begin to get a sense of this by looking at the provision that language makes for 'plug-ins.' A plug-in, as every web browser knows, is an independent routine that your browser can 'call' when needed, for example, to decompress a downloaded file. Language uses demonstratives to construct docking places for these devices, as illustrated in Figure 10.5.

Beethoven looked like this:

The opening of his 5th symphony sounds like this: <here one actually whistles>.

This guy is famous for this theme: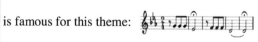

Figure 10.5 Linguistic expressions with plug-ins

In your head, though, it is *all* plug-ins, a fact that has, I think, been obscured by the exaptation of language, especially written language, for expressive purposes quite foreign to its original biological function of facilitating communication in the service of social coordination. The expressive power of language is impressive, but hardly universal. It is, I think, much better at communicating thoughts than it is at expressing them. Failure to notice the distinction has led to the view that the only thoughts that can be communicated are the ones that can be expressed. When we put this together with Davidson's Conjecture, we get the result that the only thoughts that can be communicated are those that have truth-conditional contents—propositions, in short. It is a short step from this position to the widespread view that the only thoughts we can have are the propositional attitudes, and hence that there is no thought or mental representation whose content language cannot adequately express. In our hearts we all know this is wrong, but recent philosophical tradition has taught us to live with it or suffer professional extinction.

It is nearly universally assumed that the communicative meanings of linguistic utterances are the same as their representational meanings. The idea goes like this: I have the thought that p that I wish to communicate to you. I construct a sentence that means (representationally) that p, and you decode it—i.e. you figure out what its representational meaning is, and conclude that that is what I meant to tell you. This story could be right. But it is important that we not just assume it. To see that it isn't inevitable, imagine a communicative system that works like this: there are instructions that tell you how to assemble nonlinguistic representations—pictures, say—from elements—pixels—you have available. In this system, the instructions and the messages communicated need have no meanings in common. Language *might* work like that. Sentences might be recipes for assembling thoughts, or even images, in the heads of others. If so, then the truth conditions of my sentences, if they have any, will tell us nothing about what I communicate. This is because I can communicate an accurate picture to you without saying anything true about the scene pictured. The truth-conditions of my sentences yield the limelight to the accuracy of the thoughts or other cognitive states they help to assemble.

To get a clearer view of the sort of possibility I have in mind here, consider the following communication system. You have a set of numbered storage bins. In these are little model houses, trees, ponds, lawns, roadways, signs, street lights, etc. You also have a table with a grid marked on it, with rows numbered and columns lettered. You get instructions like this:

- Put an item from bin 23 on 7A.
- Center an item from bin 14 on 8C.
- Put an item from bin 12 on 8D–8H.

The result will be a model village. You assemble this representation on the basis of instructions that are built from a vocabulary that is utterly incapable of expressing any of the things represented by the model. The signal system and the representations it helps to assemble are representationally disjoint.

This sort of example demonstrates the possibility of a communication system in which the meanings the communicative symbols communicate are not the meanings they have. Could this be true of natural language? We are, I think, already in a position to see that it very likely is true of natural language. The words 'house', 'tree', 'pond', and so on, do not express the knowledge that constitutes your understanding of houses, trees, and ponds. They are signals that activate that knowledge, bring it on line, and, somehow, orchestrate its assembly into a more or less unified conception.

10.5. Beyond the propositional attitudes

I used to think (Cummins 1996*a*) that nonlinguistic schemes could express propositions. For example, I thought we could take pictures to express propositions by following Stalnaker (1984) in thinking of a proposition as a set of possible worlds. Since a picture will 'hold' in some possible worlds and not others, it partitions the set of possible worlds, and hence expresses a proposition. I now think, however, that Haugeland (1990) was right: sentences and propositions were made for each other, and so we must look elsewhere for the contents of nonlinguistic propositions.

The striking thing about maps, diagrams, partitioned activations spaces, pictures, graphs, and other nonlinguistic representations is that they are not true or false, but more or less accurate. A sentence either hits its propositional target, or it fails. Nonpropositional representations, however, are better evaluated in terms of a graded notion of accuracy. Moreover, such representations are typically multidimensional. Pictures, for example, represent (relative) size, shape, color, and (relative) location simultaneously. The possibility thus arises that two pictures might be incomparable in overall accuracy, since one might do better on some dimensions—size and shape, say—while the other does better on others—color and location.[9] The concepts of truth and falsehood, and the Tarskian combinatorial semantics we have come to associate with them, will be no help at all in understanding how these nonpropositional representations fit or fail to fit their targets. Representational meaning for nonpropositional representations will have to be understood in different terms, as will their semantic structures.

A consequence of the graded and multidimensional nature of many nonlinguistic representations is that they do not partition up the set of possible worlds in any neat way. What we get instead is a kind of shading along a number of interdependent dimensions. Since I cannot think of a more catholic notion of propositions than the one Stalnaker endorses, I have to conclude that most, perhaps all, nonlinguistic representations do not express propositions and are not true or false.[10] But they evidently do represent. They represent how their targets are, with greater or less accuracy, along various dimensions. If we really want to understand meaning, we need to understand not only the representation of propositions, but the graded and multidimensional representation of nonpropositional contents as well. And if we want to understand the kind of meaning that is involved in mental representation, and hence in language understanding, we had best understand the kind of representation effected by the sort of dynamic partitioning of neuronal activation spaces that our synapses learn to effect. It would amaze me if truth-conditional semantics had anything significant to offer to this crucial research problem.

---

[9] It seems likely that high accuracy on one dimension will often have to be paid for in lower accuracy in others, given limited resources. The eye, for example, gains considerable resolution and color information via foveation, but loses light sensitivity in the process. A map that shows all the streets of London on one page will be either too big to use in the car, or be viewable only with magnification.

[10] Vagueness in language introduces problems that appear similar on the surface. Whether they are genuinely related to the kind of multidimensionality and gradedness we find in pictures, models, and graphs is not at all clear.

References

Alston, W., *Philosophy of Language* (Englewood Cliffs, NJ: Prentice Hall, 1964).

Austin, J. L., *How to Do Things with Words* (Oxford: Clarendon Press, 1962).

Bach, K., and Harnish, R. M., *Linguistic Communication and Speech Acts* (Cambridge, Mass.: MIT Press, 1979).

Bennett, J., *Linguistic Behavior* (Cambridge: Cambridge University Press, 1976).

—— 'The Meaning-Nominalist Strategy', *Foundations of Language*, 10 (1973), 141–68.

Churchland, P. M., 'Conceptual Similarity Across Sensory and Neural Diversity: The Fodor/LePore Challenge Answered', *Journal of Philosophy*, 95 (1998), 5–32.

Cottrell, G., 'Extracting Fratures from Faces Using Compression Networks: Face, Identity, Emotions and Gender Recognition Using Holons', in D. Touretsky, J. Elman, T. Sejnowski, and G. Hinton (eds.), *Connectionist Models: Proceedings of the 1990 Summer School* (San Mateo, Calif.: Morgan Kaufmann, 1991).

—— Metcalfe, J., 'EMPATH: Face, Emotion and Gender Recognition Using Holons', in R. Lippman, J. Moody, and D. Touretsky (eds.), *Advances in Neural Information Processing Systems*, iii (San Mateo, Calif.: Morgan Kaufmann, 1991).

Cummins, R., 'Intention, Meaning and Truth Conditions', *Philosophical Studies*, 35 (1979), 345–60.

—— 'Methodological Reflections on Belief', in R. Bogdan (ed.), *Mind and Common Sense* (Cambridge: Cambridge University Press, 1991*a*).

—— *Representations, Targets, and Attitudes* (Cambridge, Mass.: MIT Press, 1996*a*).

Davidson, D., 'Theories of Meaning and Learnable Languages', in Y. Bar-Hillel (ed.), *Proceedings of the 1964 International Congress for Logic, Methodology, and Philosophy of Science* (Amsterdam: North Holland, 1965).

—— 'Truth and Meaning', *Synthese*, 17 (1967), 304–23.

Elman, J., 'Grammatical Structure and Distributed Representations', in S. Davies (ed.), *Connectionism: Theory and Practice: Vancouver Studies in Cognitive Science*, iii (New York: Oxford University Press, 1992).

Fodor, J., *The Language of Thought*. (New York: Crowell, 1975).

—— *Psychosemantics* (Cambridge, Mass.: MIT Press, 1987).

—— 'Psychosemantics, or Where do Truth Conditions Come from', in W. Lycan (ed.), *Mind and Cognition* (Oxford: Basil Blackwell, 1990*b*).

—— McLaughlin, B., 'Connectionism and the Problem of Systematicity: Why Smolensky's Solution Doesn't Work', *Cognition*, 35 (1990*c*), 183–205.

—— Pylyshyn, Z., 'Connectionism and Cognitive Architecture', *Cognition*, 28 (1988), 3–71.

Gelman, S., 'Concepts and Theories', in R. Gelman and T. K. Au (eds.), *Perceptual and Cognitive Development: Handbook of Perception and Cognition*, 2nd edn. (San Diego, Calif.: Academic Press, 1996).

Grice, P., 'Meaning', *Philosophical Review*, 66 (1957), 377–88.

Haugeland, J., 'Representational Genera', in W. Ramsey, S. Stich, and D. Rumelhart (eds.), *Philosophy and Connectionist Theory* (Hillsdale, NJ: Lawrence Erlbaum, 1991).

Laasko, A., and Cottrell, G., 'Qualia and Cluster Analysis: Assessing Representational Similarity Between Neural Systems', *Philosophical Psychology*, 13 (2000), 46–76.

Lewis, D., *Convention* (Cambridge, Mass.: Harvard University Press, 1969).

McClelland, J., and Rumelhart, D., *Explorations in Parallel Distributed Processing: A Handbook of Models, Programs, and Exercises* (Cambridge, Mass.: MIT Press, 1988).

Schiffer, S., 'Truth and the Theory of Content', in H. Parret and J. Bouraresse (eds.), *Meaning and Understanding* (Berlin: Walter de Gruyter, 1981).

—— 'Intention Based Semantics', *Notre Dame Journal of Formal Logic*, 23 (1982), 119–59.

Sejnowski, T., and Rosenberg, C., 'Parallel Networks that Learn to Pronounce English Text', *Complex Systems*, 1 (1987a), 145–68.

Smith, E., and Medin, D., *Categories and Concepts* (Cambridge, Mass.: Harvard University Press, 1981).

Smolensky, P., LeGendre, G., and Miyata Y., 'Principles for an Integrated Connectionist/Symbolic Theory of Higher Cognition', *Technical Report 92–08* (Institute of Cognitive Science, University of Colorado, 1992).

Stalnaker, R., *Inquiry* (Cambridge, Mass.: MIT Press, 1984).

Tarski, A., 'The Concept of Truth in Formalized Languages', in *Logic, Semantics and Metamathematics* (Oxford: Oxford University Press, 1956).

11

Meaning and Content in Cognitive Science

ROBERT CUMMINS AND MARTIN ROTH

11.1. Introduction

What are the prospects for a cognitive science of meaning? As stated, we think this question is ill-posed, for it invites the conflation of several importantly different semantic concepts. In this chapter, we want to distinguish the sort of meaning that is an explanandum for cognitive science—something we are going to *call* meaning—from the sort of meaning that is an explanans in cognitive science—something we are not going to call meaning at all, but rather *content*. What we are going to *call* meaning is paradigmatically a property of linguistic expressions or acts: what one's utterance or sentence means, and what one means by it. What we are going to call *content* is a property of, among other things, mental representations and indicator signals. We will argue that it is a mistake to identify meaning with content, and that, once this is appreciated, some serious problems emerge for grounding meaning in the sorts of content that cognitive science is likely to provide.

11.2. Representation and indication

Cognitive science appeals to two main sorts of things that have contents: representations and indicator signals. We are going to spend some space

Also published in Richard Schantz (ed.), *Prospects for Meaning* (de Gruyter, forthcoming). This paper appears with the kind permission of de Gruyter.

describing these and then turn to why it is dangerous to think of their contents as meanings.

11.2.1. Indication

In the theory of content, 'indication' is used to talk about detection. Familiar examples include thermostats, which typically contain a bimetallic element whose shape detects the ambient temperature, and edge detector cells.[1] Other examples include the lights in your car's dashboard that come on when the fuel or oil level is low, and magnetosomes, which are chained magnetic ferrite crystals that indicate the direction of the local magnetic field in certain anaerobic bacteria.

When thinking about detection, it is important to distinguish the mechanism that does the detection from the state or process that signals that the target has been detected. The cells studied by Hubel and Wiesel—the so-called edge detectors—are indicators, but the pattern of electrical spikes they emit when they fire are indicator signals. Similarly, thermostats are indicators, while the signals are currents that result when the bimetallic element bends so as to close an open circuit.

11.2.2. Representation

Familiar examples include maps of all kinds, scale models, graphs, diagrams, pictures, holograms, and partitioned activation spaces. Cognitive maps (see below for discussion) are paradigm examples of what we mean by representations in the mind/brain. They are structured, and their content is grounded in that structure rather than in correlations with other events or states.

11.2.3. Indication vs. representation

Though causal and informational theories of representational content generally assert that representational content is, or is inherited from, indicator content, indication and representation should be kept distinct. For starters, indication is transitive, whereas representation is not. If S_3 indicates S_2, and S_2 indicates S_1, then S_3 indicates S_1. If a photosensitive cell pointed

---

[1] David Hubel and Torsten Wiesel (1962), who discovered such cells, write: 'The most effective stimulus configurations, dictated by the spatial arrangements of excitatory and inhibitory regions, were long narrow rectangles of light (slits), straight-line borders between areas different brightness (edges), and dark rectangular bars against a light background.'

at a light in your car's dashboard is attached to an audio device that plays a recording 'the water temperature is high' whenever the light goes on, then, if the light indicates low oil pressure, so does the recording. Notice that what it indicates has nothing to do with what it means. Representation, on the other hand, is not transitive. A representation of the pixel structure of a digitized picture of the Sears Tower is not a representation of the building's visual appearance, though the latter may be recovered from the former because a representation of the pixel structure encodes the building's visual appearance.

The transitivity of indication implies that indicator signals are arbitrary: given transitivity, in principle anything can be made to indicate anything else. Because indicator signals are arbitrary, systematic transformations of whatever structure the signals may have cannot systematically alter their contents. But structural transformations can systematically alter the contents of representations, and such transformations are what make representations useful. Consider, for example, software that 'ages' a digitized image of a face, i.e. returns an image of that face as it is likely to look after some specified interval of time. Nothing like this could possibly work on an input that was required only to indicate a certain face—a color, say, or a name— because there is no correlation between the physical characteristics something must have to be a signal that indicates the appearance of a face at age 18 and the physical characteristics of that face at age 18. It follows from the nature of indication that the structural properties of an indicator signal have no significance. Indicator signals demonstrate that their targets are there, but are silent about what they are like. Representations, on the other hand, mirror the structure of their targets (when they are accurate), and thus their consumers can cognitively process the structure of the target by modifying the structure of its representation. But unlike indicator signals, representations are typically silent about whether their targets are 'present.' Only incidentally and coincidentally do they detect anything.

Because edge detector cells all generate the same signal when they detect a target, you cannot tell, by looking at the signal itself (e.g. the spike train), what has been detected. Rather, you have to know which cells generated the signal. This follows from the arbitrariness of indicator signals, and is therefore a general feature of indication: indicators are source-dependent in a way that representations are not. In sum, then, because indication is transitive, arbitrary, and source-dependent while representation is intransitive, nonarbitrary, and not source-dependent, indication and representation are different species of content carriers.

11.3. Meaning in cognitive science

We will discuss a number of reasons why it is dangerous to think of the sorts of contents had by representations and indicator signals as meanings. The first is that meaning is linked to understanding. Meaning is idle unless someone understands what is meant. But the representations and indicator signals of cognitive theory are not supposed to be *understood*; they are supposed to be computationally *processed*. Equating content with meaning engenders a regrettable tendency to think that the processing of a representation or indicator signal is supposed to amount to *understanding* it.[2] Critics are quick to point out that it doesn't, and they are right. Cognitive science hopes to explain what it is to understand an utterance by appeal to the processing of representations and indicator signals, so the notion of content applied to representations and indicator signals had better not presuppose understanding anything. We trivialize the problem of understanding, and hence of meaning, if we suppose that utterances are simply translated into sentences of the language of thought which are already understood simply because it is the language of thought.

Another reason why it is dangerous to think of contents as meanings is that it suggests that a theory of content is, or is something that grounds, a *semantics* for content. This would be harmless were it not for the fact that semantics now means, for all intents and purposes, specifying references and truth conditions of the sort famously recommended by Davidson in 'Truth and Meaning' (1967). With the publication of that seminal article, meanings came to be references and truth conditions, and semantics came to be the now familiar combinatorial truth-conditional semantics pioneered by Tarski (1956). As a consequence, the idea that mental representations or indicator signals have meanings became the idea that they have references and truth conditions—what else is there, after all?—and the theory of

---

[2] Notice, too, that this makes any attempt to equate understanding a sentence with information flow a nonstarter. If you tell me something I already know, I can understand what you say although the information associated with your utterance is zero.

content was seen as the attempt to say what fixes the references and truth conditions of the things cognitive processes process (Fodor 1990*b*).

If you want to have truth-conditional semantics, however, you need your bearers of meaning to have logical forms, so you need them to be language-like. The idea that mental representations and indicator signals have meanings thus leads, through the Davidsonian Revolution, to the Language of Thought (LOT). This is a Bad Thing. It is a Bad Thing because, so far as we know, the representations and indicator signals required by cognitive science don't have logical forms, and are not candidates for truth-conditional semantics. They are, in this respect, in good and plentiful company. Pictures, scale models, maps, graphs, diagrams, partitioned activation spaces, magnetosomes, tree rings, fish scale ridges, sun burns, idiot lights, and light meters all have *contents*, and none of them are candidates for truth-conditional semantics.[3]

There is another route to the idea that content is meaning. You start with propositional attitude psychology, aka folk psychology, aka BDI psychology (for Belief, Desire, Intention psychology). Propositional attitudes require propositional contents, and propositions are the sorts of things expressed by sentences and only sentences. So, if you think the mind is a BDI machine, you are going to think there must be a language of thought (LOT), as Fodor famously and correctly argued (1975). This language of thought actually has to be a *language*, in that it has to be in the proposition expressing business. Moreover, as Fodor has also famously argued, if we are going to accommodate the productivity of the attitudes, that language is going to have to have a combinatorial semantics of just the sort Davidson argued we should find for natural language. So: BDI, LOT, and truth-conditional semantics are quite literally made for each other. BDI, to repeat, requires propositional contents, and LOT is the only way to have them. The only remotely plausible or worked out semantics for language (hence LOT) is the now standard truth-conditional semantics. BDI, LOT, and truth conditional semantics (TCS) are thus tightly knit together. It is a neat package, and working it out has been a major industry in the philosophy of mind, an industry that, following Fodor and Pylyshyn (1988), we might call the classical program. Unfortunately, however, there are compelling reasons for thinking that *the brain doesn't work that way*.

---

[3] LOT sentences might represent propositions (or the structure of a natural language sentence), but they do not, in the sense intended above, represent anything that isn't structured like a sentence. They might, of course, encode such a structure. See Cummins *et al.* (2001), Ch. 4, this volume, for further discussion.

11.4. Against the classical program

There are many compelling reasons for rejecting the classical program. Here are some of the most prominent concerns.

11.4.1. There are no portable symbols in the brain

LOT proposes to get complex representations from semantic primitives via the usual combinatorics. The semantic primitives in question are typically indicator signals. But indicator signals are source-dependent. As we pointed out above, an edge detector with a vertical line as target emits the same signal as one with a horizontal line as target. Thus, LOT theories must assume that indicator signals are somehow typed, and typed by something other than their source, since this will be absent in non-detection uses in complex expressions. The occurrence of a |cat| in a detection case will be a different brain event than the occurrence of a |cat| in a |There is a cat on the mat|. What makes both occurrences of |cat| tokens of the same type? It cannot be 'shape' (e.g. of the spike train), since that does not correlate with content. It is not clear what this *could* be. There appears to be no evidence that, for example, the occurrence of a given pattern of activation in one area of the brain is informationally related to the occurrence of the same pattern in another area. However, representations, because their content is grounded in their structure, do allow for portability of representation, since the same structures in different neural circuits will share content, but they do not require it.

11.4.2. A good deal of perception and cognition is not propositional

There are, basically, two routes to this idea. The first is that, given what we know about brains, they don't seem to be much like symbol systems (Sejnowski et al. 1988; Rumelhart 1989). The second is that, given what we know about BDI-LOT machines (e.g. PLANNERS, of the sort studied extensively in what Haugeland 1985 calls GOFAI), the computational demands involved in anything but the most simple tasks don't seem compatible with what we know about brains (e.g. Feldman and Ballard's 100-step-program 1982). Moreover, the currently most prominent argument for LOT, namely the systematicity of thought, either begs the essential question by presupposing BDI, or is an equally good argument for non-propositional representation of domains that do not themselves have a propositional structure, namely everything other than language (Cummins 1996*b*).

11.4.3. *The classical program is not easily reconciled with non-human cognition*

Human brains evolved, and they are, at bottom, not that different from other mammalian brains. This is not to deny that there are critically important differences between humans and non-human primates and other mammals. Nor it is to deny that the evolution of mind has been shaped by the particular adaptive problems facing each species. It is rather to emphasize how unlikely it is that human brains are fundamentally BDI-LOT machines, while non-human brains are not. The alternative is to suppose either that non-humans have no minds, or that all mammalian brains (perhaps all brains) are BDI-LOT machines. Neither option is attractive.

11.4.4. *'Naturalizing' truth-conditional semantics for the mind hasn't fared well*

It is safe to say that there is no consensus concerning the 'right' way to ground a truth-conditional semantics for LOT. It is time to consider the possibility that this is not our fault. A lot of smart people have worked hard on this for quite a while. Maybe they just haven't got it yet. But maybe it is just a bad problem.

11.5. How does content relate to meaning?

We are not going to defend any of the above claims in detail. But if you think any or all of them have a reasonable chance of being true, then it behooves you to consider alternatives to BDI and LOT and truth-conditional semantics for the mind. You should, we think, start thinking seriously about the following questions:

1. How should we understand mental content if we abandon the 'classical' picture?
2. What implications does a non-classical conception of mental content have for our understanding of *meaning*?

What we have already said about the first question motivates the second question. If the mind is not, at bottom, a propositional engine, then how is propositional thought possible? Or, to put the problem somewhat differently, how can we understand language if truth-conditional semantics correctly describes linguistic meaning, but does not correctly describe mental content? After all, it would seem to be a truism that to understand a sentence expressing the proposition that the Eiffel Tower is in Paris, you have to be able to have the thought that the Eiffel Tower is in Paris. But surely, to have the thought that the Eiffel Tower is in Paris, you have to get into a mental state whose content is the proposition that the Eiffel Tower is in Paris. Language users, it seems, *must* harbor propositional attitudes, and hence must have a LOT whose semantics mirrors that of language.

But is this apparent truism actually true? How can this picture possibly be accurate if, as the cognitive sciences seem to be telling us, mental contents are *not* propositions? If language expresses propositions—if meanings are truth conditions—then there has to be a mismatch between what goes on in your head and what you say, and between what you say and what goes on in *my* head. Imagine, for a moment, that the mind is a picture processor. Given the rather obvious fact that a picture is not worth any number of words, this seems to be a case of massive communication failure, what Cummins called forced error (1996a). We could, it seems, give a kind of reverse Fodorian argument: cognitive science says our mental states do not have propositional contents. But we do understand language. Hence the standard semantics for language must be wrong. This is temptingly radical, but not to be seriously recommended by anyone who is not prepared to abandon the standard semantics for language.

We can begin to buzz ourselves out of this bottle by noting that communicative signals do not *have* to share a semantics with the messages they communicate. A simple and familiar example of this is the transmission of pictures by pixelation. To send a grey scale picture, you need a signal system that is capable of specifying position-intensity value pairs. The picture sent, however, has a content completely disjoint from the contents of the signals.

This example demonstrates that successful communication does not require that the message communicated has the same content, or even the same *kind* of content, as the signals that communicate it. Communicative systems can be, as it were, recipes for assembling representations whose contents are utterly disjoint from the contents of the recipes themselves. So, accepting truth-conditional semantics for language doesn't *force* you to accept it for the mind. You cannot simply read off properties of mental content from properties of linguistic content—meaning—given only the fact that we understand language. In principle, linguistic signals *could be* recipes for assembling pictures (or maps or graphs or all of these or something else entirely) in your profoundly non-propositional head. This would allow us to have our truth-conditional semantics for language and a biologically realistic cognitive science too. If understanding a sentence with the content *that the Eiffel Tower is in Paris* doesn't require having a mental state with that (propositional) content, then meaning could be just what Davidson said it was, and the mind could still be what biology says *it* is.

But could this possibly be true? Isn't it just obvious, empirically, if not logically, that when I understand a sentence expressing the proposition that the Eiffel Tower is in Paris, that I have the thought that the Eiffel Tower is in Paris? We think it is. But we don't think this seemingly obvious fact (if it is a fact) runs very deep. We think Plato was right about thoughts, construed as propositional attitudes: thinking is just talking to oneself. Thoughts, construed as propositional attitudes, only happen to creatures that speak a proposition expressing language. Human language makes it possible for humans to, as it were, emulate a BDI machine. But underneath the emulator is something very different, something we share with every living creature with a brain. We certainly seem to be BDI machines to ourselves and to each other. But, of course, we cannot tell, just by ordinary interaction, or by reflecting in our philosophical armchairs, whether the mind is a BDI machine at bottom.

Somewhere in our evolutionary past, we became capable of emulating BDI machines and of using the kind of language we do. These are, we suspect, two sides of the same coin. Speaking a human natural language *is* being a virtual BDI machine. Signing apes are virtual BDI machines as well, though, it seems, much simpler ones than we are. Dennett (1991) was perhaps right to suggest that cognitive consciousness, as opposed to consciousness of the sort involved in perception, bodily sensation, and emotion, is fundamentally tied to language. It is not just to each other that we appear as BDI machines; we appear that way to ourselves, for our cognitive introspective awareness is linguistically mediated.

By thinking about thought in this way, we still give BDI a central role in explaining meaning, just as the stored chess program plays a role in explaining your computer's chess moves. However, this perspective on BDI removes its centrality in cognitive science, allowing us to focus more clearly on the primacy of content. Additionally, by construing BDI as a virtual machine, our commitment to truth-conditional semantics for propositional attitudes does not require us to think of the contents of the underlying architecture as having a truth-conditional semantics; rather, we can think of meaning and content as being semantically disjoint.

It has, we think, been a huge mistake to mix up the foundations of cognitive science with the problem of intentionality and meaning. Again, propositional attitude psychology is to blame. One thinks that the only things that have intrinsic meaning or aboutness are the propositional attitudes. Everything else is derived, meaningful only by convention. But why should one think that the propositional attitudes are intrinsically meaningful? Well, if you think we are, at bottom, BDI systems, then they have to be, because it cannot be a matter of convention what our mental states are. But if we are not BDI systems at bottom, then it *might* be a matter of convention what the contents of our propositional attitudes are: they inherit their contents from the public language sentences used to express them, and the meanings of those *are* a matter of convention.

Cognitive science needs to explain all of this. In particular, it needs to explain how a biological brain can emulate a BDI machine. But cognitive science does not need anything like the notion of meaning as a primitive. What it needs is an understanding of how information can be acquired, stored, and manipulated in a way that gives rise to intelligent and adaptive behavior, including, in the case of humans, and, perhaps some other creatures, the ability to emulate BDI machines and use a propositional language.

11.6. Non-semantic composition: the assembly of complex visual representations

As we have seen, there are strong reasons for doubting that complex representations in the brain could be *semantically* composed of source-free primitive constituents as LOT requires. In particular, it appears highly unlikely that indicator signals somehow become uniquely typed and source-independent, allowing them to float free from their roles in indication and play their required roles in complex LOT expressions as primitive terms referring to what they indicate under some set of special content-fixing conditions. How does a radically non-LOTish human brain emulate a BDI machine? It seems pretty clear that something like this begins to develop in humans during the first eighteen months of life. But it seems equally clear that the brain is not fundamentally a BDI machine, and, consequently, that most of its adaptive business, including, in our case, emulating a BDI machine, gets done by processing non-propositional representations and indicator signals.

Because the combinatorics of TCS has such a strong hold on our thinking, it is worth pausing to emphasize that TCS is not the only game in town. A different picture emerges of the relation between indication and representation and of the composition of complex representations generally, if we examine the role the sort of indicators discovered by Hubel and Wiesel play in the construction of visual images. One account of this is to be found in recent research by David Field and Bruno Olshausen (Field 1987, 1994; Olshausen and Field 1996, 1997, 2000).

Natural images contain much statistical structure as well as redundancies (Field 1987), but early visual processing effectively retains the information present in the visual signal while reducing the redundancies. In the 1950s, Stephen Kuffler (1952) discovered the center—surround structure of retinal ganglion cells' response, and Joseph Atick (1992) showed that this arrangement serves to decorrelate these cells' responses. As Horace Barlow (1961) had suspected, sensory neurons are assembled to maximize the statistical independence of their response. Olshausen and Field recently showed that the same is true of neurons in the primary visual cortex. While Hubel and Wiesel discovered that neurons in the primary visual cortex are sensitive to edges—thus their functional description as edge detectors—they did not know what the functional relevance of this structure was (1988). According to Olshausen and Field, edge detection allows neurons in the primary visual cortex to respond in a maximally independent way to visual signals, thus producing sparsely coded representations of the visual field. They demonstrated this by constructing an algorithm that could identify the minimal set of maximally independent basis functions capable of describing natural images in a way that preserves all the information present in the visual signal. Because natural images typically contain edges, and because there are reliable higher order correlations (three-point and higher) between pixels along an edge, it turns out that natural images can be fully described as composites of about a hundred such basis functions (see Figure 7.2). Given the statistical structure of natural images in the environment, there was sure to be such a set of functions, but the striking thing is that these basis functions are similar to those Hubel and Wiesel found forty years before: spatially localized and oriented edges. Recently, O'Reilly and Munakata (2000) showed how to train a neural network using conditional principle components analysis to generate a similar set of basis functions.

To see how visual representations are assembled out of these basis functions, consider a vector of V1 cortical cells connected to the same retinal area via the same small subset of LGN cells. Each cell has a receptive field similar to one in the minimal set of basis functions in Figure 11.1. An

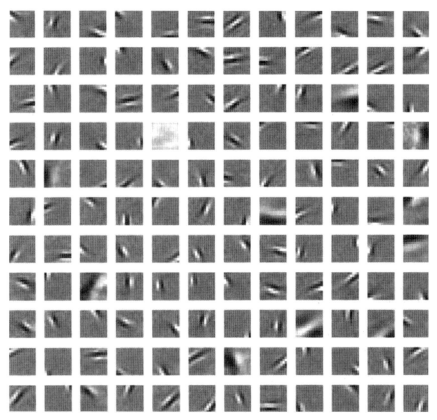

Figure 11.1 Optimal basis function set to represent natural images (from Olshausen & Field 2000)

incorrect way to understand the assembly of such visual representations is as the activation of a subset of such basis functions whose content is based solely on the information each cell receives from the relevant retinal region. If this were the case, cells in the primary visual cortex would serve to indicate activity in the LGN and, ultimately, of features in the visual field. Indeed, it would be simple to determine what is currently observed if the basis functions were completely independent and the noise factor was known, but neither is true. As a result, many distinct visual representations are compatible with the information present in the visual field. Lewicki and Olshausen (1999) have shown, however, that it is possible to infer a unique visual representation if the system has information about the probability of observed states of affairs and the probability of visual representations given observed states of affairs. Instead of assembling a visual representation from a set of indicator signals alone, the visual system may construct the representation from indicator signals and relevant probabilistic information about the visual environment.

The account that emerges here consists in the assembly of an image from a set of indicator signals that are surprisingly few in number, indicate multi-point correlations between adjacent pixels in the (whitened version of) the input, and whose success as detectors of their proprietary targets is due, to a large extent, to recurrent circuitry that effectively computes a Bayesian function in which the prior probabilities are determined by the features of neighboring areas of the developing image. Most important for our purposes, perhaps, their representational content is semantically disjoint from the image they compose in the same way that pixel values are semantically disjoint from the representational content of a computer graphic. Like maps and scale models, such representations have their content as a consequence of their geometry rather than their origins. Because such representations have the source independence that indicator signals lack, they are candidates for the disciplined structure sensitive transformations that representations afford. Since such representations literally share the static and dynamic structure of their targets, properties of the targets can be learned by transforming the representations in ways that reflect the ways in which nature constrains the structure of, and structural changes in, the targets. As a result, faces can be aged, objects can be rotated or 'zoomed,' and three-dimensional projections can be computed. None of this is possible in a system in which visual representations are semantically composed from constituents whose contents are determined by their indicator role.

11.7. Escaping the grip of propositional representation

It is useful, in this connection, to think about the above example in relation to another relatively well-entrenched form of non-propositional representation, namely cognitive maps (Tolman 1948). The hypothesis of cognitive maps is designed to explain the striking ability of living creatures such as rats and humans to get from point A to point B, via a novel route, without directions. The hypothesis is based on an analogy with the use of written maps by humans: if you have a map, you can get from point A to point B via a novel route without directions, and there seems to be no other way to do it. You can get specific directions, or you can get a map and get from anywhere to anywhere (in principle). If you can get from anywhere to anywhere via novel routes, and there is no external map in the offing, or, as in the case of rats, no ability to use one, then there must be an internal map. This might be something like a memorized map, but, instead of having its origins in an external map, it is built up from a combination of exploration and background knowledge about such things as which direction you need to go, and how streets or paths or whatever are laid out. Smallville, USA, in which streets are laid out in square blocks with numerical names in order running north–south, and, say, presidential names in order running east–west, is a particularly transparent example. If you know this fact about Smallville, and you know your numbers and presidents, and you can see at what intersection you are located when you are at an intersection, you can get from anywhere to anywhere. When we do this sort of thing, we more or less consciously have a kind of street map schema in mind. But there needn't be any reflective consciousness involved. We may do the whole thing unreflectively, as the rats presumably do. However it is done, it seems unavoidable that, if one can get from point A to point B via a novel route without directions, a map, however schematic, and however available or unavailable to introspection, must be there, somehow, underlying the ability.

Cognitive maps are paradigmatic examples of mental representations. To do their causal work in us and in rats, and their explanatory work in cognitive science, they do not need any special causal connection with the environment, nor do they need to have any historical properties. These were all rung in to ground *meaning*, not to underwrite their explanatory power. What they must have instead, and all they must have instead, is a structure that is reasonably similar to the route structure of the environment the traveler happens to be in.

It has seemed to many that nothing could count as a cognitive map (or any other representation or indicator signal), unless it is 'usable' by the traveler or one of its subsystems. After all, if the map were, say, etched into the inner surface of the rat's skull, it wouldn't do much good. But that is a misunderstanding of the same sort we have been warning against: representations like maps (or indicator signals, for that matter) do not need to be understood or grasped or used by the systems that harbor them to count as contentful. To see this, it suffices to consider the fact that it must be possible to learn (or develop, or evolve) the ability to exploit content one cannot *currently* exploit. Since you cannot learn (or develop, or evolve) the ability to exploit content that isn't there, there must be unexploited content. Indeed, it must be possible for an individual to harbor representations aspects of which that individual cannot even *learn* to exploit, if we are to allow, as we surely must, for the possibility that the species might evolve the ability to exploit that content in the future. For example, all neural network models of learning presuppose that the brain learns to exploit previously unexploited structure in its representations, for the process of weight adjustment made over time makes no sense unless we assume that the representational content of the input pattern remains the same throughout learning. It is precisely such unexploited content in the input patterns that the network is learning to use. But if a network can learn a task, it can evolve the same ability. Neither the learning nor the evolution makes sense if we suppose the representations don't represent unless and until they are thoroughly exploited (Cummins *et al.* 2006, Ch. 8, this volume).

All sorts of creatures harbor cognitive maps. They are not sets of beliefs. They do not have propositional contents. They are not candidates for truth-conditional semantics. They do not have to be understood, or 'grasped' or even exploitable, by the creatures that harbor them to have the contents they do. They need no causal connections with the environment or historical properties (which, to repeat, was all about fixing reference, anyway) to have the contents they do. They just need to share geometrical properties with the environment. They need, in short, to be reasonably good maps.

And maps, while complex, are not built up out of semantic primitives whose meanings combine to yield the content of the complex.

A similar lesson emerges when we think about how content is determined in connectionist networks. Recently, Paul Churchland has characterized the representations that he thinks underwrite such cognitive abilities as recognizing faces and representing grammatical structure as points, regions, or trajectories in neuronal activation spaces, and contrasts such representations with language-like schemes that express propositions (1998).

What are the representational contents of such trajectories and partitioned activation spaces? Consider a network that learns to discriminate families in terms of facial resemblance (1998). The points in such a space are what Churchland calls prototype points. They are centers of attraction, where the clustered points correspond to related family members. These prototype points reflect the way that training the network partitions up the relevant activation space. Furthermore, the underlying geometry is remarkably constant across different networks trained to the same task, including ones with differing input encodings and with differently dimensioned hidden layers. We can think of this geometry as representing an objective structure in the families' face space, and that trained networks discover this and represent it via a structurally similar activation space. According to Churchland, we can think of the prototype points as something like individual concepts in a conceptual space. Recurrent networks pose a different case because they allow for temporally extended representations, and are best conceived in terms of trajectories in activation space rather than points. This approach works nicely for Elman's well known grammar network (1992). For our purposes, the important point is that such contents are not propositional, they are not grounded in whatever causal connections the points may enjoy with distal properties, and they represent in virtue of shared structure.

Those of us interested in what the explanatory primitives of cognitive science are should concede that there is, to a first approximation anyway, no meaning in the head. Not because we are externalists, but because meaning isn't what's wanted. There *is* a kind of content in the heads (and other bodily parts, down to the molecules) of intelligent creatures, but it isn't meaning as that is generally understood. Meaning proper, whatever it turns out to be, is an explanandum for cognitive science, not an explanans. And for those of us who are worried about the pitfalls of trying to read off the fundamentals of cognition from the human case, meaning should probably be pretty far down on the agenda, except as it arises in connection with human language processing. And there, one must beware of the kind of translation theory of language understanding that makes LOT and BDI seem inevitable.

11.8. Conclusion

So: what we need at the foundations of cognitive science is representation and indication, and we need the concept of unexploited content—content that is there to be exploited, but which the system has not yet learned or evolved to exploit. Content, in short, that is not a function of use.

We do not need psychosemantics as generally conceived. As this is usually conceived, it makes sense only in a BDI + LOT framework. But it is likely doomed even there, because the conventions governing the semantics of the sentences that express the contents of the propositional attitudes are, obviously, just the conventions governing the sentences of a natural language, and these are going to yield meanings—references and truth conditions— that do not match the non-convention governed mental/neural states that are, or should be, the bread and butter of cognitive science. You are not going to find an evolved natural content for every convention governed sentence or its constituents. Our language doesn't reduce to Aristotle's, let alone to an imagined language of thought that is presumed to differ little if at all from the code running in the brains of our Pleistocene ancestors.

What we do need (though not everyone would welcome it) is a scientific explanation of meaning. This we evidently do not have at present. But we think our prospects would improve if we were to conceive the problem as a problem about language and communication, and not as a problem about the contents of psychological states. The trend has been to derive linguistic and communicative meaning from something else, the contents of propositional attitudes. Sentences express propositions because they express *thoughts*. This, by itself, isn't so bad. The trouble comes when we go on to think that *thoughts,* being the cogwheels of the mind, must have their propositional contents intrinsically, non-derivatively. Thoughts must be things having 'natural' (i.e. non-conventional) propositional contents. The conventions of language simply link linguistic expressions to intrinsically meaningful thoughts. We are now deeply committed to a BDI theory of the mind, and the LOT that goes with it. The concepts of representation and indication fundamental to the science of cognition get hijacked and pressed into service as grounders for meaning, and this grounding business becomes the goal of the theory of mental content. Linguistic meaning is then conceived as just LOT meaning worn by conventional symbols, and LOT meaning is just, well, functional role, or the role of primitive LOT symbols in detection, or ... We completely lose sight, in philosophy, anyway, of the success that cognitive science has achieved in understanding such things as cognitive maps and edge detectors and visual images/maps. And we make our job seem easier than it is by failing to see the gap between meaning and content. It is a large gap, and it needs to be filled by something other than hand-waving.

References

Atick, J., 'Could Information Theory Provide an Ecological Theory of Sensory Processes?', *Network*, 3 (1992), 213–51.

Barlow, H. B., 'Possible Principles Underlying the Transformation of Sensory Messages', in W. A. Rosenblith (ed.), *Sensory Communication* (Cambridge, Mass.: MIT Press, 1961), 217–34.

Churchland, P. M., 'Conceptual Similarity Across Sensory and Neural Diversity: The Fodor/LePore Challenge Answered', *Journal of Philosophy*, 95 (1998), 5–32.

Cummins, R., *Representations, Targets, and Attitudes* (Cambridge, Mass.: MIT Press, 1996a).

—— 'Systematicity', *Journal of Philosophy*, 93 (1996b), 591–614.

—— 'Truth and Meaning', in J. K. Campbell, M. O'Rourke, and D. Shier (eds.), *Meaning and Truth: Investigations in Philosophical Semantics* (New York: Seven Bridges Press, 1999).

—— Poirier, P., 'Representation and Indication', in P. Staines and P. Slezak (eds.), *Representation in Mind* (Oxford: Elsevier, 2004), 21–40.

—— Blackmon, J., Byrd, D., Poirier, P., Roth, M., and Schwarz, G., 'Systematicity and the Cognition of Structured Domains', *Journal of Philosophy*, 98 (2001), 167–85.

—————— Lee, A., May, C., and Roth, M., 'Representation and Unexploited Content', in G. McDonald and D. Papineau (eds.), *Teleosemantics* (New York: Oxford University Press, 2006).

Davidson, D., 'Truth and Meaning', *Synthese*, 17 (1967), 304–23.

Dennett, D., *Consciousness Explained* (New York: Little, Brown, 1991).

Elman, J., 'Grammatical Structure and Distributed Representations', in S. Davies (ed.), *Connectionism: Theory and Practice: Vancouver Studies in Cognitive Science*, iii (New York: Oxford University Press, 1992).

Feldman, J., and Ballard, D., 'Connectionist Models and their Properties', *Cognitive Science*, 6 (1982), 205–54.

Field, D. J., 'Relations between the Statistics of Natural Images and the Response Properties of Cortical Cells', *Journal of the Optical Society of America A*, 4 (1987), 2379–94.

—— 'What is the Goal of Sensory Coding?', *Neural Computation*, 6 (1994), 559–601.

Fodor, J., *The Language of Thought* (New York: Thomas Y. Crowell, 1975).

—— 'Psychosemantics, or Where do Truth Conditions Come from', in W. Lycan (ed.), *Mind and Cognition* (Oxford: Basil Blackwell, 1990*b*).

—— Pylyshyn, Z., 'Connectionism and Cognitive Architecture: A Critical Analysis', *Cognition*, 28 (1988), 3–71.

Haugeland, J., *Artificial Intelligence: The Very Idea* (Cambridge, Mass.: MIT Press/ Bradford Books, 1985).

Hubel, D. H., *Eye, Brain, and Vision* (New York: Scientific American Library, 1988).

—— Wiesel, T. N., 'Receptive Fields, Binocular Interaction and Functional Architecture in the Cat's Visual Cortex', *Journal of Physiology*, 160 (1962), 106–54.

King, J., 'Structured Propositions and Complex Predicates', *Nous*, 29/4 (1995), 516–35.

Kuffler, S., 'Neurons in the Retina: Organization, Inhibition and Excitatory Problems', *Cold Spring Harbor Symposia on Quantitative Biology*, 17 (1952), 281–92.

Lewicki, M. S., and Olshausen, B. A., 'A Probabilistic Framework for the Adaptation and Comparison of Images Codes', *Journal of the Optical Society of America A*, 16 (1999), 1587–1601.

Olshausen, B. A., and Field, D. J., 'Emergence of Simple-Cell Receptive Field Properties by Learning a Sparse Code for Natural Images', *Nature*, 381 (1996), 607–9.

—— —— 'Sparse Coding with an Overcomplete Basis Set: A Strategy Employed by V1?', *Vision Research*, 37(1997), 3311–25.

—— —— 'Vision and the Coding of Natural Images', *American Scientist*, 88 (2000), 238–45.

Rumelhart, D., 'The Architecture of Mind: A Connectionist Approach', in Michael Posner (ed.), *Foundations of Cognitive Science* (Cambridge, Mass.: MIT Press, 1989).

Sejnowski, T., Koch, C., and Churchland, P. S., 'Computational Neuroscience', *Science*, 241 (1988), 1299–306.

Tarski, A., 'The Concept of Truth in Formalized Languages', *Logic, Semantics and Metamathematics* (Oxford: Oxford University Press, 1956).

Tolman, E., 'Cognitive Maps in Rats and Men', *Psychological Review,* 55/4 (1948), 189–208.

12

Representational Specialization: The Synthetic A Priori Revisited

12.1. Introduction

Anyone familiar with the history of Western philosophy is familiar with the idea that our knowledge of the world is limited, by our representational resources, especially our perceptual and conceptual resources. The empiricist version of this theme has it that all of our ideas are derived from perceptual or reflective *experience*. Locke, Berkeley, and Hume all held that all of our ideas are derived from sense and reflection, and subsequent empiricist philosophy has not challenged this in any serious way. Rationalists have allowed for innate ideas of various sorts not derived from experience, but have not challenged the claim that what can be known is constrained by what concepts and percepts we can have. Indeed, this seems a truism: how could one possibly know about what one cannot conceive or perceive?

I think it is possible to challenge this truism, but I do not intend to do that here. Rather, I want to focus on its critical applications, i.e. attempts to rule out this or that as unknowable on the grounds that there is no plausible source for the underlying representations. Those uses of the 'truism' have been, I think, largely unsuccessful. Perhaps the most famous example of what I have in mind is the final paragraph of Hume's *Enquiry*:

When we run over libraries, persuaded of these principles, what havoc must we make? If we take in our hand any volume; of divinity or school metaphysics, for instance; let us ask, Does it contain any abstract reasoning concerning quantity or number? No. Does it contain any experimental reasoning concerning matter of fact and existence? No. Commit it then to the flames: for it can contain nothing but sophistry and illusion. (Hume 1748)

A. J. Ayer (1936) famously dismissed ethics and theology on the same grounds.

Critiques of this nature cannot hope to get off the ground unless there is a route to claims about what can be represented that is prior to claims about what can be known: For example, there must be a route to the claim that all of our ideas are derived from sense and reflection (a claim badly in need of unpacking before its credentials can be examined) that is prior to—i.e. does not presuppose—the claim that we cannot know about things that we cannot experience. Evidently, any story about representation that takes it to be, or to depend on, a kind of knowledge will undermine a critique that moves from the alleged origins of representations to limits on representational resources and thence to limits on what can be known.

12.2. A Kantian thought experiment

To prepare the ground for the discussion to follow, I begin with a thought experiment that owes its inspiration to Kant's *Aesthetic*. Imagine a perceptual system—call it *Cubic*—that represents objects by coloring the surface of cubes in a three-dimensional packed array of such cubes, like a Rubik's cube that is 10,000 × 10,000 × 10,000. This gives colored blobs of various sizes and shapes in a three-dimensional space. It is easy to take this the wrong way and imagine the system *looking at* such a cube, noticing that you cannot see the cells inside, and concluding that there is no perceptual representation of the insides of objects on this scheme. On the contrary, the scheme I am imagining here contains information about the colors of the insides of things that are larger than one cell. An uncolored cell inside a large object representation represents an unresolved ambiguity between, say, an apple (red outside, white inside) and a hollow plastic apple (red outside, hollow inside). It is also tempting, for some of us, anyway, to think of this symbolically, as a three-dimensional matrix with cells bound to RGB values. That would be a mathematical description of Cubic, but Cubic itself, as I want you to imagine it, involves $10 \, K^3$ cubes packed together, and a mechanism for coloring them. It is, if you like, an *implementation* of the matrix scheme.

If we assume that representations of this sort are the only representations that Cubic can generate, then a number of propositions will be synthetic and a priori for Cubic:

(V1) Every object is colored.

(V2) Every object has a determinate size and shape.

(V3) No two objects can occupy the same place at the same time.

(V4) Every object has a determinate location relative to every other object.

(V5) Every object is a determinate distance from every other object.

Of course, Cubic does not represent any of these propositions. Indeed, Cubic cannot represent any propositions at all.[1] Its only representational targets are colored shapes in three-dimensional space. Nevertheless, *we* are in a position to see that these propositions are somehow inevitable for Cubic, even though they are, in fact, all empirical, and all false. These propositions will be a priori for Cubic in the sense that Cubic cannot represent a counter-example to any of (V1)–(V5). A representational target for Cubic that violates any of (V1)–(V5) cannot be accurately represented in Cubic. If Cubic attempts to represent such a target—for example, something like an electron that has a size but no shape, no color, and no determinate location relative to its neighboring particles, it will get it massively wrong. The result will be a case of forced error: an attempt to represent a target that Cubic does not have the resources to represent accurately (Cummins 1996a: ch. 2). (V1)–(V5) are, of course, synthetic propositions, as the electron case illustrates. So we have here a toy case of the synthetic a priori. It is a *relativized* a priori—relativized to Cubic, or the representational scheme Cubic uses—but so also was Kant's notion relativized to *human* cognitive architecture.

It is, of course, odd to talk of propositions a priori for Cubic, given that it cannot represent propositions.[2] It is tempting to say, instead, that (V1)–(V5) must hold of the world *as it is represented by Cubic.* This is harmless enough, provided we mean by it simply that Cubic cannot represent a state of affairs that would be a counter-example to any of (V1)–(V5). It is not harmless if we understand this to mean that there is something called Cubic's phenomenal world, the *world-as-represented-by-Cubic,* and that (V1)–(V5) are true—indeed necessarily true—of *that.* There is no such world, and so this kind of talk is

---

[1.] It might *encode* propositions (see below), but I am assuming here that Cubic has no means to exploit such a possibility.

[2.] Do not be confused by the fact that *we* can read off (infer) propositions from one of Cubic's representations. Cubic has nothing like a *language;* it has no resources for representing propositions.

not harmless: it wrongly suggests that there is a 'world', other than the actual world, that Cubic represents, and represents just as it is—a phenomenal world about which Cubic cannot be mistaken, or anyway, about which it cannot be mistaken in the ways picked out by (V1)–(V5). We need to insist that Cubic represents the actual world, and represents it in a way that ensures that no representation of a counter-example to (V1)–(V5) can possibly occur. From our God-like positions, we can see that the representations Cubic constructs are necessarily inaccurate in certain respects, but, to borrow a phrase from Descartes, this is nothing to Cubic. (V1)–(V5) are part of the synthetic a priori content inherent in the form of P's intuitions and their representational functions—their proprietary targets.[3] It is because the targets of P's representations are objects in space that (V1)–(V5) are about objects in space. It is because of the particular form of Cubic's representations that it must represent those objects in a way that satisfies (V1)–(V5).

You don't have to be the Village Empiricist to suspect that Cubic cannot escape the limitations imposed by (V1)–(V5) without modification to its resources for perceptual representation. But it can. Let us now add a non-perceptual scheme for propositional representation, a language of thought: a scheme that will enable the expanded system to represent, among others, the propositions expressed by (V1)–(V5) and their negations. Call this expanded system P-Cubic (Propositional-Cubic). It is a tempting Kantian idea to think of P-Cubic's *experience,* its epistemic access to the world, as consisting of its perceptual representations, and to point out that P-Cubic could never have an experience that directly contradicted any of (V1)–(V5). This would not be exclusively a contingent fact about the external world, but also and correlatively a consequence of the form of P-Cubic's representational resources. (V1)–(V5) would be synthetic for P-Cubic—not conceptual truths—but they would be a priori in the sense that no disconfirming experience is possible for P-Cubic. For P-Cubic, colored shapes in a Cartesian 3-space would be the a priori form of outer intuition, i.e. of perceptual object representation. The form of P-Cubic's perceptual representations constrains not only what it can accurately perceive, but also, indirectly, what it is rational for it to think is true. P-Cubic could contemplate the negation of, say, (V1), but could never

---

[3.] See Cummins (1996a: chs. 1 and 8) for more on targets.

have an experience disconfirming (V1). Or so goes one version of the Kantian story and its empiricist predecessors. It is beguiling, but it is fundamentally mistaken.

Begin with a relatively trivial point. We have to distinguish between an experience of an uncolored object, and an experience of an object as uncolored, i.e. between experiencing a colored object, and experiencing an object *as colored*. By construction, it is impossible for P–Cubic to experience an uncolored object *as uncolored*. But P–Cubic might well experience an uncolored object, because P–Cubic might experience uncolored objects, yet experience them as colored. These will all be cases of forced error, of course, and so it might seem that P–Cubic could not *know* that it was experiencing an uncolored object, and hence that P–Cubic could not know there were such things. But this is mistaken: P–Cubic might well *discover* the existence of uncolored objects, their locations, and their trajectories, without ever experiencing such objects as such, or even without experiencing them at all. Even a rudimentary naïve mechanics, gleaned from what *is* available in perception, could provide P–Cubic with persuasive evidence of what is not; for example, an imperceptible wall on a pool table. What makes this possible is precisely the fact that P–Cubic can represent and evaluate propositions that are true of possibilities that it cannot experience as instances of those possibilities, but for which P–Cubic can have persuasive indirect evidence. Because P–Cubic's propositional representations do not have the same contents as P–Cubic's perceptual representations—because its concepts are not *copied* from its percepts, but do apply to the objects represented in those percepts—P–Cubic is in a position to infer how things should look on the pool table if there is an invisible quarter circle barrier around one of the pockets. This, more or less, is how we generally find out about the unperceived.

Thus, though P–Cubic's knowledge is limited by the form and representational function of its perceptual scheme, it is limited in a rather subtle and complex way, not in the simple way contemplated by Hume. Hume gets his critical leverage by assuming that ideas are copied from impressions, the implication being that the only representational targets available to us are those available to the perceptual systems. This is more than empiricism about evidence; it is a doctrine about mental representation for which Hume has no defense whatever.

12.3. What is implicit in representational form and function

There are two morals I want to draw from this Kantian thought experiment. The first has already been drawn, viz., that we *can* know what we cannot experience. This, obviously, is not news, but I think the discussion of P-Cubic illustrates the point in a way that exhibits nicely how radical empiricism can seem unavoidable if you assume a kind of representational monism. Unlike Cubic, P-Cubic deploys two schemes that have different targets and different forms. Kant's representational pluralism—percepts and concepts—gave him the wherewithal to avoid Hume's claim that it is impossible to know about what you cannot represent perceptually, but it is arguable that he did not fully exploit it.

The second moral, of more interest to me here, is this: *every* representational scheme generates representations with a certain proprietary form or format that defines that scheme and constrains both what can be represented and how the representations can be processed.[4] These constraints can and should be conceived as enforcing presuppositions about the scheme's target domain (the domain it is supposed to represent), assumptions that are implicit in the form of the scheme's representations in the way that (V1)–(V5) are implicit in the form of the representations generated by Cubic. Notice that there are two correlative parts to this idea. One is that representational schemes are aimed at proprietary targets, and their normal uses presuppose that the representations the scheme generates represent those proprietary targets and nothing else. The other is that the formal properties that define the scheme constrain how its targets are represented in a way that can be thought of as enforcing presuppositions about the target domain. I am going to call this pair of ideas the *representational specialization thesis,* or just the *specialization thesis,* for short.[5] Here are three simple examples of what I have in mind.

12.3.1. Maps

Your standard paper road map assumes that its targets are street and intersection structures. Because the map itself is flat, it gets linear distances more or less wrong in more or less hilly terrain. Ordinary globes of the Earth involve a comparable assumption. Notice how form and function interact here. A floor plan whose target is a flat two-dimensional structure has the same formal properties as the street map, but is limited to targets that do not violate the assumptions about distance built into the format. Stairs are not in the target domain, except where they begin and end, hence do not engender forced distance errors.

12.3.2. Notations for sound

Standard musical notation is useless for representing most sounds: speech, the sound of a construction site, the sound of a receding train whistle. Attempts to represent any of these with standard musical notation will result in forced error. This is because there are assumptions about the target domain that are implicit in the scheme—that pitch is not continuous, for example: only pitches in the chromatic scale are representable. Since the violin is not fretted, it can play pitch sequences that cannot be represented discretely. Moreover, the notation abstracts away from the difference between a violin and an oboe playing a middle C. This is no problem provided the music meant for the violins is given to the violin section and the music meant for the oboes is given to the oboe section, and the two sections are tuned together.

Phonetic writing of the sort to which there is a ready transcription to what you are now reading represents speech as a sequence of word-length phonetic sequences. It is hopelessly inaccurate if used for representing any sound other than speech. The system simply assumes that everything is a phonetic element of speech—typically, though not necessarily, in a particular language. Those are its proper representational targets. The result is an abstract normalization of the actual wave forms—exactly what is needed for the sound to formant mapping required for communication.

12.3.3. Palette systems

These are familiar from the graphics programs available on every computer. Presentation software, for example, allows a certain set of standard shapes: circles, lines, rectangles, callouts, etc., which can be sized and (sometimes) rotated. The frustrating assumption is that everything you want to draw is some relatively simple combination of these shapes at various sizes and rotations. These schemes also assume that their targets are two or three-dimensional. There are specialized pallet systems for such things as flow charts and circuit diagrams, their intended targets and attendant assumptions being obvious from their functional designations. Their formal properties specialize them in ways that make them mostly useless for targets not in their intended domains.

The specialization thesis should be more or less obvious from the fact that we have developed a large variety of representational systems for different representational targets. No one would attempt to represent a Beethoven sonata with the resources of map-making or even graphed waveforms, nor would one attempt the architectural plans for a new building in musical notation. Yet the idea persists that target neutral representation is somehow possible; that language (or symbol strings) in particular is somehow target neutral and hence fundamental. Thus, while my demystified version of the synthetic a priori may make sense to empiricists, it may seem to be of little importance: if there is target neutral representation, then the specialization thesis is false in its full generality, and the phenomena it emphasized can be dismissed as a curiosity that has no deep philosophical implications.

12.4. Target neutrality

There are a variety of routes to the idea of target neutrality. The most influential, I think, is the idea that maps and musical notation are just special purpose 'languages,' or that all nonlinguistic systems must be, or can be, linguistically interpreted. Linguistic imperialism does not, by itself, yield target neutrality, but it makes it more plausible by dismissing all of the obvious cases of representational specialization as mere differences in language. Specialization, as the example of Cubic makes clear, is invisible from inside a single scheme system. A system using an exclusively propositional scheme could allow for the proposition that its scheme is specialized. But it couldn't, of course, represent a non-propositional target. Such targets would be as inaccessible as colorless objects are to Cubic.

A more direct route to target neutrality is the idea that language is, potentially anyway, universal, limited in its representational power only by its currently limited but extendable lexical resources.[6] One can, after all, refer to a Beethoven sonata, or specify each of the notes in an extended linguistic description, which, though cumbersome, would, it seems, specify the same piece of music. And one can pixelize a picture and render it as a set of equations, or a set of verbal expressions (the RGB value of the third cell in the second row is r,g,b). To understand what is wrong with this kind of thinking we need to understand the distinctions between representing on the one hand, and reference and encoding on the other.

12.5. Reference, representation, and encoding[7]

I have been urging the thesis that representational schemes are inevitably suited to some targets to the exclusion of others; that they are *representationally specialized*. This rather obvious fact is obscured by two phenomena that are often confused with representation:

1. Reference: one can *refer* to just about anything.
2. Encoding: one can use representations of one kind to *encode* representations of another kind, and hence to carry information about other targets indirectly.

12.5.1. Reference

Representations, as I understand them here, share structure with the things they accurately represent. Thus, an accurate street map of a city shares geometrical structure with the network of streets it maps. Sentences, on some views, share structure with the propositions they express, and, hence, can be said to represent those propositions. Terms, however, do not share structure with the things to which they refer. The phrase 'the street and

---

[6.] Syntax, one might have thought, at least limits the representable *propositions*. And so it does. But look what happens in the interesting cases, e.g. modality. Friends of modality will say that non-modal languages are specialized to non-modal propositions. Enemies of modality will insist that there are no modal propositions to represent. No non-controversial instance of specialization emerges. And yet one might say, with more than a little irony, that it is a priori for those cleaving to a Quine-approved syntax that there are no modal propositions.

[7.] For more on encoding, see 'Systematicity and the Cognition of Structured Domains,' Ch. 4, this volume.

intersection structure of Chicago' does not share geometrical structure with its referent.[8]

P-Cubic, as we have imagined it, cannot represent colorless objects, but it can refer to them. It can, therefore, theorize about such objects—invisible objects—and gather indirect evidence for their existence. Imagine, for example, that, every now and again, the balls on a pool table behaved as if they had collided with an invisible ball. A little Newtonian mechanics, and the judicious use of barriers, could create an overwhelming case for such invisible balls. (Think of Brownian motion!) Lacking a sense of touch, P-Cubic could not experience colorless objects as colorless, but it could certainly formulate and confirm propositions about such objects. This fact, while important, has no power to undermine the specialization thesis unless you think that reference is representation. I do not want to argue over the word, but I do want to call attention to a distinction between the kind of relation a street map of Chicago has to the street and intersection structure of the city, and the kind of relation that the phrase 'the street and intersection structure of Chicago' has to the street and intersection structure of Chicago. I've written extensively on this elsewhere (Cummins 1996a), so I won't belabor the point here. All that is required in the current context is the fact that a successful reference to the street and intersection structure of Chicago need not carry any information about what that structure is. It is possible, of course, to describe, even specify, that structure linguistically, but that is not a case of representing that structure, but of *encoding* it.

12.5.2. *Encoding*

A transparent example of encoding is the use of pixel matrices to encode pictures and hence the targets they represent. A *symbolic specification* of a binding of RGB values to cells in a matrix is itself a scheme the proper targets of which are cell coordinates and RGB values. But the representations it *encodes* are not (typically) representations of cell coordinates and RGB values, but of objects in space. These objects might themselves be representations. One might digitally encode a picture of a musical score, for example. When the result is displayed, i.e. decoded into a picture, one looks

---

[8.] The tendency to confuse reference with what I am calling representation, and hence referential content with representational content, makes it seem that all representation must be linguistic in character.

right through the picture: a good picture of a score *is* a score, and a good picture of a map *is* a map. A good picture of a statue, on the other hand, isn't a statue, and does not represent what the statue represents, though it provides some good clues. Digitized text, when displayed, yields token sentences that represent propositions. It is tempting, but mistaken, to think that a symbolic representation of pixel values is itself a representation of objects in space (digitized picture) or of propositions about something other than pixel values (digitized text). But these cases involve what John Haugeland once called a dimension shift (Haugeland 1978), i.e. a shift in the targeted domain of representation. A picture of your aunt Tilly's face represents her visual appearance in two dimensions—i.e. a particular two-dimensional projection of her facial topography; the pixel specifications are about pixels and their values. The two systems are semantically disjoint, except for the bizarre case in which one digitizes a text (or picture of a text) that specifies pixel values.

Another familiar example of encoding is the use of Gödel numbers to encode symbol strings.[9] Imagine a system that takes as input a sentence represented as an ordered list of words and returns its phrase structure, represented as a labeled bracketing of the underlying formants.

$$<\text{Wilbur loves the toy}> \rightarrow <[[\text{Wilbur}]^{NP}[[\text{loves}]^V \ [[\text{the}]^D \ [\text{toy}]^N]^{NP}]^{VP}]^S$$

Corresponding to this is a system that takes as input the Gödel number of a sentence and returns the Gödel number of its labeled bracketing. On the assumption that the function that takes sentences onto their phrase structures is computable, it follows that there is a purely arithmetic function— call it *g*-parse—from the Gödel number of a sentence to the Gödel number of the corresponding labeled bracketing.[10] If we did such a calculation in standard decimal notation, for example, we would be generating references to integers, not to sentences or words. Moreover, the calculation we did would depend on algorithms defined over decimal numerals, and, at a more abstract level, over integers, a kind of processing that has no application to

---

[9.] Gödel numbering: to encode a string of words, e.g. 'Mary loves John and Mary,' encode each word as a natural number and its position in the string as a prime exponent, the nth prime corresponding to the nth position. Let 'Mary' = 4, 'loves' = 1, 'John' = 3, 'and' = 2. Since 'Mary' occurs in the first and fifth positions, we get 1^4 and 7^4; 'loves in position 2 yields 2^1; John in position 3 yields 3^3; 'and' in position 4 yields 5^2. The string is encoded as the product of these numbers: $1^4 \times 7^4 \times 2^1 \times 3^3 \times 5^2 =$ 2441. Since every number has a unique prime factorization, factoring a number gives us the words and their positions (assuming the numbers have been assigned to words).

[10.] G-parse is, for example, expressible as a composition of plus, times, and minimization.

words and sentences at all. The scheme would assume that every object in the domain has a unique prime factorization, and (at the level of notation) that shifting left implements multiplication by ten. All of this *specialization*— proprietary targets and proprietary processing—becomes invisible if we think of the system using Gödel numbers as 'doing the same thing' as the system that uses words and labeled brackets. But it is not doing the same thing, as is evident from the fact that *g*-parse is insensitive to whether or not the input number encodes a grammatical sentence, or even whether it encodes a sentence or words at all. (Remember: no decoding takes place, just arithmetic.) It is thus not built into the form of this scheme that everything in the domain is a word or sentence or syntactic category.

Because encodings do not, by themselves, presuppose what is built into the form of the schemes they encode, there is a sense in which they allow one to float free of representational specialization, at least to float free of the presuppositions of the scheme *encoded*. Encoding allows for contents that cannot be represented or referred to in the encoded scheme. We could allow for a variant of P-Cubic that encodes its spatial representations by binding locations (cells) to objects, and colors to cells. It is natural for us to think of such a scheme as symbolic and propositional—as a set of equations. But it need not work that way. We might have visual cells, object cells, and color cells all oscillating (activation or intensity or . . .) at distinctive frequencies. An object is encoded by the set of visual cells oscillating at the same frequency as a given object cell. A cell is colored red if it oscillates at the same frequency as a given color cell—the 'red' cell. This would allow for uncolored objects (oscillation corresponding to no color cell). It would not allow for objects whose representations are not uniformly colored, though it would allow for masses of variegated color that are not objects. As this example makes clear, encodings impose their own constraints on the encoded system's target domain, and on its own domain: the representations of the encoded system. The presuppositions of the encoded system may be violated, but not those of the encoding system.[11]

Encodings, of course, need not be encodings of another representational scheme. Encodings can themselves be encoded, and so can the world. Thus, a variant of Cubic might encode objects in space directly via the oscillation

---

[11.] It is important not to confuse linguistic description with encoding. Describing a picture is not the same as encoding it. But we can use language to specify encodings, as in the discussion of Gödel numbering in n. 9 above.

scheme sketched above, and, of course, a symbolic encoding—a set of equations—could encode those oscillation patterns. Moreover, P-Cubic need not rely on reference and encoding to cognize a world that does not satisfy (V1)–(V5). If we add to P-Cubic's arsenal some representational resources that are both non-propositional and non-perceptual, we open up the possibility of not merely referencing or encoding, but of *representing* the mechanics of objects in space in a way that abstracts away from color, size, and shape. This, of course, is exactly what, for example, vector diagrams of the objects on a pool table do. Such diagrams do not represent everything about the balls on the table: they represent only relative positions of centers of mass and their momenta. This, of course, is exactly the kind of abstract representation that is needed to get the mechanics right.[12] The example illustrates the possibility of accurately representing the objective structure of things one cannot experience as having that structure.[13]

When we take all of this into account, the simple picture of being epistemologically limited or even trapped in the presuppositions of one's representational scheme (or language) dissolves away. Only creatures whose resources are limited to a single language, or a single representational scheme, or a single encoding scheme, or creatures with a variety of resources but with no overlap whatever in the targets of those resources, need be limited in the way empiricism and Kant imagined. Figuring out in advance—a priori, as it were—what is knowable by a complex creature with multiple representational and encoding schemes at its disposal, and a language to help manage them and to invent new ones, is probably a fool's errand. Limitations perhaps there are, but they are difficult to discern, and nothing of the kind imagined by Kant, let alone Hume, is in the cards.

12.6. Representational specialization and world making

We get a different perspective on essentially the same point by considering a further Kantian-sounding consequence of the target specificity of

---

[12] If you took a snapshot of a pool table with a 'Newton camera,' it would show a bunch of coplanar arrows.

[13] This representation is not inaccurate because it does not represent color or shape, for its target is simply the relative positions and momenta. Inaccuracy in this instance would be error in position or in the magnitude or direction of a momentum vector.

representational systems, viz., that a given system can seem to create its targets. A speaker of English (or whatever) hears words, sentences, and meanings that a non-speaker does not. One needs to be in the grip of a theory that draws a sharp distinction between perception and inference to follow Berkeley and say that the non-speaker has his or her ears and the use of them as well as the speaker, so the difference cannot be in what is *heard*. Inference, very likely of a non-propositional sort, there surely is in speech perception, for it is quite obvious that speakers hear things that non-speakers do not. And it is equally clear experimentally that non-speakers hear things—for example, certain phonetic contrasts—that speakers do not (see Dupoux *et al.* 1997). Reflection on these and similar experimental facts can make it seem plausible that words, sentences, and meanings are all somehow *created* by the knowledgeable listener. This sounds way too Kantian to the contemporary analytic ear, however. It seems preferable to say instead that the words are there in the speaker's mind, and the hearer (unconsciously) infers them from the auditory signal. But how different are these two, at bottom? The inference in question, after all, must be constrained by a set of forced options, a hypothesis space, if you like, that limits the possibilities to known words, or anyway to pronounceable syllables, in a known language.[14] The upshot seems to be an analogue of Cubic for language perception: for a system specialized for speech perception in a given language, everything that cannot be treated as legitimate speech elements will simply be treated as noise. For such a system, the whole auditory world is indeed a text. A familiar extension of the point is to argue that conceptual schemes create their own objects, or even that they create the objects of the perceptual schemes they are thought to regiment.[15]

There is a sense in which representational specialization, especially perceptual representation, does create the world we live in. Walk down a street in a city that speaks a language you do not know. There is speech and there are signs everywhere, but it is all just *stuff*. No words heard or seen, at least not as such. But what *is* the *stuff*? What are the lines and shapes and colors and pitches and volumes and timbres? Wouldn't these disappear *as such* too

---

[14.] A foreign word or phrase here and there is ok, but fluent speech that changes language every word is impossible: the syntax simply won't allow it.

[15.] See Haugeland (1998: chs. 10 and 13). Dogs, Haugeland would claim, cannot see tennis balls *as such*. For a discussion, see Ch. 9 in this volume.

if we took away the resources for representing them? A familiar argument for nativism starts here: some representational resources must be innate, otherwise none could be learned, for there would be no *experience-of* to learn from. It is not the nativist response I want to pursue, however, but the transcendental idealist response: no world to know without thought, no thought without representational resources, no representational resources without the a priori limitations imposed by the form of those resources. My point about this is simple: even if all of this is true, it does not have the consequences it appears to have for a representationally pluralistic system, as we have seen. The source of the idea that representational specialization has serious implications for knowledge and world making does not derive from representational specialization itself, but some form of representational *monism* explicit or implicit in other doctrines. It is implicit in the doctrine that all of our ideas are copied from our impressions, and that our impressions can be catalogued in a short list of proper objects of perception: color, shape, size, texture, pitch, volume, timbre, etc., qualities that can be perceived *as such*. And it is explicit in the doctrine that all representation resolves somehow into language, so that the world turns out to be a set of propositions or a 'text.'

Think again of P-Cubic, and imagine that P-Cubic's propositional resources are limited to first order combinations of terms whose referents are given *as such* in perception. Even that, as we saw, does not limit P-Cubic to the presuppositions of its perceptual system. But it does limit P-Cubic's propositional targets to those expressible in a first order language with a limited empiricist lexicon. These limitations are evidently the product of two factors: representational specialization and a doctrine about the limitations of P-Cubic's lexicon. The latter assumption is not a matter of form, but of function. It is the assumption that the function of all primitive terms in P-Cubic's language of thought is to refer to 'sensible qualities,' an assumption that has no non–circular justification that I know of. For the justification of the limitation is always that the only knowable propositions are among those allowed by the restriction. You cannot argue to an ontology from a premise about limited representational resources, then argue for limiting those resources on epistemological grounds. Our resources do limit us, but they are what they are, not what some antecedent restriction on what is knowable implies that they ought to be. Moreover, as I hope the discussion above has made clear, it is no simple matter to say what limitations are actually faced by creatures with a plurality of schemes and a plurality of strategies for exploiting them.

References

Ayer, A. J., *Language, Truth, and Logic* (London: Victor Gollancz, 1936).

Clapin, H. (ed.), *Philosophy of Mental Representation* (Oxford: Oxford University Press, 2002).

Cummins, R., *Representations, Targets, and Attitudes* (Cambridge, Mass.: MIT Press, 1996a).

Dupoux, E., Pallier, C., Sebastian, N., and Mehler, J., 'A Destressing "Deafness" in French?', *Journal of Memory and Language*, 36 (1997), 406–21.

Haugeland, J., 'The Nature and Plausibility of Cognitivism', *Behavioral and Brain Sciences*, 1 (1978), 215–26.

—— 'Representational Genera', in W. Ramsey, S. Stich, and D. Rumelhart (eds.), *Philosophy and Connectionist Theory* (Hillsdale, NJ: Lawrence Erlbaum, 1991).

—— *Having Thought* (Cambridge, Mass.: Harvard University Press, 1998).

Hume, D. (1748), *An Enquiry Concerning Human Understanding*, in J. A. Selby-Bigge (ed.), *Hume's Enquiries* (Oxford: Clarendon Press, 1963).

13

Biological Preparedness and Evolutionary Explanation

DENISE DELLAROSA CUMMINS AND
ROBERT CUMMINS

13.1. Introduction

Evolutionary explanations of cognitive phenomena are often thought to imply that the cognitive capacities targeted for evolutionary explanation are *innate* and *modular*. We argue that neither of these implications is necessitated by evolutionary explanations of particular cognitive effects. Instead, we argue that issues of innateness should be conceived in terms of *canalization*, i.e. the degree to which the development of a trait is robust across normal environmental variations (Waddington 1975; McKenzie and O'Farrell 1993; Ariew 1996). Evolutionary pressures can affect the degree to which the development of a trait is canalized. High canalization can be the consequence of biasing learning/acquisition processes in ways that favor the development of concepts and cognitive functions that proved adaptive to an organism's ancestors. The end result of these biases is an adult organism that exhibits a number of highly specialized cognitive abilities that have many of the characteristics associated with modules: functional specialization, reliable emergence in spite of considerable environmental variability, and some degree of informational encapsulation.

Originally published in *Cognition*, 73 (1999), 37–53. We would like to thank three anonymous reviewers for helpful comments. Portions of this paper were presented by the first author at the 10th Annual Meeting of the Human Behavior and Evolution Society, University of California-Davis, June 1998. The original publication was seriously garbled, failing to distinguish quotations from author's text. These errors have been corrected.

This perspective makes it evident that criticisms of innate cognitive modules are not *ipso facto* criticisms of evolutionary explanations of cognitive capacities. Since evidence for modularity in the developed organism is compatible with a high degree of neural plasticity in the early stages of development, it is possible to have an evolutionary explanation of cognitive modules that does not assume these modules to be innate in the sense in which this means unlearned or present at birth or coded in the genes. Of course, an evolutionary approach to cognition is compatible with modules that are innate in this sense. Our point is simply that it need not presuppose them.

We begin by discussing two factors that appear to be prominent in motivating interest in evolutionary approaches to cognition. We then characterize how evolutionary explanations of cognitive phenomena that appeal to innate modules are typically interpreted. We go on to review some of the criticisms that have been levelled against this approach. Finally, we expound and defend a conception of the relation between natural selection and cognitive development that is responsive to worries about innate modules yet compatible with an evolutionary explanation of specialized and relatively independent cognitive mechanisms in adult organisms.

13.2. The motivation for an evolutionary approach to cognition

Two factors appear to be prominent in motivating researchers to adopt an evolutionary approach to cognition. The first is simply that cognitive psychologists are in the business of explaining cognition in biological organisms, and biological organisms are the product of evolutionary forces. To put it more succinctly:

> If you are a materialist, then you are committed (at least implicitly) to the view that *The mind is what the brain does.*

That is, our cognitive and emotional functions are instantiated as neurological processes. Unless you are a creationist, you are also committed to the view that

> *The brain (like all other organs) was shaped by evolution.*

If you accept these two premises, you are also committed to accepting their logical conclusion, namely, that

The mind was shaped by evolution.

This much we believe is uncontroversial.

A second factor is the need to account for domain-specificity effects in cognition, their early emergence in development, and their apparent adaptiveness. As illustrations, consider the following three episodes in the recent history of psychology.

Consider first simple inductive learning processes. Early learning theories rested on the assumption that an association could be made between any two stimuli through repeated pairings, yet it subsequently became apparent that some associations were learned more readily than others. This 'fast-tracked' learning typically involved contingencies that had significant survival advantages during an organism's evolutionary history. Humans (and other primates) appear predisposed to acquire fear responses to classes of animals that proved dangerous to our ancestors, such as spiders and snakes (Seligman 1971; Öhman 1986; Cook and Mineka 1989, 1990). It is also notoriously easy to acquire taste aversions to foods that make us ill even if the time between ingestion and illness is quite long (Etscorn and Stephens 1973; Bernstein and Borson 1986; Logue 1988; Garcia *et al.* 1989). Perhaps the most dramatic demonstration is the oft-replicated Garcia effect. If animals are allowed to drink quinine-adulterated water in a room with flashing lights, those subsequently shocked will avoid drinking while the lights are flashing but are indifferent to bitter-tasting water, while those subsequently irradiated to produce nausea will avoid bitter-tasting water but are indifferent as to whether lights are flashing while they drink (Garcia and Koelling 1966). As Hilgard and Bower (1975: 574) put it: 'One might say that the animal is innately preprogrammed to see certain cues and responses as "naturally fitting" together, so that they are readily learned.' These favored associations often appear to be ones that have adaptive value.

As a second example, early theories of cognitive development proposed during the 1950s rested on the assumption that infants were little more than sensory-motor systems, and that complex concepts were constructed from these simple building blocks through experience with the environment (Piaget 1952). But the last two decades of research on infant cognition has forced developmental psychologists to re-examine their assumptions about the infant mind. Some types of domain-specific knowledge appear to emerge quite early in infancy, before infants have had sufficient time to induce this knowledge through experience. These data seem to indicate that infants are cognitively predisposed to interpret the world in terms of agents and objects whose behaviors are constrained by different sets of principles (e.g. Leslie and Roth 1994; Spelke 1994).

A third example comes from research on higher cognition. During the 1970s, theories of human reasoning were proposed in which reasoning was presumed to be a content-free process, sensitive only to syntactic properties of reasoning problems. Subsequent research reported such robust domain-specific effects that even the staunchest proponents of the syntactic view of reasoning began incorporating domain-specific parameters in their models (Braine and O'Brien 1991; Rips 1994). Many of these 'privileged' domains turn out to be ones that developmentalists identified as 'early emerging' and that can plausibly assumed to have had adaptive value, such as causality, frequency, ontological category, and certain social reasoning strategies (Cosmides 1989; Cosmides and Tooby 1992, 1994; Gigerenzer and Hug 1992; Cummins 1996a, b, c, d, 1997, 1998a, b, c, 1999a, b, 2000, 2002).

In each case, psychologists had to rethink their theories in order to account for biases in learning and cognition that are apparent in their data. In the case of biological organisms, a plausible interpretation is that early-emerging, domain-specific, adaptive capacities are the result of evolutionary forces.

13.3. Characterization of the innate modules view

According to some researchers, the early emergence and domain-specificity of many cognitive capacities is evidence that evolution has produced a mind best characterized as a collection of innate and independent modules, each of which arose in response to environmental pressures during a species's evolution.

[O]ur cognitive architecture resembles a confederation of hundreds or thousands of functionally dedicated computers (often called modules) designed to solve adaptive problems endemic to our hunter-gatherer ancestors. Each of these devices has its own agenda and imposes its own exotic organization on different fragments of the world. There are specialized systems for grammar induction, for face recognition, for dead reckoning, for construing objects and for recognizing emotions from the face. There are mechanisms to detect animacy, eye direction, and cheating. There is a 'theory of mind' module...a variety of social inference modules...and a multitude of other elegant machines.   (Tooby and Cosmides 1995: pp. xiii–xiv)

We argue that human reasoning is guided by a collection of innate domain-specific systems of knowledge. Each system is characterized by a set of core principles that define the entities covered by the domain and support reasoning about those entities. Learning, on this view, consists of an enrichment of the core principles, plus their entrenchment, along with the entrenchment of the ontology they determine. In these domains, then we would expect cross cultural universality; cognitive universals akin to language universals.   (Carey and Spelke 1994: 169)

I have argued that the normal and rapid development of theory-of-mind knowledge depends on a specialized mechanism that allows the brain to attend to invisible mental states. Very early biological damage may prevent the normal expression of this theory-of-mind module in the developing brain, resulting in the core symptoms of autism.   (Leslie 1992: 20)

The relevant notion of a cognitive module derives from Fodor (1983). But, whereas Fodor held that modules were largely peripheral mechanisms, the modules at issue here know no such boundaries. Nor are all of Fodor's characteristics always, or even typically, assumed. Rather, the key features are (1) domain specificity, both informationally and computationally; (2) universality, i.e. present in every normal mind in the species; and (3) relative encapsulation—insensitivity to collateral information. This characterization differs somewhat from the 'Darwinian module' typically ascribed to evolutionary psychology.

To sum up, a (prototypical) Darwinian module is an innate, naturally selected, functionally specific and universal computational mechanism which may have access (perhaps even unique access) to a domain specific system of knowledge of the sort we've been calling a Chomskian module.   (Samuels et al. 1999)

Encapsulation is not mentioned in this quote, but we retain this characteristic from Fodor's original formulation because, without it, it is difficult to distinguish a module from a mere 'subroutine.' We do not include being naturally selected, since the origin of such modules, if there are any, is largely what is at issue.

Part of the motivation for the innate modules view is that, without the assumption of innate modules, there seems little latitude for evolutionary explanations of cognitive phenomena. For example, if there is no innate theory of mind module, it might seem the adaptive consequences of having a theory of mind could have no specific effect on selection. It could only have the indirect effect of reinforcing whatever general purpose architecture makes a theory of mind learnable in the environments in which our ancestors found themselves. While not utterly trivial, this is certainly not the basis for a new subdiscipline, and certainly not for evolutionary psychology as currently practiced. The innate modules view, on the other hand, *seems* to be just what is needed to ground a rich evolutionary cognitive psychology. If there *is* a theory of mind module, and it is heritable, then it might have spread through the population because it was adaptive.

The underlying line of thought here seems to be this: for an evolutionary explanation of a cognitive capacity to be viable, we must assume (*a*) that the capacity is specified in the genes, since the genes are the mechanism for the inheritance of evolved traits; and (*b*) that it is modular, since the independent evolution of specialized capacities requires that these be largely decoupled from other independently evolved systems. We have not seen this argument explicitly advanced by evolutionary cognitive psychologists. We offer it here as a plausible explanation of the link between evolutionary cognitive psychology and the assumption of innate modules.

To sum up: there appear to be two basic lines of argument for the innate modules view. One is that the existence of innate modules would explain the well-documented domain specificity and early emergence of many cognitive capacities. The other is that the evolution of cognition seems to require an architecture of relatively independent and heritable capacities.

13.4. Objections to innate modules

The objections to the innate modules view divide into two classes. The first and most fundamental consists of arguments from neural plasticity. The second consists of arguments defending the sufficiency of a few general-purpose learning mechanisms to account for the type of phenomena typically urged on innate modules. We briefly review these two lines of argument in turn.

13.4.1. Neural plasticity

The modularity part of the innate modules view—the idea that the mind/brain is a collection of relatively independent computational units—is consistent with much of what we know about the adult brain, which exhibits a great deal of functional specialization. Specific neural circuits subserve specific cognitive functions, and damage to those circuits typically produces selective impairments in cognition, not across-the-board reduction in intellectual function (Broca 1861; Wernicke 1874; Warrington and Weiskrantz 1968; Farah and Brown 1989; Gigerenzer and Hug 1992; Squire 1992). It is the belief that 'innate' means 'present at birth' that is the source of criticisms leveled against evolutionary psychology primarily because it does not sort well with what we understand about neural plasticity during development.

The environment has profound effects on the (developing) brain. Such effects are clearly seen during sensitive periods, which are time periods during development when an organism is particularly sensitive to certain external stimuli.   (Banich 1997: 508)

It is obvious from the dramatic cellular events that go on during gestation that the nervous system is tremendously plastic during development: it can change form, including the type and location of cells and how they are interconnected with one another.   (Gazzaniga et al. 1998: 484)

. . . representational constraints (the strongest form of nativism) are certainly plausible on theoretical grounds, but the last two decades of research on vertebrate brain development force us to conclude that innate specification of synaptic connectivity at the cortical level is highly unlikely. We therefore argue that representational nativism is rarely, if ever, a tenable position.   (Elman et al. 1996: 361)

The plasticity of the developing brain seems to point to a 'general problem solver' view of intellectual function, one in which the nature of cognitive functions simply reflects environmental contingencies. Natural selection has shaped a brain that is plastic enough to extract the statistical topography of the current environment, whatever that might turn out to be. Specific circuitry is developed in response to current environmental demands as needed in order to ensure survival within a particular niche.

13.4.2. Innate modules are unnecessary to account for domain-specificity effects in cognition

The second objection to the modules view is that they are unnecessary to account for domain-specificity in cognition. Innate modules were advanced to explain early emergence and domain-specificity in cognition. They therefore rest on 'poverty of the stimulus' arguments. Poverty of the stimulus arguments for nativism proceed by attempting to show that some capacity or other cannot be learned because there is inadequate time (e.g. early emergence), inadequate computational power, inadequate information in the environment (e.g. the Garcia effect and other domain-specific effects), etc. Replies are therefore attempts to show that one or another learning architecture is actually up to the job, or that the opposition has underestimated the available information or resources.

We suggest that for higher-level cognitive behaviors, most domain-specific outcomes are probably achieved by domain-independent means.   (Elman *et al.* 1996: 359)

. . . the general framework for induction proposed by Holland, Holyoak, Nisbett and Thagard (1986) stresses the importance of constraints of various degrees of generality in determining whether and how readily knowledge about a regularity in the environment will be induced. Two of the most general constraints they proposed involve the role of failed expectations concerning goal attainment in triggering inductions, and the role of knowledge about variability of classes of objects and events in determining the propensity to generalize. Within this framework, it is clear that pragmatically useful inductions will often be triggered . . .
(Cheng and Holyoak 1989: 308)

Our principal criticism of [domain-specific] approaches put forward to account for biases and content effects is that they lack the generality of our model . . . Domain-specific knowledge may influence the parameters in our model, and the utilities subjects use . . .   (Oaksford and Chater 1994: 626)

We do not propose to rehearse this debate here. We merely remind the reader that these arguments need to be made case by case, and that a sound case against an innate module for some cognitive capacity is not *ipso facto* a case against its selection.

The argument from neural plasticity and the criticisms of poverty of stimulus style arguments address innateness, not modularity. Of course, if cognitive capacities are not innate, they are not innate and modular. Still, there is a close connection between these criticisms of innateness and wariness about modularity. If general purpose learning mechanisms account for cognitive capacities, it would be somewhat surprising if these capacities were highly modular. Not that general learning mechanisms could not produce modules—they surely could—but it is not clear why they would. Any argument against domain-specific learning would therefore appear to be also a prima facie argument against domain-specific computational mechanisms, and hence against encapsulation.

13.5. Objections to general-purpose learning

The widely recognized difficulty with a general-purpose learning approach is that it does not explain the 'biases' that are plainly evident in the newborn brain. Although it is possible, for example, to force auditory cortex to acquire the capacity for visual processing, the result is not normal vision (Roe et al. 1992). Similarly, it is highly unlikely that the hippocampus is suited to do either visual or auditory processing. Thus, there are neurological biases present at birth, and these are the result of millions of years of evolution operating on the ontogeny of the modern mammalian brain. This means that the developing brain is not entirely plastic.

Throughout development, however, non-plasticity is also a hallmark of the brain. For example, early in gestation undifferentiated precursor cells become fated to express the characteristics of the brain region where they migrate to and remain. Thus, plasticity and non-plasticity occur during prenatal development.

(Gazzaniga et al. 1998: 485)

Moreover, biases seem to exist not just with respect to sensory/perceptual functions, but with respect to cognitive development as well. As mentioned earlier, the explosion of data on infant cognition that has come about in the last decade indicates that the infant mind is cognitively predisposed to interpret the world in terms of agents and objects whose behaviors are constrained by different sets of principles. With respect to agents, they appreciate the inherently reciprocal nature of social interactions (Vandell and Wilson 1987), and the meaning of emotional facial expressions (Campos and Stenberg 1981; Stenberg and Hagekull 1997). With respect to objects, they appreciate that objects are permanent entities that cannot occupy the same space at the same time (Baillargeon 1987, 1994; Spelke 1994) whose movements are constrained by physical causality (Leslie 1987; Leslie and Keeble 1987) and principles of biomechanical movement (Bertenthal 1984, 1985). They also appreciate the abstract concept of number and arithmetic operations (Starkey et al. 1990; Wynn 1992). A purely general-purpose learning account of human development would be faced with the unwelcome task of explaining data such as these as biases in the environment that are exploited by the learner. This is reminiscent of the behaviorist tendency to posit histories of reinforcement required by their learning theories without any direct evidence that such histories existed, or of the tendency of neo-Gibsonians to posit affordances when confronted with perceptual capacities their theories could not otherwise explain.

13.6. A third interpretation: evolution affects degree to which cognitive traits are canalized

As diametrically opposed as these positions seem to be, there in fact exists a common ground which they occupy and upon which a coherent evolutionary psychology can be founded. The following quotations exhibit this common ground.

There can be no question about the major role played by our biological inheritance in determining our physical form and our behaviors. We are not empiricists. What troubles us about the term innate is that, as it is often used in cognitive and developmental sciences, it suggests an overly simplistic view of how development unfolds. To say that a behavior is innate is often taken to mean, in the extreme case, that there is a single genetic locus or set of genes which have the specific function of producing the behavior in question, and only that behavior.

(Elman *et al.* 1996: 357)

...a better way of thinking about it is that the brain has to be assembled, and the assembly requires project scheduling over an extended timetable. The timetable does not care about when the organism is extruded from the womb: the installation sequence can carry on after birth. The process also requires, at critical junctures, the intake of information that the genes cannot predict.   (Pinker 1997: 238)

In other words, rather than assume that early emerging and specialized cognitive capacities are either innate or learned, we may suppose instead that organisms do not inherit modules fully formed, but have a *biological preparedness* (Seligman 1971) to very quickly develop specialized cognitive functions for solving classes of problems that were critical to the survival and reproductive success of their ancestors. Conceiving of cognitive functions in this way puts them on a par with other biological traits that can differ in their degree of *canalization*, that is, in the degree to which the environment plays a role in their expression (Waddington 1975; McKenzie and O'Farrell 1993; Ariew 1996).

13.6.1. Nature, nurture, and canalization

The nature–nurture debate in cognitive psychology is generally a debate about what knowledge (rules, theories, concepts) is innate, and what is learned. Couching the issue in terms of canalization or biological preparedness, however, allows us to see things quite differently. Consider a jointly authored paper. We might ask who authored which sections or paragraphs or even sentences. This is how people tend to think of the nature vs. nurture issue in the cognitive realm. But it could also happen that both authors are responsible for every sentence, with the *degree* of responsibility varying from sentence to sentence, or section to section. The suggestion is that we should think of our cognitive abilities as all thoroughly co-authored. From this perspective the question is not which concepts or capacities are contributed by the genes, and which by learning, but rather how canalized the development of a given concept or cognitive capacity is: how much variability in the learning environment will lead to the same developmental end-state? An advantage of this way of thinking is that we see at once that little or nothing in development is inevitable, even though it may be (nearly) universal. And when we investigate things in this light, we are led to ask which variations in the learning environment will divert the stream into a different and perhaps preferable canal. (See Lewontin 1974 for a similar analysis of the contributions of genes and environment.)

This perspective does not rule out innate concepts (representational nativism) or innate computational modules, but neither does it require them. Our concern, to repeat, is to articulate a framework for an evolutionary cognitive psychology that is maximally flexible. Evolutionary cognitive psychology requires relatively independent heritable cognitive traits. These could result from innate modules, but they could also result from developmental/learning biases that interact with the environment in such a way as to yield highly canalized cognitive traits.

13.6.2. Two examples of canalization

Consider first the neurological changes that subserve the development of vision and language. Binocular columns (used in depth perception) are not present at birth, but appear in the visual cortex during a critical period after the infant has received visual input (Banich 1997: 472). Other visual cortical cells show diffuse line orientation 'preferences' at birth, firing maximally to lines of a particular orientation (e.g. vertical), but responding to lines of other orientations as well, albeit to a lesser degree (Hubel 1988). After receiving visual input, however, these cell preferences are sharpened so that they respond maximally *only* to lines of a particular orientation (Blakemore 1974). Further, if visual input is restricted to only a single orientation (e.g. the animal is exposed only to lines of vertical orientation), the majority of cells will shift their preferences to match their visual experiences, responding maximally to lines of vertical orientation even if their initial preferences were for lines of other orientations (Blakemore and Cooper 1970; Hirsh and Spinelli 1970). The animal, in short, is blind to all line orientations except that to which it was exposed during this critical period. Development of visual cognitive functions depends on tightly coupled transactions between neurological predispositions and environmental inputs. Under normal circumstances, binocular columns will form in a particular area of visual cortex, and initial diffuse biases in visual cortical cells will sharpen into definite response preferences as a result of environmental stimulation during a critical period of development. The neurological predispositions are there at birth, but require an environmental 'co-author' to fully develop into functions that subserve visual cognition.

Next, consider language development. Like vision, language development also shows a complex pattern of interplay between innate biases and environmental input. Deaf babies will begin to babble vocally just as hearing babies do, but their babbling declines and eventually ceases, presumably because they don't receive the auditory feedback hearing babies do (Oller and Eilers 1988). Babbling deaf babies are practicing sounds that they have never heard, a phenomenon that is perhaps best explained as the unfolding of a biological program that requires environmental feedback to fully develop. Infants are also born with the capacity to hear all phonetic contrasts that occur in human communicative systems, yet within the first year of life they lose the capacity to distinguish among phonemes that are not marked in their language community (Eimas 1975; Kuhl 1987). Thus, they initially exhibit an auditory bias in processing speech sounds that treats the phonemes of human language as signal and everything else as noise, and subsequent language inputs modify this bias to include as signal only the phonemes of the child's native tongue. There also appears to be a critical period for language acquisition that ends approximately at puberty: children who do not acquire their first language during this critical period fail to acquire the rules governing the use of grammatical morphemes and the syntactic constraints necessary for forming grammatical sentences (Curtiss 1977; Pinker 1994). Further, the ability to extract the grammatical rules of a natural language is selectively impaired in certain genetic disorders (Gopnik 1990a, b).

There are two important lessons to be drawn from these familiar examples. The first is that biological preparedness comes in degrees, and is probably best conceived in terms of canalization. A combination of genetic and environmental factors causes development to follow a particular pathway, and once begun, development is more or less likely to achieve a particular end-state depending on the type and amount of environmental stimulation the organism receives. Limb development is highly canalized in humans (humans everywhere grow limbs in the same way) but not perfectly so, as the example of Thalidomide shows. Language is highly canalized, though not so highly as limb development. Tennis and chess are comparatively low on the canalization scale.

The second lesson to be drawn from the examples lately rehearsed is that the environment can influence trait development in many different ways. The most interesting of these to the psychologist is learning. It is important to keep in mind that learning can affect the development of even highly canalized traits. Thus language, though highly canalized, is still learned. Biology puts strong constraints on what properties a language must have to be learnable (as a first language), and it virtually guarantees that language will be learned in a huge variety of environments. This is what is meant by the claim that language acquisition is highly canalized. Few doubt that the high canalization of language acquisition is to be explained by a specific biological preparedness for language acquisition. But our genetic endowment does not determine which language we will acquire or even whether we will acquire any. This is determined largely by the learning environment.

The important point is this: as long as we continue to pose the question 'Which cognitive traits are learned and which are innate,' we will continue to run the risk of misconceiving the issue. Maybe everything is some of each, the question being how much. In the next section, we provide an illustration of how this could work for 'higher' cognition.

13.7. How preparedness and environmental input can constrain higher cognition

As an example of how genetically encoded biases and environmental input can combine to channel the development of higher cognitive functions, consider the development of social reasoning. Newborns (no more than a few minutes old) show a distinct bias for looking at faces as compared to other equally complex stimuli (Goren *et al.* 1975). Ten-week-old infants have been found to distinguish among emotional facial expressions (Entremont and Muir 1997). Within the first year of life, they also engage in *social referencing*, looking at their caregivers' reactions to novel stimuli (e.g. Stenberg and Hagekull 1997). By 2 years of age, they can succeed at tasks that require them to grasp another's goals, desires, or preferences (e.g. Bartsch and Wellman 1989; Flavell *et al.* 1990; Meltzoff 1995), and can readily identify violations of arbitrary social rules (Cummins 1999*a*). By 3 years of age, children spontaneously adopt a violation detection strategy when attempting to determine whether or not a social rule is being followed, but not when attempting to determine whether a conditional utterance is true or false, and the magnitude of this reasoning bias is equivalent to the magnitude found in the adult literature (Cummins 1999*a*). Children also find it easier to recognize instances of cheating than instances that prove a rule false (Harris 1996; Cummins 2000).

These early-emerging and robust domain-specific effects can be explained as the result of a biological preparedness to (*a*) distinguish agents from other objects; (*b*) entrain one's attentions on facial expressions; and (*c*) attempt to engage in reciprocal interactions with agents as opposed to objects. This cluster of social cognitive biases ensures that infants will be provided ample opportunity to notice contingencies between agents' actions and their consequences, and, hence 'fast track' the induction of social norms and the development of agent models necessary for complex social interaction. Just as there is a biological predisposition to acquire language, but which language is acquired depends on the surrounding language community, so too does there seem to be a biological predisposition to acquire social norms (i.e. the rules or conventions that constrain social behavior), but which norms are acquired depends on the surrounding social environment.

It seems necessary to posit a biological component to account for the acquisition of these aspects of social cognition because certain aspects of social cognition seem to depend on having the right neurological substrates. If there is a failure of biological preparedness, for example, if a neurological impairment produces failure to attend to social stimuli, then impairments in social learning and social reasoning will occur. Turner syndrome is a genetic abnormality in which a female lacks all or part of one X-chromosome. Individuals with only a maternally inherited X-chromosome show marked social difficulties, particularly on measures of social insight and adeptness (McGuffin and Scourfield 1997). Autism is a neurodevelopmental syndrome whose most vivid impact at the cognitive level is an impaired ability to reason about social stimuli (e.g. Leslie and Roth 1993; Baron-Cohen 1995). The selective impairments in social reasoning seen in Turner syndrome and autism may occur because the neurological substrates necessary for detecting and attending to social stimuli are congenitally absent or fail to develop normally.

That specialized pathways develop as a result of this 'nature–nurture' interaction is perhaps best supported by the selective cognitive impairments reported in syndromes such as prefrontal lobe syndrome. Prefrontal lobe syndrome is a pattern of impaired reasoning performance that results from bilateral damage to the ventromedial prefrontal cortical lobes. In humans, this syndrome is characterized by an impaired capacity to reason effectively about socio/emotional stimuli while leaving other types of intelligent reasoning virtually untouched (Damasio 1994). Monkeys with bilateral prefrontal ablations (both ventromedial and dorsolateral) show diminished self-grooming and reciprocal grooming behavior, greatly reduced affective interactions with others, diminished facial expressions and vocalizations, and sexual indifference (Damasio 1994: 74–5). They can no longer relate properly to others in their troop and others cannot relate to them. Damage to other sections of the cortex—even those resulting in paralysis—do not impair these social skills. The selective impairment of social reasoning that characterizes prefrontal lobe syndrome suggests that neural substrates exist whose primary purposes are the processing and integration of social reasoning functions.

Biological preparedness makes acquisition of reasoning skills and norms specific to the social domain nearly inevitable in normal environments when the neurological substrates are intact. But, although social reasoning and norm acquisition is highly canalized, *which* types of social skills and social norms a normal infant will acquire depends on the social stimuli to which it is exposed. Rhesus monkeys are notorious for their aggressive natures, while stump-tail monkeys typically are characterized by cohesive group life, high social tolerance, and frequent reconciliation after fights. Co-housing juveniles between the two species, however, produces a dramatic shift in social interaction strategies among the rhesus (de Waal and Johanowicz 1993). Those co-housed with stump-tailed macaques adopt many of the cooperative and conciliative behaviors typically seen only in stump-tails. As this example shows, social mammals are biologically predisposed to acquire the social norms that exist within their troops. That is the aspect of their cognition that is canalized. Which norms are acquired, however, depends on the social environment they find themselves in.

Acquisition of social reasoning skills and norms, then, is the result of a complex interaction of learning and innate components. But these innate components are not usefully conceptualized as innate modules, or as innate rules or theories or concepts. They are more usefully conceptualized in terms of biases in learning, especially in categorization and attention, that function to canalize the development of a specialized social reasoning system whose form is relatively invariant, but whose specific content tends to reflect the individual's socializing group. Because these biases are heritable, are relatively decoupled neurologically from other cognitive traits, and lead to highly canalized adaptive abilities, it is plausible to propose that they were selected for.

13.8. Closing comments

By invoking the concepts of biological preparedness and canalization, one can readily explain how a highly plastic developing brain could end up like a Swiss Army knife. Highly specialized functions need not be present at birth. Instead, the majority of comparative, developmental, and neuroscientific evidence weighs in on the side of fast-track learning through biological 'biases' or predispositions that entrain the focus of our attention on the environmental stimuli and contingencies that really mattered to the survival and reproductive success of our ancestors. Our biological predispositions impose the framework that is necessary to learn the things most vital for survival in a complex social environment, while neurological plasticity allows our actual environmental experiences the final say in whether and how those predispositions are expressed.

References

Ariew, A., 'Innateness and Canalization', *Philosophy of Science*, 63 (1996), S19–S27.

Baillargeon, R., 'Object Permanence in 3 1/2- and 4 1/2-month-old Infants', *Developmental Psychology*, 23 (1987), 655–64.

—— 'How do Infants Learn about the Physical World?', *Current Directions in Psychological Science*, 3 (1994), 133–40.

Banich, M. T., *Neuropsychology: The Neural Bases of Mental Function* (Boston, Mass.: Houghton-Mifflin, 1997).

Baron-Cohen, S., *Mindblindness: An Essay on Autism and Theory of Mind* (Cambridge, Mass.: MIT Press, 1995).

Bartsch, K., and Wellman, H. M., 'Young Children's Attribution of Action to Beliefs and Desires', *Child Development*, 60 (1989), 946–64.

Bernstein, I. L., and Borson, S., 'Learned Food Aversion: A Component of Anorexia Syndromes', *Psychological Review*, 93 (1986), 462–72.

Bertenthal, B. I., 'Infant Sensitivity to Figural Coherence in Biomechanical Motions', *Journal of Experimental Child Psychology*, 37 (1984), 213–30.

—— 'The Development of Sensitivity to Biomechanical Motions', *Child Development*, 56 (1985), 531–43.

Blakemore, C., 'Developmental Factors in the Formation of Feature Extracting Neurons', in F. G. Worden and F. O. Smith (eds.), *The Neurosciences, 3rd Study Program* (Cambridge, Mass.: MIT Press, 1974).

—— Cooper, G. F., 'Development of the Brain Depends on Visual Environment', *Nature*, 228 (1970), 477–8.

Braine, M. D. S., and O'Brien, D. P., 'A Theory of If: A Lexical Entry, Reasoning Program, and Pragmatic Principles', *Psychological Review*, 98 (1991), 182–203.

Broca, P., 'Paul Broca on the Speech Centers', in R. J. Herrnstein and E. G. Boring (eds.), *A Source Book in the History of Psychology* (Cambridge, Mass.: Harvard University Press, 1861).

Campos, J. J., and Stenberg, C., 'Perception, Appraisal, and Emotion: The Onset of Social Referencing', in M. Lewis and L. Rosenblum, *Infant Social Cognition: Empirical and Theoretical Considerations* (Hillsdale, NJ: Erlbaum, 1981).

Carey, S., and Spelke, E., 'Domain-Specific Knowledge and Conceptual Change', in L. A. Hirshfeld and S. A. Gelman (eds.), *Mapping the Mind: Domain Specificity in Cognition and Culture* (Cambridge: Cambridge University Press, 1994).

Cheng, P. W., and Holyoak, K. J., 'On the Natural Selection of Reasoning Theories', *Cognition*, 33 (1989), 285–313.

Cook, L. M., and Mineka, S., 'Observational Conditioning of Fear to Fear-Relevant versus Fear-Irrelevant Stimuli in Rhesus Monkeys', *Journal of Abnormal Psychology*, 98 (1989), 448–59.

—— 'Selective Associations in the Observational Conditioning of Fear in Rhesus Monkeys', *Journal of Experimental Psychology: Animal Behavior Processes*, 16 (1990), 372–89.

Cosmides, L., 'The Logic of Social Exchange: Has Natural Selection Shaped How Humans Reason? Studies with the Wason Selection Task', *Cognition*, 31 (1989), 187–276.

—— Tooby, J., 'Cognitive Adaptations for Social Exchange', in J. Barkow, L. Cosmides, and J. Tooby (eds.), *The Adapted Mind: Evolutionary Psychology and the Generation of Culture* (New York: Oxford University Press, 1992).

—— 'Origins of Domain Specificity: The Evolution of Functional Organization', in L. A. Hirshfeld and S. A. Gelman (eds.), *Mapping the Mind: Domain Specificity in Cognition and Culture* (Cambridge: Cambridge University Press, 1994).

Cummins, D. D., 'Evidence of Deontic Reasoning in 3- and 4-year-olds', *Memory and Cognition*, 24 (1996a), 823–9.

—— 'Evidence for the Innateness of Deontic Reasoning', *Mind and Language*, 11 (1996b), 160–90.

—— 'Dominance Hierarchies and the Evolution of Human Reasoning', *Minds and Machines*, 6 (1996c), 463–80.

—— 'Human Reasoning from an Evolutionary Perspective', *Proceedings of the 18th Annual Meeting of the Cognitive Science Society*, 18 (1996d), 50–1.

—— 'Rationality: Biological, Psychological, and Normative Theories', *Cahiers de Psychologie Cognitive (Current Psychology of Cognition)*, 16 (1997), 78–86.

—— 'Social Norms and Other Minds: The Evolutionary Roots of Higher Cognition', in D. D. Cummins and C. A. Allen (eds.), *The Evolution of Mind* (New York: Oxford University Press, 1998a), 30–50.

—— 'Can Humans Form Hierarchically Embedded Mental Representations? Commentary on R. W. Byrne and A. E. Russon, "Learning By Imitation: A Hierarchical Approach"', *Behavioral and Brain Sciences*, 21 (1998b), 687–8.

—— 'Biological Preparedness and Evolutionary Explanation', presented at the meeting of the Human Behavior and Evolution Society (University of California-Davis, July, 1998c).

—— 'Early Emergence of Cheater Detection in Human Development', presented at the 11th Annual Meeting of the Human Behavior and Evolution Society (University of Utah, Salt Lake City, June, 1999a).

Cummins, D. D., 'Cheater Detection is Modified by Social Rank', *Evolution and Human Behavior*, 20 (1999*b*), 229–48.

—— 'How the Social Environment Shaped the Evolution of Mind', *Synthese*, 122 (2000), 3–28.

—— 'Adaptive Cognitive Mechanisms: Reasoning about Social Norms and Other Minds', in R. Elio (ed.), *Common Sense, Reasoning and Rationality: Vancouver Studies in Cognitive Science*, 11 (Oxford: Oxford University Press, 2002).

Curtiss, S., *Genie: A Psycholinguistic Study of a Modern Day Wild Child* (New York: Academic Press, 1977).

Damasio, A. R., *Descartes' Error: Emotion, Reason, and the Human Brain* (New York: Grosset/Putnam, 1994).

De Waal, F. B., and Johanowicz, D. L., 'Modification of Reconciliation Behavior Through Social Experience: An Experiment with Two Macaque Species', *Child Development*, 64 (1993), 897–908.

Eimas, P. D., 'Speech Perception in Early Infancy', in L. B. Cohen and P. Salapafek (eds.), *Infant Perception* (New York: Academic Press, 1975).

Elman, J. L., Bates, E. A., Johnson, M. H., Karmiloff-Smith, A., Parisi, D., and Plunkett, K., *Rethinking Innateness: A Connectionist Perspective on Development* (Cambridge, Mass.: MIT Press/Bradford Books, 1996).

Entremont, B., and Muir, D. W., 'Five-Month-Olds' Attention and Affective Responses to Still-Faced Emotional Expressions', *Infant Behavior and Development*, 20 (1997), 563–8.

Etscorn, F., and Stephens, R., 'Establishment of Conditioned Taste Aversions with a 24-Hour CS-US Interval', *Physiological Psychology*, 1 (1973), 251–3.

Farah, M., 'The Neuropsychology of Mental Imagery', in J. W. Brown (ed.), *Neuropsychology of Visual Perception* (Hillsdale, NJ: Erlbaum, 1989).

Flavell, J. H., Flavell, E. R., Green, G. L., and Moses, L. J., 'Young Children's Understanding of Fact Beliefs versus Value Beliefs', *Child Development*, 61 (1990), 915–28.

Fodor, J., *The Modularity of Mind* (Cambridge, Mass.: MIT Press/Bradford Books, 1983).

Garcia, J., and Koelling, R. A., 'The Relation of Cue to Consequence in Avoidance Learning', *Psychonomic Science*, 4 (1966), 123–4.

—— Brett, L. P., and Rusiniak, K. W., 'Limits of Darwinian Conditioning', in S. B. Klein and R. R. Mowrer (eds.), *Contemporary Learning Theories: Instrumental Conditioning Theory and the Impact of Biological Constraints on Learning* (Hillsdale, NJ: Erlbaum, 1989).

Gazzaniga, M. S., Ivry, R. B., and Mangun, G. R., *Cognitive Neuroscience: The Biology of the Mind* (New York: W. W. Norton, 1998).

Gigerenzer, G., and Hug, K., 'Domain-Specific Reasoning: Social Contracts, Cheating, and Perspective Change', *Cognition*, 43 (1992), 127–71.

Gopnik, M., 'Feature Blindness: A Case Study', *Language Acquisition: A Journal of Developmental Linguistics*, 1 (1990a), 139–64.

—— 'Feature-Blind Grammar and Dysphasia', *Nature*, 344 (1990b), 715.

Goren, C. C., Sarty, M., and Wu, P. Y. K., 'Visual Following and Pattern Discrimination of Face-Like Stimuli by Newborn Infants', *Pediatrics*, 59 (1975), 544–9.

Harris, P. L., and Nuñez, M., 'Understanding of Permission Rules by Preschool Children', *Child Development*, 67 (1996), 1572–91.

Hilgard, E. R., and Bower, G. H., *Theories of Learning* (Englewood Cliffs, NJ: Prentice Hall, 1975).

Hirsh, H. V. B., and Spinelli, D. N. (1970). Visual Experience Modifies Distribution of Horizontally and Vertically Oriented Receptive Fields in Cats', *Science*, 168 (1970), 869–71.

Holland, J. H., Holyoak, K. J., Nisbett, R. E., and Thagard, P. R., *Induction: Processing of Inference, Learning, and Discovery* (Cambridge, Mass.: MIT Press, 1986).

Hubel, D. H., *Eye, Brain, and Vision* (New York: Scientific American Library, 1988).

Kuhl, P. K., 'Perception of Speech and Sound in Early Infancy', in L. B. Cohen and P. Salapafek (eds.), *Infant Perception* (New York: Academic Press, 1987).

Leslie, A. M., 'Pretense and Representation: The Origins of Theory of Mind', *Psychological Review*, 94 (1987), 412–26.

—— 'Pretense, Autism, and the 'Theory of Mind' Module', *Current Directions in Psychological Science*, 1 (1992), 18–21.

—— 'ToMM, ToBY, and Agency: Core Architecture and Domain Specificity', in L. A. Hirshfeld and S. A. Gelman (eds.), *Mapping the Mind: Domain Specificity in Cognition and Culture* (Cambridge: Cambridge University Press, 1994), 119–48.

—— Keeble, S., 'Do Six-Month-Old Infants Perceive Causality?', *Cognition*, 25 (1987), 265–88.

—— Roth, D., 'What Autism Teaches Us about Metarepresentation', in S. Baron-Cohen, H. Tager-Flusberg, and D. Cohen, *Understanding Other Minds: Perspectives from Autism* (Oxford: Oxford University Press, 1993), 83–111.

Lewontin, R. C., 'The Analysis of Variance and the Analysis of Causes', *American Journal of Human Genetics*, 26 (1974), 400–11.

Logue, A. W., 'A Comparison of Taste Aversion Learning in Humans and Other Vertebrates: Evolutionary Pressures in Common', in R. C. Bolles and M. D. Beecher, *Evolution and Learning* (Hillsdale, NJ: Erlbaum, 1988).

McGuffin, P., and Scourfield, J., 'A Father's Imprint on his Daughter's Thinking', *Nature*, 387 (1997), 652–3.

McKenzie, J. A., and O'Farrell, K., 'Modification of Developmental Instability and Fitness: Malathion Resistance in the Australian Sheep Blowfly', *Genetica*, 89 (1993), 67–76.

Meltzoff, A. N., 'Understanding the Intentions of Others: Re-enactment of Intended Acts by 18-Month-Old Children', *Developmental Psychology*, 31 (1995), 838–50.

Oaksford, M., and Chater, N., 'A Rational Analysis of the Selection Task as Optimal Data Selection', *Psychological Review*, 101 (1994), 608–31.

Öhman, A., 'Face the Beast and Fear the Face: Animal and Social Fears as Prototypes for Evolutionary Analysis of Emotion', *Psychophysiology*, 23 (1986), 123–45.

Oller, D. K., and Eilers, R. E., 'The Role of Audition in Infant Babbling', *Child Development*, 59 (1988), 441–9.

Piaget, J., *The Origins of Intelligence in Children* (New York: International University Press, 1952).

Pinker, S., *The Language Instinct* (New York: W. Morrow, 1994).

—— *How the Mind Works* (New York: Norton, 1997).

Rips, L. J., *The Psychology of Proof* (Cambridge, Mass.: MIT Press/Bradford Books, 1994).

Roe, A. W., Pallas, S. L., Kwon, Y. H., and Sur, M., 'Visual Projections Routed to the Auditory Pathway in Ferrets: Receptive Fields of Visual Neurons in Primary Auditory Cortex', *Journal of Neuroscience*, 12 (1992), 3651–64.

Samuels, R., Stich, S. P., and Tremoulet, P. D., 'Rethinking Rationality: From Bleak Implications to Darwinian Modules', in E. LePore and Z. Pylyshyn (eds.), *What is Cognitive Science?* (Oxford: Blackwell, 1999).

Seligman, M. E. P., 'Phobias and Preparedness', *Behavior Therapy*, 2 (1971), 307–20.

Spelke, E., 'Initial Knowledge: Six Suggestions', *Cognition*, 50 (1994), 431–45.

Squire, L., 'Memory and the Hippocampus: A Synthesis of Findings from Rats, Monkeys, and Humans', *Psychological Review*, 99 (1992), 195–231.

Starkey, P., Spelke, E. S., and Gelman, R., 'Numerical Abstraction by Human Infants', *Cognition*, 36 (1990), 97–127.

Stenberg, G., and Hagekull, B., 'Social Referencing and Mood Modification in 1-Year-Olds', *Infant Behavior and Development*, 20 (1997), 209–17.

Tooby, J., and Cosmides, L., 'Foreword', in S. Baron-Cohen, *Mindblindness: An Essay on Autism and Theory of Mind* (Cambridge, Mass.: MIT Press, 1995) pp. xi–xviii.

Vandell, L., and Wilson, K. S., 'Infants' Interactions with Mother, Sibling, and Peer: Contrasts and Relations between Interaction Systems', *Child Development*, 58 (1987), 176–86.

Waddington, C. H., *The Evolution of an Evolutionist* (Ithaca, NY: Cornell University Press, 1975).

Warrington, E. K., and Weiskrantz, L., 'New Method of Testing Long-Term Retention with Special Reference to Amnesic Patients', *Nature*, 217 (1968), 972–4.

Wernicke, C., 'The Aphasia Syndrome Complex: A Psychological Study on an Anatomical Basis', in G. H. Eggard (ed.), *Wernicke's Works on Aphasia* (The Hague: Mouton, 1874).

Wynn, K., 'Addition and Subtraction by Human Infants', *Nature*, 358 (1992), 749–50.

14

Cognitive Evolutionary Psychology Without Representational Nativism

DENISE DELLAROSA CUMMINS, ROBERT CUMMINS, AND PIERRE POIRIER

14.1. Introduction

14.1.1. Does a viable evolutionary cognitive psychology require the assumption of innate cognitive modules?

A viable evolutionary cognitive psychology requires that specific cognitive capacities be (i) heritable and (ii) 'quasi-independent.'[1] They must be heritable because there can be no evolutionary response to selection for traits that are not. They must also be quasi-independent—i.e. there must be additive genetic variance—because adaptive variations in a specific cognitive capacity could have no distinctive consequences for fitness if effecting those variations required widespread changes in other traits and capacities as well. If, for example, the emergence of a *theory of mind* in young

Originally published in *Journal of Experimental and Theoretical Artificial Intelligence*, 15/2 (April–June 2003), special issue: 'Cognitive Science in the New Millennium: Foundations, Directions, Applications, and Problems', 125–41.

[1] The term is Lewontin's (1978): 'Quasi-independence means that there is a great variety of alternative paths by which a given characteristic may change, so that some of them will allow selection to act on the characteristic without altering other characteristics of the organism in a countervailing fashion; pleiotropic and allometric relations must be changeable.' The point is that, from a genetic point of view, an intermediate grade of trait interaction/independence is required: too much interaction (universal pleiotropy) means that there is basically one evolutionary unit that must evolve as a unit; too little interaction (complete additivity) blocks the developmentally concerted integration of complex phenotypes because the component genes/effects are always being divided up in reproduction. In between is the realm of quasi-independence.

children is simply the consequence of the operation of a general purpose learning device, then the adaptive consequences of having a theory of mind (assuming there are some) would simply be a factor in the selection of the general purpose learning device in question. While this sort of relation between evolution and cognition would not be completely trivial, it would hardly justify a new subdiscipline of cognitive evolutionary psychology.

The dominant paradigm in evolutionary cognitive psychology attempts to satisfy these constraints by proposing that the mind can be characterized as a collection of *innate cognitive modules*. This position is succinctly captured by the following quotation:

[O]ur cognitive architecture resembles a confederation of hundreds or thousands of functionally dedicated computers (often called modules) designed to solve adaptive problems endemic to our hunter-gatherer ancestors. Each of these devices has its own agenda and imposes its own exotic organization on different fragments of the world. There are specialized systems for grammar induction, for face recognition, for dead reckoning, for construing objects and for recognizing emotions from the face. There are mechanisms to detect animacy, eye direction, and cheating. There is a 'theory of mind' module... a variety of social inference modules... and a multitude of other elegant machines. (Tooby and Cosmides 1995: pp. xiii–xiv)[2]

Since what is innate is heritable, the requirements of heritability and quasi-independence would be satisfied by innate cognitive modules on the plausible assumption that modules are relatively decoupled from each other and from other traits. By 'innate,' proponents of the dominant paradigm do *not* mean 'present at birth,' but rather encoded in the genome. For example, secondary sex characteristics are innate in that their development is encoded in the human genome but they are not present at birth. The relevant notion of a cognitive module derives from Fodor (1983). But, whereas Fodor held that modules were largely peripheral mechanisms, the modules at issue here know no such boundaries. Nor are all of Fodor's characteristics always, or even typically, assumed. Rather, the key features are: (1) domain specificity, both informationally and computationally; (2) universality—i.e. present in every normal mind in the species (assuming it

[2] Cosmides and Tooby are not the only proponents of this view. See also e.g. Leslie (1992) and Carey and Spelke (1994).

has gone to fixation); and (3) relative encapsulation—insensitivity to collateral information.[3]

When we say that this paradigm is dominant, we do not mean to suggest that it is widely accepted but rather that advocates and critics alike take the view in question to be the main theoretical contender defining the field. This is unfortunate because reliance on many innate cognitive modules has been heavily criticized in psychology and philosophy for its logical and theoretical incoherence as well as its incompatibility with what is known about developmental neurobiology (which we discuss in some detail below). These criticisms have been cited as evidence that an evolutionary cognitive psychology is not viable.

However, a viable evolutionary psychology does not require the existence of such modules in order to satisfy the heritability and 'quasi-independence' constraints. These requirements could also be satisfied by heritable learning biases, perhaps in the form of architectural or chronotopic constraints, which operated to increase the *canalization* of specific cognitive capacities in the ancestral environment (Cummins and Cummins 1999). Chronotopic constraints are constraints on the time course of development (Elman *et al.* 1996). A trait is said to be more or less canalized as its development is more or less robust across environmental variations (see Waddington 1957, 1975; Ariew 1996). As an organism develops, cognitive capacities that are highly canalized as the result of heritable learning biases might produce an organism that is behaviorally quite similar to an organism whose innate modules come 'on line' as the result of various environmental triggers.

Taking this possibility seriously is increasingly important as the case against the view that domain-specific knowledge/processors are genetically encoded (a view sometimes referred to as 'representational nativism') becomes increasingly strong (Elman *et al.* 1996; see also Samuels 1998, for a critique; Karmiloff-Smith *et al.* 1998, for an answer). The implications of the outcome of this debate are relevant not just to proponents and opponents of evolutionary cognitive psychology; they are directly relevant to

---

[3] This characterization differs somewhat from the 'Darwinian module,' ascribed to evolutionary psychology by Samuels *et al.* (1999). They define a Darwinian module as 'an innate, naturally selected, functionally specific and universal computational mechanism which may have access (perhaps even unique access) to a domain specific system of knowledge of the sort we've been calling a Chomskian module.' Encapsulation is not mentioned in this quote, but we retain this characteristic from Fodor's original formulation because, without it, it is difficult to distinguish a module from a mere 'subroutine.'

the broader question of how we characterize knowledge and its acquisition. While behavior geneticists and social scientists continue to argue about the relative importance of genes and environment in the development of personality and behavior, the initial either/or character of this debate has given way to an interactionist consensus. Nevertheless, there is still considerable vagueness and confusion about the conceptual framework needed to articulate specific interactionist proposals. This is especially true with respect to higher cognition: it is not clear how knowledge can be 'jointly authored,' and hence the debate tends to slip back into a debate about which knowledge, beliefs, or behavioral traits are innate, and which are learned. Conceptualizing matters in terms of learning-bias-induced canalization of domain/task-specific cognitive capacities, however, offers the promise of extending the interactionist perspective to cognition. One might ask of a jointly authored paper who wrote which sections, or paragraphs, or even sentences. But it could happen that both authors are jointly responsible for every sentence, with the *degree* of responsibility varying from place to place. This suggests thinking of all of knowledge as co-authored. It suggests that the question is not which concepts (or rules or whatever) are contributed by the genes and which by learning, but how canalized the development of a given concept or body of knowledge happens to be (Cummins and Cummins 1999). Many important pieces of an interactionist story about cognition are already to be found in the literature. In this chapter, we take some steps toward synthesizing this material, and articulating the conceptual resources for making this proposal specific.

To understand the learning-bias-and-canalization (LBC hereafter) framework gestured at above, we begin (section 14.2) by summarizing the reasons for scepticism about the dominant massive innate modularity paradigm. Evolutionary psychology has been criticized both for requiring massive innate modularity, and for being conceptually vague, confused, lacking explanatory force, and ill-founded empirically. A careful and rigorous formulation and analysis of LBC meets objections to massive modularity as well as questions about conceptual clarity and explanatory force. Only the science proper can speak to the issue of empirical grounding. Next, in section 14.3 we survey some of the recent developments that we believe are promising pieces of an LBC interactionist synthesis. In section 14.4, we briefly sketch the LBC framework. Finally, as an aid to rigor and theoretical viability, we also propose a series of simulations designed to demonstrate the feasibility of the processes postulated by the framework, and to test the rigor of its formulations. The goal of this kind of simulation work is primarily to investigate how selection could lead to learning biases that increase the canalization of fitness enhancing cognitive capacities. To some extent, this has already been done (see our literature review). Much is required, however, and we describe what we take to be the next step in section 14.5.

14.2. Arguments against the direct genetic specification of knowledge

To understand the motivation for the framework we propose for cognitive evolutionary psychology, one needs to appreciate the challenges facing the innate modules framework that currently predominates in evolutionary cognitive psychology. We begin, therefore, with a discussion of two influential lines of argument against direct genetic encoding of knowledge: the poverty of genetic resources and the plasticity of cortical tissue. We do not necessarily endorse these arguments, but they are sufficiently persuasive to motivate a careful and complete formulation of a framework for evolutionary cognitive psychology that can accommodate them.

14.2.1. The poverty of genetic resources

Innate cognitive modules will certainly require innate knowledge of some sort, either in the form of explicitly represented knowledge or in the form of knowledge implicit in the logic and structure of special purpose processors. Either way, direct genetic specification of an innate module will, as far as we know, require specifying synaptic connections in the cortex. (It might require more than this—e.g. neuron differentiation—but it will surely require at least a specification of synaptic connections.) Even if one supposes with Fodor and Pylyshyn (1988) that the level of synaptic connections is not the appropriate level for the specification of cognitive function, cognitive capacities still must be implemented as patterns of synaptic connectivity. If cognitive capacities are specified in the genome, the genome must encode for specific patterns of synaptic connections.

The problem is that the human genome does not appear to have the resources to directly specify a significant amount of cortical connectivity.

It is now known that human genotypes contain many fewer genes than previously thought (around 30,000–40,000 instead of 100,000; International Human Genome Sequencing Consortium 2001). Among these, it is estimated that from 20–30 percent (Wills 1991) to perhaps as many as half (Thompson 1993) may be implicated in brain development. However, our brains literally contain trillions of synaptic connections and 5,000 to 15,000 genes are clearly insufficient to directly encode all of these (Churchland 1995; Buller and Hardcastle 2000; see also McCullough 1951). Moreover, it seems that very few of the genes involved in brain development are concerned with cortical development. Most of the genes involved in brain development are dedicated to making sure our sensory transducers are properly hooked up. Winberg and Porter (1998) report that fully 4 percent of them are concerned with the sensory cells located inside our nose! If there are innate *cognitive* modules, these surely will be found in the cortex and not, for example, in the 'lowly' pons.

14.2.2. *The plasticity of cortical tissue*

The data just summarized mesh nicely with neuroscientific data suggesting that the human cortex is deeply immature at birth, leading some to claim that we are not really born with a cortex but with a proto-cortex (O'Leary 1989, 1997). If the pattern of connectivity in some area of the cortex were genetically pre-specified, then it should be impossible to transplant it to another area without bizarre consequences. If, for example, cells in the visual cortex are pre-programmed to finely connect themselves so as to subserve specifically visual processing, then surely they could not function properly when transplanted to the auditory cortex. But it has been shown that such transplants are possible, and that visual cortex cells transplanted to the auditory cortex do connect themselves in a manner that is relevant to auditory processing (O'Leary et al. 1992; see Samuels 1998 for a critique).

14.3. Alternatives to nativism

It is one thing to cast doubt on the feasibility of nativism; it is quite another to provide a feasible alternative that accounts for the data. We therefore briefly review some theory and research that, perhaps, has the potential to account for highly canalized, early emerging cognitive modules.

Quartz and Sejnowski (1997; see also Quartz 1999) argue that 'cortical development involves the progressive elaboration of neural circuits in which experience-dependent neural growth mechanisms act alongside intrinsic developmental processes to construct the representations underlying mature skills' (Quartz 1999: 48). The growth of dendritic trees is determined both by general endogenous mechanisms and by environment-driven activity. Moreover, it has been shown recently that dendritic trees have the computational properties of neural networks with hidden layers (Quartz and Sejnowski 1997: 549). Indeed, some researchers have suggested that patches of dendrite membrane might be the basic computing units of the brain (Koch *et al.* 1982; Jaslove 1992). It would follow that the representational capacities of dendritic trees grow as a result of general endogenous mechanisms interacting with environment-driven activity. These results enhance the plausibility of so-called constructive learning algorithms developed for neural networks—learning algorithms that allow a network to be dynamically reconfigured during training through the addition or deletion of nodes and weights (Fahlman and Lebiere 1990; Frean 1990; Hanson 1990; Hirose *et al.* 1991; Azimi-Sadjadi *et al.* 1993; Wynne-Jones 1993).

These ideas apply to the issue of nativism in a number of ways. For example, classic results from formal learning theory (e.g. Gold 1967) seem to show that language cannot be learned unless the child comes equipped with rich innate knowledge to restrict the set of grammars that have to be tested against evidence. These analyses assume that language learning is search through a fixed (time-invariant) hypothesis or representation space (a form of parametric regression). However, 'constructive learning' does not assume a fixed representation space. Indeed, its main feature is the *growth of the representation space*: 'The constructive learner builds its hypothesis space as it learns' (Quartz and Sejnowski 1997: 553). Accordingly, the classic results from formal learning theory do not apply to constructive learning. This does not mean that constructive learners actually can solve learning problems that formal analysis appeared to rule out, but it does remove a formidable and influential barrier and suggest a positive strategy for research. A number of formal and empirical results reviewed by Quartz and Sejnowski provide reason for optimism.

Some of these results come from experiments with artificial neural networks. Since we cannot review all of the relevant literature here, we discuss what is perhaps the most influential example.

In their book, *Rethinking Innateness*, Elman and his colleagues (1996) distinguish three types of nativism: representational, architectural, and chronotopic.[4] Representational nativism (RN) is the direct 'innate structuring of the mental/neural representations that underlie and constitute *knowledge*' (Bates *et al.* 1999: 591). Architectural nativism is the 'innate structuring of the information-processing system that must acquire and/or contain these representations' (Bates *et al.* 1999: 592). These might include, for instance, a specification of the basic computing units (their types and internal properties), the local architecture (e.g. number of layers in a structure), and the global architecture (e.g. pathways between global regions). Finally, chronotopic nativism is the 'innate structuring of the timing of developmental events' (Bates *et al.* 1999: 592).

The role of chronotopic constraints is illustrated by a famous experiment of Elman's (1993). Elman showed that a simple recurrent network subject to no chronotopic constraints is unable to learn a relatively complex grammar (an artificial grammar with central embedding and long-distance dependencies). In this case, only the architecture of the network is innate (i.e. specified by the modeler). A representational nativist might point out that the negative result was predictable and suggest that innate knowledge, in the form of a pre-specified pattern of connectivity between the network's units, is necessary to reduce the search space that has to be explored by the learning algorithm. But Elman found out that he could get the network to learn the grammar without innate knowledge (pre-specified connection weights) by simply adding a *chronotopic constraint, viz., decreasing the noise faced by the network's context units as a function of time*. In a simple recurrent network, the context units function as a short-term memory (STM) so, in effect, high noise means a rapidly fading STM, and decreasing noise through time means augmenting the STM's fidelity. This suggests that a plausible developmental trajectory—more and more faithful STM—can enable otherwise impossible learning.[5] This developmental trajectory was studied

---

[4] The original distinction between representational and architectural nativism is from Narayanan (1992).

[5] An added bonus is a possible explanation of the so-called critical learning period for language, since it is the plausibly irreversible change in STM that matters, not its ultimate fidelity.

independently, from a linguistics point of view, by Newport (1990; see also Goldowsky and Newport 1990).

14.4. The LBC (learning-bias-and-canalization) framework

We believe the foregoing discussion opens up possibilities for evolutionary explanations and analyses of cognitive capacities that are considerably more liberal and complex than the reigning innate modules approach exemplified by the work of Cosmides and Tooby (1987, 1994a, b, 1995, 1997). While the elements of LBC are not novel, we believe the particular synthesis we propose, and the correlative analysis of fundamental concepts, is.

LBC does not require a genetically problematic representational nativism, yet it does appear to satisfy the two fundamental criteria set out above for the viability of evolutionary cognitive psychology: heritability and quasi-independence. We discuss these in turn.

14.4.1. Heritability

The LBC framework assumes that there was variability in learning biases in ancestral populations. A learning bias can not only make acquisition of a cognitive trait possible, it can make it more likely. That is, it can increase the canalization of a cognitive trait. When such a trait proves adaptive, there will be a tendency for selection to spread the bias(es) responsible for increased canalization through the population. The end result is a population with a highly canalized cognitive trait.

Learning biases might themselves be the result of a kind of limited RN, since encoding these would not be as costly as encoding specific cognitive traits. More attractive, however, is the idea that variation in such traits as cortical architecture and its chronotopic properties amount to learning biases. This makes it more difficult to conceive of the resulting biases as specific to particular learning tasks—e.g. language or cheater detection—but it makes their genetic specification and heritability much more plausible, given that evolving a set of representations requires genetically coding each connection. While this nativist solution might work well for small networks, its applicability decreases drastically as the number of connections increases.

While the heritability of such traits as architectural and chronotopic constraints in ancestral populations is eminently plausible, it is, in the present state of knowledge and technology, difficult—perhaps impossible—to demonstrate the historical heritability of particular architectural and chronotopic constraints bearing on the acquisition of specific cognitive capacities. This is primarily because heritability is zero where there is no variance, and we can expect such things as the developmental course of STM involved in language learning to have gone to fixation in the current population. In this instance, then, we must be satisfied by two lines of argument. The first involves appeal to the fact that a strong genetic component in the architecture of the cortex and its chronotopic properties seems undeniable. Second, we can construct simulations that illustrate how heritable constraints of this kind can, in fact, give rise to learning biases that canalize observed effects. Language, for example, does get learned and, given the growing body of evidence against innate modules, there is a strong presumptive argument in favor of constraints and biases that can, in principle, account for the learning observed, including not just the end result but its typical developmental profile and observed departures from it.

14.4.2. Quasi-independence

If we assume that learning biases are not themselves representationally implemented, then, as remarked above, they will not be intrinsically specific to particular learning tasks, and this will impact the degree to which the cognitive traits they enable can evolve independently. This is both good news and bad news. The good news is that a demonstrable coupling between cognitive traits would provide strong evidence for a bias that grounded both, since the existence of such a bias would immediately explain the coupling. The hypothesis thus has the capacity to generate some interesting and falsifiable predictions. The bad news is that, as we noted in the introduction, some degree of independence among cognitive traits seems required to make evolutionary analysis a useful and interesting tool in cognitive psychology. It is worth noting that, even if learning biases proved to be quite general, it would not follow that they could not give rise to a modular functional architecture. A single bias could canalize development of several domain-specific capacities. For instance, Jacobs et al. (1991) have shown how mixtures of expert networks exposed to a what/where problem ... will always assign the 'where' task to the expert network which possesses a linear activation function. The implication is that networks do not necessarily need to be designed to carry out particular tasks. Rather, the task will select the network which has the appropriate (i.e. innate) computational properties.   (McCleod *et al.* 1998)

Two considerations tend to modify the point just made. First, architectural modularity might allow for learning biases that are not representationally based to have consequences for only one or a few cognitive traits. If, for example, there is an STM specific to language learning or some aspect of visual processing, then the chronotopic constraints on it might evolve primarily or exclusively under the control of the adaptive consequences they have for language learning or that aspect of visual processing. A second and closely related consideration is that specific types of input are known to be capable of causing the specialization of the local neural circuitry that receives it early in development (Elman *et al.* 1996). Hence, an innate specification of input connections can serve to specialize circuitry while effectively decoupling it from circuitry grounding other types of processing.

LBC has a number of special features that require emphasis:

(1) Learning has its costs. Learning takes time, energy, and cognitive resources. During the learning period, an organism is at a disadvantage *vis-à-vis* a counterpart that does not have to learn the target capacity. Learning typically entails making mistakes, and these can be costly. If learning is done in the infant/juvenile period, care must be provided by parents, etc.

(2) Learning has its advantages. Learning allows for the possibility that an organism can adapt to new environments. Hence, learning can sometimes give rise to a capacity that is more highly canalized than one that is completely innate in conditions in which the novel environment fails to 'trigger' development of the innate capacity or leads to the development of a 'capacity' that is not capable of fulfilling its function in the novel environment.

(3) Learning allows for the possibility of overcoming neural defects due to trauma or developmental problems. Direct specification of synaptic connections and structure in the genome would seem to leave the organism vulnerable in this respect.

(4) LBC would appear to allow more easily for gradual evolution of cognition, since the relevant architectural and chronotopic constraints can be introduced and gradually modified antecedent to the appearance of the target cognitive capacity.

(5) LBC is compatible with innate modules (though the arguments that motivate us to take it seriously are not), as well as with the innate developmental recipe approach associated with Pinker (1994, 1997). Direct comparison of LBC with other frameworks at both the conceptual level and the simulation level is a major goal of the project.

14.5. The role of simulation in this research

The simulation of adaptive behavior (SAB) is now a recognized subfield of psychology with its own periodicals (e.g. *Adaptive Behavior, From Animals to Animats*, both from MIT Press) and series of conferences (*International Conference on Adaptive Behavior*). As Miller and Todd (1994) rightly point out, there is a clear link between SAB and work in evolutionary psychology, a link that goes both ways: human evolutionary psychology can inform SAB by providing target behaviors to simulate and SAB can inform evolutionary psychology by testing the computational realizability of putative evolutionary stories (i.e. whether a proposed story could have taken place by the application of known evolutionary mechanisms). This aspect of SAB is particularly important in the present context since, as all researchers who have attempted the simulation of complex nonlinear processes know only too well, the dynamics of nonlinear processes is often counterintuitive and difficult to rationally anticipate from the armchair. Simulation plays several different related roles in our work:

- *Rigor and precision*: it has repeatedly been our experience that simulation exposes lacunae, vagueness, and ambiguity in the formulation of theories and hypotheses at every level of detail.
- *Hypothesis generation*: simulation not only helps to refine and elaborate hypotheses, it often suggests novel hypotheses. The example of chronotopic constraints from Elman rehearsed above is a striking case in point.

- *Prediction generation*: the interaction of architectural and chronotopic constraints on network design and development with learning and selection is extremely complex. We suspect the only sure way to reliably generate predictions from hypotheses about such interactions is to run simulations.
- The simulation of adaptive behavior provides us with the means to test the sufficiency of the LBC framework and to compare it in detail with competitors.

In the literature on simulations, two distinct algorithms are alternately at work. First, a neural network 'learns' various environmental contingencies during the life of the organism whose behavior it directs, and develops a set of representations through its interaction with that environment. Second, a genetic algorithm 'evolves' a population of networks through differential reproduction and mutation of some of the network's parameters.[6] In what follows, we briefly review some the relevant literature in this field and explain how our work proposes to adapt this research to our study of cognitive modularity.

Three degrees of RN have emerged in this literature: *full* representational nativism, *minimal* representational nativism (after Clark 1993), and *no* representational nativism (or *representational* constructivism).[7] *Full RN* is the view that systems are born with a full set of representations or develop such a set without the help of learning mechanisms. Work in the simulation of adaptive behavior has shown that it is possible to evolve representations in connectionist nets as 'easily' as it is to teach them: any set of representations (underlying such behaviors) that can be learned by a neural network can also be evolved by a genetic algorithm (see Yao 1993 for a review). In an evolved population of neural networks, all or most individuals in the population are born with the representations, which are therefore literally innate. For instance, Nolfi *et al.* (1994) evolved a population of animats (simulated organisms), controlled by a neural network and selected for their ability to find food items on the basis of information about distance and direction to food.

---

[6] Mutation is only one of the genetic parameters that can be used to implement such a search procedure. Another well-known parameter is crossover, which is known to work well computationally (Holland 1975) but is difficult to apply to neural networks (Yao 1993).

[7] Although we adopt Clark's expression, what we describe as minimal representational nativism is not exactly what he describes with the term since, contrary to us, he refuses to distinguish architectural and representational constraints on development.

Neural networks can easily be trained by back-propagation to achieve such behaviors and, as Nolfi *et al.* (1994) have shown, they can also be evolved to do so. An experiment by Floreano and Mondada (1996) shows how sophisticated these evolved representations can be. They used a simple recurrent network (Elman 1990) to let some of the robot's representational capacities be carried by the network's internal dynamics. Although the network only contained four hidden units, they found that two of them sustained an intricate topological map of the robot's environment, a map that varied systematically as a function of the robot's current orientation and the state of its rechargeable battery. These hidden units, in fact, seemed to function as 'place cells,' which are known to exist in the rat's hippocampus (O'Keefe and Nadel 1978), indicating, perhaps, that this type of internal organization is an especially efficient way to implement navigation behavior. Full representational nativism is thus a viable option from a purely computational point of view. However, to get a genetic algorithm to evolve a set of representations, each connection weight must be coded on an (artificial) chromosome. While this solution might work well for small networks, its applicability decreases as the number of connections increases. Moreover, maintaining a large genotype is not without costs of its own (both in computers and in nature), and it is reasonable to think that, if the same end state can be reached with a smaller genotype, the very process that evolves the set of representations will also select those networks that can achieve the result with as small a genotype as possible.

Minimal RN is the view that systems are born with (or develop without the help of learning mechanisms) the minimal set of representations necessary to learn the full set underlying a given behavior. Nolfi and Parisi (1997) constructed a network comprising two modules: one (the standard module) whose function was to drive the wheels of a small robot and one (the teaching module) whose function was to send a teaching signal to the other module.[8] The connection weights of both modules were evolved through a genetic algorithm, but the weights of the standard module were also adjusted throughout the life of the robot by back-propagation (on the basis of a teaching signal it received from the teaching module). The weight changes caused by back-propagation were discarded at reproduction time, in order to ensure Darwinian (not Lamarckian) evolution. Finally, successive

---

[8] For a similar system, see Ackley and Littman (1991).

generations of robots were alternately 'raised' in bright and dark environments (a difference that has a major impact on their infrared sensors). Robots were selected as a function of their ability to navigate the environment quickly while avoiding obstacles. As a control, Nolfi and Parisi also evolved a population of simpler robots comprising only a standard module. The robots in the control population are born with the innate representations needed to behave successfully in both environments. However, the fitness of the control population was quickly surpassed by that of the two-module network. The control networks evolve a strategy that works in both environments but that is optimal in neither. The two-module robots adopt different and superior strategies depending on whether they are in a bright or dark environment. Evolution has given the teaching module the representations necessary to differentially teach the standard module according to the environment in which the robot is learning. It is interesting to note that neither module evolved a set of representations efficient for navigating while avoiding obstacles; their success remained dependent on learning. Unlike the control population, the two-module robots are not born knowing how to behave. They are born with a set of representations that predispose them to learn the set of representations underlying the best strategy for the environment they happen to occupy.

Representational constructivism is the view that all representations are learned from the interaction between the network and its environment. Too often, however, representational constructivism is confused with the view that everything cognitive is learned. Elman *et al.*'s (1996) distinction between representational, architectural, and chronotopic constraints on development allows us to rethink the nature/nurture debate within cognitive science. Perhaps evolution only fixes the architectural and chronotopic constraints necessary to canalize learning towards the set of representations underlying the modules' cognitive abilities.[9] Indeed, Elman's famous (1993) experiment (described above) is one such instance, where only architectural and chronotopic constraints were innate. However, these were not 'evolved' but rather fixed by trial and error. It would be interesting to see which constraints a process of simulated evolution like the one described

[9] Or perhaps evolution fixes those first, and as much as possible, resorting to fixing representations (connection weights) only when the space of possible architectural and chronotopic biases has been fully explored and no set of biases has been found that could canalize learning towards the proper set of representations; a solution that would correspond to minimal representational nativism (see above).

above would fix in the network's genotype. In any case, some researchers have evolved only chronotopic or architectural characteristics of learning networks. For instance, Floreano and Mondada (1996) devised an experiment in which a robot that is not born with a navigation module learns it very quickly (in fewer than ten sensory-motor loops—i.e. ten sweeps of the back-propagation algorithm) *because of what it is born with*. Instead of evolving the connection weights to and from the hidden unit, Floreano and Mondada evolve a set of 'meta-properties' for each connection: whether the connection is driving or modulatory, whether it is excitatory or inhibitory, what learning rule it uses (one of four variants of the Hebb rule) and what its bias is. Because the meta-properties are evolved in the environment in which the robot's network controller will eventually have to learn the task, and because the connection weights are not coded on the chromosome, the genetic algorithm does not evolve a capacity to navigate but an ability to quickly learn navigation. The capacity is not innate but highly canalized through a motor learning bias:

Learning of the evolved controller relies on simple genetically inherited abilities. For example, the controller analyzed above always starts by moving backward until it finds some object; then it rotates to the right until its rightmost sensors become active and synapses begin to change. These two simple motor programs result from weak sensory signals (mostly noise) filtered and amplified through the synaptic matrix of excitatory and inhibitory weights. They represent the basis from which learning can start to operate and are similar to instincts in that they are both genetically inherited and represent primitives upon which the organism can start to explore its environment. In other words evolution not only shapes the learning modality, but also bootstraps learning by selecting basic behaviors useful for learning.   (Nolfi and Floreano 2000: 172)

To test the in-principle sufficiency of the LBC framework, and to investigate its implications, simulation experiments need to be designed to explore the way in which the development of a given adult state (in particular, the representations that are thought to constitute a cognitive module) can be canalized by the presence of innate learning biases. In such simulations, learning and evolution interact as previously, but evolution (as simulated by the genetic algorithm) is constrained not to evolve a set of representations (or a *full* set of representations) but a set of architectural and/or chronotopic (or some *minimal* representational) learning biases that, in any standard environment, will lead to the acquisition (via back-propagation or some other connectionist learning algorithm) of the necessary representations. These simulations should be designed to allow comparisons between innate-module scenarios (full-RN) with LBC scenarios (minimal or no-RN). Note that an LBC scenario involves architectural and chronotopic nativism, but no representational nativism. We describe two such simulations here to give the flavor of the work that needs to be done.

14.5.1. Simple food finding task

In evolutionary biology, fitness is defined as reproductive success—that is, the number of living offspring an individual produces that go on to reproduce themselves. Inclusive fitness means an individual's own fitness plus his or her effect on the fitness of any relative. Maximizing fitness means maximizing reproductive success. In engineering applications, fitness is typically defined *prior to reproduction* in terms of a 'fitness function,' which evaluates the performance of each individual phenotype with respect to some predetermined criterion. Those individuals that achieve the highest fitness values are allowed to reproduce. In the simulations described below, we choose food consumption as the criterion of interest and define our fitness function in terms of the number of food items eaten during a specified period of time. A natural strategy is to use a sigmoid function (which is common in neural network models) wherein fitness values change very little until a certain threshold of intake is achieved, then fitness increases linearly with food intake until an upper threshold is achieved at which point it tapers off. Those achieving the highest fitness values will be allowed to reproduce.

A typical simulation would consist of a main program and four subroutines embedded in each other: a neural net embedded in a critter embedded in an environment embedded in a genetic algorithm. The main program attaches a net to a critter, puts the critter in an environment where it gets to move around and eat, then applies the genetic algorithm. Computations proceed as follows: there is an input (a direction to move), which causes activation to spread through a simple recurrent net ($4 \times 4 \times 4$ in the current pilot). The output is a move. The critters ($n = 20$) make twenty-seven moves and then fitness (amount of food consumed) is measured. (For details about learning, see below.) The one top individual is allowed to reproduce. For the others, a roulette scheme (commonly used with genetic algorithms) is used: the roulette represents the total sum of fitness in the population, and each critter gets a portion of the roulette proportional to its own fitness. The roulette is spun twenty times and whichever critter 'wins' gets to reproduce. Mutation occurs randomly, with a few individuals being mutated a great deal, while others are not mutated at all. While biologically unrealistic, this is more realistic than very slight mutations to every synapse of every individual (common in the connectionist literature) and has a substantial engineering track record. Other mutation plans need to be tested as well. Unfortunately, crossover is not currently feasible with neural nets.

The environment consists of a surface overlaid by a grid. The critters can move forward, backward, left, and right on the grid. The environment is contoured in various ways so that moves can be classified as up or down various gradients. This might be, for example, smell (stronger, weaker, same), altitude (up, down, same), light (brighter, darker, same), etc. Food can be found (with greater or less statistical likelihood) by following certain gradients up or down, and ignoring others.

14.5.1.1. Learning   All critters start out with a set of random weights. Full RN critters do not learn, only LBC and mixed condition critters learn. LBC and mixed critters are trained using back-propagation to predict the results of possible moves—up, down, same—across the gradients in the environment. The prediction task is useful because the correct response is simply (some part of) the next input, making back-propagation learning more realistic. They are not trained to make moves that take them towards food since, a priori, there is no reason to prefer one gradient over another, or going 'up' to going 'down.' Rather, they are reinforced for moves that generate/ increase some 'pleasant' stimulus. Evolution determines which stimuli can be discriminated and which, among those, are 'pleasant'—i.e. which generate reinforcement signals. This allows the critters to learn to follow a gradient even though the payoff is remote.[10]

14.5.1.2. Selection: what is reproduced   In the pure LBC condition, connection weights are not reproduced. Instead, architectural constraints (e.g. number

---

[10] Learning has costs, e.g. delayed reproduction, and the costs of prenatal and juvenile investment by parents.

of nodes, number of layers, connection patterns, connection meta-properties, and activation functions), chronotopic constraints (e.g. time course of realized changes in the network over the lifetime of the individual), and learning rule parameters (e.g. learning rates and intervals) are reproduced. In the mixed condition, some connection weights are also reproduced, viz., those in some subnetwork. In the full RN condition, the connection weights are reproduced *in addition to* what is reproduced in the pure LBC and mixed conditions.

14.5.2. *Social encounters*

Critters travel randomly through an environment, collecting food. When one critter encounters another, it can share food, withdraw, or attempt to take the other critter's food by force. Both critters have the same options. Outcomes are determined by relative dominance rankings. Dominance ranking is encoded as a property list, which includes size, health, facial expression, posture, and observed encounters with other critters. When one critter encounters another, their respective property lists are encoded in the input activation vectors to each other. A property list is used rather than a simple relative ranking because it allows relative dominance to be learned from the list. Advanced variations include the possibility of being aided by 'friends' recruited by sharing resources.

- *Selection* works analogously to the first task.
- *Learning*: as in the first task, networks are trained to predict the outcomes of possible moves, given dominance information or information bearing on dominance. In this instance, we can assume immediate feedback concerning the move actually made, since the outcome of an encounter is determined immediately.

Simulations like these are designed to test whether the LBC condition can be at least as effective as the RN condition in generating a population with highly canalized cognitive capacities. To do this, we compare critters whose target capacities evolve in the RN condition with critters that evolve learning biases that enable effective acquisition of the target capacities, either by evolving representations (connections) in a learning subnetwork (the mixed condition), or by evolving non-representational constraints that fast-track learning of the target capacity.

14.5.3. Evaluation

Populations are compared in terms of average fitness, where the fitness of an individual is, as before, assumed to be proportional to task success during a lifetime. Individuals and populations can also be tested for plasticity, since one of the manifest advantages of learning is that it has the potential to allow the organism to acquire the target capacity in altered environments, thus opening up the possibility that the LBC scenario might lead to organisms with more highly canalized capacities than RN. This is an important consideration, since it tends to undermine universality as an argument for representational innateness. A universally acquired capacity is likely to be one acquired in a variety of environments. Too much environmental variability has the potential to lead to the extinction of capacities dependent on representations specified in the genome.

Simulations like those just described would hopefully advance our understanding a step beyond the results reviewed above by making direct fitness and canalization comparisons between RN, mixed, and non-RN scenarios, and by introducing social encounters (generally studied only in RN conditions) in a way directly relevant to evolutionary hypotheses concerning innate social reasoning modules.

14.6. Conclusion

We believe that the emergence of evolutionary cognitive psychology is an important development in cognitive science, one that may leave a lasting effect on the whole field. This promise can only be realized, however, if the research is conceptualized in a framework that is consistent with what is known about the complex interactions between evolution, neural architecture and its development, and learning. The LBC framework described here shows considerable promise of effecting the needed 'interactionist' synthesis in connection with the evolution of cognition. It avoids massive innate cognitive modules and the problematic representational nativism it engenders. In its place, it motivates us to look for the evolution of non-representationally based learning biases that interact with development and the environment to produce highly canalized and early emerging cognitive capacities.

Evolutionary cognitive psychology is intrinsically problematic because brains are soft, leaving no historical record, and because the traits of interest have (presumably) gone to fixation and cannot be readily studied in fruit flies or bacteria. It can, however, be studied in artificial creatures. Ethology, especially primatology, can provide invaluable clues. By telling us which capacities develop when and under what environmental conditions, developmental psychology continues to provide explananda that can, in principle and in fact, be used to distinguish among evolutionary hypotheses when these are framed with sufficient detail and rigor (see D. Cummins 2004 for some telling examples). This will not be enough for those who want the scientific equivalent of a smoking gun. To those, we offer the following reminder: no one has ever predicted a tide from Newton's theory of gravity (or any other theory of gravity) and the hypothesis that lunar gravitation causes the tides. Yet this is a textbook example of good science because it allows us to understand the tides in terms of simulations ranging in complexity form passing a magnet over a newspaper with another magnet under it, creating a wave, to computer simulations (e.g. http://webphysics.ph.msstate.edu/jc/library/9-PP). (We are grateful to Franz-Peter Griesmier for this example.) No one dismisses this explanation as a 'just so' story because it cannot be directly tested. Interactions between evolution, development, and learning of the sort contemplated within the LBC framework suggested here have the potential to allow us to understand cognition in a ways that standard cognitive and developmental psychology and neuroscience cannot hope to achieve alone.

References

Ackley, D. H., and Littman, M. L., 'Interaction between Learning and Evolution', in C. G. Langton *et al.* (eds.), *Proceedings of the Second Conference on Artificial Life* (Reading, Mass.: Addison-Wesley, 1991), 487–509.

Ariew, A., 'Innateness and Canalization', *Philosophy of Science*, 63 (1996), S19–S27.

——'Innateness is Canalisation: In Defense of a Developmental Account of Innateness', in V. Hardcastle (ed.), *Biology Meets Psychology: Constraints, Connections, Conjectures* (Cambridge, Mass.: MIT Press, 1999), 117–38.

Azimi-Sadjadi, M. R., Sheedvash, S., and Trujillo, F. O., 'Recursive Dynamic Node Creation in Multilayer Neural Networks', *IEEE Transactions on Neural Networks*, 4 (1993), 242–56.

Baron-Cohen, S., *Mindblindness: An Essay on Autism and Theory of Mind* (Cambridge, Mass.: MIT Press, 1995).

Bates, E., Elman, J. L., Johnson, M. H., Karmiloff-Smith, A., Parisi, D., and Plunkett, K., 'Innateness and Emergentism', in W. Bechtel and G. Graham (eds.), *A Companion to Cognitive Science* (Oxford: Blackwell 1999), 590–601.

Buller, D., and Hardcastle, V. G., 'Evolutionary Psychology, Meet Developmental Neurobiology: Against Promiscuous Modularity', *Brain and Mind*, 1 (2000), 307–25.

Carey, S., and Spelke, E., 'Domain-Specific Knowledge and Conceptual Change', in L. A. Hirshfeld and S. A. Gelman (eds.), *Mapping the Mind: Domain Specificity in Cognition and Culture* (Cambridge: Cambridge University Press, 1994).

Churchland, P. M., *The Engine of Reason, the Seat of the Soul: A Philosophical Journey into the Brain* (Cambridge, Mass.: MIT Press, 1995).

Clark, A., 'Minimal Rationalism', *Mind*, 102 (1993), 587–610.

—— (1998) 'What's Knowledge Anyway?', *Mind and Language*, 13 (1998), 571–5.

Cosmides, L., and Tooby, J., 'From Evolution to Behavior: Evolutionary Psychology as the Missing Link', in J. Dupré (ed.), *The Latest on the Best* (Cambridge, Mass.: MIT Press, 1987), 278–306.

—— 'Beyond Intuition and Instinct Blindness: Toward an Evolutionarily Rigorous Cognitive Science', *Cognition*, 50 (1994*a*), 41–77.

—— 'Origins of Domain Specificity: The Evolution of Functional Organization', in L. A. Hirshfeld and S. A. Gelman (eds.), *Mapping the Mind: Domain Specificity in Cognition and Culture* (Cambridge: Cambridge University Press, 1994*b*).

—— 'From Function to Structure: The Role of Evolutionary Biology and Computational Theories in Cognitive Neuroscience', in M. Gazzaniga, *The Cognitive Neurosciences* (Cambridge, Mass.: MIT Press, 1995), 1199–210.

—— 'The Modular Nature of Human Intelligence', in A. B. Scheibel and J. W. Schoof (eds.), *The Origin and Evolution of Intelligence* (Boston, Mass.: Jones & Bartlett Publishers, 1997), 71–101.

Cummins, D. D., 'The Evolution of Reasoning', in J. P. Leighton and R. J. Sternberg (eds.), *The Nature of Reasoning* (Cambridge: Cambridge University Press, 2004), 339–74.

Cummins, R., 'Biological Preparedness and Evolutionary Explanation', *Cognition*, 73 (1999), B37–53.

Elman, J., 'Finding Structure in Time', *Cognitive Science*, 14 (1990), 179–211.

—— 'Learning and Development in Neural Networks: The Importance of Starting Small', *Cognition*, 48 (1993), 71–99.

—— Bates, E. A., Johnson, M. H., Karmiloff-Smith, A., Parisi, D., and Plunkett, K., *Rethinking Innateness: A Connectionist Perspective on Development* (Cambridge, Mass.: MIT Press/Bradford Books, 1996).

Fahlman, S. E., and Lebiere, C., 'The Cascade-Correlation Architecture', in D. Touretsky (ed.), *Advances in Neural Information Processing Systems* (San Mateo, Calif.: Morgan Kaufmann, 1990).

Floreano, D., and Mondada, F., 'Evolution of Plastic Neurocontrollers for Situated Agents', in P. Maes, M. Mataric, J.-A. Meyer, J. Pollack, and S. Wilson (eds.), *From Animals to Animats 4: Proceedings of the International Conference on Simulation of Adaptive Behavior* (Cambridge, Mass.: MIT Press, 1996), 402–10.

Fodor, J., *The Modularity of Mind* (Cambridge, Mass.: MIT Press/Bradford Books, 1983).

——Pylyshyn, Z., 'Connectionism and Cognitive Architecture: A Critical Analysis', *Cognition*, 28 (1988), 3–71.

Frean, M., 'The Upstart Algorithm: A Method for Constructing and Training Feedforward Neural Networks', *Neural Computation*, 2 (1990), 198–209.

Gold, E. M., 'Language Identification in the Limit', *Information and Control*, 10 (1967), 447–74.

Goldowsky, B., and Newport, E. L., 'The Less is More Hypothesis: Modeling the Effect of Processing Constraints on Language Learnability', unpublished manuscript (Rochester, NY: University of Rochester, 1990).

Hanson, S. J., 'Meiosis Networks', in D. Touretsky (ed.), *Advances in Neural Information Processing Systems II* (San Mateo, Calif.: Morgan Kaufmann, 1990), 533.

Hirose, Y., Yamashita, K., and Hijiya, S., 'Back-Propagation Algorithm which Varies the Number of Hidden Units', *Neural Networks*, 4 (1991), 61–6.

Holland, J. H., *Adaptation in Natural and Artificial Systems* (Ann Arbor: University of Michigan Press, 1975).

International Human Genome Sequencing Consortium, 'Initial Sequencing and Analysis of the Human Genome', *Nature*, 409 (2001), 860–921.

Jacobs, R. A., Jordan, M. I., and Barto, A.G., 'Task Decomposition through Competition in a Modular Connectionist Architecture: The What and Where Vision Tasks', *Cognitive Science*, 15 (1991), 219–50.

Jaslove, S. W., 'The Integrative Properties of Spiny Distal Dendrites', *Neuroscience*, 47 (1992), 495–519.

Johnson, M. H., *Developmental Cognitive Neuroscience: An Introduction* (Oxford: Blackwell, 1997).

Karmiloff-Smith, A., Plunkett, K., Johnson, M. H., Elman, J. L., and Bates, E., 'What does it Mean to Claim that Something is 'Innate'? Response to Clark, Harris, Lightfoot and Samuels', *Mind and Language*, 13 (1998), 588–97.

Koch, C., Poggio, T., and Torre, V., 'Retinal Ganglion Cells: A Functional Reinterpretation of Dendritic Morphology', *Philosophical Transactions of the Royal Society of London: Biological Sciences*, 298 (1982), 227–63.

Leslie, A. M., 'Pretense, Autism, and the 'Theory of Mind' Module', *Current Directions in Psychological Science*, 1 (1992), 18–21.

Lewontin, R. C., 'Adaptation', *Scientific American*, 239 (1978), 157–69.

McCullough, W. S., 'Why the Mind is in the Head', in L. A. Jeffress (ed.), *Cerebral Mechanisms in Behavior: The Hixon Symposium* (New York: Hafner, 1951), 42–111.

McLeod, P., Plunkett, K., and Rolls, E. T., *Introduction to Connectionist Modelling of Cognitive Processes* (Oxford: Oxford University Press, 1998).

Miller, G. F., and Todd, P. M., 'A Bottom–Up Approach with a Clear View of the Top: How Human Evolutionary Psychology Can Inform Adaptive Behavior Research', *Adaptive Behavior*, 3 (1994), 83–95.

Narayanan, A., 'Is Connectionism Compatible with Rationalism?', *Connection Science*, 4 (1992), 271–92.

Newport, E. L., 'Maturational Constraints on Language Learning', *Cognitive Science*, 14 (1990), 11–28.

Nolfi, S., and Floreano, D., *Evolutionary Robotics* (Cambridge, Mass.: MIT Press, 2000).

—— Parisi, D., 'Learning to Adapt to Changing Environments in Evolving Neural Networks', *Adaptive Behavior*, 5 (1997), 99–105.

—— Elman, J. L., and Parisi, D., 'Learning and Evolution in Neural Networks', *Adaptive Behavior*, 3 (1994), 5–28.

O'Keefe, J., and Nadel, L., *The Hippocampus as a Cognitive Map* (New York: Oxford University Press, 1978).

O'Leary, D. D. M., 'Do Cortical Areas Emerge from a Protocortex?', *Trends in Neuroscience*, 12 (1989), 400–6.

—— 'Areal Specialization of the Developing Neocortex: Differentiation, Developmental Plasticity and Genetic Specification', in D. Magnusson *et al.* (eds.), *The Lifespan Development of Individuals: Behavioral, Neurobiological and Psychosocial Perspectives. A Synthesis* (Cambridge: Cambridge University Press, 1997), 23–37.

—— Schlaggar, B. L., and Stanfield, B. B., 'The Specification of Sensory Cortex: The Lessons from Cortical Transplantation', *Experimental Neurology*, 115 (1992), 121–6.

Pinker, S., *The Language Instinct* (New York: W. Morrow, 1994).

—— *How the Mind Works* (New York: Norton, 1997).

Quartz, S. R., 'The Constructivist Brain', *Trends in Cognitive Sciences*, 3 (1999), 48–57.

—— Sejnowski, T. J., 'The Neural Basis of Cognitive Development: A Constructivist Manifesto', *Behavioral and Brain Sciences*, 20 (1997), 537–96.

Samuels, R., 'What Brains Won't Tell Us About the Mind: A Critique of the Neurobiological Argument Against Representational Nativism', *Mind and Language*, 13 (1998), 548–70.

—— Stich, S. P., and Tremoulet, P. D., 'Rethinking Rationality: From Bleak Implications to Darwinian Modules', in E. Lepore and Z. Pylyshyn (eds.), *What is Cognitive Science?* (Oxford: Blackwell, 1999).

Thompson, R. F., *The Brain: A Neuroscience Primer* (New York: Freeman, 1993).

Tooby, J., and Cosmides, L., Foreword, in S. Baron-Cohen (1995: pp. xi–xviii).

Waddington, C. H., *The Strategy of the Genes* (London: Allen & Unwin, 1957).

—— *The Evolution of an Evolutionist* (Ithaca, NY: Cornell University Press, 1975).

Wills, C., *Exons, Introns, and Talking Genes: The Science Behind the Human Genome Project* (New York: Basic Books, 1991).

Winberg, J., and Porter, R. H., 'Olfaction and Human Neonatal Behavior: Clinical Implications', *Acta Paediatria*, 87 (1998), 6–10.

Wynne-Jones, M., 'Node Splitting: A Constructive Algorithm for Feed-Forward Neural Networks', *Neural Computing and Applications*, 1 (1993), 17–22.

Yao, X., 'A Review of Evolutionary Artificial Neural Networks', *International Journal of Intelligent Systems*, 8 (1993), 539–67.

15

Connectionism and the Rationale Constraint on Cognitive Explanation

15.1. The rationale constraint

Cognitive science wants to explain cognitive capacities. Capacities are dispositions, specified by articulating what Ruth Millikan (1984: 20) calls a law *in situ*, a law specific to a particular type of mechanism or system. A *cognitive* capacity is a disposition to satisfy some set of epistemic constraints that define 'correct' or 'good' performance. The capacity to play chess, to recognize faces, to find one's way home, to learn a language, and to perceive the local environment are cognitive capacities in this sense.

There is a tradition going back at least to Aristotle according to which cognitive capacities generally depend on the capacity for reason and inference. Helmholtz (1856) held that perception is unconscious inference. Chomsky (1965) spearheaded the cognitive revolution with the idea that speaking and understanding a language is to be explained as the unconscious application of a theory of that language. Fodor (1975) argued that the acquisition of cognitive capacities is a species of scientific inference, the formulation and confirmation of the sort of unconscious theory whose application underlies cognitive performance on the Chomskian model.

The fundamental assumption behind this tradition is that reasoning explains cognition: where there are epistemic constraints being satisfied, the underlying process is an inferential process. We can express this idea as a constraint on the explanation of cognitive capacities. I call it the

Originally published in *Philosophical Perspectives*, 9. *AI, Connectionism and Philosophical Psychology* (1995), 105–25. This paper appears with the kind permission of *Philosophical Perspectives*.

Rationale Constraint. It says that you haven't explained a cognitive capacity of *S*—i.e., a capacity of *S* to satisfy epistemic constraints—unless you have shown that manifestations of the target capacity are caused in *S* by a process that instantiates a justifying argument—a *rationale*—for those manifestations. In the sense intended, the partial products algorithm is a rationale for the products that are computed by executing it, and a chess program, if it is any good, is a rationale for the moves it generates. Processes that generate cognitive behavior ought, in short, to be mechanized epistemology.

The argument for the Rationale Constraint is simple. A cognitive function, as I shall understand it, is a function whose arguments and values are epistemologically related.[1] Suppose the causal process that mediates between the arguments and values of such a function is not the execution of a rationale. Then it would seem that either (i) the capacity has been unmasked as non-cognitive, for example, as the result of a look-up procedure (cf. Block 1978: 281–2); or (ii) we are left with no idea how the underlying causal process could guarantee that the characteristic epistemic constraints get satisfied, and explanation fails. Failure to satisfy the Rationale Constraint, in short, is either evidence that we aren't dealing with genuine cognition, or that we have an unexplained coincidence on our hands. Imagine, for example, a device that consistently generates outputs interpretable as reasonable conclusions given an input interpretable as a set of premises about some domain. There seem to be only two viable explanations: (i) the thing is reasoning; (ii) the thing is a fake—we are looking at the results of a perhaps elaborate look-up table, and not at the manifestations of a truly productive capacity. What appears to be ruled out is the possibility that a truly productive capacity to satisfy some set of epistemic constraints requires nothing like argument generation. For it seems that the selection of appropriate implications in an unbounded number of different cases would have to involve generating intermediate conclusions in an argument-like way. At least in the productive case, justified outputs appear to be a mystery (or a cosmic coincidence) in the absence of a justifying process that produces them. I'll have more to say about the argument for the Rationale Constraint as the discussion progresses, but, for now, I take it that the prima facie case

---

[1] Broader, or just plain different, definitions of cognitive functions are defensible. Nothing hangs on this terminological issue. I'm just interested in the class of functions, whatever they are called, that have the property indicated.

for the Rationale Constraint is strong enough to shift the burden of justification or criticism to those would deny it.

15.2. Connectionism and the rationale constraint

Cognitive capacities are difficult to specify with any precision. No one knows how to specify a law *in situ,* satisfaction of which is sufficient for having the ability to plan a party, eat in a restaurant, or comfort a friend. Even formal domains present difficulties. What, after all, does a good chess player do? More than obey the rules, of course. But what more, exactly? It seems the only way to specify an interesting chess function is to write a chess program, i.e. to give a precise formulation of a rationale for making chess moves.[2] This 'specification problem' (Cummins 1989: 111 ff.) makes a difficulty for orthodox computationalism whose methodology is basically the same as that of any programmer: Given a specification of a function, find an implementable algorithm for computing it.[3] If you are *not* given a specification of a function to compute, you have to fall back on some form of the Turing test: make a machine that is indistinguishable from humans *in the relevant respects, when they are exercising the target capacity.* Not hopeless, perhaps, but a swamp on anyone's view. One of the reasons the study of language has become so predominant in cognitive science is that the capacities to speak, understand, and acquire a natural language are (i) clearly cognitive; (ii) complex enough to be challenging; and (iii) specifiable with a great deal of precision. A good strategy in science is to attack problems to which your methodology happens to apply.

Connectionists can, in principle, finesse the specification problem because it is possible to 'train' a network to have a cognitive capacity without having even the beginning of an analysis of it; one simply needs a good training set. A successful network, however, is not, by itself, an explanation. A working

---

[2] Part of the problem is that different players, or the same player on different occasions, will do different things faced with the same board position. There is, therefore, no function from board-positions to board-positions, which constitutes *the* function chess players satisfy, in the way that there is a function from number pairs to numbers that is *the* function multipliers satisfy. But this is distinct from the problem I want to focus on here, which is that there appears to be no way to formulate a chess function at all without articulating a rationale, hence no way of specifying the explanadum prior to the discovery of an explanans.

[3] This is the 'classic' methodology described by Marr (1982). He somewhat misleadingly calls specifying a cognitive function giving a computational theory. (It's misleading because what Marr calls a computational theory specifies a function to compute, but not how to compute it.)

network may be nearly as difficult to understand as a brain in at least this respect: no rationale will typically be discernible in the spread of activation. Orthodox computationalists, on the other hand, can only succeed by writing a program that articulates a rationale for the target capacity. Unlike connectionists, they cannot succeed as engineers yet fail as scientists.

One natural and inevitable connectionist response to this situation is to point out that the orthodox approach is hamstrung by the specification problem: better let the network solve the problem, the argument goes, and afterwards study the working result in an attempt to figure out how the magic is done. But there is a more radical connectionist response that I want to discuss, which is to deny the Rationale Constraint itself. This is, for example, an implication of the line that Paul Smolensky and his colleagues have been developing (e.g. 1988, 1992), and it raises some issues in the philosophy of psychology that deserve to be surfaced.

The basic argument I want to consider, then, is this:

- The Rationale Constraint is incompatible with connectionism in its most interesting form.
- Connectionism is a viable framework for the explanation of cognition.
- Hence, the Rationale Constraint must be abandoned.

Of course, one person's modus ponens may be another's modus tollens: Someone (not me) may choose to see this as an argument against connectionism rather than an argument against the Rationale Constraint. However that may be, the focus of this discussion will be on the first premise, which I'll call the incompatibility thesis.

As I see the geography of this issue, there are two general lines of thought that might underlie the incompatibility thesis. I'll begin by setting them out briefly and uncritically, then turn to discussion.[4]

15.2.1. *The semantic arguments*

The fundamental idea here is that the explanation of a cognitive capacity and its specification take place on different semantic dimensions.[5] I've seen three ways of working out this idea.

---

[4] This isn't a literature review. I've tried to cover all the arguments I know about, but I've organized the various points in my own way to facilitate exposition and discussion.

[5] See Haugeland (1978) for the distinction between dimensions and levels of analysis. The fundamental point about the level—dimension distinction is that levels within a dimension are semantically

Version A: when a fully distributed[6] connectionist system satisfies a cognitive function, the causal process that mediates the argument-to-value connection is defined over 'sub-symbols.' For present purposes, the point about sub-symbols is that they are manipulated locally by processes that have no access to the 'big picture.' These micro-processes operate at the single node (activation) or single connection (weight) level and therefore have no access to the distributed representations over whose semantic contents the target cognitive function is defined.

Version B: when a connectionist system satisfies a cognitive function, it computes over representations that have no interpretation in the domain in which the target cognitive capacity is specified. Whatever it is that a set of weights or an activation pattern means, neither have meanings in the semantic space in which the target cognitive function is defined. This is supposed to follow directly from (i) the claim that connectionist representation and symbolic representation are more or less incommensurable; and (ii) the claim that target cognitive capacities are specified symbolically.

Version C: a connectionist system satisfies a cognitive function only approximately. Only under idealization do the values actually computed correspond to the values of a properly specified cognitive function. The causal process that actually mediates the argument-to-value connection in a network therefore cannot be interpreted as a rationale for the values of the target cognitive function because these are not the values that are actually computed.

15.2.2. *The computational arguments*

The second general line of argument that has been leveled at the Rationale Constraint is that connectionist computation has a fundamentally different form than reasoning. I've seen this argument run in a variety of ways, but I think they all boil down to one of the following.

Version A: connectionist computation is essentially a matter of discovering or exhibiting statistical correlations, whereas most rationales are not.

---

homogeneous, a lower level simply a being more refined analysis of the level above, while dimensions differ in their semantic interpretations. A LISP program and its assembly code implementation are typically on different dimensions because the LISP is about lists and the things listed, whereas the assembly code is about memory locations.

[6] By a 'connectionist system' I shall generally mean a fully distributed system. Exceptions will be explicitly noted in the text.

Version B: connectionist systems can mimic classical rationalizers by computing over encodings of classical representations. Since the encodings do not preserve the constituent structure of the representations they encode, network computations cannot be executions of the rationales they mimic.

Let's look now at each of these lines of argument in some detail.

15.3. The semantic arguments

What I am calling the semantic arguments for the incompatibility of connectionism and the Rationale Constraint are based on the idea that connectionist representations don't represent rationales, or anyway, not the right rationales—not the rationales that rationalize the system's cognitive capacities.

15.3.1. The 'sub-symbols' argument

The term 'sub-symbols' was introduced by Smolensky (1988) to describe the semantic role of an individual unit in a distributed representational scheme. A scheme for representing a domain D is fully distributed just in case every unit involved in the representation of one member of D is also involved in the representation of every other member of D. What we have, in short, is each element in D represented by a different pattern of activation on the same pool of units. To see why Smolensky calls the individual units in a distributed scheme sub-symbols, think of each representation of an element of D as a symbol. Since the scheme is distributed, these representations will be patterns of activation over a pool of units. No single unit represents any element in D though it does make a contribution to the representation of each element in D. Thus, the individual units in the pool can be thought of as sub-symbols, parts of a symbol, if you like.

What I am calling the sub-symbols argument is a semantic argument because it attempts to drive a wedge between the causal organization of a network and the semantic interpretation under which it satisfies a cognitive function. The crucial premise is that connectionist computation is local in a way that entails that it operates on sub-symbols but never on the symbols themselves that are the arguments and values of a cognitive function. On this assumption it would follow that connectionist systems don't execute rationales, because their computational processes are insensitive to the relevantly significant states. The assumption that the system is fully distributed amounts to the assumption that the relevant rationale cannot be defined over the contents (if any) represented by the individual units. The assumption that computation is local, however, amounts to the claim that the causal structure of the system is discernible only in terms of the interaction of individual units. The two assumptions together decouple the causal structure from the cognitively relevant representational states, with the consequence that the relevant causal structure cannot be seen as an implementation of a rationale for the cognitive function satisfied.

The sub–symbol argument evidently stands or falls with the assumption of local computation. In a nutshell, the problem with the assumption of local computation is that the causal dynamics of a network is specified as a function on activation *vectors*, not at the individual unit level. Connectionist computation consists in computing output activation vectors from input activation vectors and weights, and this is just to say that the representation computed—output vector—is a function of the input representation— input vector—and stored representations—the weights.[7] We think of the dynamics in terms of vectors because it is the entire activation vector at t, not the activation of any particular unit, that, together with the weights, determines the activation of each unit at t', and hence the activation vector at t'. The assumption of local computation, as it figures in the sub–symbol argument, appears patently false.

And yet, the idea hangs on.[8] I think what keeps the assumption of local computation alive is the intuitive sense that activation vectors are rather artificial. Unlike velocities and accelerations, they seem to be simply a notational artifact: one speaks of activation vectors to save ink, but it is just a gimmick for talking about each individual unit in turn. In the case of velocity, for example, we use the coordinates to specify a speed and direction. Some object is actually moving at a certain speed in a certain direction, and we pick coordinates in a way that makes for convenient representation. The coordinates are conventional. In the connectionist case, however, the coordinates are not conventional, for they are the activations of individual units, and the actual values of these matters.

---

[7] By 'input' and 'output' here I don't mean just final input or output, but also intermediate input and output, i.e. input and output on a given processing cycle.

[8] I point no fingers. If the shoe fits . . .

We can, for convenience, put activation values in a standard order and treat them as coordinates, but there is no direction or net magnitude out there that we are trying to capture. We are trying to capture the individual activations.

To neutralize this intuition completely would require a healthy chunk of metaphysics that I'm in no position to provide. But we can get a sense of what is wrong by contrasting the connectionist case with an uncontroversial case of the sort the sub-symbol argument contemplates. Imagine, then, that you are given a set of instructions for crossing a field. They specify a start position and time, and consist of a series of instructions from the following set: {go left, go right, go straight, go back, go n steps}. Every step is to be exactly one yard, and you are to take one step per second. Now if we give a lot of people instructions like this, they can be made to spell out various things on the field like a marching band at a football game. Imagine we arrange things so that they spell out proofs. These will be intelligible from the stands, but not to the individual marchers. Indeed, it is obvious that nothing anyone does is sensitive to the representations relevant to the proof; no one's actions are sensitive to the epistemic constraints whose satisfaction makes the process a proof. Causally speaking, though, the individual actions are all there are. Each person follows their instructions and that's all there is to it.

Now, we *could* specify the states of this system in vector notation: the state of the system is given by a vector whose elements are the positions of the various persons on the field. To transform one vector into another, however, we need the instructions for each marcher. Can we, as it were, aggregate these instruction sets into one function that effects the needed transformations? Of course. But—and here is the crucial point—the resulting combined function is a fraud, because the position of person A does not, by hypothesis, depend on the prior positions of any other marchers, and hence does not depend on the prior position vector. Since it is only position vectors that have interpretations in the proof, it follows that proof states don't determine other proof states, though they do predict them. Proof states are artifacts, and the 'law' that predicts later ones from earlier ones is an artifact as well. (See Cummins 1978, for the notion of an artifactual regularity.) This contrasts with connectionist systems precisely because the activation of output units does depend on the entire input vector and hence on something that *does* have a relevant representational significance.[9]

What I'm calling the sub-symbol argument, then, fails to undermine the Rationale Constraint because its attempt to demonstrate that connectionist causal structure is insensitive to distributed representation depends on the indefensible assumption of local computation.

15.3.2. *The incommensurability argument*

Version B of the semantic argument concedes that connectionist networks compute over distributed representations, but alleges that those representations are not representations of the arguments and values of cognitive functions. I'll call this argument the incommensurability argument, because it is based on the 'incommensurability thesis,' namely that distributed connectionist representational schemes are incommensurable with the (typically symbolic) schemes that must be used to specify cognitive functions.

As it stands, the incommensurability argument is incoherent because it assumes that connectionist systems can satisfy cognitive functions, even though they cannot represent the arguments and values of those functions. To be sure, one could reconcile the thesis that symbolic representation and connectionist representation are incommensurable with the thesis that connectionist systems satisfy cognitive functions by abandoning the view that cognitive functions must be specified symbolically. I have some sympathy with this view. But the result leaves us with no argument against the Rationale Constraint unless we add a premise to the effect that rationales can only be specified symbolically. This premise is worth examining in

---

[9] Some dialectics. (1) Later proof states do depend on earlier ones. Delay a few people, and all subsequent states will be different. *Reply*. True enough. But *strategically* delay several marchers so that you get e.g. 'p&p' rather than 'p&q' and the result will not be *relevantly* different: you won't, except by wild coincidence, get something that follows from the previous steps, you'll get garbage. This shows that the interpretation does not individuate states in a way that tracks their causal significance. (2) In a connectionist system, the activation of unit A at t depends on *its* entire input vector. But A's input vector may be only a part of the vector that has a relevant interpretation. (3) All an individual unit can know is a weighted sum of the activations of the units to which it is connected. Even neglecting differences in weights, if I am connected to two neighbors, A and B, I cannot tell the difference between both of them having an activation of 1 and A having an activation of 2 while B has an activation of 0. Hence, I am insensitive to differences in the input vector that make a representational difference. *Reply*. Both (2) and (3) are quite right, but beside the point. It is the output *vector*, not some single unit, that needs to be sensitive to differences in input vectors. Moreover, there needn't be sensitivity to every difference; what's wanted is sensitivity to differences that matter. The test of whether there is enough discrimination is in performance: if performance is good enough, then so is the capacity to discriminate different representational states.

some detail, for it would, together with the incommensurability thesis, make connectionism and the Rationale Constraint incompatible.

Why might one think that a rationale can only be specified symbolically? Let's begin by getting some bad reasons out of the way.

'Epistemic constraints are defined over propositions, not over things like images'   This just turns on an ambiguity in 'proposition'. As philosophers use the term, a proposition is not itself a representation but something represented, a set of possible worlds, say. In this sense, it is at least arguable that epistemic constraints are defined over propositions, for one might hold that epistemic constraints only make sense when applied to things with truth conditions.[10] Evidence, for example, is evidence for the truth of something, so a process cannot be constrained by the evidence unless that process traffics in propositions somehow. But holding that epistemic constraints are defined over propositions in this sense doesn't yield the conclusion that rationales can only be specified symbolically unless you *also* hold that only symbolic schemes can represent propositions. But surely there is no reason to believe this. A picture, for example, can hold in some possible worlds and not others just as well as a sentence.

As psychologists use the term, a proposition is a symbolic representation. In this sense of the term, it simply begs the question to suppose that epistemic constraints can only be defined over propositions. Either way you understand 'proposition,' then, we have no argument here for thinking that rationales have only symbolic specifications.[11]

'To be epistemically discriminating you have to be logically discriminating; but logical relations are defined over symbolic structure'   Again, we have an ambiguity. If 'logical relations' is understood semantically, then they are relations among propositions, and hence independent of how the propositions are represented. If 'logical relations' is understood syntactically, the question is begged, since syntax is, of course, particular to a representational scheme. The relations of interest among the formulas of symbolic logic are, of course, defined over symbolic syntax. But the relations of interest among

---

[10]   I am aware of at least one reason why one might deny even this. It goes back to Locke and Hume who held that epistemic relations are relations among ideas, and also (according to some recent commentators—see e.g. Owen 1993) that ideas don't express propositions. Perhaps, then, reasoning can be understood as a process that traffics in things subpropositional, i.e. in things with satisfaction conditions rather than truth conditions.

[11]   This is a view I have since abandoned.

the representations in a non-symbolic system like that of Barwise and Etchemendy (1990*a*, *b*) are defined over properties of those non-symbolic representations.[12]

Indeed, the existence of non-symbolic representational schemes for reasoning seems to refute outright the idea that rationales can only be specified symbolically. But the symbolist might reply that non-symbolic reasoning is limited in a way that unsuits it for cognition generally. Only symbolic schemes, they will say, allow for (i) content-independent reasoning; and (ii) unbounded reasoning competencies. The alleged boundedness of connectionist competencies will come up for discussion later on when we consider computational arguments against the rationale constraint. I'll restrict my attention here to the claim that non-symbolic representational schemes don't allow for content-independent reasoning.

There are two questions we need to ask about content-independence. First, *is* reasoning content-independent? And second, is it true that non-symbolic representational schemes cannot support content-independent reasoning? The answer to both questions, I think, is 'no.'

Is reasoning content-independent? In logic, we teach our students that deductive validity turns on form, not content. Although we usually temper this message with warnings about non-deductive inference and about inferences like that from being red to being colored, the central message remains that the sort of semantic relations that are central to inference can be seen to be invariant across contents. For most of us, modus ponens and simplification are paradigms of good reasoning, and they are content-independent.[13]

But logic, as many people have pointed out, is not a theory of reasoning, it is a theory of validity. One of the few really clear lessons of the last three decades of research in artificial intelligence, I suppose, is that reasoning

[12] Our epistemological concepts have been developed in a symbolic framework. We want to hold people accountable to epistemological norms, and this means that those norms have to be applicable to, and articulated in, language. Moreover, decades of positivist and neo-positivist epistemology were couched explicitly in symbolic terms. Indeed, for many years, articulation of epistemological principles in the language of symbolic logic was a more-or-less explicit requirement for serious research. Non-symbolic epistemology is even rarer than non-symbolic logic. But these may be just what's required to understand human cognition at its most fundamental level.

[13] That content-independent inference is seen as the base case is brought out by the fact that there is a whole literature in psychology on content effects in reasoning. (See Evans 1989; D. Cummins, under review.) The underlying assumption is that content effects are somehow deviations from proper reasoning. Often, they are treated outright as errors.

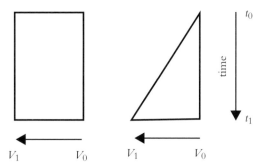

Figure 15.1 The area of the rectangle represents the distance traveled by a body moving at uniform velocity V_1 for a time t_1; the area of the triangle represents the distance traveled by a uniformly accelerated body beginning at rest and traveling for a time t_1, when it achieves a velocity of V_1

needs to be domain specific to be effective, because it needs to be driven by lots of contingent knowledge—the more the better, so long as it can be efficiently accessed. While the jury is admittedly still out on this question, it surely cannot be simply assumed at the current time that human reasoning is or even can be content-independent.

We needn't worry too much about it in the current context, however, because it simply isn't true that only symbolic schemes can support content-independent reasoning. A now familiar example is the Galilean geometrical scheme for reasoning about relations between distance, velocity, and time. In this scheme, vertical lines represent time, with time increasing from top to bottom and horizontal lines beginning at a vertical line and projecting left represent velocities, with velocity increasing from right to left. The area of the rectangle in figure one represents the distance traveled by a body that travels at uniform velocity v for a time t_1. The area of the triangle in Figure 15.1 represents the distance traveled by a body that begins at rest at t_0 and achieves a velocity v at time t_1.[14] Galileo used this scheme to reason about motion, as just described. But the scheme can be used to reason about the relations of any three quantities that are related as base, height, and area. And, of course, it can be used to reason geometrically, as it was before Galileo adapted it to mechanical problems.

[14] For further details, see Haugeland (1985: 19–23).

A final point before we leave the incommensurability argument. People do engage in symbolic reasoning. A connectionist who accepts the incommensurability thesis must somehow account for this fact. The obvious strategy here is to think of symbolic reasoning not as an explanans, but as an explanandum on a par with, or perhaps parasitic on, language use. According to this line of thought, people don't have cognitive capacities because they can reason symbolically; they rather have the cognitive capacity to reason symbolically because they can reason non-symbolically.[15] Whether connectionism can handle the capacity for language and other symbolic tasks is an open and difficult question. But it is somewhat peripheral in the current context. Given the incommensurability thesis, making connectionism prima facie consistent with the Rationale Constraint requires only that there be non-symbolic rationales.

The incommensurability argument, then, fails to demonstrate any incompatibility between connectionism and the Rationale Constraint. Even if we grant that connectionist representation and symbolic representation are incommensurable, there is no reason to think that non-symbolic reasoning is either impossible or an inaccurate picture of the inferential processes that underlie human cognitive capacities.

15.3.3. *The approximation argument*

Think about those XOR networks you cut your teeth on: they don't compute XOR no matter how long they are trained. First, the outputs aren't ones and zeros, but stuff like 0.9s and .11s. Table 15.1 gives a typical trace of performance after training.

What we are calling a 'true' isn't even always the same number. More seriously, as the table shows, the network is quite happy with any numerical inputs, not just ones and zeros. Lines five and six of the table do not correspond to arguments and values to XOR.

'Now, then,' the argument I have in mind continues, 'what goes for XOR goes for connectionist computation generally. You don't get cognitive functions computed, but only approximations to them; more or less close simulations, if you like. The causal process that mediates the argument-to-value

---

[15] If there is a language of thought, why do only humans have language? On the view that basic cognition is non-symbolic, this question has a straightforward answer: language and other symbolic processing are very special achievements; they are *very hard* for brains. Hence, only the very best brains can do them.

Table 15.1 Performance of typical XOR Network after training.

Input 1	Input 2	Output
1	1	.10
1	0	.90
0	1	.91
0	0	.09
0	.5	.76
.4	0	.59
.4	.7	.88
.3	0	.38

connection in the connectionist system cannot realize a rationale for the target cognitive function, for the system doesn't compute that function.'

I call this the 'approximation' argument because I want it to remind you of certain passages in Smolensky (1988). But the argument I've given is somewhat misnamed, for the idea is not that connectionist systems compute approximations to XOR, but that XOR can be viewed as a normalized (high numbers become ones, low numbers zeros) and restricted (only one and zero inputs count) version of the function the network actually computes. Moreover, the argument as I've presented it is self-defeating in the same way that the incommensurability argument is self-defeating. You can't argue against the Rationale Constraint on the grounds that connectionist systems cognize but don't satisfy the constraint, if part of your argument is that connectionist systems don't compute cognitive functions. We can rescue the argument from this embarrassment by supposing that, contrary to the appearances our symbolically biased epistemology generates, cognitive functions are actually like the functions connectionist systems compute in being more or less continuous.[16] Indeed, I have more than a little sympathy for this line. But it evidently lets the Rationale Constraint off the hook, unless we add the premise, lately scouted, that rationales can only

[16] This appears to be the line taken in Smolensky et al. (1992). If I understand them rightly, they argue that grammaticality is really a matter of degree, but that this is masked (to some extent, though not as much as MIT high churchers would have you believe) by the fact that the system always opts for the parsing with the maximum harmony. Like XOR networks, things only begin to look black and white when you ignore everything that doesn't reach some threshold.

be formulated for the normalized and restricted functions we *thought* were the targets. Since, as we've seen, there is no reason to believe that connectionists cannot have rationales in, as it were, their own terms, the present argument fails to show that successful connectionism is an embarrassment to the Rationale Constraint.

So much for the 'semantic arguments.' They don't work. The computational arguments, though not conclusive, do better.

15.4. The computational arguments

The fundamental idea behind this form of argument is that connectionist computation has a fundamentally different form than reasoning. Connectionist principles of computation, then, could not be principles of rationale execution. I'll discuss two versions of this line of thought, the second far more serious than the first.

15.4.1. *The correlation-engine argument*

The thought here is that connectionist systems are, in their 'learning' phase, simply correlation detectors. A trained network is then simply a correlation table with the added wrinkle of being able to automatically extrapolate between entries. No doubt connectionist networks can be used to implement other processes, but, so the argument goes, that is beside the point: At the dimension of analysis where the system is distinctively connectionist, it is simply a correlation engine. Since, however, it is obvious that rationales of the sort that rationalize cognitive performance are not typically (or ever?) algorithms for the discovery and exhibition of correlations, it follows that connectionist systems violate the Rationale Constraint.

Remember when people used to say, 'All computers really do is manipulate ones and zeros'? The reply we all learned was this: true enough, but irrelevant, because orchestrated manipulation of ones and zeros amounts to the execution of any symbolic algorithm you like. One then points out that, on the assumption (rather more suspect these days than in the golden age when we learned all this) that cognitive functions are computable functions, computers can have cognitive capacities.

It is tempting to reply to the correlation-engine argument in a similar vein: 'Maybe, at bottom, connectionist systems are just correlation-engines, but who cares what happens *at bottom*.' The correlation-engine argument anticipates this reply, however, by insisting that it is precisely at the dimension of analysis where the system is distinctly connectionist that it is a correlation-engine. It is conceded in advance (for the sake of argument) that connectionist systems can implement rationales of the sort that the Rationale Constraint requires. The argument insists, quite correctly, that the issue is not whether cognitive processes can be *implemented* as connectionist processes, but whether cognitive processes are properly *analyzed* as connectionist processes. The claim on offer is that rationale execution does not boil down to the discovery or exhibition of correlations. Since connectionist systems are correlations engines, either they don't compute cognitive functions, or the Rationale Constraint must be abandoned.

This argument is generally taken to be a knock on connectionism, but it could just as well be taken, by a convinced connectionist, as a refutation of the Rationale Constraint. Either way you take it, however, the argument suffers from a terminal naiveté about connectionist computation. Connectionist systems do, of course, correlate inputs and outputs, but so does every computational system. The claim that connectionist systems are correlation engines must come to more than this triviality. In the light of the fact that connectionist systems are able to solve quite general parsing problems, as we will see in the next section, there appears to be no reason to accept the bald claim that connectionist systems are *mere* correlation engines.

15.4.2. The SLM argument

The correlation-engine argument is naive, but it is based on a promising strategy: show that rationale execution and connectionist computation are fundamentally different. To establish this difference, one needs some fix on the form of rationales and on the form of connectionist computation. The idea that connectionist systems are correlation engines fills the bill nicely, because no one seriously supposes that rationales boil down to the discovery or exhibition of correlations. That idea fails because no one is in a position to argue that connectionist systems are correlation engines in the relevant sense. But there are other routes one might take to the conclusion that rationale execution and connectionist computation don't mix. The most interesting one is found in Smolensky *et al.* (1992; hereafter 'SLM').

The cornerstone of the SLM approach is Smolensky's well-known tensor product (tp) scheme for encoding classical representations. The notion of an encoding is crucial to what follows. Let R be a representational scheme. $<E, f>$ is an encoding of R iff $f:E{\rightarrow}R$, but E does not preserve the formal structure of the elements of R. Gödel numbers are a familiar encoding scheme. Morse code, however, is not, since it preserves form, being just a different spelling of an alphabet-based scheme in which spelling is irrelevant anyway. The tp scheme is an encoding in this sense since it does not preserve the constituent structure of the classical (in the sense of Fodor and McLaughlin 1990) representations it encodes. SLM reports development of a LISP-like programming language, TPPL, which allows for the expression of classical rationale-embodying algorithms. One takes the representations computed over by a TPPL algorithm and constructs a tp encoding. A network is then constructed, using a variation of back-propagation, that can be proved to be weakly equivalent to the TPPL algorithm. Since the tp encoding does not preserve the constituent structure of the classical representations employed by TPPL, it follows that the network does not execute a rationale defined over those representations.

SLM constitutes a serious challenge to the Rationale Constraint. It appears to establish that a connectionist system can mimic a classical rationalizer computing over representations that merely encode, but are not isomorphic to, the representations computed by that classical rationalizer. How are we to square this result with the Rationale Constraint? There are, I think, just three possibilities:

- Find some flaw in the SLM argument.
- Argue that the connectionist system does execute a rationale for the target capacity, though not one defined over the representations whose encodings the network utilizes. The network somehow finds its own rationale.
- Abandon the Rationale Constraint, and find some way to defuse the argumentation that supports it.

Is the SLM argument sound?   A rationale typically defines a competence that is unbounded under idealization away from resource constraints. Idealization away from resource constraints, however, is possible only for systems whose architecture supports a distinction between the algorithm executed and the memory/time it utilizes. Consider adding machines: they do not compute plus, but a finite restriction of plus. Nevertheless, they are said to compute the full infinite function because the restriction is due to a resource limitation. Add more memory, and you relax the restriction, because the algorithm the device executes is perfectly general: it is defined for the representations of any addends whatever. A look-up table, by contrast, is inherently finite. If you are using a look-up table, adding scratch paper and patience won't help you with addends not covered explicitly in the table.[17]

   The idea that a finite device can have the sort of unbounded competence typically characterized by a rationale, then, depends on a distinction between the algorithm executed on the one hand, and the resources—time and memory—available to it on the other. Schwarz (1993) argues, however, that connectionist networks do not support this distinction, and hence cannot be genuinely productive. His argument is simple. There are only two ways to add memory to a connectionist network: add units or add precision to units already available. Since physical networks are finite, and since physical units have bounded precision, to idealize away from memory constraints in a network amounts to asking how the network would behave were more units or more precision added. If we add units to a fully distributed network that computes f, however, it will, in general, no longer compute f. For, when we add a unit, we must, in general, readjust all the weights. But to alter the weights is to alter the algorithm. You haven't added memory to an existing network, the original network has been replaced by a different one. The same point holds for adding precision. To add precision requires altering the weights

---

[17] It is important to distinguish idealizing away from resource constraints from idealizing away from attention lapses and the like. Performance may differ from competence—there may be errors, in short—because of factors like interruptions. But idealizing away from these sorts of error inducers at most makes for correct computation of some finite function. Strictly speaking, to get an unbounded competence, you not only have to idealize away from resource constraints, you have to idealize away from physical breakdown as well.

to allow for distinctions among previously indistinguishable activations. And altering weights amounts to substituting a new network.

A crucial and controversial assumption of Schwarz's argument is that weight change in a connectionist framework is analogous to algorithm change (reprogramming) in a classical framework, and hence that changing weights amounts to building a different system. This will seem odd to those used to thinking about networks that learn, for, when a network learns, the weights change, yet surely the network retains its identity through learning. To understand what Schwarz has in mind, therefore, it is important to distinguish learning functions, which are functions from input vectors (and, in supervised learning, targets) to weight changes, from I/O functions whose domains and ranges are sets of activation vectors. Training alters the latter functions, but preserves the former. Schwarz's assumption, then, is that we should individuate connectionist systems by I/O function, at least for purposes of assessing the productivity issue.

The argument for this assumption appears to be as follows. Classical systems are individuated by algorithm. When we add memory to an adding machine, we don't change the way inputs are processed, we just make space for bigger ones. But when we add memory to a network, we change the way every input is processed, and this amounts to reprogramming the system. This argument is seriously flawed, however, by a misconception of classical systems. The function determined by a classical algorithm is a function from input and internal state (i.e. the state of memory), to output and internal state. It is important to see things this way because we want to be able to say that a change in stored knowledge, while it changes the input–output properties of the system, does not change the algorithm executed. When we program a classical system, we program it to behave differently as a function of different stored knowledge. This is what allows us to describe learning coherently as a change in the stored knowledge of a system that persists through that change. If we think of things this way, we shall be forced to admit that there is a sense in which, when stored knowledge is altered, the processing of every input is altered too, for since the algorithm executed is sensitive to stored knowledge, a change in stored knowledge makes the processing of each input subject (at least in principle) to different constraints. But this is evidently not to say that changing stored knowledge amounts to writing a new algorithm and hence to building a new system.

We should think of connectionist systems analogously. If we do, we will think of a point in weight space as a point in stored knowledge space. A connectionist algorithm, then, is a recipe for computing a function from an input vector and a point in weight space to an output vector and a point in weight space.[18] From this point of view, we do not build a new network when we change weights any more than we build a new classical system when we change its stored knowledge, and this is what allows us to coherently describe learning as a change in the stored knowledge of a persisting system.[19]

The productivity issue, as we've seen, turns on whether it makes sense to idealize away from memory constraints, and, for connectionism, this depends on how connectionist networks are individuated. Schwarz is quite right in supposing that if we make identity of computational route from input to output a necessary condition of system identity, then we cannot coherently idealize away from memory constraints in connectionist systems.[20] But the argument proves too much, for if we make identity of computational route from input to output a necessary condition of system

---

[18] Strictly speaking, it is a function from a point in activation space and a point in weight space to another point in activation space and another point in weight space. An input or output vector needn't specify the activations of every unit, yet the activation of any unit can affect subsequent performance.

[19] It is instructive to see how the same confusion can arise in thinking about production systems. We think of programming a production system as a matter of writing productions, and this makes it seem that adding or subtracting productions amounts to building a new (though related) system. But if we think of things this way, we shall have to say that any change in stored knowledge amount to changes in the system, and it will be impossible to describe a system that learns. We should rather think of the productions we write as items in the long-term memory of a system that consists of a production interpreter, a working memory, and a conflict resolution system. Construed thus, two production systems that differ only in which productions they incorporate are the same system with different stored knowledge.

[20] This claim depends on the assumption that there is, in general, no point in weight space that will produce correct behavior for all real valued activations. When there is such a point, the required idealization will go through even on Schwarz's assumption about how connectionist systems should be individuated, since adding precision would not require a move away from this point. A corresponding point cannot be made about adding units, however. To see this, imagine an indefinite supply of units fully connected to existing units with zero weights. Adding units amounts to making some of these weights non-zero, and hence amounts to changes in weight space. In the special case in which the old connections remain the same, and the new ones simply add scratch space, as in SIMPLIFIER (Cummins 1991b), it is arguable that we haven't built a new system, but this will hardly be the standard case. A possibility not considered by Schwarz is that outputs might be given as a finite but unbounded temporal sequence of activation vectors. This allows, in principle, for functions with infinite ranges. But, again, the crucial issue is whether there is some point in weight space that would, given enough time, suffice for the computation of any value in an infinite range. For many functions, such as addition, this presents no problem because the digits can be processed sequentially, with only enough memory required to handle

identity, we cannot coherently describe learning in either classical or connectionist systems. Schwarz is right to point out that there is, in connectionist systems, an internal relation between how large memory is and what is in it, while the relation between memory size and memory content is external in classical systems. But you cannot, so far as I can see, promote this into an argument against productivity in connectionist systems.[21]

Schwarz's argument bears on our question only on the assumption that finite competencies—capacities that are finite even under idealization from resource constraints—are not genuinely cognitive. The underlying idea is that finite competencies can be mimicked by a look-up table, and hence are always subject to 'unmasking.' I'm not at all sure we should find this persuasive. Even in the finite case, it seems that output could bear any or all of the standard epistemological relations to input and initial state, and hence qualify as cognitive behavior under the only standard of cognitiveness that we have, namely epistemic constraint satisfaction. But we are right to concentrate on unbounded competencies when discussing the bearing of SLM on the Rationality Constraint, for a network that is weakly equivalent to a *finite* TPPL rationale *might* well be simply a look-up device, hence not cognitive at all. The cognitiveness of a finite system seems to depend on the presence of a rationale. An SLM-based attack on the Rationale Constraint cannot rest on the existence

---

carries. In effect, the system satisfies a finite function—sum two digits and carry—which amounts to an infinite function when the inputs and outputs are read as temporal sequences. But this trick won't work in general. Many other functions, such as speech production, will require idealization from memory constraints because early outputs in the temporal sequence can depend on later ones. (Think e.g. of verb agreement in English questions.)

[21] There is another line of thought that seems to be influencing Schwarz. It goes like this. Identity of I/O function is a necessary condition of identity of algorithm computed. Changing the weights changes the I/O function computed, hence changes the algorithm, hence amounts to introducing a new system. We have to be careful how we think of an I/O function here. Evidently, when we add memory to an adding machine, it produces outputs it didn't produce before, from inputs it didn't accept before. If we think of I/O functions this way, then adding memory changes the I/O function of an adding machine, hence (by the argument on offer) the algorithm it executes, and this is not the conclusion Schwarz wants. To avoid this, we have to think of the I/O function as the one that would be computed but for resource limitations. But if we do that, identity of I/O function is no longer an independent condition on algorithm identity. As remarked above, Schwarz is apparently thinking that when we change the weights in a network, all the outputs are then computed in a new way, whereas, when we add memory to an adding machine, the computation isn't changed at all. But this is an artifact of the example. In general, when we change stored knowledge, we do change how each output is computed, in that the computational path from input to output is, at least in principle, different for each input–output pair. Imagine adding to the look-up table in an adding machine to handle 1 + 10 directly. Assuming the table is searched sequentially, and that this is the first entry, the contemplated change will alter the computational path initiated by every input. But it doesn't alter the algorithm at all.

of finite networks that are only weakly equivalent to TPPL rationalizers, since such an attack cannot presume the cognitiveness of a finite system while at the same time arguing that it executes no discernable rationale.

Fond as I am of the Rationale Constraint, I'm prepared to concede that the encoding argument shows that the SLM strategy works: you can design a network that is weakly equivalent to a classical rationalizer by having it compute over non-structure preserving encodings of the representations utilized by the classical rationalizer. There is, however, still a way that a defender of the Rationale Constraint can assimilate this result, for it is still open to defenders of the Rationale Constraint to suppose that systems like those proposed by SLM do in fact execute rationales, though not, of course, the same rationales as their TPPL counterparts.

To get this line of defense off the ground, it is helpful to begin with an idea of Haugeland's (1991), namely, that symbolic representational schemes and activation vector/weight matrix schemes belong to different genera of representational schemes. For present purposes, the essential point is that schemes from different *genera* are semantically more or less disjoint, only very approximate translation being possible.[22] The incommensurability argument, scouted above, made use of this idea to support the claim that connectionist systems cannot execute rationales defined over symbolic representations. We can accept this point, I argued, without prejudice to the Rationale Constraint, provided we could make room for rationales defined over activation vectors and weight matrices. But which rationales are those?

I don't know. We know so little about non-symbolic representational schemes, and our epistemological concepts are so closely wedded to the linguistically expressed and hence symbolic rationales they were developed to evaluate, that we can only speculate at present. Non-symbolic rationales are possible, as the work of Barwise and Etchemendy (1990a, b) demonstrates. Taking heart from this, friends of the Rationale Constraint may take a major goal of connectionist research to be the articulation of such principles of connectionist representation as will make possible the formulation and study of connectionist rationales. Meanwhile, those who, like me, are friendly to both the Rationale Constraint and to connectionism,

---

[22] Simple example: you cannot, as Locke and Berkeley agreed (*Essay Concerning Human Understanding*, IV. vii. 9; 'The Principles of Human Knowledge', Introduction) represent triangularity pictorially, though you can symbolically. Conversely, any verbal description of me is bound to hold in a different set of possible worlds than a picture of me.

needn't be dismayed by a showing of mere weak equivalence between a symbolic rationalizer and a connectionist network, for it is demonstrable that not all reasoning is symbolic, and it is at least possible that we will, one day, be able to discern non-symbolic reasoning in the disciplined spread of activation. I hope so. It is uncontroversial that there is reasoning in the brain, and that there is spreading activation there. But it is increasingly controversial to suppose that the brain is a symbol-cruncher in (very deep) disguise. *We* are symbol users, of course, but we should recognize our symbol use for what it is: an astounding bit of cultural technology. The fact that we can use symbols no more *entails* that our brains are symbol users than the fact that we use can-openers entails that our brains use them. If you think that the brain is in the spreading activation business, and you also think that it is reasoning that explains epistemic constraint satisfaction, then you had better take seriously the possibility of a connectionist epistemology.

Why not simply abandon the Rationale Constraint? Because it is very compelling. It says simply that a process cannot preserve an epistemological virtue *V* (or any other, for that matter) without being sensitive in some way to *V*-making factors. Bugs that cannot detect drawn lines cannot consistently run drawn mazes. If you design a bug that embarrasses my principle, I will take it as a research problem, not a refutation. I will do this because it is very dangerous to abandon compelling constraints on explanation. We can always respond to a theory that doesn't deliver the kind of understanding we want by training ourselves and our students to be more easily amused, but this will only trivialize science and produce hollow scientific successes. No doubt the progress of science can and should inform our conception of scientific explanation. But we should not repeat the mistake of the deductive-nomological model of explanation and confuse predictive or deductive success with explanatory success.[23]

SLM, it is interesting to notice in passing, wears its D-N patch on its sleeve:

Now we see that the principles of SSP [sub-symbolic paradigm] do indeed provide a non-Classical explanation for the systematicity and productivity of higher cognition. To recapitulate, less formally: the patterns of activity which are mental

---

[23] We'd all love a hidden variable solution in quantum mechanics, because that would allow us to satisfy a fundamental constraint on explanation that currently goes begging. There is no hidden variable solution to be had, but we haven't all simply abandon the constraint. It's the tension this situation generates that makes one of the main employment opportunities for philosophers in the middle of physics.

representations have a combinatorial (tensor product) structure which mental processes are sensitive to; the constituents in these representations figure crucially in the statement of certain high-level regularities (e.g., systematicity and productivity) in behavior; the combinatorial structure of the representations figures centrally in the explanation of this behavior (*via* mathematical deduction); but the constituents do not have causal power in the sense of figuring in mental algorithms for generating behavior: These causal algorithms can *only* be stated at a level lower than that of mental constituents, the level of individual connectionist units.   (1992: 44)

SLM has demonstrated (mathematically deduced) a weak equivalence, but the absence of a strong equivalence, between a classical rationale and a process of spreading activation. Should we say: *that explains how the network gets the correct answers*? Or should we ask: *how in the name of heaven does the spreading activation get it right*? I'm inclined to think I'm not alone in thinking we should be pressing this question, for it is this question that motivates the very considerable research devoted to understanding the so-called 'hidden representations' in connectionist systems (e.g. Rosenberg 1987; Sanger 1989).[24]

References

Barwise, J., and Etchemendy, J., 'Visual Information and Valid Reasoning', in W. Zimmerman (ed.), *Visualization in Mathematics* (Washington, DC: Mathematical Association of America, 1990a).

—— 'Information, Infons, and Inference', in R. Cooper, K. Mukai, and J. Perry (eds.), *Situation Theory and its Applications* (Stanford, Calif.: CSLI Publications, 1990b).

Block, N., 'Troubles with Functionalism', in N. Block (ed.), *Readings in the Philosophy of Psychology*, i (Cambridge, Mass.: Harvard University Press, 1978), 268–305.

Chomsky, N., *Aspects of the Theory of Syntax* (Cambridge, Mass.: MIT Press, 1965).

Cummins, D. D., 'Evidence for the Innateness of Deontic Reasoning', *Mind and Language*, 11 (1996), 160–90.

—— 'Rationality: Biological, Psychological, and Normative Theories', *Current Psychology of Cognition*, 11 (1997), 78–86.

—— (under review), 'Pragmatics, Logical Form, and Human Defeasible Reasoning'.

Cummins, R., 'Explanation and Subsumption', *PSA 1978*, 1 (1978), 163–75.

—— *The Nature of Psychological Explanation* (Cambridge, Mass.: MIT Press/Bradford Books, 1983).

---

[24] Author's note: since writing this, Martin Roth (Roth, 2005) has suggested a startling solution to this problem.

——*Meaning and Mental Representation* (Cambridge, Mass.: MIT Press, 1989).

——'The Role of Representation in Connectionist Models of Cognition', in W. Ramsey, S. Stich, and D. Rumelhart (eds.), *Philosophy and Connectionist Theory* (Hillsdale, NJ: Lawrence Erlbaum, 1991*b*), 91–114.

Evans, J. St. B. T., *Bias in Human Reasoning* (Hillsdale, NJ: Lawrence Erlbaum, 1989).

Fodor, J., *The Language of Thought* (New York: Thomas Y. Crowell, 1975).

Haugeland, J., 'The Nature and Plausibility of Cognitivism', *Behavioral and Brain Sciences*, 1 (1978), 215–26.

——*Artificial Intelligence: The Very Idea* (Cambridge, Mass.: MIT Press/Bradford Books, 1985).

——'Representational Genera', in W. Ramsey, S. Stich, and D. Rumelhart (eds.), *Philosophy and Connectionist Theory* (Hillsdale, NJ: Lawrence Erlbaum, 1991).

Helmholtz, H. von (1856) *Handbook of Physiological Optics,* ed. J. P. C. S. Southall (New York: Dover Reprint, 1963).

Hinton, G., 'Learning Distributed Representations of Concepts', *Proceedings of the Eighth Annual Conference on Artificial Intelligence* (Amherst, Mass., 1986).

Reprinted in Morris R. G. M. (ed.), *Parallel Distributed Processing: Implications for Psychology and Neurobiology* (Oxford: Oxford University Press, 1989).

Millikan, R., *Language, Thought, and Other Biological Categories* (Cambridge, Mass.: MIT Press/Bradford Books, 1984).

Owen, D., 'Locke on Reason, Probable Reason and Opinion', *Locke Newsletter*, 24 (1993), 33–79.

Rosenberg, C. (1987) 'Revealing the Structure of NETtalk's Internal Representations', *Proceedings of the Ninth Annual Meeting of the Cognitive Science Society* (Seattle, Wash., 1987), 537–54.

Reprinted in Roth, M., 'Program Execution in Connectionist Networks', *Mind and Language*, 20/4 (2005), 448–67.

Sanger, D., 'Contribution Analysis: A Technique for Assigning Responsibilities to Hidden Units in Connectionist Networks', *Technical Report CU-CS-435–89* (Department of Computer Science, University of Colorado at Boulder, 1989).

Schiffer, S., *Remnants of Meaning* (Cambridge, Mass.: MIT Press/Bradford Books, 1987).

Schwarz, G., 'Connectionism, Processing, Memory', *Connection Science*, 1 (1992), 207–26.

Smolensky, P., 'On the Proper Treatment of Connectionism', *Behavioral and Brain Sciences*, 11 (1988), 1–74.

——LeGendre, G., and Miyata Y., 'Principles for an Integrated Connectionist/Symbolic Theory of Higher Cognition', *Technical Report 92-08* (Institute of Cognitive Science, University of Colorado, 1992).

16

'How does it Work?' vs. 'What are the Laws?'

Two Conceptions of Psychological Explanation

16.1. In the beginning

In the beginning, there was the deductive nomological (DN) model of explanation, articulated by Hempel and Oppenheim (1948). According to DN, scientific explanation is subsumption under natural law. Individual events are explained by deducing them from laws together with initial conditions (or boundary conditions), and laws are explained by deriving them from other more fundamental laws, as, for example, the simple pendulum law is derived from Newton's laws of motion.

It is well-known that DN is vulnerable to a wide variety of counter-examples (e.g. Kim 1962; Salmon 1998). As a result, DN is not widely defended. But it is, I think, still widely believed that scientific explanation is subsumption under law. This is something of a scandal: given DN's miserable track record in spite of spirited defense by many ingenious believers, one is led to ask why so many cleave so faithfully to a doctrine that has proved so indefensible?

There are two factors that work to keep DN in place. First, there is the fact that every experimental paper one picks up involves the explanation of some data by appeal to some hypothesis or other. It is tempting to conclude that philosophers' continued failure to articulate this practice in some defensible way is a point against philosophers, not against DN. And second,

Originally published in F. Keil and R. Wilson (eds.), *Explanation and Cognition* (Cambridge, Mass.: MIT Press, 2000), 117–45. This paper appears with the kind permission of the MIT Press.

there is the fact that there is no widely understood and compelling alternative to DN on the market. If cognitive psychology has taught us anything, it is that no one willingly gives up a well-worn idea without having something to put in its place. I propose to examine these two factors in turn.

16.2. Two pitfalls

In psychology, DN gets a spurious plausibility from the fact that data are routinely said to be 'explained' or 'accounted for' by some hypothesis or other. But this is likely to be misleading in at least two ways.

First, when psychologists talk about explaining or accounting for some percentage of the variance, the 'hypothesis' in question is that that the experimental treatment will have some real effect. One is looking to reject the null hypothesis in favor of its complement, namely the hypothesis that whatever differences there are between the treatment group and the control group are not due to chance (random variation). But this sort of hypothesis isn't a law or anything like a law. The word 'hypothesis' as it is used in statistical analysis, and the word 'hypothesis' as it is used to refer to a conjectured theory or law, are little more than homonyms: they share the element of conjecture and little else. While there is nothing wrong with either use of the word, in the present context, we do well to keep the two senses distinct. With this in mind, I will use 'proposed law' to refer to a hypothesis in the second sense.

The second way in which talk of explanation in the context of the statistical analysis of data is likely to be misleading is that, even though experimenters sometimes are attempting to test a theory or an hypothesis in the second sense (i.e. a proposed law or regularity), this is an exercise in confirmation, not explanation. We say that a law or theory accounts for or explains the data, but this simply means that the data *confirm* the law or theory. When a law is confirmed by some data set, this is evidence that the law *describes* the data (to some reasonable approximation). The now classic illustration of this is Balmer's formula (Hempel 1966):

$$\lambda = 3645.6 \frac{n^2}{n^2 - 4}$$

This formula specifies the wavelengths of the emission spectrum of hydrogen. Finding spectral lines in the places predicted by the formula confirms the law, but no one thinks the law explains why the lines are where they are.

Defenders of DN concede that Balmer's formula and similar cases are cases in which subsumption under law is not explanatory. They then take their task to be formulating a criterion that will distinguish cases like Balmer's formula from genuinely explanatory laws. There is wide consensus, however, that this has not been done successfully, and the suspicion grows that it *cannot* be done successfully. I think we should take seriously the possibility that it cannot be done because there isn't any difference: no laws are explanatory in the sense required by DN. Laws simply tell us what happens; they do not tell us why or how. Molière, satirizing scholastic appeals to occult properties and 'virtues,' tweaks the doctors of his time for explaining that opium puts people to sleep because it has a dormitival virtue. But isn't this just what subsumption under law always amounts to? Does the Law of Effect explain why giving a pigeon Pigeon Chow whenever it pecks a key increases the rate of key pecking? Or does it just restate the phenomenon in more general terms? Surely the correct moral to draw here is that the Law of Effect is an *explanandum*, not an *explanans*.

In science, when a law is thought of as an *explanandum*, it is called an 'effect.' Einstein received his Nobel Prize, not for his work on relativity, but for his explanation of the photo-electric effect. In psychology, such laws as there are are almost always conceived of as, and even called, effects. We have the Garcia effect (Garcia and Koelling 1966), the spacing effect (Madigan 1969), the McGurk effect (MacDonald and McGurk 1978), and many, many more. Each of these is a fairly well confirmed law or regularity (or set of them). But no one thinks that the McGurk effect explains the data it subsumes. No one not in the grip of the DN model would suppose that one could *explain* why someone hears a consonant like the speaking mouth appears to make by appeal to the McGurk effect. That just *is* the McGurk effect.

The mistaken idea that accounting for data by subsuming it under law is explanation is also fostered by a confusion between explanation and prediction.[1] A law that predicts a certain data point or data set is said to

---

[1] I do not mean to suggest that DN theorists were confused about this. On the contrary, they held that explanation and prediction are just two sides of the same coin. The point is rather that DN conflates explanation and prediction, which are, I claim, orthogonal.

'explain' it. But prediction and explanation are separable in ways that DN cannot accommodate. It is possible to understand how a mechanism works, and hence to be in a position to explain its behavior and capacities—the effects it exhibits—without being able to predict or control its behavior. This is true generally of stochastic or chaotic systems. It is also true of systems whose relevant initial states are unknowable or simply unknown. In possession of a machine table for a Turing machine, I can explain all of its capacities, but, lacking knowledge of its initial state, I may be unable to predict its behavior (Moore 1956). Less interestingly, but just as important, some systems are simply intractable. We can explain the swirling trajectory of a falling leaf, but it would be hopeless to predict it.[2] Finally, many systems are well understood in one or another idealized form, but their actual behavior cannot be predicted because the relevant boundary conditions are seldom or never realized.

So, systems can be well-understood yet unpredictable. What about the converse? Can a system be predictable without being understood? Certainly. For centuries, the tides have been predicted from tide tables. Their predictability was not improved at all by Newton's successful explanation of them.[3] Consider also the plight of the seventeenth-century scientist confronted with the fact that pounding a nail makes it hot. Caloric theory, the going theory of heat at the time, treated changes in heat as diffusion phenomena. Your coffee cools because the caloric in it diffuses into the surrounding cup and air until equilibrium is reached. The fire reheats it because the caloric in the fire diffuses into the pot and surrounding air, and thence to the coffee, and so on. But pounding a nail will make it hot regardless of the temperature of the hammer.[4] This phenomenon—call it

---

[2] Cartwright (1983) denies that we can explain the trajectory of a falling leaf. But all she argues for is that we cannot predict it. She seems to think it follows from this that we have no reason to believe that the laws of mechanics accurately subsume it. A more conservative view is that we understand falling leaves quite well. No one seriously thinks this is an outstanding mystery of nature on a par with the nature of consciousness, say. The problem is just that prediction is intractable.

[3] This is an interesting case in a number of ways. Newton's successful explanation in terms of the moon's gravitational influence does not allow prediction, which is done today, as before Newton, by tables. So here we have in a single instance a case in which prediction is neither necessary nor sufficient for explanation. Moreover, we have a case in which explanation seems to come apart from truth. The Newtonian mechanics on which the explanation is based have been supplanted, yet the explanation is still accepted.

[4] Friction was thought to release otherwise bound caloric, but this will not help with a cold hammer and nail.

the 'Galileo effect' after the man who made it famous—is relatively easy to quantify. You can be in a position to predict what is going to happen, and even be able to quantify those predictions, yet still have no idea *why* it happens. Conversely, once in possession of the mechanical theory of heat, one sees that pounding a nail is like poking a cube of Jell-O: more vibration equals more heat. But this insight does not improve predictability at all; it explains the Galileo effect, but it is the statement of the effect itself that generates the predictions.

16.3. Why the laws of psychology are *explananda*

From the perspective I've been urging, it emerges that a substantial pro-portion of research effort in experimental psychology isn't expended dir-ectly in the explanation business; it is expended in the business of discovering and confirming effects. An effect, I've been arguing, is an *explanandum*, not an *explanans*. In psychology, we are overwhelmed with things to explain, and somewhat underwhelmed by things to explain them with. Why is that?

I want to begin by mentioning a sociological factor just so it can be set to one side. The fact is that it is very difficult to publish a paper that simply offers an explanation of an effect. Most journals want reports of experiments. Explanation, such as it is, is relegated to the 'discussion' section, which is generally loose and frankly speculative compared to the rest of the paper. Discussion sections are often not read, and their contents are almost never reported in other articles. The lion's share of the effort goes into the experiments and data analysis, not into explaining the effects they uncover. Any other course of action is a quick route to a plot in Tenure Memorial Park.

This is not mere tradition or perversity. It derives from a deep-rooted uncertainty about what it would take to really explain a psychological effect. What, after all, would a successful explanatory theory of the mind look like?

We can be pretty sure what it wouldn't look like. It wouldn't look like a *Principia Psychologica*. Newtonian mechanics was laid out as an axiomatic system, self-consciously imitating Euclidian geometry, a widely influential paradigm in the seventeenth century, and has since been the dominant paradigm of an explanatory theory in science. It is arguable whether this is a really useful paradigm in any science. Certainly mechanics, even Newtonian mechanics, is never presented that way today. Still, if the goal is to lay out the fundamental principles of motion, the axiomatic approach makes a kind of sense. There are, one might suppose, a small number of fundamental principles governing motion, and these, together with some suitable definitions, might enable the derivations of equations specifying the (perhaps idealized) behavior of any particular mechanical system: a pendulum, a spring, a solar system, and so on. What makes this seem a viable approach is the idea that motion is the same everywhere, whatever moves, wherever and whenever it moves. It is also this sort of idea that grounds the widespread conviction that physics is the most fundamental science.

Conversely, what grounds the idea that psychology and geology are not fundamental sciences is the thought that psychological and geological systems are special. The principles of psychology and geology and the other so-called special sciences do not govern nature generally, but only special sorts of systems. Laws of psychology and geology are laws *in situ*, that is, laws that hold of a special kind of system because of its peculiar constitution and organization. The special sciences do not yield general laws of nature, but rather laws governing the special sorts of systems that are their proper objects of study. Laws *in situ* specify effects—regular behavioral patterns characteristic of a specific kind of mechanism.

Once we see that the laws of a special science are specifications of effects, we see why theories in such sciences could not be anything like Newton's *Principia*. Who would be interested in an axiomatic development of the effects exhibited by the liver or the internal combustion engine? What we want is an explanation of those effects in terms of the constitution and organization of the liver or engine. At the level of fundamental physics, laws are what you get because, at a *fundamental* level, all you can do is say how things are. We don't think of the fundamental laws of motion as effects, because we don't think of them as specifying the behavior of some specialized sort of system that behaves as it does because of its constitution and organization. The things that obey the fundamental laws of motion (everything) do not have some special constitution or organization that accounts for the fact that they obey those laws. The laws of motion just say what motion *is* in this possible world. Special sorts of systems, on the other hand, exhibit distinctive characteristic effects. In general, then, it seems that special sciences like psychology should seek to discover and specify the effects characteristic of the systems that constitute their proprietary domains, and to explain those effects in terms of the *structure* of those systems, that is, in terms of their constituents (either physical or functional) and their mode of organization (see Cummins 1983: chs. 1 and 2, for how this kind of explanation applies to psychology).

16.4. Effects and capacities

What I have been calling psychological effects are not the only, or even the primary, *explananda* of psychology. I have been concentrating on effects because I have been criticizing the idea that psychological explanation is subsumption under law, and psychological laws specify effects. The primary *explananda* of psychology, however, are not effects (psychological laws) but *capacities*: the capacity to see depth, to learn and speak a language, to plan, to predict the future, to empathize, to fathom the mental states of others, to deceive oneself, to be self-aware, and so on. Understanding these sorts of capacities is what motivates psychological inquiry in the first place.

Capacities are best understood as a kind of complex dispositional property. Standard treatments typically assume that dispositions are specified by subjunctive conditionals along the following lines:

> Salt is water-soluble = If salt were put in water, then, *ceteris paribus*, it would dissolve.

This sort of analysis is valuable because it makes it clear that to have a dispositional property is to satisfy a law *in situ*, a law characterizing the behavior of a certain kind of thing. Capacities and effects are thus close kin.

For this sort of analysis to work, we have to know what precipitating conditions (putting x in water) generate which manifestations (x dissolves). For many psychological capacities, it is a matter of some substance to specify exactly what they are. The specification of a capacity is what Marr (1982) called the 'computational problem.' This can be extremely nontrivial. How, after all, should we specify the capacity to understand Chinese? Or it can be relatively simple, as in the case of calculational capacities (the capacity to add or multiply, for example). So one reason we do not think of the capacity to learn a natural language as an effect is just that it is relatively ill specified. As a consequence, the primary *explananda* of psychology—capacities—are not typically specified as laws, nor is it clear that they always can be (see discussion of capacity to play chess under 'computationalism' in section 16.6).

But there is a more interesting reason. Many of the things we call 'effects' in psychology are in fact incidental to the exercise of some capacity of interest. An analogy will help to clarify the distinction I have in mind. Consider two multipliers, M1 and M2. M1 uses the standard partial products algorithm we all learned in school. M2 uses successive addition. Both systems have the capacity to multiply: given two numerals, they return a numeral representing the product of the numbers represented by the inputs. But M2 also exhibits the 'linearity effect': computation is, roughly, a linear function of the size of the multiplier. It takes twice as long to compute $24 \times N$ as it does to compute $12 \times N$. M1 does not exhibit the linearity effect. Its complexity profile is, roughly, a step function of the number of digits in the multiplier.

The 'linearity effect' is incidental to the capacity to multiply in M1. It is, as it were, a side-effect of the way M1 exercises its capacity to multiply, and that is why we call this fact about computation time an 'effect' and the multiplication a 'capacity.' Of course, the 'linearity effect' might be computed. We could design a system M3 that not only computes products, but computes reaction times as well, timing its outputs to mimic a successive addition machine. M3 might be quite difficult to distinguish from M1 on behavioral grounds, though it need not be impossible. The timing function might be disabled somehow without disabling the multiplier. More subtly, computation of the relevant output times might itself be nonlinear, in which case M3 will not be able to fool us on very large inputs (assuming it can process them at all). Or it might be that the 'linearity effect' in M3 is cognitively penetrable (Pylyshyn 1982), in which case it cannot be incidental. Thus, it can be a matter of substantive controversy whether we are looking at an exercise of a capacity or an incidental effect. This is precisely what is at issue between the friends of imagery and their opponents: are the rotation and scanning effects (for example) incidental effects of rotating or scanning a picturelike representation, or is it the exercise of a capacity to estimate rotation or scanning times involving real physical objects? (See, for example, Pylyshyn 1979.)

As the primary *explananda* of psychological theory, capacities typically do not have to be discovered: everyone knows that people can see depth and learn language. But they do have to be specified, and that, to repeat, can be nontrivial. As secondary *explananda*, effects typically *do* have to be discovered. Much more important, however, is the different bearing that explaining effects as opposed to capacities has on theory confirmation. Given two theories or models of the same capacity, associated incidental effects can be used to distinguish between them. This is important for two reasons. First, it is always possible in principle, and often in fact, to construct weakly equivalent models of the same capacity. To take an extreme case, Smolensky *et al.* (1992) have shown that, for any parser written in a LISP-like language called 'tensor product programming language' (TPPL), it is possible to construct a distributed connectionist network that effects the same parses. With respect to parsing *per se*, then, there is nothing to choose between the two models. However, they predict very different incidental effects. Second, even when two models are not weakly equivalent, they may be on a par empirically, that is, close enough so that differences between them are plausibly attributed to such factors as experimental error, idealization, and the like. Again, incidental effects that may have no great interest as *explananda* in their own right may serve to distinguish such cases.

We can expect, then, to see a good deal of effort expended in the explanation of incidental effects that have little interest in their own right: no one would construct a theory just to explain *them*. But their successful explanation can often be crucial to the assessment of theories or models designed to explain the core capacities that are the primary targets of psychological inquiry.

16.5. Functional analysis

A theory may explain a dispositional property by systematic analysis—i.e. analyzing the system that has it, or it may proceed instead by analyzing the disposition itself. I call the application of property analysis to dispositions or capacities 'functional analysis.'

Functional analysis consists in analyzing a disposition into a number of less problematic dispositions such that programmed manifestation of these analyzing dispositions amounts to a manifestation of the analyzed disposition. By 'programmed' here, I simply mean organized in a way that could be specified in a program or flow chart. Assembly line production provides a transparent illustration. Production is broken down into a number of distinct and relatively simple (unskilled) tasks. The line has the capacity to produce the product by virtue of the fact that the units on the line have the capacity to perform one or more of these tasks, and by virtue of the fact that when these tasks are performed in a certain organized way—according to a certain program—the finished product results. Schematic diagrams in electronics provide another familiar example. Because each symbol represents any physical object having a certain capacity, a schematic diagram of a complex device constitutes an analysis of the electronic capacities of the device as a whole into the capacities of its components. Such an analysis allows us to explain how the device as a whole exercises the analyzed capacity, for it allows us to see exercises of the analyzed capacity as programmed exercises (i.e. organized) of the analyzing capacities.

In these examples, analysis of the disposition goes together in a fairly obvious way with componential analysis of the disposed system, analyzing dispositions being capacities of system components. This sort of direct form–function correlation is fairly common in artifacts because it facilitates diagnosis and repair of malfunctions. Form–function correlation is certainly absent in many cases, however, and it is therefore important to keep functional analysis and componential analysis conceptually distinct. Componential analysis of computers, and probably brains, will typically yield components with capacities that do not figure in the analysis of capacities of the whole system. A cook's capacity to bake a cake analyzes into other capacities of the 'whole cook.' Similarly, Turing machine capacities analyze into other Turing machine capacities. Because we do this sort of analysis without reference to a realizing system, the analysis is evidently not an analysis of a realizing system but of the capacity itself. Thus functional analysis puts very indirect constraints on componential analysis. My capacity to multiply 27 times 32 analyzes into the capacity to multiply 2 times 7, to add 5 and 1, and so on, but these capacities are not (so far as is known) capacities of my components.

The explanatory interest of functional analysis is roughly proportional to (1) the extent to which the analyzing capacities are less sophisticated than the analyzed capacities; (2) the extent to which the analyzing capacities are different in kind from the analyzed capacities; and (3) the relative sophistication of the program appealed to, that is, the relative complexity of the organization of component parts or processes that is attributed to the system. Item (3) is correlative with (1) and (2): the greater the gap in sophistication and kind between analyzing and analyzed capacities, the more sophisticated the program must be to close the gap.

Ultimately, of course, a complete theory for a capacity must exhibit the details of the target capacity's realization in the system (or system type) that has it. Functional analysis of a capacity must eventually terminate in dispositions whose realizations are explicable via analysis of the target system. Failing this, we have no reason to suppose we have analyzed the capacity as it is realized in that system.

16.6. Existing explanatory paradigms in psychology

Here is the territory traversed so far:

1. Psychological explanation is not subsumption under law.
2. Psychological laws are not general laws of nature, but laws *in situ*, namely, specifications of effects, not explanatory principles.
3. The primary *explananda* of psychology are capacities.
4. Effects and capacities in special kinds of systems are generally to be explained by appeal to the structure of those systems.
5. Much of the effort in psychology, and almost all of the methodology, is devoted to the discovery and confirmation of effects.

It is striking that, while there is an extensive body of doctrine in psychology about the methodology appropriate to the discovery and confirmation of effects, there is next to nothing about how to formulate and test an explanation.[5] This is not surprising. If you think that explanation is subsumption under law, then you will see the discovery and testing of laws as

---

[5] There is hypothetico-deductivism (HD): explanations are 'theories,' which are tested by deducing from them what effects should be exhibited. Explanations are then tested by determining whether the effects they predict are real.

the same thing as the formulation and testing of explanations. It may be a measure of the ubiquity of DN thinking that the methodology of hypothesis testing is nowhere complemented by a comparably sophisticated methodology of explanation testing. On the other hand, it may be that explanation testing simply does not admit of formulation in an explicit methodology because successful explanation has as much to do with the knowledge and cognitive capacities of the explainers as it does with the logical properties of the explanation, a possibility I will return to below. Whatever the cause, psychologists faced with the task of explaining an effect generally have recourse to imitating one or another of the explanatory paradigms established in the discipline. These are familiar enough, but a brief review in the present context will prove illuminating.

There are five general explanatory paradigms that are influential in contemporary psychology:

1. Belief–desire–intention (BDI) explanations.
2. Computational symbol-processing explanations.
3. Connectionist explanations.
4. Neuroscience explanations.
5. Evolutionary explanations.

16.6.1. Belief–desire–intention

This is by far the most familiar explanatory model, and the model of common-sense psychological explanation, Freudian psychodynamics, and a great deal of current developmental, social, and cognitive psychology. It is what Dennett praises as 'explanation from the intentional stance,' and what Churchland deplores as 'folk psychology' (Churchland 1981; Dennett 1987). Underlying BDI is a set of defining assumptions about how beliefs, desires, and intentions interact. These assumptions are seldom if ever made explicit, just as one does not make explicit the mechanical assumptions about springs, levers, and gears that ground structural explanations of a mechanical machine. Everyone knows that beliefs are available as premises in inference, that desires specify goals, and that intentions are adopted plans for achieving goals, so it does not have to be said explicitly (except by philosophers).

It is truly amazing how powerful this scheme of things is, particularly if unconscious beliefs, desires, and intentions are allowed. But there are problems. The most fundamental of these is something I call 'Leibniz's Gap'. Here is Leibniz's formulation of the Gap:

Moreover, we must confess that the perception, and what depends on it, is inexplicable in terms of mechanical reasons, that is, through shapes and motions. If we imagine that there is a machine whose structure makes it think, sense, and have perceptions, we could conceive it enlarged, keeping the same proportions, so that we could enter into it, as one enters into a mill. Assuming that, when inspecting its interior, we will only find parts that push one another, and we will never find anything to explain a perception. And so, we should seek perception in the simple substance and not in the composite or in the machine.   (Leibniz 1714: sec. 17)

There is, as Leibniz points out in this famous passage, a gap between the concepts of BDI psychology, and those we use to describe the brain. So, even if we are convinced that the mind is the brain, or a process going on in the brain, physical observation of the brain seems to give us data in the wrong vocabulary: synapses rather than thoughts. When we look at a brain, even a living brain, we do not see thoughts. Or, not to beg the question, we do not see anything we readily recognize as thoughts. If you had a Newton camera and took a snapshot of a billiard game in progress, you would see vectors with centers of gravity at their tails. If you had a psychology camera and took a snapshot of a living brain, you would, according to BDI psychology, see beliefs, desires, intentions, and their canonical relations. But to build a psychology camera, you would need to somehow bridge Leibniz's Gap by correlating observed brain properties, events, and processes with beliefs, desires, and intentions, and this, at least for now, is beyond us. Thus, the wide Leibnizian gap between BDI psychology and the brain is destructive to satisfying psychological explanation. Lacking some precise suggestion about how beliefs, desires, and intentions are instantiated in the brain, we are left wondering whether even the most powerful BDI analysis of some psychological effect might specify *a way* to achieve the effect, but not *the way*, that is, the way the brain does it. This objection is a 'philosophical' objection in that it is independent of how predictively successful BDI analyses turn out to be. If we knew there was only one way to achieve the psychological effects we find in the laboratory and in the field, then the fact that a psychological effect had a satisfactory BDI analysis would constitute evidence that the brain must somehow realize the structure that analysis specified. But, of course, we do not know that there is only one way to design a mind like ours, and, lacking this knowledge, we do not know whether the predictive inaccuracies that accompany any scientific theory are due to the fact that the human mind is not a BDI device or to the fact that our theory is idealized, that measurement is imperfect, and so on.

Another serious conceptual problem with BDI has to do with the nature of the propositional attitudes–belief, desire, intention, and their kin—that are its workhorses. BDI psychology requires a conception of the attitudes that allows for beliefs, desires, and intentions that not only are not conscious, but that cannot be made conscious. Although most philosophers and psychologists find this acceptable, it has not gone unchallenged (Searle 1992). Somewhat more seriously, BDI requires that the attitudes be 'atomistic,' which is to say, that they can exist in relative isolation. In a BDI framework, standard accounts of linguistic or visual processing, for example, require beliefs about phrase structures and zero-crossings in subsystems that are relatively isolated informationally from other aspects of cognition. No psychologist working on concepts and their acquisition would think that merely being able to see, or to understand language, is sufficient for having the concept of a phrase structure or a zero-crossing. Yet having beliefs about phrase structures and zero-crossings seems to require having these concepts. Thus, atomism about the attitudes, though it has its defenders (Fodor and Lepore 1992) is by no means uncontroversial (Stich 1983; Block 1986).[6]

Finally, it is not clear that psychological phenomena can generally be reduced to the interaction of propositional attitudes, even if these are broadly construed to include such things as the language processor generating a representation of the phrase structure of the current linguistic input. BDI seems best suited to so-called higher cognition, and in particular, to high-level reasoning and planning. Even here, there are formidable critics. Eliminativists (e.g. Churchland 1981) have argued that BDI, whether it be 'folk theory' or grounded in an innate theory of mind, is, in fact, discredited theory.

---

[6] It is interesting that, as the phenomena become more 'specialized,' intention and desire tend to drop out. There is surely some truth in the idea that the game of life is to form intentions (plans) that will get things moved from the desire box (Desire[I am rich]) to the belief box (Believe[I am rich]). But it is a stretch to think that this is the fundamental loop in language processing or vision.

16.6.2. Computationalism

Computationalism (the brain is a computer and the mind is what it is doing) is just BDI minus some of the baggage. Computationalism is a 'top–down' strategy. In the hands of the computationalist, that strategy begins by identifying a task or capacity to be explained: the capacity to learn a language, or converse, or solve a problem, etc. It then attempts to specify that capacity as a function or relation: what inputs produce what outputs under what circumstances. Finally, that characteristic function or relation is analyzed into components that have known computational realizations. (In practice, this means analysis into components that can be programmed in LISP or some other standard programming language.)

This strategy involves three assumptions and a precondition that are worth noting:

1. *Psychological functions are computable.* This is actually a rather strong and daring assumption. Most dynamical systems found in nature cannot be characterized by equations that specify a computable function. Even three bodies moving in Newtonian space do not satisfy this assumption. It is very much an open question whether the processes in the brain that subserve cognition can be characterized as the computation of a computable function.

2. Another underlying assumption of top–down computationalism as it is usually characterized (and as I have just characterized it) is that psychological capacities can be specified independently of their analyses. But this is pretty patently false in many cases: there is, for example, no input–output function the computation of which would constitute playing intelligent chess. Or rather, there are a great many. Think of a chess system as a move generator, that is, as a function from board positions (current) to board positions (the move). In a given situation, intelligent chess players might make any number of different moves. Indeed, the same player might make different moves on different occasions. In practice, then, the only way to specify a chess function is to actually write an algorithm for computing it. We cannot, in general, expect to specify a cognitive function before we analyze and implement it, and this introduces a methodological difficulty. If we cannot specify the *explanandum* independently of the *explanans*, how are we to compare competing explanations? We can, of course, determine which theory

better predicts whatever observational data there are—that is, we can determine which does a better job predicting whatever known effects there are—but this tells us only which underlying theory is more likely true, not which generates the better explanation. The distinction is important. It is well-known that, if it is possible to accommodate the data at all, it is possible to accommodate them with a theory that says nothing whatever about the underlying mechanisms or their analysis, that is, in a way that has no explanatory force whatever (Craig 1953; Putnam 1965). This problem is underappreciated because a tendency to focus exclusively on accommodating effects leaves explanatory issues out of the picture from the start.

3. A third underlying assumption of the top–down strategy, closely related to the second assumption, is that we will be able to recognize and characterize the relevant inputs and behaviors antecedently to serious attempts to explain how the latter are computed from the former. Here the difficulty is that pre-analytic conceptions of behavior and its causes may seriously misrepresent or distort what is actually going on. Connectionists sometimes complain that there is no reason to think that cognition in the brain is the manipulation of representations that correspond to our ordinary concepts. Top–down strategists therefore run the risk of characterizing the *explananda* in terms that are crosscut or that distort the causally relevant categories. This is analogous to the almost irresistible temptation in biology to believe that the morphological traits of importance and interest to us must correspond to our genes in some neat way. Computationalists are wont to reply that what Dennett (1987) calls the intentional stance— predicting and explaining behavior in terms of beliefs, desires, and intentions—is enormously successful, and hence that it cannot be fundamentally wrong to characterize cognition in something like these common-sense terms. The same can be said for Ptolemaic astronomy, or Newtonian mechanics, however. Considerable explanatory and predictive success is possible with a fundamentally mistaken or even incoherent theory.

So much for the assumptions. Now for the precondition:

A successful application of the top–down strategy requires that the target explanandum *is analyzable*. Everyone who has ever tried their hand at programming is familiar with this constraint. You cannot write a program that computes bids in bridge or computes square roots, if you do not know how to compute bids in bridge or compute square roots. But many psychological capacities are interesting *explananda* precisely because we have no idea how the task is done. This is why artificial intelligence plays such a central role in computationalism. It requires very considerable ingenuity to discover a way—any way—to construct three-dimensional specifications of visual space from retinal images, or to make it happen that, in problem solving, two short sessions are more effective than one long one.

But even with success, there is a problem. Having figured out *a* way to compute a cognitive function, what reason is there to think that that is how our brains do the job? I do not mean to suggest that there is no way of addressing this problem, only that it is a problem that is bound to arise in a top–down framework. Computationalists are thus inevitably left with a narrowed but still substantial Leibnizian Gap: the gap between a computational description of psychological processes and a bioneural description of the processes in the brain.[7]

16.6.3. Connectionism

The top–down strategy is *explanandum* driven: you begin with a capacity to explain, and try to find a computational architecture that will have it. The bottom–up strategy is *explanans* driven: you start with a specification of the architecture, and try to find a way to make it do the task.[8] What connectionists have in common is the assumption that cognitive capacities are built out of a stock of primitive processes designed explicitly to be rather brainlike. They begin with the building blocks of a simplified and idealized brain, and attempt to create systems that will behave in a recognizably cognitive way. The connectionist thus seeks to narrow the Leibnizian Gap even further

---

[7] The gap is narrowed relative to BDI because a computational analysis will at least have demonstrated the physical—indeed computational—realizability of the processes they postulate. BDI explanations are always subject to the eliminativist worry that the fundamental processes postulated have no physical realizations at all. Still, it is arguable that many computationalist explanations only make sense on the controversial assumption that beliefs, desires, and intentions have reasonably straightforward computational realizations. I return to this point below.

[8] In practice, most computationalists are actually bottom–uppers to some extent. This is because, as a graduate student, you apprentice in a research group that is more or less committed to a given architecture, and your job is to extend this approach to some new capacity. It is just as well: pure top–downism, as described by Marr (1982), is probably impossible. Computationalist architectures, however, are not well-grounded in the brain, so the problem just rehearsed remains.

to that between a genuinely bioneural description of the brain, and the simplified and idealized 'neural networks' that are their stock in trade.

But a much narrowed Gap is not the only payoff. As it happens, it is possible to program connectionist networks to do tasks that the programmer does not know how to do. All that is required is a sufficiently representative 'training set'—a set of inputs paired with their correct responses. Thus the precondition of top–down computationalism discussed above can be avoided. You can program a network to do a task you have not the faintest idea how to do. There is a downside to this, however: once you have trained a network, you may still have little if any idea how it does the task. Because studying an artificial network is much easier than studying a living brain, you are still substantially ahead. But you are not home free.

Moreover, it is seldom noticed that one of the lately discussed assumptions required by the top–down approach is also required by bottom–uppers. Training sets must be specified somehow, and the problem of how to conceptualize inputs and behaviors is no easier for connectionists than it is for top–down computationalists. While connectionists need not assume that networks operate on internal representations that correspond to ordinary common-sense concepts, they are no better off than top–down computationalists when it comes to conceptualizing the target *explananda*.

Before we leave the topic of underlying assumptions and enabling conditions, it is worth pausing to note that some of the central enabling assumptions of computationalism are shared by connectionism. Both assume that the mind is basically a cognitive engine and only secondarily a seat of emotion, feeling, and sensation. Both assume that consciousness is inessential to the understanding of cognition. And both assume that cognition does not require a biological brain, let alone an immaterial soul. Both are thoroughly functionalist and materialist. And both are representationalist in that both assume that cognition is to be understood as disciplined transformation over states whose primary function is the representation of information relevant to the cognitive capacity being exercised. The differences that divide computationalism and connectionism are practically invisible against the scale that measures the distance between them and the behaviorism of Watson or Skinner, or the structuralism of Titchener.

16.6.4. *Neuroscience*

Everyone who is not a dualist believes that mental processes are processes that go on in the brain. If one's goal is a science of the mind, however, observation of the brain seems to yield results on the wrong side of Leibniz's Gap. The computationalist response to this problem is to try to understand cognitive processes in abstraction from the brain or any other 'hardware' in which they might occur. The computationalist strategy is to first articulate a computational theory of cognition, and then to inquire into how the implicated computational processes might be carried out in the brain. This strategy has some evident merits. Because no one doubts that computational processes can be physically realized, computationalism is free from any dualist taint. Yet the problem of bridging Leibniz's Gap is conveniently put off until some future date when we will surely know more about both cognitive and neural processes. An evident drawback, however, is that there is no guarantee that cognitive processes are computational processes at all, let alone that cognition in biological brains will turn out to be the kind of processes we are led to investigate by following a strictly top–down approach. Although that approach has had some notable successes, it has also had some notable failures. It would not be unreasonable to conclude that the difficulties faced by computationalism might be due to insufficient attention being paid to the only processes we know for sure are sufficient to subserve mentality in general, and cognition in particular, namely brain processes. Perhaps we should simply accept the fact that, as things currently stand, studying the brain puts us on the wrong side of Leibniz's Gap, but hope that, as our knowledge increases, the outlines of a bridge over the Gap will eventually appear.

Connectionists attempt to take a middle ground here, starting in the middle of the Gap, as it were, and trying simultaneously to bridge to either side. Most neuroscientists, it seems, are at least tolerant of the connectionist strategy. But they are inclined to argue that connectionist models are such vastly oversimplified models of the brain as to be misleading at best. If we are going to bridge Leibniz's Gap, we are going to have to know a great deal more about the brain than we do now. This much is agreed on all sides. So why not get on with it? And, since the brain is the only known organ of mentality, whether natural or artificial, it seems only sensible to begin by trying to understand how it works. Any other strategy arguably runs the risk of being a wild goose chase, an attempt to make mentality out of stuff that just is not up to the job.

This line of argumentation has been around at least since the seventeenth century, but because there was no very good way to study the brain, it has had few practical consequences until relatively recently. Steady technological progress, however, is beginning to make Leibniz's thought experiment a reality. As a result, the problem he articulated so eloquently is forced upon us anew, for, marvelous as the new technology is, it does not, and cannot, provide 'psychology glasses,' lenses through which observed brain anatomy and activity emerge as psychological faculties and thought processes.

Technology can take us to the brink of Leibniz's Gap, but only theory can bridge it. There are two conceptions of how neuroscience might contribute to the bridge. According to one approach, concepts generated by neuroscience proper to articulate its data and theory should be used to reconceive the mental from the bottom–up, discarding mentalistic concepts that have no clear neuroscientific reconstruction, and simply replacing ones that do (Churchland 1987). Psychology on the mental side of Leibniz's Gap will either be assimilated or perish. Well-confirmed effects remain as *explananda* on this view, with the caveat that the concepts used in their articulation must not be tainted too deeply by concepts that have no acceptable neuroscientific reconstruction.[9] Psychological capacities of the sort that constitute the primary *explananda* of more top–down approaches are viewed with suspicion—guilty (until proven innocent) of not cutting nature at the joints. I call this approach the 'strong neuroscience program.'[10]

As things stand, the strong neuroscience program is almost impossible to put into practice. Standard descriptions of dissociations, of tasks done during functional magnetic resonance imaging (fMRI), and so on are up to their eyebrows in terminology from the 'wrong' side of Leibniz's Gap. A more

---

[9] The history of science is full of effects that were not real in the sense that subsequent science rediagnosed the inevitable failures to fit the data precisely as conceptual error rather than experimental error.

[10] The use of 'strong' and 'weak' to distinguish two conceptions of the role of neuroscience in psychological explanation, and the use of these words to distinguish two analogous conceptions of the role of evolutionary theory in psychological explanation, should not be taken as terms of approbation or abuse. They are modeled after Searle's well-known distinction between strong and weak AI (Searle 1980). Perhaps I should emphasize as well that I am not here attempting to characterize neuroscience, but only its abstract role in psychological explanation. The same goes for my remarks about evolution in the next section.

common and more ecumenical conception of the role of neuroscience treats it as a source of evidence designed primarily to arbitrate among functional analyses formulated in other terms, terms from unreduced psychology residing on the other side of the Gap from 'pure' neuroscience. There are serious methodological issues here that are matters of controversy in psychology, neuroscience, and philosophy, but it is clear in a general way how weak neuroscience bears on the issue of psychological explanation: it passes the buck. On this conception, psychological effects and capacities are explained as the effects or capacities of BDI, computationalist, or connectionist systems, and these are assumed to be instantiated somehow in the brain. Neuroscience enters this picture as a source of evidence, arbitrating among competitors, and ultimately, as the source of an account of the biological realization of psychological systems described functionally.

16.6.5. Evolutionary explanations

Like neuroscience, evolution can be regarded as either a source of psychological explanations or as a source of evidence bearing on one or another non-evolutionary theory that generates its own psychological explanations, and this generates a distinction between a strong evolutionary program and a weak evolutionary program analogous to the distinction between the strong and weak neuroscience programs. The evidential role of evolution is relatively easy to specify. Functional analyses attribute functions to the analyzed systems. A source of evidence that a system really has a given function, or has a component with a given function, is that such a function would have constituted an adaptation, or the likely corollary of an adaptation, for the system's ancestors.[11] Conversely, a functional analysis that proposes functions in a biological system that have no plausible evolutionary rationale are suspect on the grounds that nature is not being carved at the joints. Again, there are important methodological issues here, but they do not bear on the nature of psychological explanation, only on the confirmation of the theories that generate them.

---

[11] Corollary: x was an adaptation, and y is a likely precondition or consequence of having x, so whatever evolutionary argument exists for x confers some plausibility on y as well. I don't mean to suggest that adaptation and selection is all there is to evolution. But non-selectionist scenarios for the evolution of a psychological function are bound to be relatively difficult to construct or confirm.

The strong evolutionary program is based on the idea that evolution might actually explain a psychological capacity or effect. This idea is difficult to articulate and assess. At best, it seems that evolution might explain why a certain psychological capacity or effect is pervasive in a given population. It could, to put it crudely, explain *why* we see depth, but not *how*. Thus, an evolutionary explanation and an explanation generated by one of the other paradigms would not be direct competitors in the same explanatory game. This is obscured by the fact that evolutionary reasoning could favor some functional analyses over others, which entails that evolutionary explanations could be incompatible with explanations generated by one of the other frameworks (BDI, computationalism, connectionism, neuroscience). But evolutionary explanations do not seek to answer the same question as those generated by the other frameworks. Hence, as long as there is no incompatibility in the functional analyses each postulates, there is no reason why we should have to choose between an evolutionary explanation and, say, a connectionist explanation or a BDI explanation.

16.7. Two problems for psychological explanation

The first three of the familiar frameworks just rehearsed—BDI, computationalism, and connectionism—are, as they should be, *analytical* frameworks. That is, they are frameworks for analyzing (decomposing) complex capacities into more primitive components. The strong neuroscience program aspires to be an analytical framework, and is perhaps well on the way to becoming one. Weak neuroscience and the weak evolutionary program do not pretend to be explanatory frameworks in their own right, hence offer no alternative to the analytical approach. Finally, what I have called the 'strong evolutionary program' is, I think, best construed as explaining the prevalence of an effect or capacity in a population, and thus leaves untouched the question of what the mind is and how it works.

Our survey of the currently viable explanatory frameworks thus reveals that, although there is still considerable lip service paid to DN, actual theory building and explanation construction takes place in frameworks that are not designed for the elaboration of laws but rather are designed for the elaboration of functional analyses. The foundational problems for psychological explanation, then, are special versions of the problems that arise for functional analysis generally. If we leave aside strictly epistemological problems, problems about how functional analyses are to be 'discovered' or confirmed, and focus solely on how they work as explanations, two central issues emerge.[12] The first might be called the 'realization problem.' Functional analysis always leaves one with a gap between the functional characterization of a system and the various nonfunctional characterizations that are assumed to apply to the system whose functional analysis is at issue.[13] In psychology, this is what I have called 'Leibniz's Gap.' The second problem might be called the 'unification problem.' Functional analyses are usually generated to explain some particular capacity or effect, or a closely related set of them. Researchers concerned with some aspect of vision may be sensitive to the issue of unifying their account with those directed at some other aspect of vision. But they are less likely to concern themselves with making their analyses fit with the analyses of those researching language or emotion or reasoning.

16.7.1. Leibniz's Gap: intentionality and consciousness

The realization problem, in the form of Leibniz's Gap, looms for every current explanatory framework surveyed above, with the exception of strong neuroscience, which holds that concepts not proprietary to neuroscience itself need not be taken seriously. While attractive philosophically because it eliminates the Gap, strong neuroscience is, as remarked above, nearly impossible to put into practice as an explanatory strategy simply because the vast majority of the *explananda* are formulated in terms that either explicitly or implicitly draw on concepts that have no known counterparts in neuroscience. Indeed, neuroscience that does honor eliminativist constraints seems, at present anyway, to have little to do with psychology. I propose, therefore, to put the strong neuroscience program

---

[12] I do not mean to suggest that these problems are trivial or unimportant. Indeed, I think they are many and deep. But these are problems about confirmation, not about explanation. One of the many unfortunate consequences of DN is that it (intentionally) blurs the distinction between confirmation and explanation.

[13] As many have pointed out (see e.g. Lycan 1987), the distinction between functional and nonfunctional levels of organization is relative. Realizing systems are seldom characterized in non-functional terms. They are rather characterized in terms of functions that differ from those whose realization is at issue. A logic circuit, for example, might be analyzed in terms of AND gates, OR gates, and INVERTERS. The realization of this circuit might then be specified in terms of resistors, transistors, and capacitors. These are themselves, of course, functional terms, but their realization is not at issue, so they count as nonfunctional relative to the gates and invertors whose realization is being specified.

aside and concentrate on frameworks that must, in one way or another, face Leibniz's Gap.

There is no special mystery about what counts as a satisfactory solution to realization problems generally. Every time we design an artifact to satisfy a functional characterization and then build it, we solve a realization problem. This shows that there is no special philosophical mystery about what it is to realize a functionally specified system. Difficulties arise, however, in special cases in which there is a fundamental unclarity in one or more of the primitives of the analytical framework. There is deep uncertainty about whether beliefs, desires, and intentions can be computationally realized, not because we do not understand what realization requires, but because we are unclear about beliefs, desires, and intentions. There is no comparable worry about whether a given computationally specified system is realized in the brain. There is uncertainty, of course, but it is a different kind of uncertainty. We know what it takes to realize a computationally specified system, we just don't know if what it takes is in the brain. But we don't know what it takes to realize a belief or desire.[14] Do any of the many sophisticated planners currently in the literature actually have beliefs, desires, and intentions? And if they do not, should we conclude that planning doesn't require belief, desire, and intention, or should we conclude that computationalist planners are mere imitators of mental activity? Everyone recognizes these as Philosophical Questions, which, in this context anyway, means mainly that everyone recognizes that they are questions that, as things now stand, cannot be addressed experimentally. And, of course, there is an exactly parallel, and perhaps related (Searle 1992), set of problems about consciousness.

It is important to see that the Leibnizian Gap between intentional states like belief, desire, and intention, on the one hand, and computationalist, connectionist, or neuroscience concepts, on the other, is not just a problem for BDI. It is a problem for any framework that either characterizes its *explananda* in intentional terms, or assumes (tacitly or explicitly) a realization of intentional states in its proprietary mechanisms and processes—whether these be the computational manipulation of data structures, the spread of activation disciplined by connection weights, or synaptic connections and spiking frequencies. I think it is pretty obvious that both kinds of

[14] Except trivially: a normal brain. All this does is rule out dualism.

intentionalist taint are ubiquitous, though not universal, in psychology and artificial intelligence. I submit that this is why so much psychological explanation, while it is often compelling and informative, is almost always ultimately unsatisfying. What is more, we do not know whether the problem is just that we do not really understand intentional states, or that, as eliminativists claim, there is nothing to be understood. We never solved the realization problem for entelechies either, but that was a knock on vitalism, not a failure of philosophical analysis.

All of this is old news, of course. But it is worth reminding ourselves that there is nothing wrong with psychological explanation that a solution (or dissolution) of the problem of intentionality and consciousness would not cure.

16.7.2. The unification problem

There is, however, a *de facto* problem that plagues psychological explanation, and that is its evident lack of unification.

The first and most obvious problem is that there are four quite different explanatory frameworks operative in contemporary psychology: BDI, computationalism, connectionism, and (strong) neuroscience. While the first two and the second two are reasonably close together, it remains true that explanations constructed in one framework are seldom translatable into explanations in another. The gap between BDI and computationalism, on the one hand, and connectionism and (strong) neuroscience, on the other, is particularly wide and typically competitive.

It is a commonplace in science to attack different problems from the perspective of different explanatory models. To explain the flow of water and wave propagation, one typically models water as a continuous incompressible medium. To explain diffusion and evaporation, one models water as a collection of discrete particles.[15] But it is important to see how this situation differs from the situation that prevails in psychology. The different models of water are brought in to explain different effects. While water cannot be both a continuous incompressible fluid and a cloud of free molecules, each model is directed at a different set of problems. There is no competition between the models

---

[15] The example is from Paul Teller, in conversation.

concerning the solution of the *same* problem.[16] In contrast, it is notorious that connectionist and computationalist models compete in just this way, a classic example being the explanation of the acquisition of the past tense in English (Rumelhart and McClelland 1986; Pinker and Prince 1989). In this respect, contemporary psychology resembles seventeenth-century mechanics in which Cartesians and Newtonians competed to explain the same phenomena within different frameworks. There is, of course, no way to resolve this kind of competition other than to let the science take its course. In the meantime, however, every explanation in psychology is, to some extent, undermined by the deep disunity that afflicts the field in its current state of development. Until the field is unified in some way—by the victory of one of the current competitors, by the emergence of a new framework, or by a successful realization hierarchy (BDI realized computationally, realized as a connectionist network, realized in the brain)—the suspicion remains that some or all of the explanations currently offered are fundamentally flawed because they are articulated in a fundamentally flawed framework.

In addition to the disunity across frameworks, there is considerable disunity within each framework, particularly within computationalism and connectionism.[17] Both frameworks allow for an enormous variety of models based on very different principles.[18] Attempts at unity are not unknown: in the computationalist camp, Anderson's ACT* (1996) and Newell's SOAR (1990) spring to mind, as does Grossberg's ART (1982) in the connectionist camp. But it is an understatement that these are not

---

[16] I do not mean to suggest that this situation is entirely unproblematic. It is certainly tempting to suppose that there is a deep disunity here—unless both models of water can be treated as acceptable idealizations or simplifications grounded in a deeper single model.

[17] Functional analyses tend to proliferate when there are no strong restrictions on the primitives. Computationalism, in principle, allows any computable function as a psychological primitive. Connectionism is somewhat less permissive, but there is still a bewildering variety of network architectures currently on offer. Strong neuroscience, insofar as it exists as an explanatory framework at all, imposes very few constraints on functional architecture beyond those dictated by gross anatomy and (often controversial) dissociation effects (the classic is Ungerleider and Mishkin 1982). BDI is probably the most unified of the currently viable explanatory frameworks because it is defined by a choice of primitives. Still, there have been few systematic attempts to make the principles of interaction among these principles explicit. An exception is Freudian psychodynamics. While this is (extended) BDI, most of its fundamental principles—for example, repression—would be regarded as dubious by many BDI researchers.

[18] As Smolensky *et al.* (1992) have pointed out, explanation in these frameworks tends to be model-based rather than principle-based.

widely accepted; the prevailing bewildering diversity of models tends to undermine confidence in any.

Having said all of this, I do not think we should worry much about disunity. The ordinary practice of good science will take care of disunity eventually. There is a far greater danger in forcing more unity than the data warrant. Good experimentation, like good decision-making generally, can tell us which of two models is better, but it cannot tell us how good any particular model is. The best strategy, then, is to have a lot of models on offer on the grounds that, other things equal, the best of a large set is likely better than the best of a small one.

16.8. Conclusions

I have been urging that explanation in psychology, like scientific explanation generally, is not subsumption under law. Such laws as there are in psychology are specifications of effects. As such, they do not explain anything, but themselves require explanation. Moreover, though important, the phenomena we typically call 'effects' are incidental to the primary *explananda* of psychology, viz., capacities. Capacities, unlike their associated incidental effects, seldom require discovery, though their precise specification can be nontrivial. The search for laws in psychology is therefore the search for *explananda*, for it is either the search for an adequate specification of a capacity or for some capacity's associated incidental effects. Laws tell us what the mind does, not how it does it. We want to know how the mind works, not just what it does.

Capacities and their associated incidental effects are to be explained by appeal to a combination of functional analysis and realization, and the currently influential explanatory frameworks in psychology are all frameworks for generating this sort of explanation. Thus, in spite of a good deal of lip service to the idea that explanation is subsumption under law, psychology, though pretty seriously disunified, is squarely on the right track. Its efforts at satisfying explanation are still bedeviled by the old problems of intentionality and consciousness. This is where psychology and philosophy meet. Psychology need not wait on philosophy, however. The life sciences made a lot of progress before anyone knew how life was realized.

References

Anderson, J., *The Architecture of Cognition* (Mahwah, NJ: Lawrence Erlbaum Associates, 1996).

Block, N., 'Advertisement for a Semantics for Psychology', in P. French, T. Uehling, and H. Wettstein (eds.), *Midwest Studies in Philosophy*, 10. *Studies in the Philosophy of Mind* (Minneapolis: University of Minnesota Press, 1986).

Cartwright, N., *How the Laws of Physics Lie* (Oxford: Clarendon Press; New York: Oxford University Press, 1983).

Churchland, P. M., 'Eliminative Materialism and Propositional Attitudes', *Journal of Philosophy*, 78 (1981), 67–90.

Craig, W., 'On Axiomatizability within a System', *Journal of Symbolic Logic*, 18/1 (1953), 30–2.

Cummins, R., *The Nature of Psychological Explanation*. (Cambridge, Mass.: MIT Press/Bradford Books, 1983).

Dennett, D., *The Intentional Stance* (Cambridge, Mass.: MIT Press/Bradford Books, 1987).

Fodor, J., and Lepore, E., *Holism: A Shopper's Guide* (Oxford and Cambridge, Mass.: Basil Blackwell, 1992).

Garcia, J., and Koelling, R., 'The Relation of Cue to Consequence in Avoidance Learning', *Psychonomic Science*, 4 (1966), 123–4.

Grossberg, S., *Studies of Mind and Brain: Neural Principles of Learning, Perception, Development, Cognition, and Motor Control* (Dordrecht: D. Reidel, 1982).

Hempel, C., *Philosophy of Natural Science* (Englewood Cliffs, NJ: Prentice Hall, 1966).

—— Oppenheim, P., 'Studies in the Logic of Explanation', *Philosophy of Science*, 15 (1948), 135–75.

Kim, J., 'On the Logical Conditions of Deductive Explanation', *Philosophy of Science*, 30 (1962), 286–91.

Leibniz, G. (1714). *The Monadology*, tr. R. Ariew and D. Garber, *Leibniz: Basic Works* (Indianapolis: Hackett, 1989).

Lycan, W., *Consciousness* (Cambridge, Mass.: MIT Press/Bradford Books, 1987).

MacDonald, J., and McGurk, H., 'Visual Influences on Speech Perception Processes', *Perception and Psychophysics*, 24/3 (1978), 253–7.

Madigan, S., 'Intraserial Repetition and Coding Processes in Free Recall', *Journal of Verbal Learning and Verbal Behavior*, 8 (1969), 828–35.

Marr, D., *Vision* (New York: Freeman, 1982).

Moore, E., 'Gedanken Experiments on Sequential Machines', in C. Shannon and J. McCarthy, *Automata Studies* (Princeton: Princeton University Press, 1956), 129–56.

Newell, A., *Unified Theories of Cognition* (Cambridge, Mass.: Harvard University Press, 1990).

Pinker, S., and Prince, A., 'Rules and Connections in Human Language', in R. Morris (ed.), *Parallel Distributed Processing* (Oxford: Oxford University Press, 1989), 182–99.

Putnam, H., 'Craig's Theorem', *Journal of Philosophy*, 62/10 (1965), 251–60.

Pylyshyn, Z., 'The Rate of 'Mental Rotation' of Images: A Test of a Holistic Analogue Hypothesis', *Memory and Cognition*, 7/1 (1979), 19–28.

—— *Computation and Cognition* (Cambridge, Mass.: MIT Press/Bradford Books, 1984).

Rumelhart, D., and McClelland, J., 'On Learning the Past Tenses of English Verbs', in J. McClelland, D. Rumelhart, and the PDP Research Group (eds.), *Parallel Distributed Processing,* ii (Cambridge, Mass.: MIT Press, 1986), 216–71.

Salmon, W., *Causality and Explanation* (New York: Oxford University Press, 1998).

Searle, J., 'Minds, Brains, and Programs', *Behavioral and Brain Sciences*, 3 (1980), 417–24.

—— *The Rediscovery of the Mind* (Cambridge, Mass.: MIT Press, 1992).

Smolensky, P., LeGendre, G., and Miyata Y., 'Principles for an Integrated Connectionist/Symbolic Theory of Higher Cognition', *Technical Report 92–08* (Institute of Cognitive Science, University of Colorado, 1992).

Stich, S., *From Folk Psychology to Cognitive Science: The Case Against Belief* (Cambridge, Mass.: MIT Press/Bradford Books, 1983).

Bibliography

Aizawa, K., 'Explaining Systematicity', *Mind and Language*, 12 (1997), 115–36.

Allen, C., Bekoff, M., and Lauder, G. (eds.), *Nature's Purposes* (Cambridge, Mass.: MIT Press, 1998).

Alston, W., *Philosophy of Language* (Englewood Cliffs, NJ: Prentice Hall, 1964).

Anderson, J., *The Architecture of Cognition* (Mahwah, NJ: Lawrence Erlbaum Associates, 1996).

Ariew, A., Cummins, R., and Perlman, M. (eds.), *Functions: New Essays in the Philosophy of Psychology and Biology* (Oxford: Oxford University Press, 2002).

Atick, J., 'Could Information Theory Provide an Ecological Theory of Sensory Processes?', *Network*, 3 (1992), 213–51.

Austin, J. L., *How to Do Things with Words* (Oxford: Clarendon Press, 1962).

Ayer, A. J., *Language, Truth, and Logic* (London: Victor Gollancz, 1936).

Bach, K., and Harnish, R. M., *Linguistic Communication and Speech Acts* (Cambridge, Mass.: MIT Press, 1979).

Barlow, H. B., 'Possible Principles Underlying the Transformation of Sensory Messages', in W. A. Rosenblith (ed.), *Sensory Communication* (Cambridge, Mass.: MIT Press, 1961), 217–34.

Barwise, J., and Etchemendy, J., 'Visual Information and Valid Reasoning', in W. Zimmerman (ed.), *Visualization in Mathematics* (Washington, DC: Mathematical Association of America, 1990*a*).

—— —— 'Information, Infons, and Inference', in R. Cooper, K. Mukai, and J. Perry (eds.), *Situation Theory and its Applications* (Stanford, Calif.: CSLI Publications, 1990*b*).

Bennett, J., *Linguistic Behavior* (Cambridge: Cambridge University Press, 1976).

—— 'The Meaning-Nominalist Strategy', *Foundations of Language*, 10 (1973), 141–68.

Block, N. (ed.), 'Troubles with Functionalism', *Readings in the Philosophy of Psychology* (Cambridge, Mass.: Harvard University Press, 1978), 268–305.

—— 'Advertisement for a Semantics for Psychology', in P. French, T. Uehling, and H. Wettstein (eds.), *Midwest Studies in Philosophy*, 10. *Studies in the Philosophy of Mind* (Minneapolis: University of Minnesota Press, 1986).

Braine, M. D. S., 'On the Relation between the Natural Logic of Reasoning and Standard Logic', *Psychological Review*, 85 (1978), 1–21.

—— O'Brien, D. P., 'A Theory of *If*: A Lexical Entry, Reasoning Program, and Pragmatic Principles', *Psychological Review*, 98 (1991), 182–203.

Braine, M. D. S., Reiser, B. J., and Rumain, B., 'Some Empirical Justification for a Theory of Natural Propositional Logic', in G. H. Bower (ed.), *The Psychology of Learning and Motivation,* xviii (New York: Academic Press, 1984).

Buller, D. (ed.), *Function, Selection, and Design* (New York: SUNY Press, 1999).

Burge, T., 'Individualism and the Mental', in P. A. French, T. E. Euhling, and H. K. Wettstein (eds.), *Studies in the Philosophy of Mind: Midwest Studies in Philosophy,* 10 (Minneapolis: University of Minnesota Press, 1979).

Butler, K., 'Towards a Connectionist Cognitive Architecture', *Mind and Language,* 6 (1991), 252–72.

—— 'Compositionality in Cognitive Models: The Real Issue', *Philosophical Studies,* 78 (1995), 153–62.

Cartwright, N., *How the Laws of Physics Lie* (Oxford: Clarendon Press; New York: Oxford University Press, 1983).

Chalmers, D. J., 'Connectionism and Compositionality: Why Fodor and Pylyshyn were Wrong', *Philosophical Psychology,* 6 (1993), 305–19.

Chater, N., and Oaksford, M., 'Autonomy, Implementation and Cognitive Architecture: A Reply to Fodor and Pylyshyn', *Cognition,* 34 (1990), 93–107.

Chomsky, N., *Aspects of the Theory of Syntax* (Cambridge, Mass.: MIT Press, 1965).

Churchland, P. M., 'Eliminative Materialism and Propositional Attitudes', *Journal of Philosophy,* 78 (1981), 67–90.

—— *A Neurocomputational Perspective* (Cambridge, Mass.: MIT Press, 1989).

—— *The Engine of Reason, the Seat of the Soul: A Philosophical Journey into the Brain* (Cambridge, Mass.: MIT Press, 1995).

—— 'Conceptual Similarity Across Sensory and Neural Diversity: The Fodor/LePore Challenge Answered', *Journal of Philosophy,* 95 (1998), 5–32.

Clapin, H. (ed.), *Philosophy of Mental Representation* (Oxford: Oxford University Press, 2002).

Cottrell, G., 'Extracting Fratures from Faces Using Compression Networks: Face, Identity, Emotions and Gender Recognition Using Holons', in D. Touretsky, J. Elman, T. Sejnowski, and G. Hinton (eds.), *Connectionist Models: Proceedings of the 1990 Summer School* (San Mateo, Calif.: Morgan Kaufmann, 1991).

—— Metcalfe, J., 'EMPATH: Face, Emotion and Gender Recognition Using Holons', in R. Lippman, J. Moody, and D. Touretsky (eds.), *Advances in Neural Information Processing Systems,* iii (San Mateo, Calif.: Morgan Kaufmann, 1991).

Craig, W., 'On Axiomatizability Within a System', *Journal of Symbolic Logic,* 18/1 (1953), 30–2.

Cummins, D. D., 'The Role of Analogical Reasoning in the Induction of Problem Categories', *Journal of Experimental Psychology: Learning, Memory, and Cognition,* 5 (1992), 1103–24.

—— 'Naive Theories and Causal Deduction', *Memory and Cognition*, 23 (1995), 646–58.

—— 'How the Social Environment Shaped the Evolution of Mind', *Synthese*, 122 (2000), 3–28.

—— (under review) 'Pragmatics, Logical Form, and Human Defeasible Reasoning'.

—— Lubart, T., Alsknis, O., and Rist, R., 'Conditional Reasoning and Causation', *Memory and Cognition*, 19 (1991), 274–82.

Cummins, R., 'Programs in the Explanation of Behavior', *Philosophy of Science*, 44 (1977), 269–87.

—— 'Explanation and Subsumption', *PSA 1978*, 1 (1978), 163–75.

—— 'Intention, Meaning and Truth Conditions', *Philosophical Studies*, 35 (1979), 345–60.

—— *The Nature of Psychological Explanation*. (Cambridge, Mass.: MIT Press/Bradford Books, 1983).

—— 'Inexplicit Information', in M. Brand and R. M. Harnish (eds.), *The Representation of Knowledge and Belief* (Tucson, Ariz.: University of Arizona Press, 1986).

—— *Meaning and Mental Representation* (Cambridge, Mass.: MIT Press, 1989).

—— 'Methodological Reflections on Belief', in R. Bogdan (ed.), *Mind and Common Sense* (Cambridge: Cambridge University Press, 1991*a*).

—— 'The Role of Representation in Connectionist Models of Cognition', in W. Ramsey, S. Stich, and D. Rumelhart (eds.), *Philosophy and Connectionist Theory* (Hillsdale, NJ: Lawrence Erlbaum, 1991*b*), 91–114.

—— *Representations, Targets, and Attitudes* (Cambridge, Mass.: MIT Press, 1996*a*).

—— 'Systematicity', *Journal of Philosophy*, 93 (1996*b*), 591–614.

—— 'The LOT of the Causal Theory of Reference', *Journal of Philosophy*, 94 (1997), 535–42.

—— 'Truth and Meaning', in J. K. Campbell, M. O'Rourke, and D. Shier (eds.), *Meaning and Truth: Investigations in Philosophical Semantics* (New York: Seven Bridges Press, 1999).

—— ' "How Does It Work?" versus "What Are the Laws?": Two Conceptions of Psychological Explanation', in F. C. Keil and R. A. Wilson (eds.), *Explanation and Cognition* (Cambridge, Mass.: MIT Press, 2000*a*), 117–44.

—— 'Reply to Millikan', *Philosophy and Phenomenological Research*, 60 (2000*b*), 113–28.

—— Poirier, P., 'Representation and Indication', in H. Clapin, P. Staines, and P. Slezak (eds.), *Representation in Mind* (Oxford: Elsevier, 2004).

—— Blackmon, J., Byrd, D., Lee, A., May, C., and Roth, M., 'Representation and Unexploited Content', in G. McDonald and D. Papineau (eds.), *Teleosemantics* (New York: Oxford University Press, 2006).

Cummins, R., Blackmon, J., Byrd, D., Poirier, P., Roth, M., and Schwarz, G., 'Systematicity and the Cognition of Structured Domains', *Journal of Philosophy*, 98 (2001), 1–19.

Davidson, D., 'Theories of Meaning and Learnable Languages', in Y. Bar-Hillel (ed.), *Proceedings of the 1964 International Congress for Logic, Methodology, and Philosophy of Science* (Amsterdam: North Holland, 1965).

—— 'Truth and Meaning', *Synthese*, 17 (1967), 304–23.

Dennett, D., *Brainstorms* (Cambridge, Mass.: MIT Press/Bradford Books, 1978).

—— 'Comment on Searle, "Minds, Brains and Programs" ', *Behavioral and Brain Sciences*, 3 (1980), 417–24.

—— *The Intentional Stance* (Cambridge, Mass.: MIT Press/Bradford Books, 1987).

—— *Consciousness Explained* (New York: Little, Brown, 1991).

Dretske, F., *Knowledge and the Flow of Information* (Cambridge, Mass.: MIT Press, 1981).

—— *Explaining Behavior: Reasons in a World of Causes* (Cambridge, Mass.: MIT Press, 1988).

Dupoux, E., Pallier, C., Sebastian, N., and Mehler, J., 'A Destressing "Deafness" in French?', *Journal of Memory and Language*, 36 (1997), 406–21.

Elman, J., 'Grammatical Structure and Distributed Representations', in S. Davies (ed.), *Connectionism: Theory and Practice: Vancouver Studies in Cognitive Science*, iii (New York: Oxford University Press, 1992).

Evans, J. St. B. T., *Bias in Human Reasoning* (Hillsdale, NJ: Lawrence Erlbaum, 1989).

Feldman, J., and Ballard, D., 'Connectionist Models and their Properties', *Cognitive Science*, 6 (1982), 205–54.

Field, D. J., 'Relations between the Statistics of Natural Images and the Response Properties of Cortical Cells', *Journal of the Optical Society of America A*, 4 (1987), 2379–94.

—— 'What is the Goal of Sensory Coding?', *Neural Computation*, 6 (1994), 559–601.

Fodor, J., *The Language of Thought* (New York: Thomas Y. Crowell, 1975).

—— 'Methodological Solipsism Considered as a Research Strategy in Cognitive Science', *Behavioral and Brain Sciences*, 3 (1980), 63–109.

—— *RePresentations* (Cambridge, Mass.: MIT Press/Bradford Books, 1981).

—— *The Modularity of Mind* (Cambridge, Mass.: MIT Press/Bradford Books, 1983).

—— *Psychosemantics* (Cambridge, Mass.: MIT Press, 1987).

—— *A Theory of Content and Other Essays* (Cambridge, Mass.: MIT Press, 1990a).

—— 'Psychosemantics, or Where Do Truth Conditions Come From', in W. Lycan (ed.), *Mind and Cognition* (Oxford: Basil Blackwell, 1990b).

—— 'Connectionism and the Problem of Systematicity (Continued): Why Smolensky's Solution Still Doesn't Work', *Cognition*, 62 (1997), 109–19.

——Lepore, E., *Holism: A Shopper's Guide* (Oxford and Cambridge, Mass.: Basil Blackwell, 1992).

——McLaughlin, B., 'Connectionism and the Problem of Systematicity: Why Smolensky's Solution Does Not Work', *Cognition*, 35 (1990*c*), 183–204.

——Pylyshyn, Z., 'Connectionism and Cognitive Architecture: A Critical Analysis', *Cognition*, 28 (1988), 3–71.

Garcia, J., and Koelling, R., 'The Relation of Cue to Consequence in Avoidance Learning', *Psychonomic Science*, 4 (1966), 123–4.

Gelman, S., 'Concepts and Theories', in R. Gelman and T. K. Au (eds.), *Perceptual and Cognitive Development: Handbook of Perception and Cognition*, 2nd edn. (San Diego, Calif.: Academic Press, 1996).

Grice, P., 'Meaning', *Philosophical Review*, 66 (1957), 377–88.

Grossberg, S., *Studies of Mind and Brain: Neural Principles of Learning, Perception, Development, Cognition, and Motor Control* (Dordrecht: D. Reidel, 1982).

Hadley, R., 'Systematicity in Connectionist Language Learning', *Mind and Language*, 9 (1994*a*), 247–72.

——'Systematicity Revisited', *Mind and Language*, 9 (1994*b*), 431–44.

——'Cognition, Systematicity, and Nomic Necessity', *Mind and Language*, 12 (1997*a*), 137–53.

——Hayward, M. B., 'Strong Semantic Systematicity from Hebbian Connectionist Learning', *Minds and Machines*, 7 (1997*b*), 1–55.

Haugeland, J., 'The Nature and Plausibility of Cognitivism', *Behavioral and Brain Sciences*, 1 (1978), 215–26.

——(ed.), *Mind Design* (Cambridge, Mass.: MIT Press/Bradford Books, 1981).

——*Artificial Intelligence: The Very Idea* (Cambridge, Mass.: MIT Press/Bradford Books, 1985).

——'Representational Genera', in W. Ramsey, S. Stich, and D. Rumelhart (eds.), *Philosophy and Connectionist Theory* (Hillsdale, NJ: Lawrence Erlbaum, 1991).

——'Understanding Dennett and Searle', in A. Revonsuo and M. Kamppinen (eds.), *Consciousness in Philosophy and Cognitive Neuroscience* (Hillsdale, NJ: Lawrence Erlbaum, 1992).

——'Objective Perception', in K. Akins (ed.), *Perception: Vancouver Studies in Cognitive Science*, v (New York: Oxford University Press, 1996).

——*Having Thought* (Cambridge, Mass.: Harvard University Press, 1998).

Helmholtz, H. von (1856) *Handbook of Physiological Optics,* (ed.) J. P. C. S. Southall (New York: Dover Reprint, 1963).

Hempel, C., *Philosophy of Natural Science* (Englewood Cliffs, NJ: Prentice Hall, 1966).

——Oppenheim, P., 'Studies in the Logic of Explanation', *Philosophy of Science*, 15 (1948), 135–75.

Hinton, G., 'Learning Distributed Representations of Concepts', *Proceedings of the Eighth Annual Conference of the Cognitive Science Society* (Amherst, Mass., 1986).

Hofstadter, D., and Dennett, D., (eds.), *The Mind's I: Fantasies and Reflections on Self and Soul* (New York: Basic Books, 1981).

Horgan, T., and Tienson, J., 'Structured Representations in Connectionist Systems?', in S. Davis (ed.), *Connectionism: Theory and Practice* (New York: Oxford University Press, 1992), 195–228.

Hubel, D. H., *Eye, Brain, and Vision* (New York: Scientific American Library, 1988).

—— Wiesel, T. N., 'Receptive Fields, Binocular Interaction and Functional Architecture in the Cat's Visual Cortex', *Journal of Physiology*, 160 (1962), 106–54.

Hume, D. (1748), *An Enquiry Concerning Human Understanding*, in J. A. Selby-Bigge (ed.), *Hume's Enquiries* (Oxford: Clarendon Press, 1963).

Johnson-Laird, P. N., and Byrne, R. M. J., *Deduction* (Hillsdale, NJ: Erlbaum, 1992).

Kaiser, M. K., Jonides, J., and Alexander, J., 'Intuitive Reasoning about Abstract and Familiar Physics Problems', *Memory and Cognition*, 14 (1986), 308–12.

Kim, J., 'On the Logical Conditions of Deductive Explanation', *Philosophy of Science*, 30 (1962), 286–91.

King, J., 'Structured Propositions and Complex Predicates', *Nous*, 29/4 (1995), 516–35.

Kuffler, S., 'Neurons in the Retina: Organization, Inhibition and Excitatory Problems', *Cold Spring Harbor Symposia on Quantitative Biology*, 17 (1952), 281–92.

Laasko, A., and Cottrell, G., 'Qualia and Cluster Analysis: Assessing Representational Similarity between Neural Systems', *Philosophical Psychology*, 13 (2000), 46–76.

Leibniz, G. (1714). *The Monadology*, tr. R. Ariew and D. Garber, *Leibniz: Basic Works* (Indianapolis: Hackett, 1989).

Lewicki, M. S., and Olshausen, B. A. 'A Probabilistic Framework for the Adaptation and Comparison of Images Codes', *Journal of the Optical Society of America A*, 16 (1999), 1587–1601.

Lewis, D., *Convention* (Cambridge, Mass.: Harvard University Press, 1969).

Livingstone, M., and Hubel, D., 'Segregation of Form, Color, Movement and Depth: Anatomy, Physiology, and Perception', *Science*, 240 (1988), 740–9.

Lycan, W., *Consciousness* (Cambridge, Mass.: MIT Press/Bradford Books, 1987).

McClelland, J., and Rumelhart, D., *Explorations in Parallel Distributed Processing: A Handbook of Models, Programs, and Exercises* (Cambridge, Mass.: MIT Press, 1988).

—— McNaughton, B. L., and O'Reilly, R. C., 'Why there are Complementary Learning Systems in the Hippocampus and the Neocortex: Insights from the Success and Failures of Connectionist Models of Learning and Memory', *Psychological Review*, 102 (1995), 419–57.

McCloskey, M., 'Intuitive Physics', *Scientific American*, 24 (1983), 122–30.

—— Cohen, N. J., 'Catastrophic Interference in Connectionist Networks: The Sequential Learning Problem', *The Psychology of Learning and Motivation*, 24 (1989), 109–65.

McDermott, D. (1976), 'Artificial Intelligence Meets Natural Stupidity', in J. Haugeland (ed.), *Mind Design* (Cambridge, Mass.: MIT Press/Bradford Books, 1981).

Macdonald, G., 'Biology and Representation', *Mind and Language*, 4 (1989), 186–200.

—— McGurk, H., 'Visual Influences on Speech Perception Processes', *Perception and Psychophysics*, 24/3 (1978), 253–7.

McLaughlin, B. P., 'Systematicity, Conceptual Truth, and Evolution', in C. Hookway and D. Peterson (eds.), *Philosophy and Cognitive Science* (Cambridge: Cambridge University Press, 1993*a*).

—— 'The Connectionism/Classicism Battle to Win Souls', *Philosophical Studies*, 71 (1993*b*), 163–90.

Madigan, S., 'Intraserial Repetition and Coding Processes in Free Recall', *Journal of Verbal Learning and Verbal Behavior*, 8 (1969), 828–35.

Marr, D., *Vision* (New York: Freeman, 1982).

Matthews, R. J., 'Three-Concept Monte: Explanation, Implementation, and Systematicity', *Synthese*, 101 (1994), 347–63.

—— 'Can Connectionists Explain Systematicity?', *Mind and Language*, 12 (1997), 154–77.

Millikan, R., *Language, Thought, and Other Biological Categories* (Cambridge, Mass.: MIT Press/Bradford Books, 1984).

—— 'Thoughts without Laws: Cognitive Science with Content', *Philosophical Review*, 95 (1986), 47–80.

—— 'Representations, Targets, Attitudes', *Philosophy and Phenomenological Research*, 60 (2000), 103–11.

Moore, E., 'Gedanken Experiments on Sequential Machines', in C. Shannon and J. McCarthy (eds.), *Automata Studies* (Princeton, NJ: Princeton University Press, 1956), 129–56.

Nagel, T., 'What is it Like to Be a Bat?', *Philosophical Review*, 83 (1974), 435–50.

Neander, K., 'The Teleological Notion of Function', *Australasian Journal of Philosophy*, 69 (1991), 454–68.

Newell, A., *Unified Theories of Cognition* (Cambridge, Mass.: Harvard University Press, 1990).

—— Simon, H., *Human Problem Solving* (Englewood Cliffs, NJ: Prentice-Hall, 1972).

Niklasson, L., and Van Gelder, T., 'On Being Systematically Connectionist', *Mind and Language*, 9 (1994), 288–302.

Olshausen, B. A., and Field, D. J., 'Emergence of Simple-Cell Receptive Field Properties by Learning a Sparse Code for Natural Images', *Nature*, 381(1996), 607–9.

—— —— 'Sparse Coding with an Overcomplete Basis Set: A Strategy Employed by V1?', *Vision Research*, 37(1997), 3311–25.

—— —— 'Vision and the Coding of Natural Images', *American Scientist*, 88 (2000), 238–45.

O'Reilly, R. C., and Munakata, Y., *Computational Explorations in Cognitive Neuroscience* (Cambridge, Mass.: MIT Press, 2000).

Owen, D., 'Locke on Reason, Probable Reason and Opinion', *Locke Newsletter*, 24 (1993), 33–79.

Papineau, D., 'Reality and Explanation', *Philosophy of Science*, 51 (1984), 550–72.

—— *Reality and Representation* (Oxford: Basil Blackwell, 1987).

Perlman, M., *Conceptual Flux: Mental Representation, Misrepresentation, and Concept Change* (New York: Springer, 2000).

Pinker, S., and Prince, A., 'Rules and Connections in Human Language', in R. Morris (ed.), *Parallel Distributed Processing* (Oxford: Oxford University Press, 1989), 182–99.

Putnam, H., 'Craig's Theorem', *Journal of Philosophy*, 62/10 (1965), 251–60.

—— (ed.), 'The Meaning of "Meaning" ', *Mind, Language and Reality: Philosophical Papers,* ii (Cambridge: Cambridge University Press, 1975), 215–71.

Pylyshyn, Z., 'The Rate of 'Mental Rotation' of Images: A Test of a Holistic Analogue Hypothesis', *Memory and Cognition*, 7/1 (1979), 19–28.

—— *Computation and Cognition* (Cambridge, Mass.: MIT Press/Bradford Books, 1984).

Rips, L. J., 'Reasoning', *Annual Review of Psychology*, 41(1990), 321–53.

—— *The Psychology of Proof* (Cambridge, Mass.: MIT Press/Bradford Books, 1994).

Rosenberg, C. (1987) 'Revealing the Structure of NETtalk's Internal Representations', *Proceedings of the Ninth Annual Meeting of the Cognitive Science Society* (Seattle, Wash., 1987), 537–54.

Roth, M., 'Program Execution in Connectionist Networks', *Mind and Language*, 20/4 (2005), 448–67.

Rumelhart, D., 'The Architecture of Mind: A Connectionist Approach', in Michael Posner (ed.), *Foundations of Cognitive Science* (Cambridge, Mass.: MIT Press, 1989).

—— McClelland, J., 'On Learning the Past Tenses of English Verbs', in J. McClelland, D. Rumelhart, and the PDP Research Group (eds.), *Parallel Distributed Processing,* ii (Cambridge, Mass.: MIT Press, 1986), 216–71.

Salmon, W., *Causality and Explanation* (New York: Oxford University Press, 1998).

Sanger, D., 'Contribution Analysis: A Technique for Assigning Responsibilities to Hidden Units in Connectionist Networks', *Technical Report CU-CS-435-89* (Department of Computer Science, University of Colorado at Boulder, 1989).

Schiffer, S., 'Truth and the Theory of Content', in H. Parret and J. Bouraresse (eds.), *Meaning and Understanding* (Berlin: Walter de Gruyter, 1981).

—— 'Intention Based Semantics', *Notre Dame Journal of Formal Logic*, 23 (1982), 119–59.

—— *Remnants of Meaning* (Cambridge, Mass.: MIT Press, 1987).

Schwarz, G., 'Connectionism, Processing, Memory', *Connection Science*, 1 (1992), 207–26.

Searle, J., 'Minds, Brains, and Programs', *Behavioral and Brain Sciences*, 3 (1980), 417–24.

—— *The Rediscovery of the Mind* (Cambridge, Mass.: MIT Press, 1992).

Sejnowski, T., and Rosenberg, C., 'Parallel Networks that Learn to Pronounce English Text', *Complex Systems*, 1 (1987a), 145–68.

—— 'Connectionist Models of Learning', in M. S. Gazzaniga (ed.), *Perspectives in Memory Research and Training* (Cambridge, Mass.: MIT Press, 1987b).

—— Koch, C., and Churchland, P. S., 'Computational Neuroscience', *Science*, 241 (1988), 1299–1306.

Sherman, S. M., and Koch, C., 'The Control of Retino-geniculate Transmission in the Mammalian Lateral Geniculate Nucleus', *Experimental Brain Research*, 63 (1986), 1–20.

Shin, S-J., *The Logical Status of Diagrams* (Cambridge: Cambridge University Press, 1994).

Smith, E., and Medin, D., *Categories and Concepts* (Cambridge, Mass.: Harvard University Press, 1981).

Smolensky, P., 'The Constituent Structure of Connectionist Mental States', *Southern Journal of Philosophy Supplement*, 26 (1987), 137–60.

—— 'On the Proper Treatment of Connectionism', *Behavioral and Brain Sciences*, 11 (1988), 1–74.

—— 'Tensor Product Variable Binding and the Representation of Symbolic Structures in Connectionist Systems. *Artificial Intelligence*, 46 (1990), 159–216.

—— 'Connectionism, Constituency and the Language of Thought', in B. Loewer and G. Rey (eds.), *Meaning in Mind: Fodor and his Critics* (Oxford: Blackwell, 1991).

—— 'Constituent Structure and Explanation in an Integrated Connectionist/Symbolic Cognitive Architecture', in C. Macdonald (ed.), *Connectionism: Debates on Psychological Explanation* (Oxford: Blackwell, 1995).

—— LeGendre, G., and Miyata Y., 'Principles for an Integrated Connectionist/Symbolic Theory of Higher Cognition', *Technical Report 92-08* (Institute of Cognitive Science, University of Colorado, 1992).

Stalnaker, R., *Inquiry* (Cambridge, Mass.: MIT Press, 1984).

Stampe, D., 'Towards a Causal Theory of Linguistic Representation', in P. A. French, T. E. Uehling, and H. K. Wettstein (eds.), *Midwest Studies in Philosophy*, ii. *Studies in the Philosophy of Language* (Minneapolis: University of Minnesota Press, 1977), 42–63.

Stich, S., *From Folk Psychology to Cognitive Science: The Case Against Belief* (Cambridge, Mass.: MIT Press/Bradford Books, 1983).

Swoyer, C., 'Structural Representation and Surrogative Reasoning', *Synthese*, 87 (1991), 449–508.

Tarski, A., 'The Concept of Truth in Formalized Languages', in J. H. Woodger (ed.), *Logic, Semantics, Metamathematics* (Oxford: Oxford University Press, 1936, 1956).

——'The Semantic Conception of Truth', in H. Feigl and W. Sellars (eds.), *Readings in Philosophical Analysis* (New York: Appleton, 1944, 1949).

Tolman, E., 'Cognitive Maps in Rats and Men', *The Psychological Review,* 55/4 (1948), 189–208.

Van Gelder, T., 'Compositionality: A Connectionist Variation on a Classical Theme', *Cognitive Science*, 14 (1990), 355–84.

——Port, R., 'It's About Time: An Overview of the Dynamical Approach to Cognition', in R. Port and T. van Gelder (eds.), *Mind as Motion: Explorations in the Dynamics of Cognition* (Cambridge, Mass.: MIT Press, 1995).

Name Index

Subject Index